REINVENTING
POLITICS

REINVENTING POLITICS

POLITICS

*Eastern Europe
from Stalin to Havel*

Vladimir Tismaneanu

THE FREE PRESS
A Division of Macmillan, Inc.
NEW YORK
Maxwell Macmillan Canada
TORONTO
Maxwell Macmillan International
NEW YORK   OXFORD   SINGAPORE   SYDNEY

The Free Press
A Division of Simon & Schuster
1230 Avenue of the Americas
New York, NY 10020

Manufactured in the United States of America

10 9 8 7 6 5 4 3 2 1

Library of Congress Cataloging-In-Publication Data
Tismaneanu, Vladimir.
Reinventing politics: Eastern Europe from Stalin to Havel/
Vladimir Tismaneanu.
p. cm.
Includes bibilographical references and index.
1. Europe, Eastern-Politics and government-1945- I. Title
DJK50.T57 1992
947-dc20 91-42878
CIP

ISBN 0-7432-1282-7

To all those who, hoping against hope,
made the revolutions of 1989 possible.

Contents

Preface

The Devil is part of our experience.
Our generation has seen enough of it
for the message to be taken extremely
seriously.
                    —Leszek Kolakowski

   This book is an attempt to explain the origins and the dynamics of
one of the most important events in this century: the breakdown of
communist regimes in Eastern Europe. More than just a historical account, the book was written while the events were still unfolding and the
author became what Raymond Aron once called a committed witness
(*spectateur engagé*). After all, as we know from Albert Camus, Hannah
Arendt, or Vaclav Havel, one cannot write dispassionately about a phenomenon like totalitarianism. We can, of course, simulate objectivity.
We could dissemble an *au-dessus-de-la-mêlée* attitude to Ceausescu's pageants, say, depicting them as exercises in political leadership, but that
would not improve the quality of our investigation. On the contrary, that
could only make it look abjectly toothless.
   Communism was not simply a variety of political regime, one of the
many forms of dictatorship mankind has experienced since ancient times.
It was unique in its attempt to mold the human psyche, in its mythological hubris, in its endeavor to regiment people and to force them to
behave in accordance with Pavlovian recipes of happiness. In comparison
with my previous book on the fate of Marxism in Eastern Europe (published by Routledge in 1988), this one is meant to be less "subjective."
Years of American academic experience have convinced me that it is
important to convey the message in a more facts-oriented way. That may
reduce its emotional charge, but in exchange I can hope to gain in
persuasive power.
   To write this book I used numerous primary materials from East European democratic movements. Special praise should be given to the

London-based *East European Reporter* and to the New York–based *Uncaptive Minds* for their efforts to help Western readers follow the sweeping changes in the former Soviet bloc. Since the 1989 upheaval, I have traveled frequently to the region and have been able to interview many of the principal actors in this ongoing drama. Most of my hypotheses were discussed with colleagues in the field, and the main theses were topics of my lectures in the courses I taught at the University of Pennsylvania and the University of Maryland (College Park) over the past six years. My students turned out to be my accomplices in the attempt to make sense of events that, in their speed and unpredictability, came close to the miraculous.

I must confess that my approach differs in some respects from the long-prevailing direction in the field of communist studies. For years I have believed (and hope I am not wrong) that studying communist elites is only a fragment—and not necessarily the most significant one—of the field of comparative communism. More important for understanding those societies, it has seemed to me, is to focus on the less visible, definitely less powerful and impressive—in terms of authority—nuclei of autonomous social and cultural initiative. I vividly remember that when I wrote a study for *Problems of Communism* on the nascent civil society in the German Democratic Republic, more than one of my colleagues in the discipline smiled skeptically. How can tiny independent communities affect the fate of a well-controlled police state like Erich Honecker's model of barracks socialism? With regard to Hungary, many thought that Kadarism, with its promise of an enlightened version of authoritarianism labeled "gulash socialism," could last a long time. The exponents of the Budapest School were in that respect the exception. The dissident enclaves were described, even by some of their representatives (as for instance Miklos Haraszti in his book *The Velvet Prison*), as quixotic examples of political naïveté. As for Romania, I clearly recall the friendly reproach of a distinguished British professor, indeed one of my mentors and the author of a classic study on Romanian communism, who once asked me if I really believed it was worthwhile to pay so much attention to the ideas of dissidents like Mihai Botez, Paul Goma, Dan Petrescu, and Dorin Tudoran. After all, in light of the monolithic image of the Ceausescu regime, what could those argonauts of dignity symbolize except the failure of a society to resist the most irrational dictatorship Eastern Europe had known since Stalin's time? I do not claim that my interpretation is the only appropriate one. However, now that the communist elites have ingloriously left the limelight, and the political stage in those countries is dominated by figures long regarded as irrelevant, such an approach seems to have been historically vindicated. Who could have predicted that Kadar's place would be taken by an obscure historian of medicine called Jozsef Antall? Who would have thought that the ruling party in the GDR would willingly give up power, or that those who would launch the onslaught on the terrorist state that claimed to represent the interests of workers and peasants would be painters, physicists, and Lutheran pastors engaged in nonviolent, antimilitaristic movements? Who could have imagined that Jaruzelski, the bespectacled Spartan general who proclaimed Martial Law in December 1981 and imprisoned the flower of the Polish opposition, would shake hands with his nemesis Lech Walesa and ensure a smooth transition to a procedural democracy?

Even more challenging for reductionist explanations remains the role of Mikhail Gorbachev and his tolerance of revolutionary change in what was rightly described as the Soviet Union's outer empire. The strategic shift in relations between the imperial center and its periphery, between the Kremlin and its former satellites, has created a new political reality. With the exception of Albania, Romania, and Serbia, the East European countries are no longer run by luminaries of the traditional communist bureaucracies. Instead, new political formations have emerged that seek their sources of inspiration in Western philosophical approaches to the issues of community, public life, and civic rights. When Gorbachev meets East European leaders, he has to deal with people whom he would have normally described as "bourgeois politicians." In July 1991 the disbandment of the Warsaw Pact during a summit in Prague officially consecrated the end of the old-fashioned alliance and the beginning of a new era in Soviet–East European relations, as well as in relations among the East European countries themselves. The shadow of Big Brother has disappeared, and the small and medium-size states in the region have to cope with this new reality. The threat of Soviet intervention to crush domestic movements for democracy in Eastern Europe seems, at least for the time being, nonexistent. Currently, those countries are faced with internal strife and countless unsolved quandaries. In some of them, ethnic minorities decry persecution fomented by the demographic majority. In Kosovo, an autonomous province in Yugoslavia's Serbian Republic, the Albanian majority has suffered under discriminatory measures taken by the Serbian government. In Romania, instead of ensuring protection for the Hungarian minority, the government has encouraged a staunchly nationalist movement called *Vatra Romaneasca* (the Romanian Hearth). In all these countries the wounds of the past continue to bleed, and the newly formed democracies still seem incapable of providing more than moral injunctions for their healing. That is not too pessimistic an assessment, but rather a matter-of-fact description of the existing situation. As

the economies continue to plummet, discontent is soaring, and regrets
for the paternalistic ways of the communist regimes are beginning to be
heard. Yes, there was poverty under communism, some say, but at least
everybody had a job and there was no anarchy in the media. Cynical
demagogues, including some former communists, have tried to exploit
the disarray among the masses. They may try again.

After 1989 Czechoslovakia, Hungary, and Poland seem to have embarked decisively on the road to an open society. The parliaments in those
countries have functioned more or less properly, as responsible legislative
bodies. Political differentiation has occurred, and parties have emerged to
express the interests of different groups. Thanks to rapid privatization, a
middle class of technocrats and entrepreneurs is taking shape. A new
political elite, committed to pluralism and a free market, is now in charge
of the orderly development of the transition. Regardless of possible setbacks, it is likely that those countries will join West European integrative
bodies, including the European Economic Community, sooner rather than
later. The same can scarcely be said of Albania, Romania, and Yugoslavia.
What one sees there is continuous fragmentation of the body politic,
endless conflict, and little hope for the creation of a national consensus.
Bulgaria stands somewhere in the middle, with the democratic forces still
scattered, but also with a declining ex-communist party that has lost both
its will for power and the mass basis it once commanded. The new equation
in the region thus indicates a widening gap between East-Central (the
former G.D.R., Czechoslovakia, Poland, and Hungary) and the rest of
Eastern Europe that in the long run might lead to the isolation of the
Balkan countries from the mainstream of European politics and the European economy. The remedy for that unsettling trend would be acceleration
of the democratic transition in Eastern Europe and the development of
strong civic movements that can, in turn, help the emergence of solid
democratic parties. Otherwise, the future might confront us with the
appearance of two Europes: one prosperous, democratic, and tolerant of
political and ethnic minorities, and the other poor, resentful, plagued with
chauvinism and civil and ethnic conflicts, and prone to allow the rise of
new dictatorships.

The West should not ignore that danger. The Balkans cannot and
should not be quarantined as the "unhealthy" area of Europe, a region
where nothing can be done to expedite the transition to democracy. In
all those countries there are courageous movements that champion precisely the values of democracy. They should be made to feel that the West
is resolutely on their side.

This book uses a comparative approach to assess the causes of the

disintegration of communist regimes in Eastern Europe (Albania, Bulgaria, Czechoslovakia, East Germany, Hungary, Poland, Romania, and Yugoslavia), the current state of the political revival in the region, and the prospects for democratic development in the foreseeable future. While comparing the very different paths away from communism, I suggest that, although the obstacles to genuine pluralism remain great, the democratic forces can win the day.

I hope the book will provide students of Eastern Europe with a detailed account of the startling changes in recent years and with an analytical framework for the ongoing political transformations. Considering the striking scarcity of such comprehensive (historical, sociological, and political) approaches, this is a pioneering attempt to sum up one of modern history's most fascinating chapters: the breakup of communism in the Soviet Union's outer empire, the dissolution of the political and economic institutions that guaranteed the conservation of communist structures, and the rediscovery of politics in countries where the very idea of citizenry had been consistently trampled underfoot. Those developments have more than immediate significance: They demand a reconceptualization and a search for notions that would capture the true meaning of such changes. Terms like authority, legitimacy, influence, leadership, power, and society now carry different meanings in Eastern Europe from the ones they had through the previous decades. Will the postcommunist democracy be identical with Western-type models of pluralism? What is the legacy of more than four decades of Leninism for the East European psyche? How will the emerging politics of Eastern Europe affect the rest of Europe and the world? Do potential crises in the region have international implications? Is the nascent politics bound to favor more stability in those countries, or less?

The main hypothesis of this book is that the causes of the East European revolutionary upheaval are primarily domestic. The paramount one is the rise and ripening of civil societies in countries long dominated by totalitarian Leninist parties. The civil society comprises the independent, nongovernmental groups, associations, and institutions that have emerged in Eastern Europe in recent year, especially after 1980. It was primarily thanks to the existence of such structures, which the Czech philosopher Vaclav Benda once called "the parallel polis," that the breakthrough could result in a smooth, nonviolent change. Some of those groups are explicitly political, others are not. By implication, however, they all represent a challenge to the totalitarian ambition of a total grip upon society. One example will suffice to convey the meaning of civil society: In political regimes where all decision-making is hypercentralized and where authority lies in the communist party (whose monopoly of power is constitutionally guaranteed), even an autonomous ecological initative clashes with such all-embracing domination. The civil society was thus a first step in the reinvention of politics outside the existing matrix of power, that is, explicitly outside and implicitly against the communist party. It was thanks to that approach to political change that a strategy was devised to build parallel institutions (independent unions, flying universities, clubs) and even an opposition counterculture in countries like Czechoslovakia, Hungary, and Poland.

The rise of those new movements cannot be separated from a number of international influences: the communications revolution and the expanding access to free information; the impact of the Helsinki process and the growing pressures from the West for domestic democratization; and the increasing links between independent groups in Eastern Europe and those in the West (such as pacifists and environmentalists).

In addition to the movements from below, the transition to postcommunism was obviously accelerated by the evident collapse of the command economies. The information revolution permitted people in the East to become aware of the immense gap between their living standards and those in the other half of Europe. The government elites, in turn, could offer no more than cosmetic remedies with little appeal to the population. The bureaucrats themselves often traveled to the West and eventually realized that the issue was not to reform the planned economy, but to get rid of its stifling mechanisms. Disillusionment with the Leninist model was rampant among both the rulers and the ruled. What followed was the complete evaporation of ideological zeal and the emergence of a cynical managerial class whose sole interest was to stay in power. The end of any communist mystique contributed to the breakdown of the existing principle of legitimacy. According to Leninist ideology, communists represented the interests of the workers. But, especially after the rise of Solidarity in Poland, that fallacy had ceased to mobilize anybody. In some of these countries, the reformers took over within the communist parties, changed their programs, and claimed to embrace the ideals of Western Social Democracy. In Romania, a violent explosion of social anger led to the overthrow of the Ceausescu regime, but not necessarily to the end of communism. This book deals extensively with the factious struggles within communist elites and their impact on society at large. Since those communist parties derived their legitimacy to a great extent from their special relationship with Moscow, it is important to focus on the Gorbachev factor and to highlight the interplay of change in the Soviet Union and the democratic renewal in Eastern Europe.

The book focuses on five major themes. They are neither exclusive nor exhaustive. They give an idea, however, about the main hypotheses of this approach, which tends to avoid the pitfalls of anecdotal history or monographic descriptivism.

The first theme, *Communism in Eastern Europe,* is primarily historical. The book examines the diversity of the precommunist traditions in Eastern Europe; the establishment of communist regimes in the aftermath of World War II; the dynamics of the Soviet bloc; Nikita Khrushchev's aborted de-Stalinization; and the main crises in the history of the bloc (Yugoslavia in 1948, Hungary in 1956, Czechoslovakia in 1968, Poland in 1980). This theme embraces as well the evolution of Soviet–East European relations and the impact of the Soviet transition from Brezhnev's period of "stagnation" to Gorbachev's perestroika and "new thinking" in international relations. An effort is made to familiarize the reader with the significant reference points in post–World War II East European political history.

The second theme, *The Rise of Civil Society,* provides a comparative approach to strategies and methods adopted by independent movements (Poland's Solidarity, Czechoslovakia's Charter 77, Hungary's Democratic Opposition) and analyzes how those groups emerged in the repressive conditions of the post-Stalinist authoritarian regimes. Illuminating platforms and other political documents are discussed to identify the theoretical and moral options of the opposition forces. For instance, it would be impossible for a student of Eastern Europe to understand the origins and the direction of the current changes without referring to Vaclav Havel's pathbreaking essay, "The Power of the Powerless." After all, the revolution in Eastern Europe has been the creation of the powerless, and the event was anticipated in the works of critical intellectuals like Havel, Janos Kis, György Konrad, Milovan Djilas, Leszek Kolakowski, and Adam Michnik.

The third theme, *The Triumph of the Powerless,* deals with the revolutionary dynamics in Eastern Europe during the 1989 upheaval and explains in concrete detail why the communist regimes fell apart. To understand the changes, the historical peculiarities for each country and for the region as a whole are most important. This theme focuses on the electoral victory of Solidarity and the formation of the first noncommunist government in Eastern Europe's post-Yalta history; the end of moderate reformist illusions and Hungary's transition to pluralism; the domestic and international dimensions of East Germany's "gentle revolution"; Czechoslovakia's "velvet revolution" and the victory of the Civic Forum; Bulgaria's awakening and the overthrow of Todor Zhivkov's dictatorship; Romania's abducted revolution and the National Salvation Front as a reincarnation of the communist party; and the disintegration of Tito's legacy in Yugoslavia, with the rise of ethnic, separatist parties and movements.

The fourth theme, *The Birth Pangs of Democracy*, discusses the chances for democracy in each country and in Eastern Europe as a whole. Again, the approach is comparative, providing the reader with an in-depth exploration of the political ideologies and inclinations of the new parties in the region. Here we discuss the obstacles to democratic development, including the inertia of the government bureaucracies, the dangers of neo-authoritarian solutions, the existence of populist temptations, and the resurgence of long-denied ethnic passions. As Kenneth Jowitt once put it, the future of Eastern Europe does not inevitably belong to benign social democratic and liberal democratic parties. It is quite possible that the region will experience unprecedented convulsions provoked by the rise of neofundamentalist "movements of rage," rooted in political despair and economic frustration.

The fifth theme—*Democracy or Ethnocracy?*—investigates the growing tension between self-centered, anti-Western, and anti-intellectual ethnic movements and the democratic groups and parties inspired by liberal values. I want to emphasize, once again, my conviction that Eastern Europe's future is not foreclosed and that the breakdown of communism has opened a multitude of possible avenues to be pursued by these long-victimized nations. One cannot ignore, however, that the ongoing changes are taking place in dramatically impoverished countries and are affecting morally traumatized populations. Crossing what Ralf Dahrendorf has called a historical vale of tears is not an exhilarating experience, which explains the current disenchantment, among many in the region, with the slow pace of economic and social recovery. Instead of the expected cornocupia, people are asked to tighten their belts further. That in turn creates opportunities for populist adventurers, charlatans, and pseudo-prophets.

I want to express here my warmest thanks to all those who made possible the completion of this project. First, my heartfelt thanks to the American Council of Learned Societies, the Bradley Foundation, the Pew Charitable Trusts, and the Foreign Policy Research Institute and its director, Daniel Pipes, for all the understanding and support so generously offered to me. I want to thank my research assistants, Joydeep Bhattacharya, Marco Bianchini, and Brett Kinsella, for having patiently and enthusiastically kept track of the amazing changes in Eastern Europe as reflected in the myriad sources I had to consult. They succeeded in organizing and keeping my files under strict control, in spite of my perpetually confusing interventions. I am also indebted to the University of Maryland's Department of Government and Politics, where I found a congenial atmosphere and great interest in my analysis of postcommunist societies.

The theoretical depth of this book owes an enormous amount to my discussions with Mihai Botez, Matei Calinescu, Daniel Chirot, Ferenc Feher, Agnes Heller, Bartek Kaminski, Maria Kovacs, Kenneth Jowitt, John Lampe, Juliana Pilon, Alvin Rubinstein, Sandor Szilagyi, Sonia Sluzar, Dorin Tudoran, and many other colleagues and friends who shared their insights with me on issues with which I was wrestling. Some of them made important suggestions that definitely led to improvements in the manuscript's clarity and poignancy. I also want to thank my Romanian friends Vasile Gogea and Mircea Mihaies, editors of the independent magazines *Astra* in Brasov and *Orizont* in Timisoara, who during their trips to Washington found the time and energy to accompany me creatively in the revision of the manuscript. Peter Dougherty, my outstanding editor at The Free Press, deserves more than special thanks for having come up with encouraging suggestions that definitely added to what was valuable in my text and certainly diminished what was superfluous or confusing. I am deeply grateful to Johnathan Sunley for providing invaluable photographs from the archives of the *East European Reporter* (London and Budapest). Finally, but most warmly, let Mary Sladek be thanked for having done all she did to make this book what it is. For her editorial, computer, and human skills, both the book and the author owe her more than words can say.

Vladimir Tismaneanu
Washington, D.C.
July 18, 1991

ONE

Victims and Outsiders
East Europe Before Communism

Central Europe as a family of small nations has its own vision of the world, a
vision based on a deep distrust of history.
History, that goddess of Hegel and Marx,
that incarnation of reason that judges us
and arbitrates our fate—that is the history of conquerors. The people of Central Europe are not conquerors. They cannot be separated from European history;
they cannot exist outside it; but they represent the wrong side of history; they are
its victims and outsiders.

> —*Milan Kundera*

The revolutionary upheaval of 1989 that led to the collapse of apparently well-entrenched communist regimes was one of those epoch-
making events that shape the world. Long-established perceptions and
beliefs about the stability of communist states were suddenly contradicted by the social and political explosions in the region. The spectacular breakdown of the Berlin Wall, the single most conspicuous symbol
of the separation between East and West, contributed to this dramatic
alteration in the political geography of Europe. The significance of the
upheaval cannot be exaggerated: Following those events, Europe looks

different. The unfettering of social and political energies in Eastern Europe and the resurgence of long-denied ethnic passions are things that matter for all those interested in the building of a peaceful and prosperous international order. If those nations manage to achieve the transition to a market economy and a pluralist political order, the world would only benefit from such an evolution. If not, and new conflicts emerge in the historically spasmodic area that we call Eastern Europe, the future of the continent will be plagued by rivalries, tensions, and strifes. We should not forget that two world wars started in the heart of Europe. The conflicts that preexisted communism have not been abolished during the four decades of state socialism. On the contrary, they continued to exist underneath the bogus veneer of Marxist-Leninist propaganda. It was only in the minds of doctrinaire communists that such things as proletarian internationalism and a socialist community of nations existed. In reality, the traditions and memories of the past continued to inspire individual and collective efforts to get rid of the totalitarian regimes. The distinction between East-Central and the rest of Eastern Europe can serve to clarify the different levels of opposition to communism. The latter region includes countries like Albania, Bulgaria, Romania, and, to a certain extent, Yugoslavia, and the former refers to Czechoslovakia, Hungary, Poland, and what used to be called the German Democratic Republic. History, including a knowledge of the religious and political traditions of these countries, can help us understand their different dynamics both under communism and in the current situation. Communism could not erase distinctions that were rooted in centuries of different political, economic, and cultural evolution. It was one thing to belong to the Hapsburg or the German empire, and another to be part of the Ottoman and Russian spheres of domination. In the Balkan part of Europe, political development during the nineteenth century was late and convoluted. In East-Central Europe, institutions were founded upon a Western concept of law and individual rights. In Southeastern Europe, civil society was underdeveloped and extremely fragile. The foundations of pluralism were precarious and vulnerable to dictatorial encroachment. In order to grasp the amplitude of and the obstacles to the current search for a democratic reconstruction in that part of Europe, history is an indispensable tool. All the countries in the region are relatively new state constructs, the product of the great national awakenings characteristic of the nineteenth century. They all owe their current size and shape to the international arrangements that followed the two crucial conflagrations of this century. At the same time, for the nations in that part of the continent, the very term "Eastern

Europe" sounds like discrimination. The 1989 revolutions, among other effects, had revived the European identities of these nations. When people took to the streets in Prague, Leipzig, Timisoara, and Sofia, they did so not only for economic reasons. Perhaps more than the economic disaster of state socialism, the universal boredom and the enclosing of the political and social universe within an asphyxiating bureaucratic dictatorship made people unhappy and frustrated in those countries. Following the euphoria of the first postrevolutionary months, it appeared that the old problems were back: Croatians protesting Serbian hegemony, Serbs indicting Croatians and Slovenes for their secessionist drive, ethnic Hungarians in Romania denouncing infringements on their minority rights, ethnic Turks in Bulgaria scapegoated by advocates of a homogeneous Bulgarian nation, Slovaks jeering President Vaclav Havel as a champion of Czech supremacy, Czechs deploring the nationalism of the Slovaks, Lech Walesa using anti-Semitic innuendo during his presidential campaign against his critics and challengers, and so forth. In all these countries, democracy appeared to be more an ideal than a procedural reality. In Southeastern Europe, the former communist parties managed to survive the first revolutionary shock. In East-Central Europe, they changed not only names but also habits and appeared to have converted to the values of social democracy. The cleavage within the region ran between the countries that had completely broken with the communist system and those that remained somewhere in the middle of the road, as in the case of Romania, Serbia, and Bulgaria. With the exception of Czechoslovakia, none of these countries could invoke a consistently democratic tradition. At the same time, one must not forget that the changes were taking place against the background of European integration and that the price for engaging in new forms of authoritarian politics could be international isolation and a perpetuation of the state of underdevelopment that had provoked the end of communism. The competition between the two tendencies—the ethnocentric versus the democratic temptation—is the most important development taking place in the aftermath of the communist defeat. In the words of Polish journalist and activist Adam Michnik:

> On top of the clash between different cultural perspectives and understandings of civilization are added controversies which turn round problems of a more concrete kind. How best should one steer politics? By means of evolution, without the use of force, or by following the logic of revolutionary upheaval and purges? Should society be open or, on the contrary, enclosed within its own particular forms? Should the new order rest on the

adoption of all the conditions imposed by democracy, or on observance of a principle of revenge against members of the former regime? In other words, should the road taken be that of Spain when released from the rule of Franco, or that of Iran whereby they escaped the dictatorship of the Shah for that of the Ayatollah?[1]

As the East European countries emerge as important actors on the international stage, their future is far from certain. Optimists would maintain that democracy is their only rational choice. Pessimists would argue that rational choices are infrequent in history and that political and cultural traditions as well as enduring mythologies could result in the rise of new authoritarian regimes based on collective anguishes and neuroses. One thing is sure: The 1989 antitotalitarian revolution opened many avenues. Whether these countries will become democracies or ethnocracies is a question that remains unanswered.

Fifty-two years ago Germany's invasion of Poland and subsequent occupation of the region led to the long war between the Axis (Germany, Italy, and Japan) and the Allies (Great Britain, France, and, after 1941, the Soviet Union and the United States). World War II left all of Europe devastated, economically and politically, creating the perfect environment for Stalinism's rapid expansion from the Soviet Union. The spread of communism through the Eastern half of Europe frightened many policy-makers and citizens in the nations of Western Europe and helped precipitate the Cold War between the United States and the Soviet Union. The Cold War in turn led to the proliferation of nuclear weapons globally and to McCarthyism in the United States, among other consequences. Hence understanding Eastern Europe is directly related to global security and national ideology issues. The nations of Eastern Europe, to cite the old children's parable, are like the small, vital nails that hold a horseshoe on a hoof: "For want of a nail the horseshoe was lost, for want of the shoe the horse was lost, for want of the horse the rider was lost, for want of the rider the message was lost, for want of the message the battle was lost—all was lost for want of a nail." For fifty years, the world limped along without the full participation of the nations of Eastern Europe, but the world had adjusted itself to the instability. The adjustment was fairly easy, for the region appeared to operate under essentially monolithic communist policies; foreign governments and businessmen understood that relations with the nations of Eastern Europe were regulated by Moscow and local communist parties. The reemergence of the multifaceted character of those nations, the distinctiveness of their peoples, cultures, and politics, has left many policy-makers, businessmen, and average citizens around the world looking for new ways to understand the region. This book provides an orientation to the politics of the nations of Eastern Europe.

An understanding of the politics and peoples of Eastern Europe and how the dynamics of that region relates to global stability requires some knowledge of history at least as far back as the beginning of this century. The post-1989 revival of Central European nostalgia, with its Hapsburgian overtones, is more than a mere cultural phenomenon. There is a tendency to idealize the times of the empire and to perceive pre–World War I Austria-Hungary as the model for a possible Central European Confederation. Opposed to that "cosmopolitan" trend, the resurrection of old myths and illusions about the predestined role of the national community, presumably endangered by foreign influences, and other archaic tribal passions long considered vanished, as well as the frequent outbursts of anti-Semitism in Hungarian, Polish, Romanian, and Slovak public life, show that the precommunist chauvinist traditions did not disappear. Politically, there is an encouraging search for the legacy of the state of law (Rechtsstaat) that existed in that region before the collapse of the Austrian-Hungarian Empire. There is also a widespread yearning for the times when Prague, Budapest, Bucharest, and Warsaw were truly European capitals, cradles for daring cultural experiments situated in the vanguard of artistic modernity. To give some examples: During the first decades of the twentieth century it was in Prague that Franz Kafka wrote his stories and novels; Budapest was the headquarters of hectic intellectual ferment exemplified by names like Georg Lukacs, Arthur Koestler, and Bela Bartok.[2] As for Bucharest, it was there that such authors as Eugène Ionesco, Mircea Eliade, and Emil Cioran made their literary debuts during the interwar period.

In that part of the world, the phantoms of the past continue to haunt the collective imagination. Sometimes they contribute to peace and reconciliation; at other times they inspire and mobilize resentments and animosities. To be able to comprehend the present mosaic of ethnic, political, and cultural strains and its implications for the future, it is vitally important to revisit the historical experience of the East European countries between 1918 and 1945, before the advent of communist regimes, in the aftermath of World War II. It may seem like a cliché, but for the nations of Eastern Europe the precommunist past is prologue. Those nations whose citizens entered communism with some limited experience with democratic values, such as free speech, will be better able to organize political systems that are tolerant and nonauthoritarian. At the same time, democratic reconstruction in those countries depends on their ability to cope with the legacy of many unresolved ethnic, social, and political issues. The exit from communism generates the eruption of long-contained explosive forces, but as the French political philosopher Jean-François Revel has noted, the old problems are at the same time new problems, characteristic of the twenty-first century—that is, insoluble in the absence of democracy and the state of law.[3]

A FRAGMENTED WORLD, 1918–45

During the nineteenth century Eastern Europe was simply part of the East. To be sure, the West knew of the existence of Hungarians, Romanians, and Poles, but the widespread attitude was one of benign neglect. Most of the countries discussed in this book emerged as independent nation-states only following the collapse of the great European empires in 1917–18.

Before World War I, the existence of Austro-Hungarian imperial domination kept many of the religious, cultural, and ethnic conflicts that have beset Eastern Europe since 1918 in check. With its unresolved tensions, the world that emerged out of the ashes of the dead empires and the Wilsonian dream of universal democracy seemed ripe for bloody explosions of intolerance and exclusiveness. The nation-states created on the basis of such noble principles as the right to self-determination ensured very little protection for minorities. The new borders were designed to accommodate the victors and their protégés. They often ignored the plight of large minorities, whose calls for cultural autonomy were considered seditious by the ruling ethnic groups. Germans and Hungarians in Czechoslovakia; Ukrainians and Jews in Poland; Hungarians, Jews, and Ukrainians in Romania were among those who experienced the consequences of ethnic harassment and even persecution.

Romania, a country that joined the Entente coalition (formed mainly by Russia, Great Britain, and France) in 1916, was rewarded under the Versailles and Trianon Treaties (1918–20) and expanded its territory by incorporating Transylvania and Northern Bukovina from Austria-Hungary and Bessarabia from Russia. Also as a result of the new international arrangements consecrated by the Versailles Treaty, Yugoslavia appeared as an entirely new political entity, with an Eastern Orthodox Serbian dynasty ruling a country that included not only Catholic Croatia and Slovenia but also predominantly Muslim Bosnia and Herzegovina. As a result of the defeat of Austria-Hungary and the region's competing ethnic ambitions, Hungary's territory was shrunk to one-

third of what it had been before 1914.[4] Hungary, itself a former part of
the multinational, Austrian-dominated empire, acquired state independence, but large Hungarian minorities were destined to live in the
newly created or substantially expanded successor states.

One of those new entities was Czechoslovakia, which included the
former imperial provinces of Bohemia, Moravia, and Slovakia. Of all the
countries in the region, although it was not spared major ethnic conflicts,
Czechoslovakia seemed the only successful democratic experiment, inas-
much as it included a well-functioning parliamentary system, a strong
presidency, and the separation of state powers, inspired by the American
Constitution. Founded in 1918, the Czechoslovak Republic showed tolerance for political opposition, including the communists, but failed to
satisfy the strong national sentiments of the Slovaks. The Founding
Father and first president of Czechoslovakia, Tomas G. Masaryk, was
convinced that economic and social development would suffice to erase
the differences between Czechs and Slovaks. He accused the Hungarians
of having invented the very notion of a Slovak nation.[5] On the other
hand, with its superior technological infrastructure, Czechoslovakia
looked like an economic paradise in comparison with the other East
European countries.

Bulgaria and Romania had been monarchies since the nineteenth
century, and Yugoslavia emerged as a kingdom after 1918. Hungary was
ruled, after a short-lived 1919 communist revolution, by Miklos Horthy,
an admiral without a fleet, who played the role of regent for a nonexistent king. Romania, following the adoption of the 1923 Constitution
(largely inspired by the Belgian model), had a multiparty system within a
constitutional monarchy. Despite the onslaughts of extreme right-wing
and left-wing movements, the parliamentary system functioned properly
until 1938, when King Carol II proclaimed his royal dictatorship and
dissolved the parties and the parliament. The period between 1923 and
1938 can thus be seen as the only genuinely democratic stage in the
country's history. Poland, reborn as a nation in 1917 following the disintegration of the Czarist empire, for most of the interwar period was a
republic run by authoritarian leaders who drew their legitimacy from their
having resisted Soviet efforts to occupy that country in 1920. Although
formally an independent kingdom, Albania was in reality Italy's economic and diplomatic client.[6]

In all those countries, attitudes toward the Bolshevik Revolution and
the Soviet state were of paramount importance. After centuries of living
under the political and cultural domination of the Austro-Hungarian
Empire, Imperial Germany, Czarist Russia, and the Ottoman Turks, most

citizens of Eastern Europe wanted to assert their ethnic identity. Nationalism was on the rise, and Sovietism, with its claim to embody the interests of the workers regardless of nationality, was perceived as a mortal threat to the new nation-states' very existence. The internationalist mystique propagated by the Communist International (Comintern), founded by Lenin in Moscow in March 1919, was able to inspire no more than tiny communities of zealots. The Soviets tried to export their revolution and did not hesitate to use the Red Army as the bearer of their expansionist dreams. For example, had the Bolsheviks managed to occupy Poland as a result of the Red Army's "March on Warsaw" in 1920, they would have turned that country into a Soviet Republic and extinguished its cultural and ethnic identity for many decades. Being anti-Bolshevik or anticommunist in Poland or Romania—states whose integrity was questioned by the Kremlin and its supporters—was equated with fighting for national survival. More than fifty-five years after the Red Army's defeat in Poland, Adam Michnik offered a neat assessment of the importance of the anticommunist triumph during what was often referred to as the "miracle on the Vistula":

> We owe to the 1920 victory over the Bolsheviks twenty years of independent Polish thought which inspired and still inspires generations. Yes, contemporary resistance to Sovietization is to a large extent possible thanks to the cultural reserves created by the interwar Republic. If the Red Army had won the Battle of Warsaw, if a Provisional Revolutionary Committee had started governing Poland, then perhaps I would be living today in Kolyma or Birobidzhan; who knows whether I'd speak Polish, whether a generation of Polish intelligentsia would not have been turned into fodder for polar bears, if Polish culture could have avoided the disaster that befell Russian culture under Stalin's rule.[7]

Michnik's hindsight explains why the policy of creating a *cordon sanitaire* against Bolshevik expansionism in Eastern Europe was so popular among large social strata, including the downtrodden. The awareness of a Soviet threat led to joint efforts by Polish, Czechoslovak, and Romanian elites to cooperate in their international initiatives. But the persistence of national animosities between successor states prevented the emergence of a coordinated pan–East European foreign policy.

Each of these countries harbored substantial social inequities. The land reforms of the early 1920s fell short of lifting the derelict-like living standards of the peasants. Except for Czechoslovakia, unemployment, primarily the intellectual unemployment created by the existence of an overpopulation of lawyers, teachers, and journalists, was all-pervasive and propitious for the rise of political extremism, including terrorism and physical violence. Social discontent led to explosions of hatred and anger. The new democratic institutions, which included parliaments and an independent judiciary, were too fragile to contain those radical onslaughts. In Romania a fascist movement was formed in the early 1920s and took the name "Legion of Archangel Michael," later known as the "Iron Guard." Exploiting social frustrations and ethnic phobias, manipulating religious symbols, and promising the spiritual purification of the country's corrupt political life, it tried to mobilize Romanians against ethnic minorities, primarily the Jews. Combining romantic anticapitalist motifs with virulent chauvinism, the Iron Guard regarded parliamentary democracy as a non-Romanian, artificial Western institution that had to be replaced by a dictatorship.[8]

By the 1930s, right-wing authoritarianism was definitely gathering momentum in all these countries, with the exception once again of Czechoslovakia, although even there a pro-Nazi movement was increasingly influential among the German minority. The failure of the Western powers to offer reliable guarantees against revisionist powers interested in redrawing the borders established by the 1920 Treaty of Trianon only helped demagogic populist movements to recruit more and more adherents. Inspired by the Nazis in Germany and the Fascists in Italy, they despised the parliamentary system and resented liberal democracy. Instead they wanted to establish dictatorships based on the cult of the leader and xenophobic-atavistic values. Such movements developed in Romania (the Iron Guard, led by Corneliu Zelea Codreanu), in Hungary under the name of the "Arrow Crosses," and Slovakia, where an extremist xenophobic party was founded by the nationalist priest Andrej Hlinka. In addition to being viciously anti-Semitic, those parties were also outspokenly supportive of Hitler's expansionist plans.

Interestingly, coincident with the mounting political tensions, Eastern Europe witnessed a unique cultural flourishing. Budapest and Bucharest, Prague and Belgrade, Krakow and Zagreb were dynamic cultural centers where young intellectuals feverishly engendered new philosophical and artistic trends. Surrealist groups and publications, for example, were extremely lively in Romania and Czechoslovakia, as were modern philosophical trends like existentialism and phenomenological philosophy. The area (which then considered itself part of Central Europe, lying as it did midway between the Urals and the western shores of the continent) was the homeland for the European avant-garde as well as the birthplace of some of the most innovative cultural currents of the cen-

tury, including the theater of the absurd, psychoanalysis, structural lin-
guistics, and analytical philosophy. In that part of the world, people
valued memory and tried to escape a perpetually cunning History. For
them History had been a slaughterhouse, a stage for continuous injustice
and defeats. Memory was the faculty that preserved the unfulfilled
dreams of freedom and expectations for a community of true citizens.
Apocalyptic sarcasm rather than metaphysical commitments was the hallmark of the Central European identity. Unlike the Russians, Germans, or
French, the Central Europeans were always aware of the fragility of their
political settings. In the words of the Czech novelist Milan Kundera:

> Central Europe as a family of small nations has its own vision of the world,
> a vision based on a deep distrust of history. History, that goddess of Hegel
> and Marx, that incarnation of reason that judges us and arbitrates our
> fate—that is the history of conquerors. The peoples of Central Europe are
> not conquerors. They cannot be separated from European history; they
> cannot exist outside it; but they represent the wrong side of this history;
> they are its victims and outsiders. It's this disabused view of history that is
> the source of their culture, of their wisdom, of their "nonserious spirit"
> that mocks grandeur and glory.[9]

The historical fatality represented by the looming proximity of the Russian and German empires caused Central European intellectuals to look
askance at millenary promises of radical ideologies like communism and
fascism. However, some intellectuals, like the Hungarian philosopher
Georg Lukacs, the Romanian writer Panait Istrati, and the Polish poet
Alexander Wat, embraced communism because they felt alienated in
their original bourgeois milieu and tried to transcend it by espousing the
messianic creed of Leninism. Later, when they realized that they had
been duped, many broke with the totalitarian faith and became its most
scathing critics. Embittered and pessimistic, disgusted with rampant hypocrisy of a philistine world, and despairing over the chances for democracy to withstand its enemies, many ended up by taking own their lives.
The case of the Hungarian-born writer Arthur Koestler, author of the
classic anti-Stalinist novel *Darkness at Noon*, published in England in
May 1941, is emblematic of the destiny of Central European intellectuals
in this century of radical illusions and devastating disenchantments.
Danilo Kis, the Yugoslav novelist, wrote in a memorable essay on Central
Europe, several years after Koestler's suicide in the early 1980s: "The
intellectual adventure of Koestler, through his *ultimate choice*, is unique
even in the most broadly defined limits of Europe. It contains the poten-

tial biography of every Central European intellectual. In its radical realiza-tion."[10] In Central Europe intellectuals played a crucial role in articulat-ing values and defending the cultural memory of nations long deprived of state existence. In Poland, Hungary, Czechoslovakia, and Romania intel-lectuals were widely perceived as moral standard-bearers. During the nineteenth century, it was the intelligentsia (a term of Russian origin denoting the morally and socially concerned segment of the intellectual class) that spearheaded the struggle for national liberation; the group continued to enjoy its missionary status even after the formation of the nation-states. Political attitudes espoused by prominent intellectuals had immediate effects on large social strata that identified themselves with those whom they trusted and often followed. More than in other places, Central European intellectuals were seen to be and acted like paragons of social and national causes.

The ferment in intellectual life during the interwar period and the various responses to utopian temptations are superbly captured by Alexan-der Wat, the Polish writer, in his conversations with Czeslaw Milosz. According to Wat, the appeal of communism for most intellectuals was associated primarily with its ability to meet the human yearning for solidarity and fraternity:

> The warmth of brotherhood. *Fraternité* . . . it all starts with *fraternité*. But it was clear that no other party, no church was providing it. The church was too large, too cold, ritualistic, ornamental. . . . The communist church had the wisdom, like the early Christian communities (though I greatly dislike analogies with early Christianity; these analogies are nearly always misleading), to base itself on the cell where everyone knew each other and where everyone loved each other. And the warmth, the mutual love found in that little cell surrounded by a hostile world made for a powerful bond.[11]

Precisely because social tensions were so high and the democratic institutions were too recent to have generated a stable pluralist political culture, totalitarian mass movements were able to gain a foothold in those countries. In March 1919 the Third International (Comintern) was founded. Its bylaws included the obligation of local communist par-ties willing to become its members to obey Moscow's directives slavishly. According to the "Conditions of Admission into the Communist Interna-tional" adopted by the Comintern's Second Congress in 1920, the deci-sions of the Moscow headquarters were binding on all the affiliate parties. Opposition to them amounted to treason and led to excommunication.[12]

World communism had found its Mecca. Following Lenin's death in 1924, Stalin turned the Comintern into an instrument for the implementation of his expansionist designs. The national branches acted as Trojan horses, disciplined contingents of fanatical supporters of every twist in the Comintern's strategy. Everywhere in the world, communist groups acted as Moscow's instrument. In Western Europe they could arouse some support from radicalized industrial workers and gullible intellectuals who ignored the true conditions in Soviet Russia. In Eastern Europe, the very proximity of the Soviet Union and the threat of Soviet aggression made the existence of those parties extremely difficult. For the communist parties in Romania and Poland, the situation was even more dramatic: They endorsed the Soviet territorial claims and could therefore be stigmatized as antinational formations. Formed in the early 1920s, from the very outset those parties championed the Soviet strategy of disrupting the newly created democratic institutions. Indeed, with the exception of Czechoslovakia, communist parties were outlawed in all East European countries. The more marginal these groups were, with their visionary and inflammatory rhetoric, the more sectarian and intransigent their internal life. The first generation of East European communist leaders was made up of people who participated in the Comintern's activities during Lenin's last years in power. They had witnessed Stalin's intrigues during the struggle for Lenin's mantle. Some of them had been supportive of Stalin's enemies in the Bolshevik leadership. Others were committed Stalinists with a high sense of discipline; they willingly participated in the Comintern-engineered purges of their own parties. To deter the dissenting elements, Stalin insisted on the need to "Bolshevize" these parties by eliminating the first generation and replacing it with more docile persons.

During the 1930s the entire elite of the East European communist parties perished in the Great Purge massacres in the Soviet Union. Because Stalin had a particular distaste for Polish communists, whom he accused of the mortal sins of Trotskyism and Luxemburgism, in 1938 he presided over the complete disbandment of the Polish communist party. Wera Kostrzewa, Julian Lenski-Leszczynski, and Alfred Warski, the historical leaders of Polish communism, were all executed. The whole exiled elite of Polish communism was ruthlessly massacred in Soviet prisons. Other parties suffered similar experiences: Milan Gorkic, the general secretary of the Yugoslav communist party, was liquidated in the Soviet Union, as were the founding fathers of Romanian communism, including Alexandru Dobrogeanu-Gherea, Imre Aladar, David Fabian, and many others.[13]

Enthralled with their internationalist delusions, convinced that by serving the Bolshevik revolution they were serving the cause of the world revolution and the emancipation of the proletariat, these devout communists accepted Stalin's murderous verdict without a murmur. The replacement of the first nuclei of communist leaders with an even more subservient generation of Moscow-trained apparatchiks led to the complete elimination of any critical trends within those parties.

Despite their unbounded obedience in relations with Moscow, some of the elites found themselves in particularly difficult situations. Moscow always treated the Romanian communist party as a kind of poor relation precisely because it was not able to overcome its marginal status.[14] On the one hand, the Kremlin imposed on them a suicidal line that prevented them from becoming mass parties; on the other, it used their marginality constantly to humiliate them. The Bulgarian Communist Party enjoyed more favorable treatment, mainly because of the international stature of its leader, Georgi Dimitrov, who, after his acquittal in the December 1933 Leipzig trial, had become a cult figure for the whole international left. Dimitrov, a political refugee in Germany, was accused by the Nazis of having masterminded the Reichstag fire soon after Hitler's takeover in January 1933. In a widely publicized trial he managed to denounce the Nazi leaders as the real perpetrators of that political provocation. He was permitted to leave Germany and went to Moscow, where he became the chief executive of the Comintern.[15] In Hungary, where a Leninist revolutionary regime headed by Bela Kun had been overthrown with the support of Romania's army in 1919, the communists barely recovered from their defeat. Kun himself was executed in the Soviet Union as an "enemy of the people," and his name disappeared for two decades from all communist references to the ill-fated Budapest Commune of 1919.

After 1938, Josip Broz, a Croatian communist who became famous under the pseudonym Tito (one of the more than seventy that he used as a clandestine militant), was entrusted to lead the clandestine Yugoslav communist party. Among the rising stars of Yugoslav communism was Milovan Djilas, a philosophy student who would later become the country' Vice President and, following his disenchantment with communism, a most vocal critic of the communist dictatorship and of Tito's autocratic behavior.

At the other end of the region's political spectrum were the strong right-wing populist movements that appealed primarily to peasants and recently urbanized social groups through the use of chauvinistic and mystical symbols and values. Unlike the communists, who criticized the status quo in the name of absolute commitment to the defense of the Soviet Union, the alleged "motherland of world proletariat," the extreme right criticized democracy and capitalism for their failure to create "an organic national body." In Romania, the far right included—in addition to the "Legion" (rechristened the Iron Guard in the 1930s), made up of exalted and hopeless young intellectuals, students, priests, and untrained workers—many smaller but extremely vociferous parties and groups, which all held anti-Western, anti-Semitic, and anti-intellectual attitudes in common. Those groups lambasted communism as a "Judeo-masonic" concoction and promised to purify the country's corrupt political life through the establishment of a dictatorial regime headed by a charismatic strongman: the Iron Guard's captain, Corneliu Zelea Codreanu. Their ideal was the formation of a political community based on the values of Romanianism and Orthodoxy. In other words, they advocated the re-placement of the secular parliamentary regime with a religiously based "national-legionary state." To achieve their aims, the members of the Iron Guard used the weapon of political terrorism. In December 1933 an Iron Guard commando assassinated the liberal Prime Minister, Ion G. Duca, well known for his pro-Western and antifascist views. The radical-ization of the far right, especially after the Nazi takeover in Germany, forced the Romanian political class to engage in repressive actions against the leaders of the fascist movement. Codreanu himself was ar-rested and murdered by King Carol II's police in 1938. A royal dictator-ship was proclaimed, and the parliamentary system was suppressed. The escalation of violence in that country seemed inevitable.

In March 1938 Czechoslovakia and, *ipso facto,* the other descendants of Austria-Hungary received a mortal blow with the signing of the Mu-nich agreements, which accepted the German claims on the Sudeten-land. In September of the same year the Wehrmacht occupied Prague, and Hitler announced the establishment of the Protectorate of Bohemia and Moravia. Slovakia jumped to proclaim its independence, and a pro-Nazi regime was established under the leadership of an arch-reactionary priest, Monsignor Tiso. In August 1939 the Nazi-Soviet Pact put an end to any illusions about the possibility of preventing war.

Soviet and German troops cooperated in the dismemberment of Po-land. Soviet Foreign Minister Vyacheslav Molotov applauded the disap-pearance of Poland from Europe's map. The Soviets, like the Nazis, could not accept the existence of the Polish republic, which Molotov disparag-ingly called "the monstrous bastard of the Peace of Versailles."[16] What had been known as Central Europe ceased to exist at the moment the totalitarian twin brothers of communism and fascism imposed their iron grip on those countries. To paraphrase Czeslaw Milosz, all the countries that had suffered the consequences of the Nazi-Soviet Pact continued to exist as a nonexistent entity in a traumatized cultural memory:

> There is probably a basic division between the two halves of Europe in the difference between memory and lack of memory. For Western Europeans, the Molotov–Ribbentrop pact is no more than the vague recollection of a misty past. For us—I say us, for I myself experienced the consequences of the agreement between the superpowers—that division of Europe has been a palpable reality, as it has been for all those in our countries who were born after the war. Therefore I would risk a very simple definition. I would define Central Europe as all the countries that in August 1939 were the real or hypothetical object of a trade between the Soviet Union and Germany. . . . Decades of pain and humiliation: *that* is what distinguishes Central European countries from their Western counterparts.[17]

In June 1940 the Soviets addressed an ultimatum to the Romanian government demanding the immediate retrocession of Bessarabia and Northern Bukovina. Completely isolated internationally, King Carol II, who had established his personal dictatorship in 1938, gave in and accepted the Soviet *diktat*. In August the Germans and the Italians imposed on Romania the Vienna Award, and Northern Transylvania was given to Hungary. Several days later the King fled Romania, and a new dictatorship was established, headed by General Ion Antonescu and the Iron Guard leader, Horia Sima. In January 1941 the Iron Guard tried to get rid of Antonescu but failed. A military dictatorship was set up, Horia Sima then left Romania for Germany, and Antonescu was proclaimed the *Conducator* of the Romanian state.

Germany attacked Yugoslavia in 1941, and several resistance movements were immediately organized. The most powerful were the nationalist Serbian movement led by General Draza Mihajlovic, known as the Chetniks, and the communist resistance directed by Tito, known as the Partisans. During that period, Hungary maintained good relations with Germany, although Admiral Horthy was outflanked from the extreme right by the ultra-chauvinistic Arrow Cross movement. In Bulgaria the militarist regime, close to Germany, strove to keep the country out of imminent conflicts. For almost two years, between September 1939 and June 1941, when Hitler attacked the Soviet Union, local communist parties in Bulgaria, Czechoslovakia, Hungary, Poland, and Romania remained in a standby posture and even lambasted the British and French "militarists" for their alleged bellicose adventurism. (Yugoslavia was the exception.) The explanation for the East European communist parties' refusal to engage in anti-Nazi actions between August 1939 and June 1941 was their subordination to the Soviet-controlled Comintern.

The August 1940 Comintern directives to those parties were to oppose strongly the attempts organized by pro-British and pro-French circles—the "imperialist warmongers," as the Stalinist propaganda called the Western democracies in the months of the honeymoon with Hitler. Like the French communists, who initially pledged to cooperate diligently with the Nazi occupiers, communists in Eastern Europe were actually sabotaging the anti-German resistance. Later they would sweep those inglorious episodes under the carpet and create the legend of the communists' crucial role in the struggle against the Nazi invaders in all the East European countries.

When Hitler attacked the Soviet Union, communications between Moscow and the communist parties in Europe were shut down. For some time those groups were free to act on their own. That explains the somewhat uncoordinated and often daring strategies adopted by domestic leaderships, including the Yugoslav communists' effort to tinker with Soviet-style institutions without Stalin's knowledge or approval. In the same vein, in Poland local communists, headed by Wladislaw Gomulka, engaged in the reconstruction of the communist party and launched a partisan movement without a direct Soviet blessing.

The main characteristic of the war years from the viewpoint of the relationship between the Kremlin and the communist parties of Eastern Europe was the partial interruption of the flow of information and support between the center and its tributaries. In each communist party, local (home) nuclei emerged as parallel and potentially alternative leaderships to the Moscow-trained exiles. In the Yugoslav case, Tito's radical propensities and his inclination to out-Stalin Stalin led him to initiatives that could only embarrass the Soviet leaders in their relations with the Western allies. It is important to remember that in 1943 Stalin decided to disband the Communist International as a gesture of good will to Churchill and Roosevelt. Later it became clear that the dissolution, justified at the time as recognition the decreased need for guidance from Moscow on the part of the maturing local communist parties, was merely a propagandistic concession linked to Stalin's desire to mitigate the Allies' dislike of the revolutionary Bolshevik legacy.

As soon as the Soviets penetrated the territory of Eastern Europe, they resumed their controls over the communist parties and installed "Muscovites" (communists who had spent the war in exile in Moscow) at the top. Ana Pauker and Vasile Luca joined Gheorghe Gheorghiu-Dej as secretaries of the Romanian Communist Party's Central Committee. In Poland, Boleslaw Bierut, the head of the Moscow-sponsored Lublin Government, became General Secretary of the Polish Communist Party and initiated a purge of the home communists headed by Gomulka.

In Czechoslovakia and elsewhere, the interrupted hegemony resumed the same pattern of Soviet domination. Hegemony was pursued with the appointment of the former Moscow emigrés Klement Gottwald and Rudolf Slansky, respectively, as President and General Secretary of the Communist Party in Czechoslovakia. In Bulgaria, the home-based communists headed by Traicho Kostov had to share power with the Muscovites Georgi Dimitrov, Vasil Kolarov, and Vulko Chervenkov. In Hungary the Muscovites took over the whole leadership of the Hungarian Communist Party and established a clique dictatorship under a leading foursome made up of General Secretary Matyas Rakosi and his faithful underlings Ernő Gerő (the former NKVD officer who had presided over the purge of the anti-Stalinist revolutionaries in Barcelona during the Spanish civil war), Mihaly Farkas, and Jozsef Revai, a former disciple of the celebrated Marxist thinker Georg Lukacs who had been converted to hard-line Stalinism.

Fewer possibilities existed in Yugoslavia for the hegemonic pattern to proceed along the same lines. Tito had succeeded in creating a powerful mass base for himself and his closest associates (Edvard Kardelj, Aleksandar Rankovic, and Milovan Djilas). During the bloody confrontations of World War II and in spite of their unabashed support for Stalin and the Soviet international strategy, the Yugoslav communists managed to turn themselves into a national movement. The Kremlin's real problem with Tito was that, although definitely full of love and admiration for Stalin, his ambition was to become Stalin's counterpart in the Balkans. Eventually that unconscious, unavowed, but very real design would bring him into first a covert and then an open conflict with the Soviet dictator.

The Yugoslav communists launched terrorist actions against their enemies—Nazi and otherwise—and instituted a secret police system whose repressive methods were directly borrowed from the arsenal of the Soviet secret police (NKVD).[18] Tito then sought to expand his influence in other Balkan countries. He sent his emissary Svetozar Vukmanovic-Tempo to develop contacts with the Greek communists, who were engaged in a civil war against supporters of a pro-Western monarchic regime. The Yugoslavs also acted as "Big Brother" toward the tiny Albanian Communist Party, headed by Enver Hoxha, a former French teacher in the city of Tirana.[19]

When Stalin decided to anathematize Tito and expel him from the world communist movement, Hoxha and his acolytes remembered the humiliation inflicted upon them by the arrogant Yugoslavs and added some of the most obstreperous notes to the Soviet-orchestrated anti-Yugoslav campaign.

MESSIANIC DELUSIONS

What were all these communist formations promising to liberate their nations? What values did they stand for, and what blueprints did they offer for their countries' renewal?

It would be easy but frivolous to say that all those engaged in clandestine communist activities during World War II were inspired exclusively by their unreserved worship of the Soviet Union. In addition to that prevailing temporal motivation, those people were convinced that their struggle against fascism was part of a universal human emancipation.

Many of the communists were outright Soviet agents, but not all. Especially among young intellectuals, the identification of the Soviet Union with the cause of human freedom was very powerful. Both during the interwar period and throughout the years of the anti-Nazi resistance, many young people joined the communist movement convinced that it offered a superior form of historical rationality. Information about the extent of the Great Purge in the USSR was scarce, so many people tended to dismiss it as fascist slander. The atrociousness of the fascist crimes and the astute manipulation by the Stalinists of democratic symbols, particularly after the Seventh Comintern Congress, when the strategy of the "Popular Fronts" (communist-controlled umbrella organizations) was adopted, made some people believe that after the war Eastern Europe would be governed by popular democratic regimes, with the communists behaving like normal political actors in the pluralistic game. The myth of a classless society where all political and economic tensions would be abolished in favor of an earthly paradise of human equality and dignity functioned as an excuse for the communist militants' willing abandonment of their reasoning powers. But the Kremlin's strategists and their East European puppets, of course, had no intention of establishing pluralism or classless societies. The Comintern's masterminds realized that the arrival of the Soviet troops in those countries would provide the communist parties with extraordinary political and logistic superiority over any of their adversaries.

Since the 1930s, Eastern Europe's communist parties had been thoroughly Stalinized. There were some residual elements of original faith in the socialist dream of world revolution, but as a rule all those elites were ready to serve the Soviet Union without hesitation. Most resented local Social Democratic parties that advocated an evolutionary road to a more just society. Following the Bolsheviks' rude propaganda techniques, the communists accused their rivals of being agents of the bourgeoisie. But because Stalin wanted to preserve his image (at least until the world war was over) as a benign and wise statesman, the pro-Soviet communists subdued their venomous rhetoric and pledged to behave as champions of national independence.

During the years of World War II, no parties were more vociferous in proclaiming their commitment to patriotic values than the communists. The fact that many of their militants served prison terms or had even been killed in fascist jails only enhanced their public image as exemplars of martyrdom and heroism. Their sacrifices, in many cases genuine, were skillfully exploited by a cynical propaganda machine that presented them as the only legitimate exponents of national interests. The communists went out of their way to polish their image and extended their hands to other political formations, creating large umbrella movements dedicated to the establishment of allegedly democratic governments. Such was the background of the illusions entertained by many in the West, including some of the most influential policy-makers, as they analyzed and responded to Stalin's "change of mind" about the necessity and feasibility of a "world revolution."

Although those illusions were rooted in wishful thinking and underrated or completely ignored the expansionist nature of the Soviet system, they were powerful enough to modify Western perceptions of the Soviet Union and to lead to a number of agreements, including those resulting from the Teheran (1944) and the Yalta (1945) conferences. At Teheran and Yalta the Soviet Union convinced its Western partners that it had the right to defend its sphere of influence in Eastern Europe. It did not matter that the language of the Yalta Declaration was imbued with flowery democratic promises: The Soviets knew how to use their internationally recognized role to impose satellite regimes in the countries of Eastern Europe.

In the name of the struggle against fascist vestiges, democratic parties in Eastern Europe were savagely persecuted, censorship was established and intensified, and secret police systems were instituted to harass all those who dared to criticize the communists. Anticommunism (or anti-Sovietism) was automatically equated with fascism. As soon as they realized that no real obstacle existed to prevent their rise to power, the local communist elites started to behave with increasing boldness.

The Soviet military presence on the territories of East European nations endowed the local communist elites with a shield of immunity that they knew how to employ successfully to further their monopolistic objectives. Across Eastern Europe, communist parties included in their official statements promises of democratic elections and respect for human rights and political tolerance; however, in practice those parties initiated continuous purges and single-mindedly established their political domination.

In order to accomplish their goals, they used splinter groups of the traditional indigenous parties and vainglorious political figures who were convinced that collaborating with the Stalinists would ensure their political survival. The communists, however, did not want to engage in any power-sharing. The logic of Leninism, with its militaristic organizational doctrine and extreme authoritarian practice, made the communists better prepared to win power in an ultimate showdown. Unlike their enemies, they were convinced that only a one-party system could solve their countries' problems. They sincerely abhorred parliamentarianism and regarded democratic structures as profoundly and incurably inept.

Unlike their rivals, the communists were not divided along ideological or moral lines. They were cohesive formations, monolithic in spirit and action. To be sure, these groups were not as monolithic as they claimed to be, but their factious strifes had more to do with the struggle for power within their sectarian boundaries than with different philosophies or strategies. The communists were educated in the spirit of unqualified support for their superiors. They obeyed the leadership's orders without murmur or scruples. In garrison-style formations, no wavering was permitted. To be a true communist, a party member had to surrender any personal claim to freedom of thought or personal honesty in favor of the suprapersonal entity called the party.

While the issue was the takeover of political power and the establishment of Soviet-style dictatorships, the communist party acted like a single body, without any trace of anarchy. The unifying feature was Stalinist dogma, the codified version of Leninism internalized by communist armies around the world. As if Stalinism were a revealed truth, the party members were expected to believe in its tenets with religious passion. Many accepted the complete renunciation of individual mental autonomy and served the "party" with the same zeal that an illuminated sect follows the dictates of a charismatic prophet. Indeed, a high percentage of mysticism existed in this abnegation, which bordered on absolute serfdom, but for the militants the experience was as an inebriating situation, a way of transcending any form of estrangement and achieving liberation through historical salvation. [20]

Party militants were sincerely convinced that the Stalinist model of society, with its rigid planning of everything human beings needed and its overall unsparing indoctrination, dubbed the education of the "new man," was superior to the conflict-ridden texture of the bourgeois world as exemplified by the contradiction between haves and have-nots and the perceived alienation of the intelligentsia. They thought importing the Soviet-style institutions to their countries would ensure modernization and rapid economic progress.

To achieve those goals of economic progress and modernization, the various East European communist parties undertook a systematic destructive operation whose chief consequence was the suppression of the civil society. That was, indeed, the main purpose of totalitarian practice in this century: to annihilate the sources of human creativity, to separate individuals from one another while making them mutually inimical, and to replace collective bonds of solidarity and support with the supremacy of the party-state, acclaimed as omnipotent and omniscient. All previous associations and groups had to disappear. The values long held to be sacred—patriotism, family, national traditions—had to be redefined in the light of communist dogmas. An overhaul of each country's cultural tradition and a revision of the moral postulates, including those derived from the European humanist tradition, were accomplished through the Marxist dogma of the class struggle.

In countries where the social contrasts were often outrageous before World War II, the communists' promises to defend the interests of the have-nots against the haves and to give selfless support to the social underdogs sounded appealing. They offered the intellectuals the opportunity to feel socially important and useful, and many intellectuals considered the chance a godsend.

Likewise, the communists abused the confidence of the working class by announcing that their party was the repository of all human virtues and was predestined by history to become the ruling force in society. Party members penetrated and eventually controlled the trade unions, which they considered to be their "transmission belts" to the working class. In reality, despite their proletarian verbiage, the communists did not trust the class in whose name they were trying to take over power: For them the workers were simply a maneuverable mass, a passive and pliable crowd, incapable of understanding its own interests. The communists acted as a pedagogical minority, enthralled with its own mission and convinced that any opposition to their party's designs was by definition criminal.

THE COMINFORM AND THE TWO CAMPS THEORY

Following the idyllic years 1944–45, when the Soviets claimed that they had no intent to establish Communist regimes in Eastern and Central Europe, things started to change in 1946. The Cold War had become increasingly intense. The Civil War in Greece, which had started in 1944, entered a more violent stage, the West hardened its opposition to communist insurrectionary tactics in various countries, and Stalin came to the conclusion that it was high time to abandon any soothing rhetoric about popular fronts and national coalitions. In the Kremlin it was a time of savage power struggles. Two factions were vying for the upper hand in the aging despot's entourage. On one side were the Moscow apparatchiks, headed by Georgy Malenkov and Lavrenty Beria. On the other, growing ever more obsessed with proving to Stalin their indefatigable commitment to the principles of international class struggle, were the former Leningrad party boss Andrei Zhdanov and his associates.[21]

For Zhdanov, first the British commitment supporting the anti-Communist forces in Greece and then the United States' decision to assist the economic recovery in Western Europe through the Marshall Plan were clear indications that the time for entente with the "bourgeois" former allies had come to an end. According to that high priest of Stalinist orthodoxy, a new stage in the irreconcilable struggle between the forces of peace and progress and those of reaction and war had begun. There was no longer any room for searches for "national roads to socialism." The battle cry sounded by Zhdanov for all communists and "progressive forces" was to close ranks around the Soviet Union, "the fortress of mankind's dreams of equality and happiness." This theory formulated by Zhdanov, at the time Stalin's chief lieutenant and the Kremlin's ideological czar, would be the alpha and omega of communist internationalism until Stalin's death in March 1953.

Zhdanov spelled out his strategy of intensification of international class warfare and elaborated on its implications for Eastern Europe during a secret meeting that took place in Poland, at Szklarska Poreba, in September 1947. On that occasion, representatives of the Bulgarian, Czechoslovak, French, Italian, Polish, Romanian, Soviet, and Yugoslav communist parties gathered to discuss a common response to what Stalin had identified as the new aggressive behavior of American imperialism. The conclave culminated in the creation of the Information Bureau of the Communist and Workers' parties with its headquarters in Belgrade. The creation of the new institution, usually referred to as the Cominform, indicated Moscow's desire to contain the centrifugal trends within world communism. Although it was intended as a successor to the Comintern, it lacked the defunct International's global stature and influence. For instance, it did not include some of the most influential parties engaged at that moment in civil wars (the Chinese and the Greek communist parties). Even more symptomatic was the absence of the Albanians and the East Germans, which meant the Cominform did not include all the actual or potential ruling European communist parties.

The Yugoslav communists were among the most vocal in calling for coordinated actions against the West and charged their colleagues from Italy and France with "defeatism," "capitulationism," and "right-wing opportunism." At the time of the secret meeting at Szklarska Poreba, Zhdanov's prestige in the Soviet Union and among communists throughout the world was at its apex; only one year had passed since he had lambasted the poet Anna Akhmatova and the satirist Mikhail Zoshchenko for their deviations from the dogmas of socialist realism, according to which "the artistic representation of reality must be linked with he task of ideological transformation and education of workers in the spirit of socialism."[22] During the anticultural campaign of 1946, Zhdanov formulated a chauvinistic, intensely anti-Western theory of the Great Russian claim to moral superiority and the obligation of the intellectuals to conform strictly to party commands:

> Our literature, which reflects a state order of much higher standards than that of any bourgeois country and a culture which is much greater than that of bourgeois countries, has the right to instruct others in a new public morality. Where can you find such a nation and such a country as we have? Where can you find such splendid human qualities as were shown by our Soviet people in the Fatherland war? . . . The writer cannot follow events. He must be the first in the ranks of the people; he must show them the way of progress but be guided by the methods of socialist realism, study our reality conscientiously, and try to understand the basis of our growth and development.[23]

During the Cominform's foundation meeting, Zhdanov pushed through the adoption of a declaration to the effect that it was the USSR that embodied the truly humanistic goals of the anti-Nazi struggle, whereas the Western powers had opposed Hitler only for greedy, imperialistic reasons. Crammed with ideological fictions and vengeful attacks on the West, the declaration was indeed a direct echo of the hardening of the Soviet domestic and international line. According to Stalin's chief ideo-

logue, the Soviet Union and other democratic countries had regarded as
their basic war aims the restoration and consolidation of democratic
order in Europe, the eradication of fascism, the prevention of any possibility of new aggression on the part of Germany, and the establishment of
lasting all-around cooperation among the nations of Europe. On the
other hand, Zhdanov maintained, the United States of America and
Great Britain had set themselves another goal in the war: to rid themselves of competitors on the market (Germany and Japan) and to establish their dominant position. Zhdanov's argument continued:

> This difference in the definition of war aims and tasks of the postwar
> settlement grew more profound after the war. Thus two camps were
> formed—the imperialist and antidemocratic camp, having as its basic aim
> the establishment of world domination for American imperialism and the
> smashing of democracy, and the anti-imperialist and democratic camp,
> having as its basic aim the undermining of imperialism, the consolidation
> of democracy, and the eradication of the remnants of fascism.[24]

Zhdanov's style was uniquely imperative and unambiguous. For him
there was no middle road between Soviet-style socialism and Western
capitalism. His Manichean vision found its corollary in the acceleration
of the satellization process in Eastern Europe.[25] The model then imposed
on Eastern Europe consisted in an extremely violent social, economic,
political, and cultural destruction of the old order; the elimination of all
potential or real political enemies; and the complete regimentation of
culture. The new structures erected on the ruins of those smashed and
increasingly atomized societies had to be carbon copies of the Soviet
ones: rubber-stamp parliaments, communist control over all spheres of
life, the establishment of concentration camps for the extermination of
politically unreliable elements, and the institution of a command economy, where private property was virtually eliminated and replaced by
state ownership of all resources.

In Romania, for instance, application of the model started in March
1945. Soviet Deputy Minister of Foreign Affairs Andrei Vyshinsky went
to Bucharest and forced King Michael to appoint Petru Groza, a communist fellow-traveler, as the country's Prime Minister. When the King
initially refused, the Soviet prosecutor-turned-diplomat raised his voice
and threatened direct Soviet intervention. In the meantime the communists mobilized their assault squads and instituted a state of terror in the
whole country. So the King gave in to the *diktat,* and the country fell into
the hands of a Soviet-appointed government. A communist, Teohari

Georgescu, became Minister of the Interior, ensuring the further deterioration of the already suffering democratic system. The transition to Sovietism was completed in December 1947 with the King's forced abdication and the proclaiming of a Romanian People's Republic.

Scenarios similar to the Romanian case can be detailed for most of Eastern Europe. In Hungary the communists waged a conquest of position, occupying one after the other all the vital centers of government. The communist leader Matyas Rakosi cynically referred to this "slicing off" of the non-Communist partners in the government coalition as "salami tactics."[26] Unlike the Hungarians, the Bulgarian communists used "frontist" tactics to emasculate their rivals and eventually to establish themselves in power.[27] In Poland, the communists had reemerged during the war under the name Polish Workers' Party, headed by the underground leader Wladyslaw Gomulka, and tried to appeal to the strong national sentiments of the population. It failed, however, to stir responsive chords among the masses, who continued to see the communists as the tool of the Soviet government. Having direct Soviet support and holding the key ministries, the communists engaged in a violent "pacification" by organizing a harsh repression against the last pockets of anticommunist armed resistance. A keen observer of Polish politics noted that:

> . . . in the immediate postwar years, the Communist Party and its allies commanded no significant popular support in the country. The great majority of Poles remained loyal to the Polish Government-in-Exile and, subsequently, supported the opposition led by the Polish Peasant Party. The Communist regime in Poland was entrenched in power only after a prolonged and, at times, fierce struggle between the Polish Workers' Party, openly assisted by the Soviet military might, and the anti-Communist political forces supported by the overwhelming majority of the Polish people.[28]

An element that ensured the vitality of the Polish anticommunist resistance was the intransigent conduct of the Catholic Church. Its supranational status, represented by subordination to the Vatican, was a source of international support at a time when the communists were trying to sever any link between local groups and institutions and the outside world. For the decades to come, the beleaguered Catholic Church would symbolize the last stronghold of Poland's civil society.

The last to fall victim to the communists' subversive tactics was Czechoslovakia. In February 1948 mass demonstrations were staged to

compel noncommunist ministers to resign because of their alleged conspiratorial activities. President Eduard Beneš had to yield to the communist leader Klement Gottwald's ultimatum. Beneš asked Gottwald to
form a new government without representatives of the democratic parties. Communist propaganda insisted that the takeover in Czechoslovakia had occurred in a nonviolent, constitutional way. The truth, however, was that the communists had prepared themselves for a military
showdown with the democratic forces and that militia units were ready
for action in factories throughout the country. Soviet Deputy Foreign
Minister Valerian Zorin's presence in Prague at the moment of the putsch
contributed to the psychological pressure on the opposition. Writing
twenty years after the February coup, during the Prague Spring of 1968, a
participant in the takeover admitted:

> We gave a distorted picture of the February story. . . . The true history of
> February, I feel, has never been faithfully narrated; only now are condi-
> tions ripening in which a critical study, among other things, could and
> should be made of the errors and half-truths and untruths uttered about
> February 1948, both at home and abroad.[29]

The Soviets even devised a theory to describe the nature of these new
regimes in Eastern Europe: According to Zhdanov, those governments
were not full-fledged "dictatorships of the proletariat" but experiments in
a new political formula called "people's democracy." Even the Cominform's official newspaper reflected the new political formula in its
name—For a Lasting Peace, for People's Democracy—a long title apparently invented by Stalin himself. This awkward name was an attempt to
force the Western media, whenever they cited the Cominform's organ, to
repeat its slogans.

The like the name of the Cominform's newspaper, the Prague coup of
February 1948 was tied to Stalin's anxiety over the temptation of the East
European communist elites to accept the Western offer for assistance
through the Marshall Plan. With the temptation of the Marshall Plan
beckoning, Stalin thought it was time to stop encouraging or accepting
any policy initiatives on the part of local communists. An important
conclusion to draw from Stalin's reaction is that the Cominform came
into being in order to coordinate, in keeping with the Soviet interpretation of the shifts in the international balance of power, both the domestic
and the foreign policies of the newly established regimes. In Stalin's view,
the imperialist contradictions were bound to intensify, the attacks on
socialist countries were likely to be more violent and frequent, and no

one could be permitted to break ranks at that particularly dangerous juncture.

Tito enthusiastically supported Stalin's new orientation but thought the moment was propitious for furthering his own hegemonic agenda. Ironically, it was precisely at the moment when the Soviet and the Yugoslav perspective on international class warfare were in the closest alignment that the clash between the two countries inevitably occurred. Tito ignored Stalin's jealous behavior and initiated a project for the creation of a Danubian confederation, including Yugoslavia, Bulgaria, and possibly Romania. Tito's secret contacts with the veteran Moscow-trained Bulgarian communist Georgi Dimitrov were correctly perceived by Moscow as a challenge to its overall supremacy, not only within the camp but also within the world communist movement.

Stalin could not bear the rise of a parallel center of power and initiative within world communism. He intensified his efforts to tame Yugoslavia's rebellious leadership. An exchange of letters between the Kremlin and Tito was begun, but to no avail. The dice had been cast, and there was no way for the Yugoslav heretic to back down. Once he had told Stalin that he rejected Moscow's condescending tutelage, he had sealed his fate and had turned into the Soviet dictator's worst enemy, a diabolical reincarnation of Menshevism, Trotskyism, and all the other "deviations" Stalin had managed to eradicate in the Soviet Union.

The conflict with Yugoslavia and Tito's excommunication from the Cominform in June 1948 gave the signal for the beginning of dramatic purges within the East European communist parties. It also indicated that Moscow's hegemony could not completely suppress domestic tendencies even within the most pro-Soviet communist formations. After all, Tito had dedicated all his life to the communist cause. He was a man with impeccable Stalinist credentials, so, in Stalin's eyes, Tito's unique fault was the desire to maintain his own and Yugoslavia's limited autonomy relative to the Kremlin.

In Stalin's view, at this particularly dangerous time, when the imperialists had decided to intensify their aggressive actions against the budding "people's democracies" and the threat of a new world war was looming large, no country or leader could be allowed to engage in national communist experiments. Nationalism, defined as the opposite of loyalty to the Soviet Union and its leader, was diagnosed as a betrayal of the sacred principles of Marxism-Leninism. From that moment on, those identified as nationalists could be charged with the most fantastic sins, including collaboration in the past with the Gestapo or, in the present, with Western intelligence agencies. That was the background of Stalin's clash with Yugoslavia. Monolithism was the religion of Stalinism, and all centrifugal trends had to be ruthlessly extirpated. Indeed, the purpose in creating the Cominform had been to coordinate all policies of the newly established regimes in accordance with the radicalization of Soviet international behavior and to prevent such clashes.

After all, the sole principle of legitimation for the ruling communist parties in the Soviet bloc was their unreserved attachment to the Soviet Union, their readiness to carry out unflinchingly all of Stalin's directives. He had invested the communist parties in Eastern Europe with power, and it was thanks to him that they had gained the ruling positions in their countries. Therefore, within the various countries of the Soviet bloc, party leaders could be allowed to enjoy the adoration of their subordinates, but their cults were only echoes of the true faith: unswerving love for Stalin. In the words of Wladislaw Gomulka, the Polish communist leader, the cult of the local leaders "could be called only a reflected brilliance, a borrowed light. It shone as the moon does."[30]

The logic of Stalinism excluded doubt and questioning, numbed critical reasoning and intelligence, and instituted Soviet-style Marxism as a system of universal truth inimical to any form of doubt. Stalin's alleged omniscience purported to settle all troubling issues and confusing situations. The logic was by definition exclusive and hortatory, a celebration of the pivotal role of cadres in a militaristic, rigidly hierarchical order. The leader was the only guarantor of ideological purity, and full submission to his orders was the only socially accepted conduct. Civic autonomy was thus destroyed, and a slavishly obedient form of political activism was the general norm. To achieve ideological uniformity and regimentation, Stalinism invented and perfected the mechanism of the permanent purge.

The purge mechanism, the basic technique of Stalinist demonology, was the modern equivalent of the medieval witch-hunt. It was eagerly adopted by Stalin's East European apprentices and adapted for their own purposes. Echoing Stalin's fervid cult, East European leaders engineered similar campaigns of praise and idolatry in their own countries. The party was identified with the supreme leader, whose chief merit consisted in having correctly applied the Stalinist line. The solutions to all disturbing questions could be found in Stalin's writings, and those who failed to discover the answers were branded "enemies of the people." Members of the traditional political elites, members of the clergy, and representatives of the nationalist intelligentsia who had refused to collaborate with the new regimes were sentenced to long prison terms following dramatic show trials or cursory in camera trials. That was the first stage of the purge in Eastern Europe. After 1949 the purges fed upon the communist elites themselves, and in that second purge many faithful Stalinists experienced firsthand the effects of the unstoppable terrorist machine they had helped set in motion.

According to the Polish-born philosopher Leszek Kolakowski, the purges had an integrative function, contributing to the destruction of the last vestiges of subjective autonomy and creating a social climate where no one would even dream of criticism: "The object of a totalitarian system is to destroy all forms of communal life that are not imposed by the state and closely controlled by it, so that individuals are isolated from one another and become mere instruments in the hands of the state. The citizen belongs to the state and must have no other loyalty, not even to the state ideology."[31] Only Stalin was privileged to interpret and reinterpret the ideological dogmas to suit opportunistic shifts in the official party line. Ideology was simultaneously vague and rigid, a mixture of prescriptions and interdictions, which the individual had to follow blindly.

As in the USSR in the late 1930s, in the Soviet bloc the ideology underlying this terrorist pedagogy was only partly irrational. While the victims recruited among politicians of the prewar political parties were innocent of the charges uttered against them, many of them embodied a political tradition, which the Stalinists were desperately trying to suppress. As for the communist victims, they belonged to a category described by Stalinist legal theory as "objective enemies." They were people who once in their lives may have expressed reservations about the sagacity of Soviet policies or, even worse, may have criticized Stalin personally. Links with Tito, of course, were used as arguments to demonstrate the political unreliability of certain East European leaders (for instance Laszlo Rajk in Hungary, who had fought in the Spanish Civil War and had maintained friendly relations with members of Tito's entourage). The purpose of the continuous cleansing was to eliminate any search for domestic initiatives and to ensure the complete Soviet domination of the East European satellites.

Domesticism, according to Zbigniew Brzezinski, was an exaggerated, even if frequently unconscious, "preoccupation with local, domestic communist objectives, at the expense of broader, international Soviet goals."[32] It was not an elaborated philosophy of opposition to Soviet hegemony, but a conviction on the part of some East European leaders, like Wladyslaw Gomulka in Poland, Lucretiu Patrascanu in Romania, and Traicho Kostov in Bulgaria, that national interests were not necessarily incompatible with the Soviet agenda and that such purposes could therefore be pursued with impunity. The fact that the "domestic" East

European leaders were mistaken became clear in later years. Most of them would either perish or be jailed on the most absurd charges.

The rise of domesticism was an international phenomenon, and Stalin realized that if the trend was not nipped in the bud it could undermine the whole system of domination and control he had been working to create in Eastern Europe. Titoism had to be exposed as a villainous attempt to restore capitalism and to break Yugoslavia away from the "fraternal family of socialist nations." It became the Cominform's main task—if not its only task—to suppress such domestic ambitions. Domesticism had to be halted once for all and unity drastically imposed. Moscow's absolute preeminence had to be recognized as sacrosanct and Stalin's views as infallible.

The fulfillment of the Stalinist design for Eastern Europe included the pursuit of a singular strategy that could eventually transform the various national political cultures into carbon copies of the "advanced" Soviet experience. Local communist parties, engaged in frantic attempts to imitate the Stalinist model, transplanting and sometimes enhancing the most repulsive characteristics of the Soviet totalitarian system, enthusiastically formulated strategic goals.

Economic Goals: Industrialization

Regarding the economy, the Stalinization of Eastern Europe meant the adoption of the command economy model. State planning commissions were formed in all the East European socialist countries. Their purpose was to designate the principal tasks of the state-owned economy. The state-planned economy was founded on the nationalization of the principal means of production.

Stalinist economic doctrine provided for a special role assigned to heavy industry, particularly the machine-building industry. In accordance with the Soviet dogma of economic autarky and self-reliance, each nation's economy was reoriented toward forced industrialization. For predominantly agricultural countries like Romania and Bulgaria, industrialization amounted to a violation of the natural economic course and the destruction of a potentially prosperous source of economic growth. All East European countries engaged in an industrial buildup that completely neglected the necessary equilibrium among various economic branches. Fascination with the Soviet industrialization precedent led to the launching of Pharaonic projects, including the building of canals and steel mills in disregard of any economic rationale. Those projects were ideologically motivated, and no questioning of their effectiveness was permitted.

Whenever they failed to produce the expected results, the blame was placed on alleged saboteurs who were trying to create obstacles in the way of the triumphant march toward the classless society.

Because the communists were convinced that both nature and society could and should be continuously transformed, they combined economic, social, and educational engineering in a repressive formula reminiscent of Oriental despotism. The classic Leninist formula—"socialism is Soviet power plus electrification"—was oversimplified and eventually reduced to the second term of the equation. During that initial stage of unchained Stalinism, socialism came to mean simply electrification plus terror. In the name of proletarian internationalism, the Soviet Union imposed unfair trade agreements on the satellite countries and forced them to establish joint enterprises with Soviet partners that definitely did not favor the East European countries. The Soviets used Romanian oil, Czechoslovak uranium, and Polish coal under purely colonial agreements. Economically as well as politically, the USSR became the metropolis, and the East European states its colonies.

Economic Goals: Agriculture

Since Soviet socialism could not exist in a society based on heterogeneous property relations, the private ownership of land had to be abolished and replaced with collective farms. The ideological underpinning of the decision to collectivize agriculture was the Marxist-Leninist belief that the peasantry by definition constituted a reactionary class and that only in large collective units could it be reeducated as selfless members of the socialist community. Total warfare against the peasantry was essential to the Stalinist effort to achieve a cohesive and entirely controllable economic body. In turn, the collective farms themselves were controllable through their dependency on the government for technological supplies, delivered through state-managed machine and tractor stations.

Political Goals: Destruction of the Civil Society

Socially, the Stalinization of Eastern Europe meant the destruction of the human bonds generally described as the civil society. A universal sense of fear was instilled in individuals, who were treated as simple cogs in the wheels of the totalitarian state machine. The legal system was redesigned to deprive the individual of any sense of protection or potential support. Revolutionary justice satisfied the communist party's thirst for social revenge against the former ruling groups and against all who might raise any doubts regarding the validity of the political and economic goals of the rulers. The whole legal system was turned upside down. New judges were appointed, and the whole judicial procedure became a mockery. The true repository of power was the communist party's political apparatus, including the organizational, the ideological, and the security police branches. The army also was purged, and new officers were recruited among workers who zealously obeyed the orders of the party leaders.

Political Goals: Regimenting Intellectual Life and Culture

In the field of intellectual life, the communists tried, with partial success, to neutralize and anesthetize all critical currents. The party smashed all forms of dissent inside and outside itself. Campaigns were undertaken to eliminate "objectivistic and cosmopolitan trends." Marxism-Leninism, as codified by Stalin, was enshrined as the only accepted ideology. It played a mobilizing role, indoctrinating the people and conditioning them to submit easily to the communist party's behests.

The ideology claimed to be exhaustive and comprehensive, a set of universal values to explain all natural, social, economic, and cultural phenomena. The Stalinist ideological project consisted in the creation of a new human type, actually an extremely flexible individual, totally controllable by the party. Soviet dissident writers aptly referred to this "new man" as *Homo Sovieticus*. The phrase *Homo Sovieticus* captures the anthropological ambition of Stalinism to carry out more than a simple social transformation. With remarkable prescience, three years after the October Revolution, in 1920, the Russian writer Yevgeny Zamyatin wrote about this suppression of human autonomy in a collectivistic Leviathan:

> [T]ake a pair of scales: on one side there is a gram, on the other—a ton; on one side "I," on the other "We," the One State. Is it not clear that to suppose that the "I" can have some sorts of "rights" in relation to the State is exactly like assuming that the gram can counterbalance the ton? Hence the rights go to the ton and the duties to the gram; and the natural path from nothingness to greatness is to forget that you are a gram and to feel instead that you are a millionth part of a ton.[33]

The social regimentation had to be total. No sphere of life, however private or intimate, could escape its impact. In all satellite countries ideological bureaucracies, the so-called Agitprop departments, were created to conduct brainwashing campaigns similar to those already tested in the Soviet Union. Hollow propaganda slogans permeated all publications. The guidance of literature was entrusted to fanatical commissars whose sole objective was to eradicate all forms of independent thought. "Socialist realism" was proclaimed the road to cultural and political perfection, and mass production of this utopian kitsch made audiences increasingly disgusted with officially sponsored creativity.

Literature, art, and philosophy lost all credibility because of their annexation by the political sphere. They became a safe haven for mendacity, hypocrisy, and moral turpitude. In all fairness, only a few intellectuals were really committed to this debased aesthetic creed. More often than not, others tended to collaborate with the regime out of fear or opportunism. Ethical suicide and chameleon behavior became pandemic among the communist intelligentsia. The most illuminating source for those who wish to understand the fascination of the East European intelligentsia with Marxism-Leninism, or the "New Faith," remains Czeslaw Milosz's classic *The Captive Mind.* Published in 1951, when the Cold War had reached its peak, Milosz's book analyzed the illusions and delusions of his colleagues who had espoused communism after the arrival of Soviet troops in Poland.

According to Milosz, the role of ideology was to neutralize the faculty of doubt and to instill in the individual boundless love and gratitude toward the party. With its claim to omniscience, ideology offered ready-made answers to any unsettling issue and promoted the individual's belief that there was no salvation outside the party:

> There is a species of insect which injects its venom into a caterpillar; thus inoculated, the caterpillar lives on though it is paralyzed. The poisonous insect then lays its eggs in it, and the body of the caterpillar serves as a living larder for the young brood. Likewise (although Marx and Engels never foresaw this use for their doctrine), the anaesthetic of dialectical materialism was injected into the mind of an individual in the people's democracies. When the individual's brain was duly paralyzed, the eggs of Stalinism were laid in it. "As soon as you are a Marxist," the party says to the patient, "you *must* be a Stalinist, for there is no Marxism outside of Stalinism."[34]

In the words of another great Polish poet, Zbigniew Herbert, the foundations of Stalinism rested upon fear, pride, a perverse joy in humiliation, and base material interests. Certain members of the intellectual elite accepted and sometimes even enjoyed this pact with the Stalinist establishment:

> The Great Linguist, Stalin, once said that one does not need to buy a nation. One simple has to have engineers of human souls. The govern-

ment needed legitimacy which was provided by the intellectuals, the so-
called "creative" intelligentsia, and especially the writers. . . . There was
a visible gap, then, between the elite and the sentiments of the nation.
These people believed that the nation is a foolish crowd to be led by the
enlightened few. Such are the beginnings of every fascist system: a self-
appointed elite imposes upon the rest its own vision of the radiant future.[35]

Overview

What happened in each of the East European countries? How was it
possible to extirpate and sterilize traditional nuclei of critical thought?
How was it possible that the apparatus, headed by tiny elites, managed to
smash all opposition and impose its autocratic rule? Who were the victims of those developments, and how were they selected?

In order to understand the success of the Stalinist experiment in
Eastern Europe, remember the prevailing role of direct Soviet intervention and intimidation. Keep in mind as well that the local Stalinist
formations were pursuing the Stalinist model of systematic destruction of
the noncommunist institutions, the disintegration of the civil society,
and the monopolistic occupation of the public space through state-
controlled rituals and institutions (Communist Youth Leagues, party-
controlled trade unions, peace councils, and other subservient mass organizations). The overall goal was to build a passive and fearful consensus
based on unlimited commitment to the political program of the ruling
elite. The true content of the political regime is described as the "cult of
personality" system. Where one person symbolizes collective, infallible
wisdom, where difference as such is considered subversive, where there is
absolutely no room for opposition attitudes, and where the social body is
threatened with extinction, the very notion of a civic culture is doomed.

The personalization of political power, its concentration in the hands
of a communist demigod, led to his forcible religious adoration and the
masochistic humiliation of subordinates. The leavening agent for this
moral and political enslavement was the Stalinist definition of internationalism as unbounded love for the USSR. In the words of an editorial
published by Czechoslovak communist daily *Rude Pravo* on May 25,
1952: "The road into the morass of treason indeed begins on the inclined
plane of reservations and doubts regarding the correctness of the policy of
the Soviet Union."[36]

Terror was theoretically justified as the *sine qua non* for the system's
survival. Stalinist doctrine maintained that the more advanced the social-

ist construction, the harsher the opposition of the defeated social groups. Therefore, the more critical becomes the need to respond in an uncompromising way to plots fomented by the "enemies of the people." Terror was sanctified and glorified as the antidote needed to conserve the socialist gains.

The catchword of the epoch in Eastern Europe was the Stalinist rationale for the Great Purge in the Soviet Union: "When one chops wood, the chips must fly." At that particular stage, the denunciation of Tito as an infiltrated spy on the payroll of Western intelligence agencies served as an argument for a redefinition of the main priorities in the people's democracies. The communist parties announced their embarkation on the "construction of socialism." The "people's democracy" was described as a new form of the dictatorship of the proletariat. Time and again, leading Cominform doctrinaires emphasized the "leading role of the vanguard party." The supremacy of the party could not be questioned, and the Soviet dictatorial pattern was reproduced without any hesitation or concern for national characteristics.

To keep strict control over all mechanisms that guaranteed social reproduction and preserved the matrix of domination in such a system, the party had to play the central role. Ideology was the main argument for doing away with actually or potentially seditious elements within and outside the party. Political police, cast in the Soviet mold and controlled by Soviet advisers, took care to fulfill the ideological *desiderata*. The political content of that ideological dictatorship in its mature incarnation (1948–53) was sheer terror and permanent propaganda warfare waged within a personal dictatorship. The main weakness of this system was its deficit of legitimacy.

Legitimacy is usually acquired through institutional solidification, stability, and a guarantee of conservation of certain values, or at least a minimal degree of national consensus. Under mature Stalinism, both in the Soviet Union and in Eastern Europe, autocratic despotism managed to ruin the functioning of the party as an autonomous institution. As terror unfolded, the party itself became a simple appendage of the General Secretary's personal office. In the words of Bertram Wolfe:

> Under a dictatorial one-party regime the party is anything but a party. It is a Praetorian guard; a privileged, dedicated, commanding caste; a band of activists to drive everyone to carry out the "Summit's" or the Leader's plans; a sounding board to broadcast infallible commands and dogmas; the eyes and the ears of an espionage system; a nucleus of penetration and control of all organizations, clubs, unions, collective farms, factories, gov-

ernment organs, army, police; a transmission belt to convey the Leader's will to a will-less nation, and to members and sympathizers in other lands.[37]

In this monolithic structure dominated by the revolutionary phalanx, the plans to reshape man, nature, and society could be frantically pursued. The Stalinist model was thus transplanted to all the East European countries satellitized by the Soviet Union after World War II: Albania, Bulgaria, Czechoslovakia, the German Democratic Republic, Hungary, Poland, and Romania. In Yugoslavia, because of Tito's obstinate rejection of Stalin's interference in his country's internal affairs and the subsequent break with the Cominform, a different pattern would emerge. The leading role of the communist party would be differently justified and applied in Yugoslavia.

With the exception of the Yugoslav leaders, all the communist formations derived their claim to legitimacy from their subservience to the Soviet Union and to Stalin himself. Even had they nourished any heretical thought, they could not have developed it, for at that moment the communists lacked any mass base. For the local populations, communists were simply agents of a foreign power. Most East Europeans perceived the communists as "them," a group of mystical militants serving a foreign despot and trying to impose a social model with no roots in the national legacies of Eastern Europe.

To ensure their monopoly of power, the communist parties engineered the methodical destruction of the traditional political cultures in the countries they were ruling. The socialist parties were dissolved, and their left-wing factions were absorbed in the so-called united workers' parties. Using both coercive and persuasive (propaganda) measures, the communists managed to recruit large segments of the industrial working class and expand their social base. In the name of the struggle against foreign powers, noncommunist parties were either banned or co-opted within rubber-stamp parliaments totally pliable and controlled by the communists. The Stalinist theory of the intensification of class warfare and its corollary, the psychology of the beleaguered fortress, became the rationale for the construction of a ubiquitous and universally feared secret police force that penetrated all walks of life and maintained an atmosphere of universal fear and mutual distrust.

The human model in this society was the selfless individual ready to inform on his closest friends and relatives. Treason on behalf of the party was considered a virtue. Failure to cooperate with the police was, of course, a political offense. In her gripping memoirs, Nadezhda Mandelstam, the widow of Osip Mandelstam, the great Russian poet who died in Stalin's Gulag during the Great Terror, poignantly captured the unbreathable climate in this type of society. Referring to a scathing remark by Anna Akhmatova, the "keening muse" of Russian poetry, as Joseph Brodsky once called her, Nadezhda Mandelstam wrote:

> At this period, astonished how people abroad—in particular Russian emigrés—utterly misunderstand our life, Akhmatova often repeated a phrase that infuriated me: "They are envious of our suffering." Such failure to understand has nothing to do with envy—it comes from the impossibility of imagining our experience and also from the deluge of lies by which reality has been twisted out of all recognition. . . . But the main thing was that it was nothing to envy. There was absolutely nothing at all uplifting in our suffering. It is pointless to look for some redeeming feature; there was nothing to it except animal fear and pain. I do not envy a dog that has been run over by a truck or a cat thrown from the tenth floor of a building by a hooligan. I do not envy people like myself, who suspected a traitor, provocateur, or informer in everyone and did not dare utter their thought even to themselves for fear of shouting them out in their sleep and giving themselves away to the neighbors on the other side of the thin walls that divide our apartments. There was, I can tell you, nothing to envy. [38]

In all East European countries, those nightmarish feelings were experienced by millions of people. The communists' attempts to destroy individual autonomy were unceasing. No one could see any promise of light at the end of the tunnel, only monstrous witch-hunts organized to affect both the noncommunist groups and, in a most atrocious way, the communist elites themselves. The Cominform provided the groundwork for the enactment of surreal show trials, where diehard communists acknowledged that they had always been traitors and spies.

T W O

Children in the Fog
From People's Democracies
to "Developed Socialism"

> And so I was living like a drunken child
> in fog. I knew nothing; that is, I knew
> and I didn't know, like all the rest of
> our circle. Only in prison did I see what
> political struggle in the communist
> camp meant, between communists,
> what mighty hatreds, what fanaticism,
> what ruthlessness that struggle could
> assume.
>
> —*Aleksander Wat*

Stalin's terminal paranoia exacerbated terror both in the Soviet Union and in the satellite countries of Eastern Europe. Convinced that Tito's autonomist heresy and his explicit challenge to the Kremlin's authority amounted to pure treason in favor of the "imperialist bloc," Stalin ordered his supporters to intensify the search for potential and real saboteurs. Stalin's rationale for the Great Terror—the 1937-formulated theory about the heightening of class struggle as socialism advances—was enthusiastically embraced by local despots in the satellite countries. In each of the East European communist countries the secret police were endowed with discretionary powers, and nobody—not even the party apparatus—felt protected against the mounting wave of repression.

PURGES AND WITCH-HUNTS

The category of "objective enemy," that is, of people who by virtue of their social status of background were capable of conspiring against the communist regime, was applied by Stalin's local henchmen to justify the terror. The purposes of the show trials that took place in the people's democracies were to create a national consensus surrounding the top communist elite and to maintain a state of panic and fear among the population. According to George H. Hodos, a survivor of the 1949 Laszlo Rajk trial in Hungary, those frame-ups were signals addressed to all potential freethinkers or heretics in the satellite countries. The trials also "attempted to brand anyone who displayed differences of opinion as a common criminal and/or agent of imperialism, to distort tactical differences as betrayal, sabotage, and espionage."[1] But those trials were not a simple repetition of the bloody purges that had devastated the Soviet body politic in the 1930s.

Although the show trial rituals in the satellite countries were similar in some respects to their Soviet predecessors, the selection of the defendants differed, as did their background. To prepare those purges, Stalin dispatched to all the satellite countries special teams of "advisers," who directly conducted the interrogations and contributed to the concoction of the diabolical scenarios that justified the death penalties for the defendants. Such Old Bolsheviks as Grigory Zinovyev, Lev Kamenev, Aleksei Rykov, and Nikolai Bukharin, who had once challenged Stalin and had represented a viable alternative to the Stalinist course, had been the victims of the Soviet show trials, but in the 1950s in Eastern Europe the chosen victims came from among the Stalinist elite itself. The show trials were introduced under the camouflage of the Cominform's break with Yugoslavia and the denunciation of Tito as the head of a "gang of murderers and spies."

The fact that the trials were held did not mean that the East European communist parties actually contained movements aimed at limiting Soviet influence and encouraging genuine national communist experiments. To be sure, differences existed between different wings, especially between local and Muscovite communists (people who had returned from Moscow exile after the end of World War II). But one should not consider those distinctions indicative of the existence of real Titoist factions throughout Eastern Europe ready to emulate the Yugoslavs in their defiance of Moscow's dictates. For Stalinism to function properly, that is, to maintain a perpetual state of national emergency and fear, conspiracies had to be continuously invented and unmasked. Nobody was above suspicion; absolutely everybody had to feel like a potential victim of the impersonal terrorist machine. The techniques and the procedures adopted in Eastern Europe were the same as those used during the Moscow show trials: The prosecution based its charges solely on the confessions of the defendants. No material proof of guilt was ever presented as the psychologically crushed people in the dock delivered their self-deprecating statements. Hodos writes:

> The show trials in Eastern Europe would have occurred even without the break between Stalin and Tito, probably even with the identical victims, as the device by which the brother parties of the postwar Soviet satellite states in Eastern Europe were subordinated to the Soviet party. Show trials were an integral part of Stalinism, and their introduction into the satellite states was a logical step, albeit with variants on the tested Soviet model. . . . The show trial is a propaganda arm of political terror. Its aim is to personalize an abstract political enemy, to place it in the dock in flesh and blood and, with the aid of a perverted system of justice, to transform abstract political-ideological differences into easily intelligible common crimes. It both incites the masses against the evil embodied by the defendants and frightens them away from supporting any potential opposition.[2]

Because the new regimes in Eastern Europe suffered economic setbacks and failed to arouse mass popular support for their social policies, they engaged in this frenzied exercise in terror and persecution. The prelude to the trials took place in Albania in May 1949, when the former Politburo member and Minister of the Interior Koci Xoxe was executed as a Titoist. As a matter of fact, in the aftermath of World War II Tito tried to extend his influence throughout Eastern Europe, but there was no indication that he ever tried to initiate a concerted opposition to Stalin. "Titoism," therefore, referred to a style of conduct more assertive of national interests than the policies dictated by Stalin to the local communist elites. In September 1949 Laszlo Rajk, Hungary's former Minister of the Interior and one of the top communist leaders after the war, admitted his guilt in a public trial and was sentenced to death together with other former prominent party figures. On that occasion, the state prosecutor's speech bordered on hysteria. He venomously linked the alleged Rajk conspiracy to Tito's treacherous activities, which were in turn conditioned by his subordination to Western warmongers engaged in the preparation of an overall attack against the people's democracies:

> American imperialism was the instigator and executor behind Tito's and Rankovic's entire political program and "putsch" plans! The American

and British intelligence services purchased Tito and his clique even during the war against Hitler, to prevent the national and social liberation of the peoples of southeastern Europe, to isolate the Soviet Union, and to prepare the third world war. . . . The putsch in Hungary, planned by Tito and his clique to be put into action by Rajk's spy ring, cannot be understood out of the context of the international plans of the American imperialists. . . . There are no extenuating circumstances, only aggravating circumstances. Our people demand death for the traitors and I, as the representative of the prosecuting authority, identify myself with this demand. The head of the snake that wants to bite us must be crushed. . . . The only defense against mad dogs is to beat them to death.[3]

In December 1949 a former Politburo member and economic czar of Bulgaria, Traicho Kostov, was indicted together with other former influential communists on charges similar to Rajk's: espionage, Titoism, and collaboration with bourgeois secret police during the party's clandestine years. In Kostov's case, the well-prepared public show was almost ruined by the chief defendant's sudden decision to refute the prosecutor's charges, but everything was put back in order following a short recess. Kostov, like the other East European leaders accused of conspiracy, eventually accepted the verdict and cooperated with the court in his own destruction. He abjured his earlier attempt to deny the charges and, according to the communist official daily *Rabotnichesko Delo,* confessed that he was nothing but a scoundrel. We cannot engage here in a long disquisition on why, for what reason, those people cooperated with their tormentors. Their behavior was motivated principally by their orthodox Leninist belief that the party was the bearer of historical truth and that they had to sacrifice their own lives on the shrine of the party's ultimate interests. Educated in a spirit of infinite dedication to Stalin and the Soviet Union, they lacked the minimal spirit of independence that would have permitted them to realize that they were trapped in a monstrous charade that had nothing whatsoever to do with the professed goals of their party. Some of them were so astounded by the enormity of the charges that they initially thought that they were victims of a counterrevolutionary coup. A few refused to accept the surreal charges leveled against them, but that small group represented the exception rather than the rule. The use of physical and psychological pressure, including threats to the lives of the defendants' relatives, also helps to explain how the confessions were extorted.

In September 1949, in a fulminating indictment entitled "The Communist Party of Yugoslavia in the Hands of Murderers and Spies," delivered to the Cominform summit in Budapest, Gheorghe Gheorghiu-Dej, the Romanian communist leader, denounced his former Politburo colleague and Romania's ex-Minister of Justice, Lucretiu Patrascanu, as a Titoist traitor and foreign agent. Patrascanu had been arrested earlier, but after Gheorghiu-Dej's speech, which anticipated the tribunal's verdict, his fate was sealed. However, because he refused to admit his guilt and engage in masochistic public confessions, Patrascanu could not be used for the staging of a show trial in Bucharest. He stayed in jail until April 1954, when he was sentenced to death and shot following a pseudo-trial.

After the same 1949 Budapest meeting, and in keeping with the international campaign against Tito's alleged supporters, the Polish communist leader Wladyslaw Gomulka was demoted, accused of a lack of revolutionary vigilance with regard to nationalism, and placed under house arrest in Poland under secret police surveillance. The Polish United Workers' Party was completely, after the purge of Gomulka's group, in the hands of the Muscovite faction headed by Boleslaw Bierut, Jakub Berman, and Hilary Minc.

At the time of the trials, the atmosphere in the people's democracies had become unbreathable: The obsession with the infiltrated enemies, the hysterical celebration of Stalin's universal genius, the humiliation of the national intelligentsias, and the assault on national tradition had created a general climate of hopelessness and anguish. For most of the population, the show trials were events that happened in another universe. The defendants were communists executed by their fellow communists. The involvement of the average citizen in these rituals was absolutely perfunctory: They had to repeat the nonsensical charges in order to become part and parcel of this new reality based on lies and fear. The average citizen was aware that the tragic fate of the ousted communist leaders could befall himself or herself as well at any moment. Irrationality had to be internalized as the system's way of functioning. Everybody was a candidate for the criminal mechanism's next strike. Any form of doubt had to be covered under the most obedient expressions of loyalty. The gigantic communist propaganda machine compelled the whole population to indulge in mass ceremonies of adherence to the party's slogans. At the same time, as if to enhance the mandatory frenzy, the model of forced (and false) stimulation of labor productivity was imported from the Soviet Union; those workers who did not perform in accordance with party orders were considered politically unreliable. The effect of the show trials was a schizoid split in the individual's mentality: The public person proclaimed precisely those values that the private one execrated.

The mechanics and the functions of the show trials can be understood by examining the structure of the groups selected for public exposure and liquidation. Between 1949 and 1951 the main victims of the trials were members of the "national communist" elites, or "home communists," as opposed to doctrinaire Stalin loyalists. Koci Xoxe, Traicho Kostov, Lucretiu Patrascanu, Wladyslaw Gomulka, and Laszlo Rajk had all spent the war years in their respective countries. They had participated in the anti-Nazi resistance movement. Unlike their Moscow-trained colleagues, who arrived in the tanks of the Red Army, they could invoke a source of legitimacy from direct involvement in the partisan movement. Some of these "home-grown" communists may have even resented the condescending attitudes of the "Muscovites," who traded on their better connections with Moscow and treated the home communists like junior partners. Stalin was aware of those factional rivalries and used them to initiate the permanent purges in the satellite countries.

In the early 1950s Stalin became increasingly concerned with the role of the Jews as carriers of a "cosmopolitan world view" and as "objective" supporters of the West. For the communists, it did not matter whether an individual was "subjectively" against the system, but rather what he or she might have thought and done by virtue of his or her "objective" status (coming from a bourgeois family, having studied in the West, belonging to a certain minority, and so forth). Morbid anti-Semitic campaigns were organized by Stalinists in the Soviet Union against Jewish writers and literary critics. The specter of a massive pogrom loomed over the Soviet Jewish population. In the people's democracies, the struggle against "rootless cosmopolitans" (a code word meaning Jews) allowed certain local communist leaders to engage in an elite purge against the "Muscovite" factions dominated by communists of Jewish extraction (many of whom had fled fascism and had sought refuge in the Soviet Union between the two wars). The elimination of those otherwise totally loyal Stalinists reached a spectacular level in Czechoslovakia, where the chief defendant in an October 1952 show trial was Rudolf Slansky, who until September 1951 had been the General Secretary of the ruling communist party and in that capacity had presided over the ruthless persecution of communists and noncommunists. Slansky and other prominent militants, most of Jewish origin, were sentenced to death and hanged in December 1952.

The Slansky group was accused of Zionist conspiracy and direct collusion with the Western espionage networks. Slansky himself, who had been the chief organizer of the previous purges in Czechoslovakia, could hardly understand the fantastic charges leveled against him. He tried several times, while in his prison cell, to commit suicide. He implored the party chairman, his former friend Klement Gottwald, to grant him a chance to explain himself, but of course he was denied any such opportunity. Since the trial had to confirm Stalin's conviction about the existence of a worldwide conspiracy determined to unsettle the communist bloc, there was no way to exonerate any of the defendants. Furthermore, the anti-Semitic charges were bound to appeal to precommunist chauvinistic prejudices widespread in the whole region.

In May 1952 the Romanian media announced the elimination of three members of the Politburo, two of whom had been the leaders of the party's Moscow emigré center during World War II. All three had been party secretaries and had shared absolute power with the leader of the domestic faction, Gheorghe Gheorghiu-Dej. Ana Pauker, a veteran communist leader who long had been lionized by international communist propaganda as an impeccable communist fighter, lost her job as Minister of Foreign Affairs and was put under house arrest. Her Muscovite ally, the Hungarian-born Vasile Luca, was accused of economic sabotage during his tenure as Minister of Finance and collaboration with the bourgeois police during the party's underground activity. Luca was arrested and died in prison in the early 1960s. The third member of the group, Teohari Georgescu, a home communist and former Minister of Internal Affairs whose principal fault consisted in his close association with the Pauker–Luca faction, was also jailed but was soon released. Georgescu thereafter worked in menial jobs.

The Romanian purge seems to have been determined by both local and international circumstances. There was a definite competition for authority and supremacy between Gheorghiu-Dej and Ana Pauker. The source of their rivalry, however, lay not in different political conceptions, as Gheorghiu-Dej later claimed, but simply in personal ambitions and vanities. While resolving his rivalry with Pauker, Gheorghiu-Dej capitalized on Stalin's interest in the "ethnicization" of East European communist elites through the elimination of the Jewish leaders, among whom Ana Pauker figured prominently. He convinced the Kremlin that he was a much more trustworthy exponent of Soviet interests and accused his opponents of deliberately practicing an adventurist course bound to destabilize the country and restore capitalism.

As for the Soviet Union itself, the anti-American and anti-Semitic campaign reached its most vicious moment in February 1953, one month before Stalin's death, with the pseudo-discovery of the "doctors' plot." According to the official story, the Kremlin's doctors—most of whom were Jewish—had long been involved in criminal activities aimed at physically annihilating the Soviet leadership. They were all arrested and subjected to horrendous psychological and physical tortures. Only Stalin's demise prevented a public trial that would have been the opening

salvo for an overall anti-Semitic purge and the forced resettlement of the
Jewish population to Siberia.[4] With the Slansky trial and the "doctors'
plot," the system had reached the limits of its irrationality. The most
grotesque accusations were brought against Soviet and East European
Jews without any concern for minimal credibility. The "party line" was
simply a plastic material used to suit the latest whims of the Soviet
dictator, and nobody, not even the local general secretaries, could feel
totally protected against potential accusations of treason. It did not matter whether the selected victim had ever expressed the slightest doubt
about Stalin's genius. The only concern for the Soviet advisers, the true
stage directors of the show trials, was to confirm Stalin's suspicions and
incessantly add new names to the list of unmasked criminals. But the
purges affected more than the top apparatus. Once unleashed, they rever-
berated throughout the whole party, resulting in a complete paralysis of
any individual autonomy. The terrorist pedagogy totally suppressed critical attitudes and made obedience the golden rule of survival.

At the moment of Stalin's death on March 5, 1953, the countries of
the Soviet bloc shared a political system based on terror, ideological
manipulation, and command economy. The institutionalization of the
purges as a mechanism of elite replacement and political mobilization was
a phenomenon characteristic of the whole bloc. According to Zbigniew
Brzezinski, the principal features of the Stalinist interstate system included the communality of the institutional organization; the acknowl-
edgement of Soviet supremacy as symbolized by Stalin's role as the leader
of world communism; the paramount role assigned to ideology as the
source of political legitimacy for the ruling elites; and the economic
exploitation of the satellite countries by the Soviet overlord.[5] In their
main characteristics, those polities could be described as totalitarian,
since the monolithic party-state had managed to absorb or annihilate all
forms of institutional autonomy. Least affected was the German Democratic Republic, primarily because the police state could not be totally
established there until the construction of the Berlin Wall in 1961 completed that country's separation from the West.

TITO'S CHALLENGE AND THE BREAKDOWN OF MONOLITHIC RULE

It would be hard to exaggerate the importance of Tito's refusal to bow to
Stalin's dictates. It was the first time a Comintern-trained and -promoted
communist dared to defy the Kremlin's supremacy and claim *his party's*

right to an independent role. Tito's 1948–49 opposition to Stalin's pressure and blackmail represented a turning point in the history of world communism. It was the first successful rejection of Stalin's claim to a monopoly of truth, a repudiation of the Stalinist concept of internationalism, and a proud assertion of national values in the face of Soviet imperialist behavior. Tito rejected the Cominform dogma according to which all communists had to be judged by their attitude toward the Soviet Union and Stalin personally. In Tito's view, it was the right of each communist party, be it large or small, to establish its political line in accordance with its own self-defined interests. Since they had directed a successful mass resistance movement against the Nazi occupiers, the Yugoslav leaders felt entitled to international recognition of their special role within world communism.

Tito's quest for recognition inaugurated national communism, a trend within world communism that elevates domestic priorities over imperial values and objectives. It was national, in contrast to the complete suppression of patriotic attachments required by Stalin. On the other hand, it was not a resumption of the nationalist movements and ideologies characteristic of Eastern Europe before communism. Tito promoted his own version of pan-Yugoslav socialist ideology, which had nothing in common with traditional Serbian, Croatian, or Slovene nationalisms. Stalin completely ignored or despised the national pride of the subjugated nations and did not realize that once Tito had decided to withstand his pressure, the Yugoslav communist could mobilize large segments of the public opinion that otherwise may have resented the new political order. "If I lift a finger, Tito will fall," Stalin informed his Politburo colleagues, according to Nikita Khrushchev.[6] The Soviet dictator failed to see in his Yugoslav nemesis more than a simple slave who had dared to dispute the authority of his master.

Likewise, at least initially, the Yugoslavs could not fully understand the origins of Stalin's wrath against them. After all, they had already behaved as the most loyal disciples of the Soviet leader. Tito was no less an industrializer than Stalin, no less committed—at the outset of his rule—to forced collectivization. Terror against the party-designated "class enemies" in Yugoslavia was consistently organized by Aleksandar Rankovic's secret police. Schooled in the Stalinist tradition, the Yugoslav leaders saw the party as the carrier of universal reason, the perfect instrument, predestined to bring about immediate answers to the most difficult questions through the application of Leninist and Stalinist dogmas. So initially Tito and his comrades clung to the Leninist-Stalinist ideological patterns and norms, and the Yugoslav leadership responded to Stalinist accusations by trying to surpass Stalin in orthodoxy.

In the first stage of the conflict, Tito was convinced that the whole dispute was the result of a regrettable misunderstanding. Tito's defiance of the Soviet protectorate was the infuriated reaction of a Stalinist against his master's arbitrariness and willfulness. It took some time for the Yugoslav leaders to engage in a full-fledged de-Stalinization. Even when they decided to do so, they conducted their break in an authoritarian manner, with methods comparable to those employed in the "people's democracies" in the struggle against "class enemies." Communists who refused to endorse Tito's views and stuck to the Cominform's abusive criticism of the Yugoslav Communist Party were labeled "Cominformists" and treated as foreign agents. Many were deported to remote Yugoslav concentration camps, including the notorious Goli Otok.[7] Others managed to escape to the neighboring "people's democracies," where they launched a propaganda war against those whom they stigmatized as the "Titoist gang of traitors." Only Tito's pressing need for popular support resulted in the decision to encourage the search for a Yugoslav "road to socialism," different from the Soviet ultra-bureaucratic and authoritarian pattern. The widely acclaimed Yugoslav "self-management," which promised the workers a role in deciding industrial objectives, was less the consequence of the desire to break with the ossified and highly ineffective bureaucratic-administrative management system practiced in the Soviet Union than the outcome of the vital need to expand the popular base for an externally threatened dictatorship.

Isolated from and slandered by the whole world communist movement, Tito abandoned many of the dogmas long held as sacrosanct. The Yugoslav model of "self-management" was imposed from above, and the spontaneous initiatives of the masses, ceaselessly invoked in the official propaganda, were kept under strict party control. In Yugoslavia domesticism was supposed to result not in the destruction of the communist system but only in its reformation along lines different from those pursued in the Soviet Union under Stalin. The origins of domesticism lay in a conflict between two competing communist centers rather than in a clash of visions between a totalitarian and a humanistic interpretation of Marxism and Leninism. For Tito and his associates, ethnic pride was more an instrument to strengthen their popular base than the deep motivation for the divorce from Moscow.

But at the same time, because foreign policy cannot be totally dissociated from domestic practices, the more critical Tito became of Stalin's imperialist behavior, the more disposed he was to criticize the Soviet system as well. In a number of theoretical documents published by Yugoslav communists in the early 1950s, the Soviet model was described as a dictatorship controlled by a huge bureaucratic machine. Those publications asserted that the Communist Party of the Soviet Union was no longer the vanguard of the world proletariat, but a clique of bureaucrats whose survival depended on the perpetuation of the purges. The Soviet system had degenerated into state capitalism administered by a new class of bureaucratic potentates. To avoid a repetition of Stalin's mistaken choices, Tito and his comrades had decided in 1950 to experiment with the transition to a model where the workers could exert direct control over production objectives. Because they were committed communists, however, the Titoists did not completely abandon the party's leading role. Communist party cells continued to function at the shop floor level, and the central government continued to control the appointment of industrial managers. The communist party nevertheless redefined its position in society as a political formation "with a voluntary and democratic character."

All those changes convinced Stalin and his associates that Tito had indeed completely abandoned socialism. For the Stalinists, the very fact that the workers were consulted with regard to their enterprises and that they were allowed to have a word in the decision-making process was considered a pernicious sign of anarchism and "bourgeois liberalism." Even after Stalin's death, the Soviet leaders could not reconcile what they saw in Yugoslavia with their own frozen dogmas and consequently stigmatized the Yugoslav model as "revisionism." Still, the Yugoslav attempts to diminish the harmful effects of excessive bureaucracy did not represent a complete systemic overhaul. On the contrary, Tito made sure that the party maintained its dominant role by outlawing any alternative political formations. Censorship was maintained and severely applied against reformers like Milovan Djilas, Tito's former lieutenant, who overstepped the party-defined limits of "creativity."

In 1953 the Yugoslav leaders decided to de-collectivize agriculture. Tito, as the spokesman, engaged in more active criticism of the Soviet model as rigid and dictatorial. Unlike the Soviet theorists, who were insisting on the need continuously to strengthen the role of the dictatorship of the proletariat, the Yugoslav communists claimed that true socialism, the type inspired by genuine Marxism, would favor the reduction of state operations and eventually the "withering away of the state." The Yugoslav "search for man," as their differing philosophy and practice of socialism were called,[8] did not include a complete separation from the dogma of the party as the repository of historical rationality. The conflict consisted rather in the determination of the Yugoslav leaders to reject the Soviet-imposed vassal status and their forceful defense of their right to national sovereignty. The special privileges of the party members, although theoretically criticized by Yugoslav communists, were not curtailed even when the well-known leader Milovan Djilas—then the country's Vice President—decided to attack the communist *nomenklatura.* First Djilas was expelled from the Communist League of Yugoslavia, and then, after he published his famous indictment of the "new class" of potentates, he was jailed as a "subversive element."[9] Tito was ready to condemn the atrocities of Stalinism and to deplore the bureaucratization of socialism, but he refused to countenance an overall criticism of the systemic origins of communist autocracy.

The thrust of Tito's divorce from Moscow consisted in an attempt to initiate a different, less repressive version of the one-party system. In his New Year's Address of 1949, Tito condemned Stalism for its sanctification of cruelty and violence:

> Those who are appeasing their conscience with the reflection that "the end hallows the means" should remember that this dictum was particularly current among the Jesuits at the time of the Inquisition. Great things cannot be accomplished by dirty means or in a dishonest manner. Great things can only be created by honest means and in honest manner—this is what we shall always believe.[10]

But when confronted with radical reformism within his own party, the Yugoslav leader resorted to the same methods for which he criticized Stalin. His mindset was not really different from that of his true mentor, nor was his goal, which amounted to the retention of absolute power in his own hands.

THE EAST EUROPEAN STALINISTS

To understand evolutions in Eastern Europe in the 1950s we have to remember the main features of the communist parties in those countries. Again, with the exception of the Czechoslovak and Yugoslav communist parties, all the Leninist formations in the region suffered from a chronic deficit of mass support. All those countries counted millions of party members but very few committed communists. The parties derived their legitimacy from their boundless and unconditional loyalty to the Soviet Union and to Stalin personally. Even the Yugoslav leaders, until the outbreak of their open conflict with Stalin, did not question the Soviet claim to domination within world communism. Stalin was universally worshipped as a godlike figure; no sacrifice was considered too great to show the communist commitment to the common cause.

All these communist parties held a common conception of internationalism as well as a similar philosophy of party dicipline. It was the duty of individual members slavishly to obey orders coming from the top. This militaristic logic was called democratic centralism. The internal life of the parties was ritualistic, extremely authoritarian, and hierarchical. They functioned in accordance with a skillfully engineered cult of the leaders, and all forms of factionalism or critical attitudes were strictly banned. In those circumstances, a climate of mechanical enthusiasm and apocryphal romanticism thrived. Those who expressed any doubts were marginalized or even exterminated.

The East European communist parties were led by tightly knit nuclei of militants united in their conviction that their countries had to follow the Soviet model without any reservation or hesitation. As a rule, the Soviet bloc parties were headed by professional revolutionaries, most of whom had been trained in the Comintern schools and whose devotion to the Soviet Union had been thoroughly tested through the years. To carry out the main objectives of Stalinism, those people established a system of terror and persecution that did not spare some of its ardent partisans. In those communist sects there was no room for personal loyalties. The only permitted attachment was to the party, which was considered superior to any of its individual components. The party established its monistic world view as the only acceptable version of truth and pilloried any other conception as objectively reactionary and dangerous. From that intolerance for nonparty truths grew a shared anti-intellectual prejudice. The Soviet-bloc parties suspected all intellectuals, including communist intellectuals, of entertaining a temptation to criticize the status quo and thus of being potential troublemakers. The Stalinists' suspicion of intellectuals and their belief that the parties embodied the class consciousness of the industrial proletariat led the parties' elites to try to expand their working class appeal.

The mind of the Stalinist elites in Eastern Europe was impressively revealed by the Polish journalist Teresa Toranska in a series of interviews conducted in the early 1980s with some of the former leaders of the Polish communist party. Her book title, *Oni* (Them), captured the universe of myths, fantasies, resentments, and delusions that made possible the self-hypnosis of those who presided over the Stalinization of Poland. The most striking and illuminating of the interviews is with the former Politburo member and Central Committee Secretary Jakub Berman (1901–84), who tried to defend the options and actions of his political generation. According to Berman, Polish communists were right in championing Stalin's policies in Poland because, he claimed, the Soviets guaranteed his country's social and national liberation. When Toranska, a Solidarity-linked journalist, maintained that the communists had brought a great disaster upon the Polish nation, Berman replied angrily:

> That's not true. We brought it liberation. . . . We didn't come to this country as its occupiers and we never even imagined ourselves in that role. After all the disasters that had befallen this country, we brought its ultimate liberation, because we finally got rid of those Germans, and that counts for something. I know these things aren't simple. We wanted to get this country moving, to breathe life into it; all our hopes were tied up with the new model of Poland, which was without historical precedent and was the only chance it had throughout its thousand years of history; we wanted to use that chance 100 percent. And we succeeded. In any case we were bound to succeed, because we were right; not in some irrational, dreamed-up way we'd plucked out of the air, but historically—history was on our side.[11]

Thus no empirical (social, cultural, moral) evidence was required to justify the communists' self-confidence. They knew they had received the mandate of history, and they were pursuing their salvationist dreams without any concern for the fate of those who may have disliked their utopian blueprints.

The sense of being entitled to impose happiness on the people, combined with a messianic belief in their parties' chosen role, made the communist elites impervious to any signals from a disheartened, potentially rebellious society. Far from trying to adjust their schemes to the concrete conditions, the parties were increasingly inclined to change and if need be to suppress society. That explains the fatal chasm between the ruling elites, "them" as the average citizens were calling those zealots, and the mass of the population, or "us." Berman's astute and often cynical rationalization of his generation's commitment to Stalinism could not conceal its mystical underpinnings. After all, the communist elites in Eastern Europe had deliberately broken with their countries' national traditions in favor of what they perceived as the supranational fraternity of the "liberators of mankind." The leaders of the Soviet-bloc communist parties were convinced, like Lenin at the moment he founded the Bolshevik party at the beginning of the twentieth century, that the people needed an external force to enlighten and teach them, that without such a vanguard party there was no hope of true emancipation. At the end of his interview with Toranska, Berman issued a passionate plea for the moral superiority of "genuine" communism. According to him, a day will come when mankind will do justice to this chiliastic dream of global revolution, and all the atrocities and crimes of Stalinism will be remembered only as passing incidents:

> [W]ithout placing my faith in the magical power of words, I am nonetheless convinced that the sum of our actions, skillfully and consistently carried out, will finally produce results and create a new Polish consciousness; because all the advantages flowing from our new path will be borne out, must be borne out, and if we're not destroyed by an atomic war and we don't disappear into nothingness, there will finally be a breakthrough in mentality which will give it an entirely new content and quality. And then we, the communists, will be able to apply all the democratic principles we would like to apply but can't apply now, because they would end in our defeat and elimination. It may happen in fifty years or it may happen in a hundred, I don't want to make prophecies, but I'm sure it will happen one day.[12]

In his absolute belief that history was on his and his comrades' side, Berman was not alone. His was a mindset characteristic of the communist elites in all Soviet satellite countries. The same words could have been uttered by Ana Pauker, the Romanian communist purged in 1952, who died in 1960, still convinced that the Soviet Union was the mainstay of all progressive mankind. Other communist leaders in Eastern Europe likewise could have offered Berman's profession of faith. Poland's leader at the moment of the country's Stalinization was Boleslaw Bierut (1892–1956), a former Soviet secret agent who had served as a Comintern instructor in Bulgaria, Czechoslovakia, and Austria during the interwar period. Hungary was run by a "foursome" made up by the communist leader Matyas Rakosi (1892–1971), who had spent fifteen years in Admiral Horthy's jails for his communist activities, and his close associates Ernő Gerő (the economic czar), Jozsef Revai (the chief ideologue), and Mihaly Farkas (the Minister of Defense). In Bulgaria, the party leader was Vulko Chervenkov (1900–1980), who in the 1930s had served as the deputy director of the Leninist School of the Comintern in Moscow. In East Germany, the party leaders were Wilhelm Pieck (1876–1960) and Walter Ulbricht (1893–1973), who had left their country after Hitler's takeover in 1933, had spent the way years in Moscow exile, and had returned to Germany in 1945. In Romania, after the elimination of the Pauker–Luca faction, the communist party was run by Gheorghe Gheorghiu-Dej (1901–65), a former railroad worker who had spent more than ten years in jails and labor camps. Czechoslovakia's leader Klement Gottwald (1896–1953) had spent the war years in Soviet exile.[13] All these people had known each other in Moscow during the interwar or war years, but the story of their relations belongs to another book.

Berman, Pauker, Rakosi, and the rest of the East European communist leaders were seasoned militants for whom Stalin's personality was an example of correct revolutionary conduct. They admired the Soviet leader's intransigence and his uncompromising struggle against oppositional factions, and they shared his hostility to the West. Educated in the Stalinist tradition, they believed in the theory of permanent intensification of the class struggle and did their best to create a repressive system where all critical tendencies could be immediately weeded out. Their minds were Manichean: Socialism was right, capitalism was wrong, and there was no middle road between the two. In their intense belief in this simplistic philosophy, they were careful to ensure that the same views would be instilled in the minds of their younger disciples in their countries. A whole propaganda system based on the principle of systematic indoctrination of the party apparatchiks with the myths of the Stalinist doctrine was established in the Soviet-bloc countries. For most of the apparatchiks, knowledge of Marxism was limited to the Comintern Vulgate, which they accepted without reservation as Stalin's title to infallibility. During their communist underground service, the Soviet-bloc communists had learned to see Stalin's catechistic formulations as the best formulations of their own thoughts and beliefs. The mental and emotional unity between the prophet and his disciples was unshakable.

When Stalin died, his East European disciples suffered like orphans: They lost more than their parties' supporter, they lost their protector, the very embodiment of their highest dreams, the hero they had come to revere, the symbol of their strength. Stalin, the true source of their authority, had passed away. Without him they barely knew how to function in an increasingly centrifugal and ambiguous world.

NIKITA KHRUSHCHEV AND THE "NEW COURSE"

Immediately after Stalin's death, the Soviet leadership began to reassess its relationship to the satellite countries. The ferocious struggle for power in the Kremlin definitely affected the stability of the Soviet-appointed ruling teams in Eastern Europe. As the Soviets moved toward a restoration of their relationship with Yugoslavia, the East European communist leaders found their own authority seriously threatened: After all, they had put all their prestige into the struggle against the Titoist deviation. Some of them had directly initiated purges against fellow communist whose execution had been justified in the name of the struggle against Tito's spies. Yet the new Soviet leaders could not tolerate the preservation of unreconstructed Stalinist fortresses in Eastern Europe at a time when the Kremlin was trying to revise some of is basic tenets.

In the summer of 1953 Khrushchev and Malenkov, respectively the Soviet party leader and the Prime Minister, summoned the Hungarian leaders to Moscow and asked them to deploy a new strategy that would ensure better living standards for the population and deflate the terror. Rakosi had to give up his prime-ministership to Imre Nagy, a former Politburo member whose dissenting views on the collectivization of agriculture had resulted in his elimination from the top leadership in the late 1940s. In the GDR, the death of Stalin contributed to the increased nervousness of the Socialist Unity Party (SED) ruling team. In June 1953 they decided to impose a 10 percent rise in work quotas at Berlin's construction sites (without a corresponding rise in salaries), which led to strikes and a spontaneous mass assault on the communist party headquarters. East German and Soviet troops smashed that first antitotalitarian insurrection in Eastern Europe. Officially dozens, but it is more likely that hundreds, died during the crackdown. In the bitter words of Bertolt Brecht, the renowned poet and playwright:

> After the uprising of the 17th June
> The Secretary of the Writers' Union
> Had leaflets distributed in the Stalinallee
> Stating that the people
> Had forfeited the confidence of the government
> And could win it back only
> By redoubled efforts. Would it not be easier
> In that case for the government
> To dissolve the people
> And elect another?[14]

The East Berlin uprising was the first in a series of spontaneous outbursts of popular rage against the repressive regimes installed with the direct assistance of the Red Army in Eastern Europe. The revolts had a dual nature: They were at once political rebellions against a social order inimical to freedom and destructive of human personality, and they were movements of national emancipation against a foreign power, that is, the Soviet Union. So the thrust of the East European revolts of 1956 included political, social, economic, and national demands. People stood up against a system perceived as fundamentally flawed. The revolts also attacked the ideological camouflage that justified the communist oppression. Marxism-Leninism, as interpreted by Stalin, came under heavy fire in the writings and public statements of intellectuals of leftist persuasion, who felt betrayed by the cynical manipulation of their romantic dreams by the ruling apparatus. Intellectuals who had refused to kowtow to party doctrine, unable to publicize their views, stayed away from what appeared to be a communist family quarrel. To give just one example, Lucian Blaga, one of Romania's outstanding poets and philosophers, could publish only translations and survived at the periphery of public life as a librarian.

Meanwhile, in the USSR the new leaders tried to reassure their supporters in the party, military, and government apparatus that the times of irrational terror were over. The Soviet leaders came to the conclusion, especially after the Berlin rebellion, that the old-fashioned methods of colonial exploitation of Eastern Europe had to be replaced. They informed their proconsuls in the East European capitals that new methods of leadership and new forms of authority were needed in the changed circumstances. The Soviets initiated a rapprochement with Tito and asked their East European vassals to do likewise. All those modifications of what had appeared as the sacred, immutable "party line" led to disarray and confusion among the East European communist elites: Matyas Rakosi and his clique in Hungary: Gheorghe Gheorghiu-Dej in Romania; Boleslaw Bierut in Poland; Antonin Novotny, Gottwald's successor, in Czechoslovakia; Walter Ulbricht and Wilhelm Pieck in the German Democratic Republic; Vulko Chervenkov in Bulgaria; Enver Hoxha in Albania—all these little Stalins realized that their political survival depended on their ability to contain the traumatic impact of the Soviet thaw in their countries. Clearly for those diehard Stalinists, once Tito's reputation was restored and the Yugoslav communists ceased to be depicted as the archenemies of progressive mankind, all the charges they had used against their rivals during the show trials would be exposed as frame-ups. So the de-Stalinization initiated by Malenkov and Khrushchev had widespread contagious effects in Eastern Europe. Not surprisingly, the local leaderships, whose legitimacy, as we have mentioned, derived from their boundless solidarity with Stalin's Soviet Union, did their best to procrastinate. While the procrastinators could not torpedo liberalization altogether, they certainly affected its pace.

Because Soviet leaders were pushing in that direction, the pressures for liberalization were too forceful to be completely ignored in the Soviet-bloc countries. Furthermore, the economic situation in all those countries was dismal. Well informed by their emissaries in Eastern Europe, the Soviet leaders understood that unless a new course was rapidly adopted, social explosions in the region were inevitable. In Hungary, the avuncular Imre Nagy, less ideological than Rakosi and his associates, was appointed Premier with Soviet blessing in July 1953. He launched a daring program of economic and political reforms. His strategy consisted in reducing the burden imposed on the industrial working class, easing the pressure on the peasants by abandoning coercive methods of collectivization, and instituting a new approach to legality that included a partial amnesty for political prisoners and the abolition of internment camps. That last measure was particularly important in Hungary—perhaps the most repressive of all East European Stalinist regimes. Nagy's decision to dismantle the Hungarian gulag earned him genuine popularity and made him a serious rival for the increasingly weakened and despised Rakosi.

Leaders in the other East European countries pursued similar liberalization strategies, but with less commitment and enthusiasm than that shown by Nagy. As the struggle for power intensified in the Kremlin, East European local bosses tried to ingratiate themselves with those Soviet leaders they considered less prone to engage in a sweeping separation from the Stalinist legacy. Khrushchev's victory over Malenkov in 1955 permitted Rakosi to reassert his supremacy and to eliminate Nagy from both the premiership and the communist party on a charge of "right-wing opportunism."

In May 1955 the Soviets took a new step toward the institutionalization of their hegemony in the region by creating the Warsaw Pact as a military alliance based on ideological affinities. In the words of Zbigniew Brzezinski, the Warsaw Pact was "the single most important formal commitment binding the [East European] states to the USSR, officially limiting their scope of independent action, and legalizing the presence (and hence the political influence) of the Soviet troops stationed on their territory."[15] Initially, the Warsaw Pact included Albania, Bulgaria, Czechoslovakia, East Germany, Poland, Romania, and the Soviet Union. After the Albanian–Soviet split in 1960, the leadership in Tirana broke with the Warsaw Pact, which the Albanians denounced as an instrument of Soviet imperialism. Albania formally left the alliance in August 1968, when the Soviet Union and its allies invaded Czechoslovakia. While the Warsaw Pact guaranteed Moscow's political and military control over the potentially rebellious satellites, an earlier alliance, the Council of Mutual Eco-

nomic Aid (CMEA), founded in 1949, ensured Soviet economic domination in the region.

The principal instrument used to perpetuate the economic dependence of these countries on the Soviet Union was "specialization in
industrial production." The principles of socialist internationalism were
reshaped to fit the new concept of limited economic sovereignty and
efforts to create supranational economic bodies entirely subordinated to
Soviet interests. Later on, after 1960, the CMEA would be the framework for carrying out the policy of economic integration of the centrally
planned East European economies. National plans had to be coordinated,
and a unified socialist market was supposed to emerge as a result of these
joint economic efforts. After the 1989 upheaval, both the Warsaw Pact
and the CMEA became increasingly irrelevant, as member countries
embarked on a path toward complete dissolution. Indeed, in February
1991 a meeting of foreign and defense ministers of the Warsaw Pact
countries took place in Budapest. It decided to disband the military
alliance by March 31, 1991.[16]

THE TWENTIETH CPSU CONGRESS: THE ANTI-STALIN BOMBSHELL

No event turned out to be more devastating for the legacy of Stalinism
than the "secret speech" delivered by Nikita Khrushchev in February
1956 to the Twentieth CPSU Congress. The reasons Khrushchev undertook the unprecendented attack against the previously adored leader
were many: First, he wanted to delegitimize his adversaries in the Soviet
party's Politburo, whose association with Stalin had been more thoroughgoing and compromising than his own (Vyacheslav Molotov, Lazar
Kaganovich, Georgy Malenkov, Kliment Voroshilov); second, the demolition of Stalin's myth was bound to restore the communist party's prerogatives as the true repository of political power—in other words, to
ensure the institutional dignity of the party oligarchy jeopardized by
Stalin's personal despotism; third, by proclaiming the "return to true
Leninism" as the new official line, Khrushchev could secure his own
image as the restorer of socialist legality and the protector of the bureaucracy against secret police terror; and fourth, the "secret speech" (its
existence was not mentioned in the official record of the Congress, and
the Soviet media published it first in 1989) permitted Khrushchev to
single out his enemies within both the Soviet elite and the world communist movement (including some leaders of communist countries, primar-

ily China's Mao Zedong) as incorrigible dogmatics, unable to keep pace with changes in the contemporary world.

The delegations of the "brotherly" parties were immediately informed about the dynamite in Khrushchev's "secret speech." They too were compelled to admit that the "bourgeois propaganda" indictment of Stalin's rule of terror had been correct: Khrushchev documented the amplitude of Stalin's destruction of the Bolshevik elite, his criminal propensities, and his direct implication in the establishment of the terrorist system. The impact of the revelations, which became public several months later when the *New York Times* obtained a copy of the speech and published its complete text, cannot be exaggerated. As Leszek Kolakowski pointed out, it was indeed a most traumatizing experience for thousands upon thousands of militants educated in the cult of Stalin to learn from world communism's most authoritative voice that "he who had been the leader of progressive humanity, the inspiration of the world, the father of the Soviet people, the master of science and learning, the supreme military genius, and altogether the greatest genius in history was in reality a paranoiac torturer, a mass murderer, and a military ignoramus who had brought the Soviet state to the verge of disaster."[17] But it was precisely the emphasis on Stalin's disturbed psychology that made Khrushchev's speech extremely tenuous and unconvincing. By insisting on the personal roots of terror, Khrushchev tried to conceal its social and institutional origins. Because he may have realized subconsciously that it required a one-party *system*, ruled with an iron fist by a phalanx of illuminated zealots convinced of the universal truth of their dogmas, for such atrocities to take place, Khrushchev saw no point in digging deeper than Stalin's personal responsibility. The system had to be preserved, and any attempt to question its legitimacy was the most dangerous of heresies. Instead of dwelling upon the structural conditions that had made possible the ascent of a psychopath to absolute power, instead of focusing on the Leninist premises of Stalinism, Khrushchev did his best to exonerate both Lenin and the Bolshevik "Old Guard."

In Khrushchev's speech, Beria appeared as the embodiment of universal evil and Stalin as a gullible pawn manipulated by this amoral adventurer. The party, Khrushchev claimed, had been decimated as a result of Beria's vicious intrigues and Stalin's morbid suspiciousness. He did not ask, however, why the party elite had not reacted to that destructive course and had sheepishly acquiesced in its own annihilation. Also missing was a strategic proposal for an internal structure to prevent the rise of such sadistic monsters to the party's pinnacle. The communists gave the population no assurances that the Stalinist aberrations would not repeat themselves in the future. Moreover, the most disturbing and ominous of Khrushchev's silences dealt with the fate of the noncommunist victims of Stalinism. There was no remorse in the "secret speech" with regard to the millions of peasants exterminated during the government-induced famine of the early 1930s, no word about the persecution of religion and of the democratic political parties, no regrets for destruction of the national elites in the Sovietized republics. In the same vein, Khrushchev made sure to identify the year 1934, when Stalin engineered the assassination of his Politburo colleague and presumed rival, Sergei Kirov, as the beginning of the disaster.

In other words, the catastrophe of Stalinism, according to Khrushchev's self-serving interpretation, began at the moment Stalin decided to launch his attack against the Stalinist bureaucracy itself. What Khrushchev deplored was not the Jacobin logic of terror but its "distorted" application against the faithful servants of the communist ideal. This was the main fallacy of Khrushchevism: the deceptive effort to rescue Leninism from any association with Stalinist lawlessness and to rehabilitate only those victims of the Stalinist terror who had unflinchingly served the Bolshevik party and its leader. There was no way, with that logic, to go further and analyze the show trials of the 1930s or reconsider the preposterous charges raised against Stalin's opponents of the Bolshevik "Old Guard." Trotsky, Zinoviev, Kamenev, Rykov, and Bukharin were still pilloried as adversaries of the party, and Stalin was even praised for his relentless struggle against those alleged conspirators. The ideological euphemism for the whole system of lies, corruption, mass murder, and universal fear was the "cult of personality." If only Stalin had been more modest and humane, the whole system would have looked different. Moreover, Khrushchev argued, Stalin's personal intentions had been above suspicion. The late leader had always been a devout communist whose means, and not ends, had to be condemned. Khrushchev admitted that the crimes took place "during Stalin's life under his leadership and with his concurrence." At the same time, however, the "secret speech" hastened to grant the deceased tyrant a strange alibi by pointing to his presumed commitment to revolutionary values:

> Stalin was convinced that this was necessary for the defense of the interests of the working classes against the plotting of enemies and against the attack of the imperialist class. He saw this from the position of the interest of the working class, of the interest of the victory of socialism and communism. We cannot say that these were the deeds of a giddy despot. He considered this should be done in the interest of the party, of the working

masses, in the name of the defense of the revolution's gains. In this lies the whole tragedy.[18]

Regardless of Khrushchev's disclaimers and rationalizations, the "secret speech" legitimized the revolt against Stalinist institutions and values. The Soviet Union tried to save as much as possible of its ideological myths, but the wave of liberalization swept irresistibly through the satellite countries. The most dynamic examples in discovering a new sense of autonomy and in attempts to relinquish the frozen Stalinist carcass turned out to be Hungary and Poland. Profound effects from the Soviet Congress also were felt in all the other bloc countries, where the party intelligentsia became increasingly radicalized and critical of the past abuses.

THE POLISH CRISIS OF 1956

The Polish communist leader Boleslaw Bierut, overwhelmed by the revelations of the Twentieth Congress, died in March 1956. What followed was a tremendous struggle for power among different factions within the party elite. To understand the characteristics of communism in Poland, it is necessary to refer to the political and intellectual origins of the party's formation, as well as to its tribulations under Stalin. Initially, the clandestine Polish Communist Party was one of the least regimented of the East European Leninist parties. Stalin strongly resented the veteran leaders of Polish communism and engineered their extermination during the Great Purge. In 1938 the Polish Communist Party was dissolved by a decree of the Executive Committee of the Communist International, which accused the Polish party of being a nest of spies and *agents-provocateurs* for the Polish secret police. That was a serious blow by Stalin against a political group that had already suffered the psychological consequences of its underground status: suspicion, sectarianism, and lack of political imagination.

One of the main reasons for Stalin's dislike of Polish communism, as Isaac Deutscher once pointed out, had to do with the never completely abandoned tradition of Luxemburgism. The luminaries of Polish communism had been formed in the radical socialist tradition of Rosa Luxemburg and had little reason either to respect or to love Stalin, although they considered the Soviet Union the symbol for their best hopes. At the same time, one should keep in mind that the Polish Communist Party had been ruthlessly Bolshevized in the late 1920s and early 1930s and that its militants had accepted the Comintern's verdict without even a gesture of protest. Isaac Deutscher correctly raised the following questions about the effects of Stalinism on the Polish communist elite:

> How did it happen, we must ask, that a Party which had to its credit decades of underground struggle and a long (seventy years long!) and proud Marxist tradition, submitted meekly to this horrible outrage— without a protest, without making any attempt to defend its martyred leaders and fighters, without even trying to vindicate its honor, and without declaring that in spite of the death sentence Stalin had passed on it, it would live on and fight on? How could this happen? We must be fully aware of the moral corrosion to which Stalinism had for so many years exposed Polish Communism in order to understand its complete collapse under the blow.[19]

It was during World War II that the Polish Communist Party reemerged as a political force active in the anti-Nazi resistance. The party's main leader was Wladyslaw Gomulka, who after the liberation of the country became General Secretary of the Polish Communist Party. But Gomulka was eventually ousted by the more powerful Muscovite faction headed by Boleslaw Bierut, Hilary Minc, and Jakub Berman. He spent the years of the intense Stalinist terror in Poland under house arrest.

Among the salient characteristics of the Polish political culture in the first decade of communist rule were the persistence of nationalism, the weakness of Marxist-Leninist ideology, and the political authority of the Catholic Church.[20] Despite the permanent ideological warfare waged by the communists against the Church, Catholicism continued to be a magnetizing force for the Poles. As de-Stalinization developed in the Soviet Union, the Polish communist elite started to split between those favorable to liberalization and the fundamentalists for whom there was no need to renounce any of the traditional dogmas. Gomulka had been released from his forced residence in 1954, and the charges against his alleged "nationalist" deviation were forgotten. In 1955 Poland became the ground for heated intellectual debates in which old-fashioned conceptions were drastically criticized by increasingly bold intellectuals. Intellectuals were exhilarated by the revelations of the Twentieth CPSU Congress. By 1956 more than two hundred discussion clubs were unabashedly examining the thorniest issues of the country's past and present. Indeed, the resurgence of interest in public opinion revived the besieged Polish civil society.

Like their peers in Hungary, Polish intellectuals searched for a new principle of socialism. Their critique of the ruling elite was rooted not in nostalgia for the old regime but rather in the belief that the true values of socialism had been forgotten by communist bureaucrats interested only in the perpetuation and expansion of their power. The insurgent intellectuals exposed the calamitous moral and psychological consequences of the dictatorship and called for the humanization of the existing order. Their approach, however, was evolutionary rather than revolutionary. They wanted to change the system from within and pinned their hopes on the presumably more open-minded faction of the party leadership. The publication in 1955 of the communist writer Adam Wazyk's "Poem for Adults" unleashed a fierce political and literary battle between the liberals and the conservatives. Wazyk denounced the party leadership's lack of sensitivity to the abysmal living standards of the working class, the absence of a fair legal system, and the all-pervasive lie as an indelible characteristic of the everyday life in Stalinized Poland:

There are people overworked,
there are people from Nowa Huta
who have never been to a theatre,
there are Polish apples which Polish children cannot reach,
there are boys forced to lie,
there are girls forced to lie,
there are old wives turned away from their homes by their husbands,
there are the weary dying of tired hearts,
there are people slandered, spat upon
there are people stripped in the streets by common bandits,
for whom the authorities still seek a legal definition,
there are people who wait for documents, there are people who wait for justice,
there are people who wait very long.

After that merciless indictment of the established order, Wazyk spelled out the principal demands of Poland's rising civil society. For him, and for his colleagues who had long believed in the Marxist creed, the solution could not come from outside the communist party. His requests were therefore addressed to an unknown enlightened leader who could eventually take over and restore the dignity of true socialism. The following lines of the poem contain the whole ethos of revisionism as an attempt to correct the evils of the system without renouncing its most important institution, the communist party itself:

We make demands on this earth,
for the people who are overlooked,

for keys to open doors,
for rooms with windows,
for walls which do not rot,
for hatred of little documents,
for holy human time,
for safe homecoming,
for a simple distinction between words and deeds.

We make demands on this earth,
for which we did not throw dice,
for which a million perished in battle:
for a clear truth,
for the bread of freedom,
for burning reason,
for burning reason.

We demand this every day.
We demand through the party.[21]

Wazyk's *cri de coeur* managed to antagonize the communist ideo-logues, who reacted in a most offended way. The poem was singled out by the party's official daily *Trybuna Ludu* as an example of "childish hyste-ria." But, as the writer Stanislaw Baranczak pointed out, it was precisely the adoption of such a "childish" perspective of moral indignation that made Wazyk's writing particularly gripping and seditious: "The reason Wazyk's poem proved so offensive was that the poet behaved like a child throwing a fit when reality does not correspond to his expectations. Wazyk offended everybody by acting like a spiteful child, by vomiting in the literary salon of 1955 and completely disregarding the rules of either anti-thaw or pro-thaw *savoir-vivre.*"[22] The disquieting tone of Wazyk's poem turned out to be a premonition of events soon to take place.

The self-confidence of Poland's communist ruling class was shattered at the moment of the Twentieth CPSU Congress. The old idols and sacred values were torn apart, and the need for an autonomous Polish way to socialism was reasserted. The meaning of the resurgence was unequivo-cal: It signified a resolute break with the Stalinist conception of the leading role of the party apparatus. To disseminate their unorthodox views, intellectuals decided to go into the factories and talk to the indus-trial workers. Polish political and intellectual life was thus increasingly polarized between the Stalinist nostalgics and the partisans of change. Domesticism, or the temptation to emphasize the distinctive peculiarities of the Polish road to socialism, was fighting a moribund version of Stalin-ist pseudo-internationalism. The calls for rapid transformation of the existing order did not, however, transcend the boundaries of the system. The Polish opposition of 1956 was still convinced of the inner perfectibility of the communist system. Changes, therefore, were to be gradual, without cataclysmic collisions or violent conflicts between rulers and ruled. The events in Poznan in June 1956, when a working-class riot was crushed with army support, contradicted the belief that those "corrections" could take place in a peaceful and quiet way.

The chasm between reformers and dogmatics further widened, making Gomulka's return to power a pressing condition for the party's very survival. Because of his persecution under the Bierut regime, Gomulka enjoyed popularity and could clean the party's tarnished image. The basic source of division within the ruling group was the attitude toward the future of Polish-Soviet relations. It was mandatory for liberals, and even more so for revisionist intellectuals, to establish full equality in relations between Poland and the USSR. As the liberals tended to radicalize, the conservatives hardened their positions and resorted to strong anti-intellectual, xenophobic, and anti-Semitic slogans. In October 1956 the crisis within the top party hierarchy had reached an explosive point. Gomulka's return to the head of the Central Committee was demanded both by the party's rank-and-file and by nonparty pressure groups. At the same time there were demands for the immediate removal of Soviet Marshal Konstantin Rokossovsky from his position as Poland's Minister of Defense (his appointment to that job had been one of Stalin's most outrageous gestures for humiliating the Polish national pride). Edward Ochab, a veteran communist who had succeeded Boleslaw Bierut as the party leader in March 1956, decided to step down and endorsed Wladyslaw Gomulka's candidacy during a tempestuous Central Committee meeting on October 19. The meeting was attended also by an uninvited Soviet delegation comprising Nikita Khrushchev, Vyacheslav Molotov, Anastas Mikoyan, and Lazar Kaganovich, who had arrived suddenly in Warsaw to watch and, if possible, to influence the course of events. In spite of the Soviet reservations, Gomulka was triumphantly elected First Secretary of the party and announced the establishment of the "Polish way to socialism." The new leader insisted on the need for autonomy in domestic policy and reassured the Soviets that Poland would remain a loyal ally within the Warsaw Pact. Unlike Tito, for whom Yugoslavia had to play a special role in world affairs as a neutral country, Gomulka deliberately limited his quest for international autonomy. He was convinced that Poland's alliance with Moscow was indispensable for the country's integrity, especially in the light of potential West German territorial claims.

Even in domestic policy, Gomulka did not dare to transcend the limits of timid reformism. He refused to recognize the party's responsibility for the economic morass and continued to cling to the dogmas of the central plan. Ideologically, Gomulka advocated the hegemony of Marxism-Leninism. He staunchly opposed a genuine dialogue with the Catholic Church, which he considered a monolithic "reactionary" bloc, and simply tried to contain its influence. As for the Church, it was a magnet for many of those who saw communist rule as government imposed by a foreign power. The innovations Gomulka permitted resulted in a softening of the domestic repression, a slowdown in industrial investments, and greater tolerance for intellectual and artistic experimentation. An out-and-out break with Stalinism would have been too ambitious and difficult for Gomulka. At the most, his dream was to reinvigorate the system, not to replace it. Certainly, during his first years in power, the climate in Poland was more relaxed than in the other East European countries, but political pluralism remained a mere *desideratum*. Gomulka capitalized on the existing malaise and promised a rapid economic recovery. He managed to deceive many intellectuals, who took him for a genuine enemy of Stalinism and applauded his coming to power.

In fact, Gomulka had no sympathy for or understanding of those who advocated a revolutionary change of the system. Basically, he was satisfied with the existing institutional framework and did not have the slightest intention of tolerating its overthrow. Without being a dogmatic of the Bierut or Rakosi type, he was even less a heretic. He looked askance at the turbulent workers' councils in Polish industry, which threatened the party's constituted authority. At the moment he consolidated his power within the communist hierarchy, Gomulka proceeded to curb spontaneous development from below and to restore the party's overall control over society. In 1957 he unleashed a purge against revisionist intellectuals, whom he accused of trying to undermine the socialist order. Freedom of the press, a Polish reality of the previous year, was severely curtailed. The proponents of democratic socialism were denied access to publication; their revisionism became the target of officially engineered slander campaigns. The revisionist position was formulated in a crystal-clear manner by Leszek Kolakowski, then a young philosophy professor at the University of Warsaw. In a short text entitled "What is Socialism?"—which was banned by the Gomulka regime—Kolakowski offered a provocative series of negative definitions of socialism, thereby pointing out what he considered to be the true content of the concept of socialism. With remarkable poignancy and wit, Kolakowski highlighted the most important elements of the revisionist creed:

Socialism is not:

A society in which a person who has committed no crime sits at home waiting for the police.

A society in which one person is unhappy because he says what he thinks, and another happy because he does not say what he is in his mind.

A society in which a person lives better because he does not think at all.

A state whose neighbors curse geography.

A state which wants all its citizens to have the same opinions in philosophy, foreign policy, economics, literature, and ethics.

A state whose government defines its citizens' rights, but whose citizens do not define the government's rights.

A state in which there is private ownership of the means of production.

A state which considers itself solidly socialist because it had liquidated private ownership of the means of production.

A state which always knows the will of the people before it asks them.

A state in which the philosophers and writers always say the same as the generals and the ministers, but always after them.

A state in which the returns of parliamentary elections are always predictable.

A state which does not like its citizens to read back numbers of newspapers.[23]

This mordant definition of what socialism is not offered one of the most accurate diagnoses of the dismal conditions imposed by the communists on the East European nations. While in Poland Gomulka managed to contain and neutralize the rebellious ferment, in Hungary a popular movement succeeded in toppling the old order and ushering in a truly pluralistic society.

FREEDOM RECONQUERED: IMRE NAGY AND THE HUNGARIAN REVOLUTION

On June 16, 1989, a solemn ceremony took place in Budapest. For more than thirty years, Imre Nagy and the other martyrs of the 1956 revolution had been besmirched by the Kadar regime's propaganda as fomenters of a counterrevolutionary conspiracy. Now, the leaders of Hungary's 1956 revolution were finally granted a proper burial. In the meantime, the official stories told to justify those who had betrayed the revolution and colluded with the Soviet invaders fell apart. Janos Kadar, the man who had accepted the Soviet *diktat* and had led the country for three decades, had been forced to resign at a party conference one year earlier. The new leaders, headed by General Secretary Karoly Grosz and Prime Minister Miklos Nemeth, were striving to gain authority by resuming the interrupted tradition of reform communism. With Gorbachev in the Kremlin, the times were opportune for their break with the ludicrous description of the 1956 uprising as a counterrevolution. From within the ruling Hungarian Socialist Workers' Party, there was growing demand for the rehabilitation of Imre Nagy and his comrades. The maverick reformer Imre Pozsgay, head of the liberal wing within the party elite, and Rezsö Nyers, the father of the economic reform of the early 1970s, joined the country's democratic opposition in its demand for the restoration of truth regarding the 1956 national uprising.

When the reform-oriented Hungarian communists tried to join in the mourning procession, they heard the following irreverent, even defiant statement by Victor Orban, one of the leaders of the FIDESZ, the Federation of Young Democrats, a new political party unashamed of its anticommunist convictions:

> We young people fail to understand many things that are obvious to the older generations. We are puzzled that those who were so eager to slander the Revolution and Imre Nagy have suddenly become the greatest supporters of the former prime minister's policies. Nor do we understand why the party leaders who saw to it that we were taught from books that falsified the Revolution are now rushing to touch the coffins as if they were good-luck charms. We need not be grateful for their permission to bury our martyrs after thirty-one years; nor do we have to thank them for allowing our political organizations to function.[24]

In its deliberate abrasiveness, Orban's statement betokened the immense gap between the revisionist illusions of the previous generations and the unambiguous refusal to embrace any form of communism on the part of Hungary's youth. The communist party was not to be credited with anything: It had ruled the country against the people's will, and no one had to be grateful for its sudden discovery of the principles of tolerance. Imre Nagy's reburial in June 1989 was thus a symbolic farewell to the idea of intrasystemic reforms. Instead of gradual change from within, the battle cry was now a resolute break with the communist system and the establishment of a pluralist order based on a free market and accountable government. More than thirty years earlier, Nagy himself had been the forerunner of this revolutionary approach. In a time of immense personal risk, he had shown the courage to embrace the cause of the plebeians against the communist oppressors.

The intelligentsia played a leading role in the earlier Hungarian antitotalitarian outburst, and for many reasons: First, the intelligentsia had been subjected, throughout the Stalinist years, to particularly vicious measures of persecution; second, its representatives considered themselves the repository of national values debased under Stalinism; third, as an enlightened elite, with certain revolutionary traditions going back to the social and national upheaval of 1848, the intelligentsia considered itself entitled to assume a leading role in the struggle against despotism; and fourth, large segments of the Polish and Hungarian intelligentsias who had espoused the values of Marxism had grown disenchanted with the manipulation of those values by the ruling bureaucracies.

As for the industrial workers, they were initially captivated by the communist promises of social justice and equality. The collectivistic ethos of early communism is Eastern Europe and the personnel policy favoring people with working-class social background served precisely to create the feeling that workers were indeed the ruling group in society. In turn, this form of exclusiveness contributed to a widening gulf between workers and intellectuals: The former perceived the latter as troublemakers, while the intellectuals considered the workers the main social base for a most suffocating regime. It was only later, in the 1970s, that organic cooperation became possible between the radical wings of both the intelligentsia and the industrial working class. By 1956 intellectuals were looking for support in the communist parties' antidogmatic wing. In Poland they tried to mobilize on their side people from the Gomulka faction. In Hungary, because the leadership seemed completely subjugated by the unrepentant Stalinists headed by Rakosi and his lackeys, the critical intellectuals looked to Imre Nagy and his partisans. Another element that had a cardinal influence for the coalescence of radical reformism was the contagious effect of Titoism in Eastern Europe. Tito's repudiation of Stalinism was regarded as a strategy to be emulated, and the Yugoslavs did not conceal their sympathy for the East European revisionists. Reformism in Eastern Europe in 1956 started as an attempt to solve structural contradictions and tensions within the existing matrix of authority and domination. It did not include, at least in its original formulations by people like Nagy or even Kolakowski, the desire to overthrow the system. The thrust of the struggle was political in that it emphasized the possibility of reformation within the status quo. Because of its failure to embrace global grievances and champion the national rejection of communism, revisionism could not embody a full-fledged and convincing alternative to the communist regime.[25]

One of the best analyses of both the grandeur and the limits of Marxist revisionism was provided by Adam Michnik, the celebrated Polish historian and civil rights activist. In his essay "A New Evolutionism," Michnik scrutinized the nature of the revisionist wave in Poland, but his conclusions are valid for the other East European countries as well. According to Michnik, the revisionist fallacy stemmed from this group's idealization of the communist party's aptitude and readiness for structural change:

> The revisionist concept was based on a specific intraparty perspective. It was never formulated into a political program. It assumed that the system of power could be humanized and democratized and that the official Marxist doctrine was capable of assimilating contemporary arts and social sciences. The revisionists wanted to act within the framework of the communist party and Marxist doctrine. They wanted to transform "from within" the doctrine and the party in the direction of reform and common sense.[26]

The main weakness of the revisionists, Michnik insisted, originated in their lack of a radical oppositional platform. Sharing the Marxist illusions with the powers-that-be, the revisionists could not realize that only such a program for sweeping change could provide them with a mass base: The "revisionists' greatest sin lay not in their defeat in the intraparty struggle for power (where they could not win) but in the character of that defeat. It was the defeat of individuals being eliminated from positions of power and influence, not a setback for a broadly based leftist and democratic political platform."[27]

Only in Hungary did the social movement from below outrun the expectations and objectives of the revisionist faction. A conjunction of factors, among which was Imre Nagy's personal decision to embrace the demands of the popular uprising, turned this movement into a revolution against totalitarianism. Hungary of 1956 was the first case in Eastern Europe where violence was used by the masses in self-defense against the repression waged by foreign troops. It is important to stress that the Hungarian revolution was not a reactionary movement aiming to restore the *ancien régime*, but an outburst of popular rage against the usurpation of the ideals of justice and equality by the communist bureaucracy. The first post–World War II democratic revolution in Eastern Europe, it created a model and a tradition that was to influence all the antitotalitarian social movements in the region for the subsequent decades.

The course of events that led to the revolutionary explosion was definitely accelerated by the stubbornness and blatant ineptitude of the

Hungarian communist elite under Rakosi and Gerö. In 1955, after the two years of experimentation in the "New Course" policy, Imre Nagy was demoted, and the Rakosi faction tried to reestablish full domination over the country. It was too late, however, for those dyed-in-the-wool Stalinists to restore their domination: The signals coming from Moscow were extremely confusing and were of no help against the powerful wind of change affecting the whole region. On the other hand, during the two years of Nagy's premiership, Hungarian intellectuals had experienced a sense of freedom that they refused to renounce under the party's pressure. Undeterred by Rakosi's threats and sick of the official lies, they engaged in a search for truth that was aptly called the "revolt of the mind."[28] For a mass revolutionary movement to develop, several premises were indispensable. First, such a challenge to communist authority is unthinkable as long as the communist elite remains monolithically cohesive. In other words, for a social crisis to become a political crisis in Soviet-type regimes, communist elites must split on ideological and personal issues. In Hungary, the conflict between the Stalinist hard-liners headed by the Rakosi–Gerö team and the revisionist faction led by Nagy made possible the mounting attacks against the police state. Another condition for such a crisis to develop into a revolutionary situation is the erosion of party authority. The revelations about the Stalinist atrocities, especially Khrushchev's "secret speech," ruined Rakosi's political credibility. Instead of trying to co-opt the revisionists, the Hungarian leaders intensified their campaigns against the rebellious party members and initiated new witch-hunts against critical intellectuals. That perceived debility in the ruling group emboldened the leadership's opponents. A broad coalition could be formed among intellectuals, students, and representatives of the industrial working class. By the summer of 1956, the political and cultural scene in Budapest was dominated by heated debates on such basic issues as the history of the communist party, freedom of the press, and rehabilitation of the victims of the Stalinist terror in Hungary. An example of this rise in civil life was the Petöfi Circle. Members of the Nagy faction inspired the Petöfi Circle, a discussion group created to debate the issues associated with the democratization of public life and methods to overcome the Stalinist legacy. Thus Nagy's supporters could publicize the ideas expressed by the former Prime Minister in a memorandum addressed to the party leadership in the first months of 1956. According to Nagy, the further development of socialism required a new approach to Marxism. Instead of being revered as a sacrosanct dogma, that philosophy had to adjust itself to changing realities. Moreover, Nagy claimed, socialism was threatened by the degeneration of political power in the Soviet-style regimes, where the people's democracy "is obviously being replaced by a party dictatorship, which does not rely on Party membership, but relies on a personal dictatorship and attempts to make the party apparatus, and through it the Party membership, a mere tool of this dictatorship." According to Nagy, this authoritarian regime did not have anything to do with humane socialism: "Its power is not permeated by the spirit of socialism or democratism, but by a Bonapartist spirit of minority dictatorship. Its aims are not determined by Marxism, the teachings of scientific socialism, but by autocratic views that are maintained at any cost and by any means."[29]

In Nagy's statement one can identify all the themes of the revisionist mythology: On the one hand, he denounced the party's absolutist grip on power as illegitimate and inherently antidemocratic. On the other hand, he stuck to the interpretation of "scientific socialism" as a doctrine of human emancipation, without noticing that the principal source of the oppressive conditions he deplored was precisely the ideological pretense to omniscience and infallibility characteristic of Marxist historical determinism. Such themes notwithstanding, Nagy challenged the "Bonapartist, individual dictatorship" in the name of a humane version of socialism based on a "constitutional, legal system of the people's democracy, with its legislature and government, with the democracy of our entire state and social life."[30] In the discussions within the Petőfi Circle those theses were further developed to an extent that went beyond Nagy's stated goals. Writers and journalists participating in the discussions did not feel constrained by the Bolshevik logic of party discipline. Unlike Nagy, they recognized the root of evil in the very ideology that had justified the monopolization of power by a gang of bloodthirsty bureaucrats. For instance, in one discussion Tibor Dery, a writer who had long been active in the revolutionary movement, raised his voice against the system that had made possible the Stalinist crimes:

> As long as we direct our criticism against individuals instead of investigating whether the mistakes spring from the very system, from the very ideology, we can achieve nothing more than to exchange evil for a lesser evil. I trust we will get rid of our current leaders. All I fear is that the limping race-horses will be followed by limping donkeys. . . . We must seek in our socialist system the mistakes which not only permit our leaders to misuse their power, but which also render us incapable of dealing with each other with the humanity we deserve. The mistakes in question are structural mistakes that curtail, to an entirely unnecessary degree, the individual's rights and that, again, increase his burdens.[31]

Like their Polish peers, Hungarian intellectuals decided that freedom was a universal concept that could not be limited by selfish class restrictions.

The party dogma, according to which all moral concepts had to be interpreted in the light of the interests of the working class as designated by the communist apparatus, was flatly rejected as a fraud. The principle of party-mindedness (*partiinost*), long held to be unquestionable, was exposed in its naked reality as a form of enslavement of the mind and an anesthetizing of the critical faculty of the intellectual. Thus, another former Stalinist writer, Gyula Hay, spelled out the intelligentsia's longing for total cultural and political freedom:

> Well, let us get it over quickly. We are talking about the *full freedom* of literature. . . . The writer, like anybody else, should be allowed to tell the truth without restrictions; to criticize everybody and everything; to be sad, to be in love, to think of death . . . to believe or disbelieve in the omnipotence of God; to doubt the accuracy of certain statistics; to think in a non-Marxist way; to dislike certain leaders; to consider low the living standard of the people.[32]

The thrust of the reform movement was toward the democratization of the communist party's structure, the launching of economic reforms that would include rapid decentralization, political liberalization, and cultural and personal freedom.

As the challenge from the revisionist circles grew more powerful, the Stalinists at the top of the party reacted erratically. They were dismayed at the new Soviet line and did not know how to deal with it. Rakosi and his associates were political dinosaurs, relics of the Stalinist age whose mindset could not grasp the need for relaxation. For them, the critical intellectuals were subversive elements ready to dismantle the existing system and restore capitalism. In March 1956, under enormous pressure from below, Rakosi had to give in and approve of Laszlo Rajk's rehabilitation. From that moment on, his fate was sealed. Since he had been the chief engineer of the show trial, he could not outlive politically the movement for historical reparation. In the summer of 1956, when Rakosi desperately tried to launch a new campaign against an alleged "conspiracy led by Imre Nagy," the Soviets decided to use their leverage and oust the increasingly embarassing Stalinist despot.

Rakosi's replacement was a most unfortunate one: The new party leader, Ernö Gerö, had been Rakosi's second in command and could lay no claim to political innocence during those times of merciless settling of accounts. Seeking to broaden and strengthen his power base by incorporating a number of committed communists who had been jailed during the Stalinist terror, Gerö rehabilitated Janos Kadar, a former Politburo member and Minister of the Interior. He also went out of his way to warm up relations with Yugoslavia, hoping that Tito's endorsement would improve his image in Hungary. Those were, however, spasmodic gestures on the part of a political group that had lost any legitimacy. The Gerö leadership was challenged by the whole Hungarian society. Despite Gerö's panicky appeals, the communist party failed to mobilize a powerful response to the mounting unrest.

The party actually had become a political corpse whose function had been to serve as a mere transmission belt for the capricious decisions of the ruling group. Far from encouraging the moral autonomy of the party members, the Rakosi–Gerö team had completely annihilated personal will and had maintained its dictatorship primarily with the help of the secret police. Confronted with the popular wrath, even the secret police failed to stand up to significant resistance and collapsed, together with the communist bureaucracy. As Gerö could offer no more than outrageous vindictive speeches, there was no doubt that his leadership represented in fact Rakosism without Rakosi. As for Nagy and his group, their main problem stemmed from their hesitation to renounce utterly their loyalty to the party. For them, the Stalin myth had been demolished, but not the romantic vision of the party as a heroic community endowed by history with a predestined liberating role. In October 1956 Nagy was reinstated in the party, but Gerö refused to appoint him as Prime Minister.

On October 23 hundreds of thousands of citizens took to the streets of Budapest demanding the establishment of a state of law, the punishment of Rakosi and his gang, the reappointment of Imre Nagy as Prime Minister, the disbandment of the secret police, and the withdrawal of Soviet troops stationed in Hungary. That revolutionary movement had both a political and a national character. Frightened by the irresistible growth of the popular insurrection, Gerö asked for Soviet help and proclaimed a state of emergency. Inaugurating a pattern to be followed by other beleaguered communist leaders confronted with popular uprisings, he delivered a provocative broadcast address, labeling the revolt as a "counterrevolution." Following Gerö's order, police shot at the peaceful demonstrators. At that moment the long-dormant Central Committee ousted Gerö, and a new leadership that included both Nagy and Kadar was elected. Once sworn in as Prime Minister, Nagy announced a program of democratization. A brief intervention on October 24 notwithstanding, the Soviet troops maintained a "wait and see" attitude. The Soviet Ambassador to Hungary, Yury Andropov, reassured Nagy that his government would not interfere in that country's internal affairs. What had started as a spontaneous mass revolt evolved into a popular revolution. Imre Nagy, the committed communist, discovered that the people wanted to dismantle the communist system completely and establish a genuine pluralistic regime. In factories revolutionary councils were formed as a form of direct democracy. To his credit, Nagy managed to sense the pulse of the historical developments in his country and embraced the popular demands for the complete overthrow of the Stalinist system. Nagy's awakening was catalyzed by the inner dynamics of the revolutionary process, the pressures exerted by members of his group, and his realization of the duplicity of the Soviet attitude toward the changes in Hungary. Thus, one could say that Imre Nagy started as a reformer and ended up as a revolutionary. He went far beyond the logic of intra-systemic change and joined the momentum of an antisystemic movement that rapidly swept away the whole edifice of bureaucratic socialism.

Prompted by the irresistible movement from below, Nagy decided to broaden the base of his government by accepting the principle of political pluralism. By the end of October 1956 Hungary had ceased to resemble a people's democracy and was moving fast toward a multiparty system. Faced with this challenge coming from one of its former satellites, the Soviet Union issued a declaration on October 30 in which it solemnly proclaimed its commitment to the principles of full equality in relations between Moscow and the states of the so-called socialist family. Recognizing that violations of those principles had taken place in the past, the Kremlin promised to respect the national sovereignty of the East European countries. Lulled by those soothing Soviet pledges, Nagy underestimated Moscow's determination to preserve the communist regime in Hungary. The limits of Soviet tolerance were tested several days later. Soviet troops directly intervened to overthrow the legal Nagy government and to smash the Hungarian resistance movement.

The second Soviet intervention was brought on by Nagy's decision to embark on the multiparty system and by the formation of a "military-revolutionary council" to lead the Hungarian armed forces. Threatened with the complete loss of influence in Hungary and noticing the inglorious collapse of the Hungarian communist party, the Kremlin decided to intervene directly and to restore bureaucratic-authoritarian order. On October 31 Nagy announced negotiations for Hungary's withdrawal from the Warsaw Pact. On November 1 Hungary proclaimed its neutrality. That set it on a course that could be followed by other satellites and had the potential to destroy the Soviet alliance system. Both internally and externally, the Hungarian revolution demolished the institutional frame-

work of the people's democracy system. Irritated by this unprecedented
defiance and influenced by the hard-liners within the world communist
movement, principally China's Mao Zedong, the Soviet leadership decided to put an end to the Hungarian pluralist experiment. Janos Kadar
disappeared from Budapest. Later Kadar would announce from a Soviet-
controlled radio station the creation of a "revolutionary government of
the workers and peasants." On November 4 Soviet troops attacked garrisons and military units loyal to the Nagy government. Nagy and his
closest associates took refuge in the Yugoslav Embassy and, following
Kadar's promises that no revenge would be organized against them, accepted the political asylum granted to the them by the Romanian government. What happened in fact was that in Romania the leaders of the
Nagy government were subjected to continuous interrogations by Soviet
secret police officers helped by Hungarian-speaking Romanian party officials. In June 1958 a pseudo-trial took place in Budapest. Imre Nagy and
several of his allies were sentenced to death and executed.

The meaning of Nagy's attempt to reconcile socialism with democracy cannot be exaggerated: In its consistency and temerity, Nagy's radical reformism went beyond the limited logic of national communism as
tested by Tito in Yugoslavia. After all, for all his staunch criticism of
Stalin's dictatorial methods, Tito had never tolerated full dissent in his
own country, let alone the emergence of a multiparty system. For the
national communists like Tito and Gomulka, the issue was to preserve
their domestic autonomy and, in the Yugoslav case, a relatively large
margin of initiative in foreign policy. National communism, as Milovan
Djilas has often said, remains essentially communist, although of a less
absolutist stripe.[33] It became increasingly clear to Nagy that the humanization of the system required the end of the communist party's illegitimate claim to monopolistic power. There was in Imre Nagy's personality
a tragic dimension stemming from a tension between his commitment to
democratic values on the one hand and his failure to recognize the
cynicism of Soviet international behavior on the other. Nagy naïvely
trusted the Soviet leaders and took their promises at face value. He was,
however, too much a moral individual to renege on his pledges to the
Hungarian nation and accept what Gomulka accepted in Poland: the
deliberate curtailment of the revolutionary movement, its manipulation
and eventual asphyxiation. The Hungarian uprising against the logic of
capitulation to foreign *diktat* was enhanced by Nagy's decision to side
with the victims rather than support the executioners for reasons of party
discipline or merely for personal survival. The glorious lesson of the
Hungarian democratic revolution was indeed that it was possible for a

mass movement inspired by humanistic ideals to overthrow a despised tyranny and to achieve a genuine breakthrough in the suffocating totalitarian universe. During the ten sublime days of the Budapest uprising, the legacy of Yalta had been fundamentally shattered. In the words of Ferenc Feher and Agnes Heller:

> In a world where superpowers cynically collaborated, in which radical causes betrayed so often their original aims, where movements with an emancipating message degenerated into various sorts of conservative and fundamentalist tyrannies, the Hungarian October, with the outlines of its socialist (because radically democratic and self-created) "new republic," emerges unspoiled and promising; a cause capable of instilling moral and social self-confidence in a nation desperately needing it. [34]

Indeed, the crushed revolution, with its unfulfilled dreams of national liberation and political emancipation, continued to haunt the collective psyche of Hungarians for decades.

Despite Kadar's first forcible, later more benign pacification, and despite his achievement of turning Hungary into the "most joyful barrack of the socialist camp," the principle of an impure Realpolitik could not triumph over the national search for historical truth. The blatant lies on which the Kadar regime was founded, the allegations about the existence of a "counterrevolutionary conspiracy" fomented by Imre Nagy and his comrades, could only backfire. Instead of erasing the memory of the heroic moments of the insurrection, the Kadar propaganda fostered nostalgia for (and even a kind of idealization of) Nagy's pluralist experiment and enhanced the general admiration for the politician who chose martyrdom over collaborationism.

Nagy's sacrifice foreshadowed a new approach to postcommunist politics. His refutation of the intrigue-ridden world of the communist bureaucracy, combined with his confidence in society's right to self-government, helped Nagy to break with the Jacobin and Bolshevik despotic paternalism and to recognize the legitimacy of civic rebellions against the terrorist status quo. In so doing, he inaugurated a political tradition of opposition that was based on nonviolence, civic dignity, and moral responsibility. Nagy's gesture of defiance to the limited Khrushchevite de-Stalinization and his belief that it was possible to overturn the unjust established order were bound to inspire future generations of dissidents in the whole Soviet bloc. The lesson of the Hungarian Revolution taught the whole communist world. Feher and Heller luminously pointed out: "The Hungarian revolution was the first to assault the unjust and oppressive world-system created by the signatories to the Yalta and Potsdam agreements. It was the Hungarian revolution that taught the lesson, after too long a period of belief to the contrary, that a totalitarian regime can be toppled from within."[35]

Unlike Imre Nagy, who believed in the sovereignty of the people, Janos Kadar preferred to yield to imperial logic and to obey Khrushchev's orders. For a number of years, he became the most hated man in Hungary. With his collusion, if not his direct supervision, Nagy and his comrades were executed in June 1958. Later, when the Soviets themselves would soften their line and Khrushchev would come under Mao's fire for "revisionism," Kadar was allowed to slow the pace of vengeful terror. In the meantime, tens of thousands had been executed, jailed, and deported. Hundreds of thousands had been forced into exile. As a consequence of the massacre engineered by Kadar and his fellow collaborationists, Hungary's intelligentsia was bled white. For years, Hungary's greatest Marxist philosopher, Georg Lukacs, who had served as Minister of Culture in Nagy's first revolutionary government, was unable to publish his works and was denounced by party hacks as a dangerous revisionist. The writers and activists involved in the Petőfi Circle either emigrated or were sentenced to prison terms.

The crushing of the Hungarian Revolution showed that by 1956 the established spheres of influence, as sanctioned by the agreements at the end of World War II, continued to exist. The Soviet Union retained the role of a guardian of orthodoxy within the Eastern bloc and made sure that heresies similar to Nagy's would not affect the other satellite countries. In the documents of the world communist conclave that took place in Moscow in November 1957, revisionism and national communism were branded as the most deleterious deviations from true Marxism-Leninism. The publication in 1958 of the Program of the Communist League of Yugoslavia offered dogmatics like Romania's Gheorghiu-Dej and East Germany's Ulbricht an opportunity to renew their attacks on Tito and Titoism. The Soviets made sure that their domination, both ideologically and militarily, would be preserved against all odds. To maintain the unity of the bloc against the national-communist temptation, Moscow was ready to suffer international opprobrium. As for Tito, after initially expressing support for Imre Nagy, he changed his attitude under relentless Soviet pressure. The Yugoslav leader did not want to be isolated again, so he accepted the Soviet allegations about the danger of a counterrevolution in Hungary. He even called the Nagy government "premature" and eventually decided to endorse the Kadar regime.

The Hungarian Revolution revealed the character of Khrushchevism

as a strategy of limited reforms from above and unambiguously demonstrated the imperialist nature of Soviet domination over Eastern Europe.
Within this Soviet internal empire, Khrushchev did not allow any development of autonomous movements in republics like the Baltic states,
Moldavia, or the Ukraine. On the contrary, under his reign Stalin's
program of Russification continued unabated. Externally, the suppression
of the Hungarian Revolution was proof of the hypocrisy of the Soviet
leadership's claim of having renounced Stalinist methods in their dealings with the satellite countries. As for the rulers in the other communist
states, they applauded the crushing of the revolution and the 1958 verdict against Nagy and his associates. Even Gomulka, who from his own
experience should have known better, described the Soviet intervention
in Hungary as "a correct and necessary action."[36] In all Eastern Europe a
new ideological tightening took place. The Stalinist forces reorganized
themselves to eliminate their liberal opponents. In East Germany, for
instance, the Marxist philosopher Ernst Bloch was forced to emigrate
after a vicious campaign was unleashed against him. Wolfgang Harich, a
young professor of Marxism who had written a program for the democratization of the country, was arrested. The party's theoretical journals emphasized the need to intensify the struggle against "bourgeois ideology
and revisionism." East Germany's intellectuals found themselves increasingly alienated from the dogmatic power. In the words of the poet Ger-
hard Zwerenz:

> The times are morose
> Writers are silent
> From fear
> And critics lecture
> At command
> And there is a literature
> Which no one believes
> But fees are paid.[37]

    In Czechoslovakia, where the economy was more prosperous than in
the other Eastern-bloc countries, the defeat of the Hungarian Revolution
reassured the neo-Stalinists, headed by Gottwald's successor, Antonin
Novotny, that there was no danger of a Soviet push for further liberalization. An abrupt stop was put to the process of political rehabilitations
initiated after the Twentieth CPSU Congress. In 1958, during the
antirevisionist campaign, and two years after the official dissolution of
the Cominform, an international journal expressing the shared views of

the world communist movement was established in Prague with the name *Problems of Peace and Socialism* (the English-language version bore the name *World Marxist Review*).[38]

After 1961 the Hungarian communists, enjoying Khrushchev's unstinting support, embarked on a less repressive domestic strategy. In order to create a minimal national consensus, Kadar broke with the exclusive Stalinist slogan, "He who is not with us is against us," and replaced it with the less intolerant and deliberately inclusive policy, "He who is not against us is with us." The Eighth Congress of the Hungarian communists took place in November 1962. Kadar announced a policy of national reconciliation and an economic strategy aimed at increasing the living standards of the population by encouraging limited private initiative and tolerating small business. He received Khrushchev's blessing in pursuing the relaxation, which became known as "goulash socialism." In March 1963 a general amnesty was declared, and thousands of Hungarian political prisoners were released. In exchange for that limited liberalization, the regime required its subjects to refrain from any criticism of the Soviet Union and to forget that its birth certificate had been signed in blood. The Party was ready to co-opt all highly skilled people who did not question its political legitimacy.

ATTEMPTS AT AUTONOMY: DESATELLITIZATION AND DE-STALINIZATION IN ROMANIA AND ALBANIA

In Romania, especially following the suppression of the Hungarian Revolution, the Stalinist leadership hardened its domestic policy. In June 1957 Gheorghiu-Dej eliminated a pro-Khrushchev faction that had tried to topple him. Interestingly, the two Politburo members eliminated on that occasion were Iosif Chisinevschi, the chief ideologue of the Stalinist period in Romania, and Miron Constantinescu, a Marxist sociologist with some revisionist propensities. Although the two had nothing in common, Gheorghiu-Dej insisted that their criticism of his role in the terror of the early 1950s was indicative of their joint antiparty activities. Khrushchev was too busy at that moment with his own struggle against the Stalinist diehards in the Kremlin to do anything in support of his presumed Romanian followers. A massive purge of the party and the intelligentsia took place in 1958, and tens of thousands were expelled from the communist party, then formally called the Romanian Workers' Party. In June 1958, as a result of previous secret negotiations between Gheorghiu-Dej and Khrushchev, the Kremlin decided to withdraw its troops from Romania. That was considered at the time an indication of the Soviets' unlimited confidence in the unflinchingly orthodox Romanian leaders and their capacity to maintain systemic stability. It was also a measure destined to convince the West that the intervention in Hungary had been a mere accident and that the Soviet Union did not intend to continue its imperialist policy toward the former satellites. Later on, it turned out that the Romanian communists headed by Gheorghiu-Dej had played a deceptive game with Khrushchev and that their goal was to ensure a margin of autonomy against any Soviet injunctions for further de-Stalinization. As a matter of fact, Romania and Albania were the only East European countries where the thaw was nipped in the bud.

No challenge to Gheorghiu-Dej's authority could coalesce in Romania, and those who dared to suggest that he had been guilty of Stalinist abuses were immediately purged. Gheorghiu-Dej's policy amounted to unwavering Stalinism: He favored breakneck industrialization and waged a merciless collectivization campaign. In the spring of 1962 Romania's agriculture was entirely collectivized. Gheorghiu-Dej announced the definitive and irrevocable victory of socialism in that country and the beginning of a new stage: "the completion of socialist construction."

For Gheorghiu-Dej, Khrushchev's second de-Stalinization campaign, inaugurated at the Twenty-second CPSU Congress in October 1961, with the removal of Stalin's body from Lenin's Mausoleum, looked ominous. Like other veteran Stalinist leaders, Gheorghiu-Dej resented the Soviet leader's erratic policies and feared that further liberalization could only undermine the foundations of the existing system. They were all convinced that further relaxation of authority would threaten their status. In this respect, Gheorghiu-Dej, like Albania's Hoxha, Czechoslovakia's Novotny, and East Germany's Ulbricht, was closer to Mao Zedong's exaltation of Stalin's merits than to Khrushchev's denunciation of the late despot's crimes.

In 1960 Enver Hoxha, the leader of the Albanian Communist Party, went to Moscow to attend the second world communist conference. On that occasion he attacked Khrushchev for his destabilizing role within world communism and maintained that the effects of the Twentieth CPSU Congress had been calamitous. One year later the Albanian indictment was repeated by the Chinese communists, who decided to give economic assistance to Hoxha after Khrushchev unleashed an economic boycott of that extremely poor country. Traumatized by the Soviet attempt to strangle them, the Albanian communists became the most vehement critics of "modern revisionism" and accused Khrushchev of being the gravedigger of world communism. For all practical purposes, Albania ceased to participate in the activities of the Eastern bloc and broke off diplomatic relations with Moscow and its satellites.[39]

Meanwhile, in Romania the limited and strictly controlled de-Stalinization amounted to nothing more than a new attack on Gheorghiu-Dej's former rivals eliminated in 1952 (Pauker and Luca) and 1957 (Chisinevschi and Constantinescu). Far from being rehabilitated, the former Politburo member Lucretiu Patrascanu, executed in 1954, continued to be vilified as a traitor to the working class. At the same time Gheorghiu-Dej ensured the rapid ethnicization of the party and government elites. Hungarian and Jewish apparatchiks were replaced by ethnic Romanians who owed to Gheorghiu-Dej their swift rise to prominence. It was at that moment that Nicolae Ceausescu, the youngest member of the Politburo, began to emerge as the leader's heir apparent.

Faced with potential Soviet intervention, Gheorghiu-Dej initiated a rapprochement with Tito and started to champion the principle of non-interference by the Soviets in other countries' internal affairs. When Khrushchev tried to push for the creation of supranational integrative bodies within the CMEA, the Romanians strongly opposed those suggestions and boycotted the Eastern bloc's summits. For Gheorghiu-Dej and his team, the only way to defend their own political hegemony was to ensure the country's economic independence. Educated in the Stalinist faith, they thought only rapid industrialization, with special emphasis on the paramount role of heavy industry, would succeed in securing that independence. They insisted that the only chance for Romania to escape foreign—that is, Soviet—pressure was to become economically self-sufficient. That was the rationale for the Romanian deviation that developed after 1962. In 1963–64 the Romanian media published a number of staunchly anti-Soviet articles, criticizing various Soviet plans to impose integration upon the East European economies. At the same time, noting the deterioration of Khrushchev's power in the Kremlin, Gheorghiu-Dej adopted a neutralist stance in the conflict between the Soviet and the Chinese communist parties. One reason Gheorghiu-Dej took such offense at Khrushchev's integrationist plans was that the Romanians thought in a new East European arrangement they would become vassals of more developed countries like East Germany and Czechoslovakia. The personal animosities between Gheorghiu-Dej, on the one hand, and Ulbricht and Novotny, on the other, played a considerable role in aggravating the friction.

In the summer of 1963 the Romanian media printed documents from both sides of the Soviet-Chinese conflict over the "general line of the world communist movement." One can assume that, far from sharing Mao's revolutionary zeal, Gheorghiu-Dej used the split between the two communist giants to create his own area of autonomy and to distance himself from the increasingly unpredictable Soviet First Secretary. In 1966 J. F. Brown observed:

> With daring shrewdness, Gheorghiu-Dej soon recognized the implications of the Sino-Soviet dispute for the East European satellites. He saw that they were now given much more scope for maneuver vis-à-vis the Kremlin than ever before. On the overt basic issues of the Sino-Soviet dispute, he was always wholly pro-Soviet; there was virtually no danger of his ever becoming a Maoist. Mao, to him, became simply a means of winning concession from the Soviet Union.[40]

In fact, Gheorghiu-Dej empathized with Mao's intransigent defense of the Stalinist legacy. Like other leftovers of the time of terror, he knew that the ultimate consequence of Khrushchev's disruptive campaigns against the "cult of personality" would be his own political elimination from the top leadership. To prevent such a denouement and to strengthen his power base, Gheorghiu-Dej turned to the weapon of nationalism: With mind-boggling rapidity, the Romanian communists, once the most subservient in their relations with Moscow, performed an about-face and started to pledge their commitment to national values. Prominent figures of the country's intelligentsia were rehabilitated, history books were rewritten in accordance with the new party line, and Russian ceased to be a mandatory foreign language taught in all Romanian schools. In April 1964, as the Sino-Soviet dispute reached an unprecedented polemical level, the Romanian Communist Party issued its "Statement with Regard to the Major Question Within the World Communist Movement." The document was very much influenced by Tito's self-ordained independence. It emphasized the right of every communist party to decide its own strategy, denied the Kremlin its privileged status within the socialist bloc, and called for new relations between communist parties and countries based on full equality and respect of national traditions and interests.

The Romanian challenge to the Soviet claim to hegemony ensured a broader popular base for Gheorghiu-Dej's leadership. Although his toughness in implementing the Stalinist line was evident to all Romanians, many were tempted to support the new national communist line. In August 1964 Gheorghiu-Dej felt secure enough to announce a general amnesty for political prisoners. Long-censored manuscripts by Karl Marx, critical of the Russian Empire's expansionist policy toward the Danubian principalities during the nineteenth century, were published. Closed party gatherings were organized where members of Gheorghiu-Dej's Politburo engaged in radical criticism of the Soviet record of plundering Romania in the 1950s. The rediscovery of national values was, of course, self-serving for Gheorghiu-Dej and his associates. Far from converting to genuine patriotism, the communist elite was trying to manipulate national symbols in order to foster its domination and absolute control over the country. At the end of Gheorghiu-Dej's rule, in March 1965, Romania could follow one of two scenarios: either emulate Tito and de-Stalinize further, allowing for ideological relaxation and an opening to the West; or emulate Albania, that is, further strengthening of the communist party's grip on power and consolidation of a nationalist authoritarianism hostile to any liberalization. What would have happened had Gheorghiu-Dej lived longer is hard to say. When he died in office at the beginning of 1965, his successor, Nicolae Ceausescu, pursued de-Stalinization only for purposes of consolidating his own power. Unlike Gheorghiu-Dej, however, who had grasped a measure of authority through his opposition to the Soviets, Ceausescu had to build his own image as a national leader. A former shoemaker's apprentice with no real education, Ceausescu distrusted intellectuals and resented any form of liberalism. He played the nationalist card but made sure to keep any critical tendencies under strict control. Ceausescu pursued an adamantly Stalinist policy in the economy but permitted, at least during his first years in power, a relative loosening of the dogmatic constraints on the country's intellectual life. Later on, he engaged in a tremendous consolidation of power and established an original version of national communism whose eclectic ideology included elements of simplistic Marxism-Leninism and far-right ethnocentrism. As an unreconstructed Stalinist, he believed in the predestined role of the communist party and defended its monopoly on power. Since the only source of legitimacy for such power was the rejection of Moscow's interference, Ceausescu exploited the national pride of the Romanians and their historical anti-Russian resentments. He became enthralled with his own propaganda and came to see himself as the incarnation of Romania's destiny. His dream was to create a strong, highly centralized, and ethnically homogeneous state; he consistently referred to the "unified working people whose unique language would consist of communist words." In comparison with other East European leaders, Ceausescu enjoyed the somewhat privileged status of ruling a country with no Soviet troops on its territory. Instead of using that advantage to democratize the political system, he established a personal dictatorship that in the 1980s would reach the most absurd dimensions.

BULGARIA: THE FAITHFUL ALLY

The Bulgarian attitude to Khrushchevism mirrored the convulsions plagu-ing the Soviet leadership. Todor Zhivkov, the Bulgarian leader, derived po-litical legitimacy from the momentous revelations of the Twentieth CPSU Congress. Indeed, in 1956 Zhivkov engineered the elimination of his former patron, the Comintern veteran Vulko Chervenkov, from the top party position. At the April 1956 plenum the foundation myth of Zhiv-kov's pretense to being the embodiment of a new face of communism was created. The struggle between Zhivkov and the Chervenkov faction lasted until the Soviet Twenty-second Congress in 1961, when Khrushchev cre-ated the political framework for sweeping de-Stalinization in the satellite countries. Even after Chervenkov's expulsion from the party, however, the Stalinists continued to oppose Zhivkov's calls for a domestic thaw. In 1962 the Eighth Party Congress consecrated Zhivkov's triumph over his Stalin-ist opponents. The hard-line Prime Minister, Anton Yugov, who had par-ticipated in the purges of the 1950s, was attacked by Zhivkov and lost all his party and government positions. But Zhivkov was himself a skillful com-munist bureaucrat whose commitment to liberalization was perfunctory. In 1963 he emulated Khrushchev's anti-intellectual outbursts, directed pri-marily against Soviet liberal artists like the poet Yevgeny Yevtushenko and the sculptor Ernst Neizvestny, and engineered a strong purge of the Bulgar-ian anti-Stalinists. Critics of his regime were deported from Sofia, and the secret police resumed persecution of those who were suspected of the slightest form of dissent. When Khrushchev was ousted in October 1964, Zhivkov immediately tried to ingratiate himself with the new Soviet lead-ership headed by Leonid Brezhnev and Aleksei Kosygin. But his power base remained very fragile, and in the spring of 1965 a conspiracy com-posed of communist veterans and high-ranking army officers almost man-aged to topple him. After the defeat of the putschists, Zhivkov stated his unconditional support for the Soviet Union. In the years to come he would make subservience the principal underpinning of his power. Later, when the Soviets ceased to support him, that was enough to enable a group of conspirators in the Politburo to eliminate him in November 1989.

CONCLUSIONS

The shock created by Khrushchev's de-Stalinization campaigns affected all East European countries. The disarray among local elites resulted in the loosening of party controls and the emergence of emancipating movements from below, especially in Poland and Hungary. Once the Stalinist anti-Tito charges were exposed as insane fabrications, the national communist temptation became rampant in the region. The demolition of Stalin's myth and Khrushchev's calls for a creative approach to revolutionary doctrine emboldened unorthodox thinkers to question the very foundations of the existing order. From the late 1950s to the early 1960s all East European countries (to varying degrees), experienced the rise of revisionist tendencies. They were boldest in Poland and Hungary, where the Stalinist edifice crumbled under the onslaught of critical currents. In Hungary, the political dynamism resulted in the complete collapse of the communist structures and the emergence of an embryonic pluralist order, smashed by Soviet troops in November 1956. After the defeat of the Hungarian Revolution, the Soviets tried to restore the uniformity of the bloc, but their attempts were bound to fail. Centrifugal trends developed in each country, and local elites refused to be treated in the old humiliating fashion.

In many respects, the initiatives in those countries came from the local leaders, forcing Moscow to comply with their decisions. For instance, Walter Ulbricht, the East German leader, could persuade the Kremlin that only the erection of the Berlin Wall could stop the demographic hemorrhage in his country. In Hungary, the Kadarite national consensus was based on tacit recognition of the impossibility of discussing the 1956 events and Kadar's personal role in the annihilation of the legal Nagy government. It was a compromise based on blatant lies, half-truths, and illusions regarding the reformability of the existing system from within. The lack of independence in Hungary's foreign policy was balanced by an increased margin of personal freedom and a limitation on the powers enjoyed by the secret police inside the country. The Romanians maintained their equal distance from both Moscow and Beijing in the increasingly bitter conflict between the two communist giants. Romania engaged in a maverick foreign policy while keeping the repressive apparatus intact and sticking to a fundamentalist Stalinist interpretation of socialist construction. Yugoslavia continued to promote its nonaligned foreign policy, but Tito made no secret of his support for Khrushchev's anti-Maoist platform. Domestically, there were new reforms in the direction of self-management, and critical Marxists established their theoretical journal, Praxis, where they called for a resolute divorce from bureaucratic socialism. They criticized Tito and the Communist League of Yugoslavia for inconsistency in their break with the authoritarian-personalistic model of socialism. Only Albania, because of its remoteness and the strength of the local repressive apparatus, could avoid any form of de-Stalinization.

The once cohesive bloc, created as a result of Stalin's imperialist occupation of Eastern Europe, showed unmistakable signs of ill health. Khrushchev's successors tried to contain those chaotic trends by developing and institutionalizing new forms of interstate relations. Under Brezhnev the coordination of foreign policy initiatives between the Soviet Union and its allies became a prime objective for the Kremlin. The Kremlin tried to create the image of a new kind of relationship, where all countries enjoyed equal rights and had similar obligations. The theoretical base of the new concept of unity was called "socialist internationalism," a notion according to which the Soviet and East European interests were necessarily convergent and any attempt to question the nature of those relations was by definition a form of deviation from the true Marxist-Leninist line. "Developed socialism" was the name for the existing order in all East European countries. It was described by communist propaganda as a stable political system based on a dynamic economy and social consensus. The truth of the matter is that the social contract of Brezhnevism was based on political immobility, widespread apathy, and mass resignation to a status quo perceived as marginally less horrible than the Stalinist period.

The social contract of post-Stalinist communist societies was based not on terror but rather on mutual guarantees exchanged between the rulers and the ruled: While the former were providing their subjects with a protective shield of social benefits, the latter were renouncing their right to rebel against an inherently unjust system. However, such a social contract, being rooted in an unviable convention, was precarious: The rulers had no genuine legitimacy, hence at the moment the economy ceased to offer enough supplies for the continuation of the agreement, the whole system would fall apart. Added to this were the questionable foundations of the regimes. First, with the exception of Yugoslavia, none could claim that it had emerged on a base of popular will; second, their self-serving ideology, Marxism-Leninism, had lost its aura of infallibility as a result of the anti-Stalin campaigns and the social upheaval of 1956; and third, unlike the seasoned Stalinists who had led the East European communist parties during the times of savage duress, the mounting elites treated Marxism as a compulsory ritualistic creed and did not feel any mystical identification with the Leninist universalistic pretense. The belief system of the Stalinist days was maintained as a hollow carcass, and very few members of the elites took its ideas seriously. They used Leninism only as a doctrinaire camouflage for the perpetuation of their monopoly of power.

THREE

༄

From Thaw to Freeze

Eastern Europe Under "Real Socialism"

> There is no such thing a nontotalitarian
> ruling communism. It either becomes to-
> talitarian or it ceases to be communism.
> —*Adam Michnik*

Nikita Khrushchev was ousted as Soviet First Secretary and Chairman of the Council of Ministers in October 1964 as a result of an
intraparty coup organized by neo-Stalinist, bureaucratic forces dissatisfied with his leadership methods, branded as "harebrained schemes."
Among the charges raised against Khrushchev by his Politburo colleagues was that, as the champion of ill-conceived reforms, he had
weakened the authority of the communist party and its ideology. Because the new leaders in the Kremlin sought to restore the unity of
world communism, gravely damaged by the intensification of the polemic with China, Khrushchev's anti-Stalin pronouncements were conveniently forgotten. The very name of the tempestuous former First
Secretary disappeared for more than twenty years from official Soviet
utterances. The de-Khrushchevization campaign launched by Leonid
Brezhnev, Aleksandr Shelepin, Nikolai Podgorny, and Mikhail Suslov,
who had engineered the October palace coup, amounted to a moderate but unmistakable effort to rehabilitate Stalin.[1]

The Soviet decision to restore ideological uniformity and intrabloc coordination did not go unnoticed in Eastern Europe. Initially, the East European local leaders feared that the change in the Kremlin would affect their own positions, but they soon realized that the Soviets would continue to support them. Like the Soviet apparatus, they resented the former First Secretary's unpredictable gestures and preferred to deal with a more routinized and therefore more stable type of Soviet leadership. The new Soviet leaders tried to breathe life into the existing international consultative bodies and emphasized their commitment to an increased degree of solidarity between the ruling parties in the Soviet bloc. With the exception of Romania's Gheorghe Gheorghiu-Dej (who died in 1965) and his successor Nicolae Ceausescu, all the rulers in the other Warsaw Pact countries accepted the reassertion of Soviet hegemony as practiced by Khrushchev's successors. Brezhnevism demanded that they ensure domestic stability and ideological conformity and refrain from personal initiatives in foreign policy. The rulers in those countries were very happy to see the end of Khrushchev's improvisations. The intensification of the Sino-Soviet conflict and the American intervention in Vietnam were used by Soviet propaganda as arguments for strengthening ties between the ruling parties in Eastern Europe.

THE PRAGUE SPRING AND THE BREZHNEV DOCTRINE

The short interlude of apparent calm in Eastern Europe came to an end in 1968 with the Czechoslovak crisis, provoked by the efforts of the Prague reformers to offer a model of socialism radically different from the Soviet one. The new leaders in Czechoslovakia tried to broaden their mass base and to enlist large social strata in the political process. Their endeavors aroused suspicion on the part of dogmatics in Czechoslovakia and the allied Warsaw Pact states, particularly in the GDR, Poland, and the Soviet Union. The new crisis was predicated on the same lack of legitimacy of the ruling elites that explained the Hungarian and Polish upheavals of 1956. In spite of the continuous attempts by communist bureaucracies to create an image of national consensus, they were widely perceived as exponents of the anachronistic Stalinist model. In Czechoslovakia, President Antonin Novotny had been directly involved in the organization of the purges in the 1950s and had consistently opposed the political rehabilitation of those who suffered during the terror. Although Rudolf Slansky and the other defendants in the October 1952 show trial had been legally rehabilitated, Novotny refused to engage in a full-fledged condemnation of the purges and boycotted any movement to reform the hypercentralized and repressive political and economic structures. The country was plagued with economic stagnation, political immobility, and moral disaffection. Voices both within and outside the communist party were calling for a break with the Stalinist model.

The assault on the party's claim to a monopoly of power began with cultural discussions that started in the early 1960s. The ideological hegemony of the party was challenged during a colloquium dedicated to the writings of Franz Kafka that took place in Liblice in 1963. On that occasion the dogma of socialist realism, according to which art was subordinated to the political values championed by the communist party, was directly questioned by Czechoslovak intellectuals. Kafka's parables of the individual threatened by the anonymous powers of an overwhelming bureaucratic Leviathan were interpreted as premonitions of modern totalitarian dictatorships. In the words of Eduard Goldstücker, chairman of the Czechoslovak Writers' Union during the Prague Spring and an authority on Kafka, the author of *The Penal Colony* had become a central factor in the struggle against the isolation provoked by Stalinism and the Cold War.[2] Concerned over this wave of potential dissent, Novotny denounced the rise of revisionism as a serious danger for Czechoslovak socialism. In the summer of 1967, during the Congress of the Writers' Union, censorship and party interference in cultural creation were directly attacked. Among those who expressed their opposition to the Novotny regime were a number of former communist writers who had grown increasingly disenchanted with the official lies. The writer Ludvik Vaculik delivered a passionate speech to protest the limitations imposed by the regime upon the exercise of basic human rights:

> Just as I do not feel very secure in a cultural-political situation which the regime apparently can drive to a state of conflict, neither do I feel safe as a citizen outside this room, outside this playground. Nothing happens to me, and nothing has happened. That sort of thing is not done any more. Should I be grateful? Not so, I am afraid. I see no firm guarantee. It is true that I see better work in the courts, but the judges themselves do not see any hard and fast guarantee. I see that better work is done by the public prosecutor's office, but do the public prosecutors have guarantees and do they feel safe? If you would like it, I should be glad to interview some of them for the newspapers. Do you think it would be published? I would not be afraid to interview even the Prosecutor General and ask him why unjustly sentenced and rehabilitated people do not regain their original rights as a matter of course, why the national committees are reluctant to return them to their apartments or houses—but it will not be published. Why has no one properly apologized to these people, why do they not have

the advantages of the politically persecuted, why do we haggle with them about money? Why can we not live where we want to? Why cannot the tailors go for three years to Vienna and the printers for thirty years to Paris and be able to return without being considered criminals?

Vaculik followed that unequivocal condemnation of the Novotny regime's procrastination over a resolute abandonment of Stalinist practices with a rejection of the party's claim to having ensured Czechoslovakia's progress during the twenty years of socialism. According to him, in the course of twenty years no human problem had been solved in Czechoslovakia—starting with such elementary needs as housing, schools, and economic prosperity and ending with the finer requirements of life, which cannot be provided by the undemocratic systems of the world, for instance the feeling of full value in the society, the subordination of political decisions to ethical criteria, belief in the value of even less important work, the need for confidence among men, and development of the education of the entire people:

> By this I do not wish to say that we have lived in vain, that none of this has any value. It has value. But the question is whether it is only the value of forewarning. Even in this case the total knowledge of mankind would progress. But was it necessary to make a country which knew precisely the dangers for its culture into an instrument for this kind of knowledge?[3]

After that speech, the war between the party apparatus and the rebellious intellectuals could not be postponed. Vaculik and a number of like-minded writers were expelled from the communist party. Slander campaigns were organized against the critical intellectuals, and the regime tried to mobilize the workers in its struggle to stifle dissenting views. But the ferment only gathered momentum, and it soon contaminated the universities, inspiring unrest among the students.

Another cause of the crisis was the regime's condescending and often humiliating treatment of the Slovaks. There was a growing movement among both intellectuals and members of the party bureaucracy in Slovakia for more autonomy in their relations with the government in Prague. Among those involved in the movement were the first secretary of the Slovak communist party, Alexander Dubcek, who had graduated from the High Party School in Moscow and whose Khrushchevite propensities were well known.[4] Another prominent supporter of increased Slovak rights within the federative republic was Gustav Husak. A professional lawyer and a communist veteran, Husak had been one of the leaders of the Slovak anti-Nazi insurrection of 1944. Convicted for alleged nationalism in one the Stalinist frame-ups in the early 1950s, Husak appeared to many to be a convinced partisan of reform.

Between October 1967 and January 1968 the political struggle at the top continued to sharpen. Deprived of genuine support among the members of the Central Committee, who saw him as the principal culprit in the country's crisis, Novotny appealed to Brezhnev and asked for direct Soviet support. After a short trip to Prague, however, the Soviet General Secretary came to the conclusion that Novotny's position was so weak and indefensible that the only solution to the crisis would be his immediate ouster. In January the plenum of the Czechoslovak Communist Party's Central Committee released Novotny from his position as first secretary and replaced him with Alexander Dubcek, the Slovak leader who had dared to challenge Novotny's authority on previous occasions. In a few weeks it became clear that the new leader's program was going beyond the expected simple tinkering with the system. In March Novotny was forced to resign as President of Czechoslovakia. His successor was Ludvik Svoboda, a respected army general marginalized by the Stalinists. Another victim of the Stalinist show trials, Josef Smrkovsky, was elected Chairman of the National Assembly. The hard-liners on the Central Committee's Presidium were replaced by party apparatchiks close to Dubcek. The party's objective was not to abolish the existing system but rather to modernize it and make it work.

The basic illusions about the reformability of the socialist system, as well as Dubcek's conviction that a centrally planned system could be made operational, appeared in the text of the most important document produced by the communist reformers: the "Action Program" adopted by the Central Committee in April 1968. Although it maintained the commitment of the Czechoslovak communists to Marxism-Leninism, the program emphasized their decision to embark on a democratization of the existing system. The party professed its determination to renounce dictatorial command methods and pledged to favor persuasion over coercion. Legality was declared to be the fundamental principle needed for the existence of a healthy body politic. Thus, the main points of the document, entitled "Czechoslovakia's Road to Socialism," included (1) new guarantees of freedom of speech, press, assembly, and religious observance; (2) electoral laws to provide a broader choice of candidates and real freedom for the four noncommunist parties integrated in the communist-controlled National Front; (3) a limitation on the communist party's prerogatives in its dealings with the parliament and the government; (4) broad economic reforms to strengthen the autonomy of the enterprises, to revive a limited number of private enterprises, to achieve a convertible currency, and to increase trade with the West; (5) an independent judiciary; (6) federal status for Slovakia; and (7) a new constitution to be drafted by the end of 1969. The program was the outcome of a compromise between the radical reformers and the conservative faction within the party's leadership. Some of the ideas sounded very promising, and others were mere repetitions of the hackneyed Leninist slogans about the party's leading role. In its general orientation the program could be invoked by the exponents of the democratic wing to pursue their search for a new model of socialism. Actually, it was an attempt to keep the party at the rudder and make it the generator of the society's reawakening:

> We are not taking the outlined measures to make any concessions from our ideals—let alone to our opponents. On the contrary: we are convinced that they will help us get rid of the burden which for years provided many advantages for the opponent by restricting, reducing and paralyzing the efficiency of the socialist idea, the attractiveness of the socialist example. We want to set new penetrating forces of socialist life in motion in this country to give them the possibility of a much more efficient confrontation of the social systems and world outlooks and allowing a fuller application of the advantages of socialism.

With its wholehearted commitment to socialist ideals, the program stopped short of a clear-cut affirmation of the new leadership's decision to engage in a sweeping break with the Soviet model of socialism.[5] Massive political rehabilitations took place, and the victims of the Stalinist repressions were allowed to organize their own associations and clubs. It was precisely at that moment of relaxation that the ambivalent nature of the Prague Spring became clear: On the one hand, it was a reform movement initiated from above by a group of communists dissatisfied with the poor economic performance and the social malaise characteristic of Novotny's rule. On the other hand, as the movement advanced and large social groups were energized by reformist ideas, the limits of the official strategy of renewal were denounced by the exponents of the emerging Czech and Slovak civil society.

Because Dubcek and his associates concluded that true socialism is inconceivable in the absence of democracy, they opened the gates for the flow of independent intiatives from below, including the formation of noncommunist or even anticommunist groups and associations. The lightning speed of the democratization inebriated the Czechoslovak intellectuals, who sided without reservation with the more radical wing of the communist leadership. At the same time, the leading nucleus of the Czechoslovak communist party failed to articulate a coherent approach to the country's basic dilemmas. Some in the Presidium were inclined to move faster toward comprehensive and unabashed reforms. Others, definitely scared by the risk of losing political power in a pluralist system, complained about the rise of right-wing forces and urged Dubcek to harden his policies. The majority of the party, however, was strongly supportive of the ideals championed by Dubcek. For them, the only choice was between socialism with a human face and a return to the suffocating Stalinist system.

The concern of domestic orthodox forces that the party-initiated reforms could unleash a spontaneous civic movement against communism was shared (and even encouraged) by the Soviet leaders and their allies. In March 1968 a summit took place in Dresden, East Germany, where all the Warsaw Pact communist leaders (minus Romania's President Ceausescu) expressed their worries about the course of events in Czechoslovakia. In the following months, during meetings between Dubcek and Brezhnev, the Czechoslovak leader tried to allay Soviet apprehensions regarding the danger of a "counterrevolution" in his country. In his criticism of Dubcek's reforms, Brezhnev voiced the irritation of communist bureaucracies not only in the Soviet Union but also in the other countries of the bloc. What they could not tolerate was the Czechoslovak ambition to build up an alternative model of socialism, a society where the individual would be treated humanely and not simply as an instrument for the fulfillment of the party's plans.

As the conflict between the Czechoslovak reformers and the other Warsaw Pact leaders deepened, the whole world communist movement was entering a new period of crisis and turmoil. The Yugoslavs and the Romanians publicly expressed their opposition to the use of foreign forces to arrest the drive toward democracy in Czechoslovakia. Similar warnings were sent to Moscow by a number of nonruling communist parties, including the French, Italian, and Spanish. It was during those months of sharp polemics on the meaning of Marxist internationalism and the right of each communist party to establish sovereignty in it political line that the birth certificate of Eurocommunism, a political platform embraced by several West European communist parties, was written. Eurocommunism challenged the Kremlin's right to dictate its line to other parties and insisted on the inseparability between socialism and pluralist democracy.[6] The Czechoslovaks' rejection of the Soviet frozen model, with its ultracentralism and suspicious attitude toward any grassroots initiative, was thus shared by a number of Western communist parties, which argued that the Leninist dogma of the dictatorship of the proletariat needed to be abandoned. At the opposite pole where the Stalinist nostalgics in China and Albania, who condemned the Prague Spring as an attempt to restore capitalism and at the same time opposed the Soviet imperial claims to domination over Eastern Europe. Although China's Chairman Mao Zedong was hostile to the revisionist course adopted by Dubcek, he criticized the Soviets for using imperialist methods in dealing with their allies. He even scornfully referred to Brezhnev and his team as the new czars in the Kremlin.

In Czechoslovakia the Soviet criticism did nothing but radicalize the reformers. The intelligentsia continued to exert pressure on the wavering leadership to broaden the political pluralism and to establish guarantees against the return to Stalinist command methods. Foreshadowing Gorbachev's calls for openness (glasnost), the Prague reformers rejected "politics behind the scenes." The Czechoslovak leaders, primarily First Secretary Dubcek and Chairman of the National Assembly Smrkovsky, engaged in direct dialogue with representatives of public opinion. In the space of a month, the slumbering Czechoslovak society awakened and became a major actor in the decision-making process. As people realized that they could have a role in changing the political course, participation ceased to be an empty slogan. In June 1968 a pathbreaking document entitled "2,000 Words to Workers, Farmers, Scientists, Artists and Everyone" appeared in the increasingly bold Writers' Union weekly *Literarni Listy*. Elaborated mainly by Ludvik Vaculik, the document symbolized a break with the logic of acquiescence and called for a divorce from the communist techniques of political control and manipulation. The manifesto demanded the acceleration of democratization, elimination of the dogmatics from the party leadership, and a rapid transition to a multiparty system. Signed by seventy well-known figures of the liberal intelligentsia and supported by the signatures of some 40,000 people across the country, the document expressed the growing discontent with the slow introduction of reforms and the inconsistencies of the official strategy of renewal. Although the dogmatics hastened to brand the document "an appeal for counterrevolution," the manifesto by no means expressed an intolerant or fanatical stance. Far from calling for revenge against those who had ruled the country for two decades, the document opposed any use of violence. On the contrary, it voiced the hopes of the overwhelming majority of Czechs and Slovaks that the communist party could convert to a truly democratic force:

> Above all, we will oppose the view, should it arise, that it is possible to conduct some sort of democratic revival without the Communists or possi-

bly against them. This would be both unjust and unreasonable. The Communists have well-structured organizations, and we should support the progressive wing within them. . . . The Czechoslovak Communist Party is preparing for the Congress which will elect a new Central Committee. Let us demand that it be better than the current one. If the Communist Party now says that in the future it wants to base its leading position on the citizens' confidence and not on force, let us believe it as long as we can believe in the people whom it is now sending as delegates to the district and regional conferences.[7]

The chief bone of contention in the political struggle within the Czechoslovak communist elite was the nature of the future leadership and the fears of the conservatives (and their Soviet protectors) that the Fourteenth Party Congress, set to take place in the summer of 1968, would sanction their elimination and endorse the program of "socialism with a human face." Increasingly concerned over the Soviet threats, Dubcek rejected the appeal but refused to give in to the neo-Stalinist forces who labeled the document a "counterrevolutionary manifesto."

The Soviet displeasure with Dubcek's delay in taking harsh measures to stop the liberalization was aggravated by the pressure on Brezhnev exerted by Polish and East German communist leaders, who were panicked at the idea that the Czechoslovak virus could infect their countries as well. In July a Warsaw Pact summit took place in the Polish capital in the absence of the Czechoslovak and Romanian leaders. The conference addressed an ominous open letter to the Czechoslovak leaders urging them to weed out the "counterrevolutionary nuclei" and to purge the media of anti-Stalinist forces immediately. The letter—which to all intents and purposes amounted to an ultimatum—made clear that from the Kremlin's perspective the pledge of noninterference in the internal affairs of other communist countries was not valid when the issue was the future of Soviet-style socialism in one of the bloc's countries. Echoing the 1956 justification for the military intervention in Hungary, the Soviets and their allies insisted that the "preservation of the people's revolutionary gains" in Czechoslovakia was not only a domestic issue for that country's leaders but also a concern for the whole "socialist community":

We neither had or have any intention to interfere in [affairs that] are strictly the internal business of your party and your state, to violate the principles of respect, independence and equality in the relations among the communist parties and socialist countries. . . . At the same time we cannot agree to have hostile forces push your country from the road of socialism and create a threat of severing Czechoslovakia from the socialist community. This is something more than only your concern. It is the common concern of all the communist and workers' parties and states united by alliance, cooperation and friendship.[8]

Brandishing the specter of anticommunist rebellion, the Warsaw Pact leaders tried to force Dubcek and his comrades to halt the reform process and renounce their ambition to construct a different type of socialism. Instead of bowing to the Kremlin's *diktat,* Dubcek rejected the Soviet charges and counterattacked in a televised speech on July 18. He defended the choices of his party and protested the accusations of opportunism and revisionism:

> After many years, an atmosphere has been created in our country, in which everyone can publicly and without fear, openly and with dignity, express his opinion and thus test whether the cause of this country and the cause of socialism is the cause of us all. By an open and honest policy, by a sincere and honest elimination of the residue of past years, our party is gradually regaining the badly shaken confidence. Therefore we are saying openly, calmly but determinedly, [that] we realize what is now at stake: there is no other path than for the people of this country to achieve the profound, democratic and socialist changes in our life. We do not want to give up in the least any of the principles we expressed in the "action program." . . . The Communist Party is relying on the voluntary support of the people; we do not carry out our guiding role by ruling over society, but by serving their free, progressive and socialist development in the most dedicated way. We cannot assert our authority by giving orders, but by the work of our members, by the justice of our ideas.[9]

It was indeed a clash of political visions between the Czechoslovaks, with their focus on the human dimension of socialism, and the bloc's leaders, who were interested exclusively in the preservation of the status quo and therefore regarded Dubcek's experimentation with democracy suspiciously.

As genuine Stalinists, the Soviet leaders did not treat citizens as autonomous political actors: For them, the party elite had to remain in full and unquestioned possession of its dictatorial attributes. Any attempt to establish a different principle of authority, especially one that recognized the sovereignty of the people, was perceived as subversive. One could hardly find two more different interpretations of the nature of socialism than Dubcek's neo-Marxist idealism and Brezhnev's cynical pragmatism. Twenty years after the brutal interruption of the Prague Spring, Antonin Liehm, one of the most active intellectuals involved in the reform movement, summed up the meaning of the Czechoslovak attempt to overhaul the ossified vision of socialism and to propose an alternative model attuned to the requirements of a modern society respectful of the individual rights of its members:

> The Czechoslovak attempt to reform "real socialism" was an attempt at a constructive answer to the collapse of the Stalinist system in its entirety. It was an attempt to create a model of a renewed, permanently self-reforming civil society. This attempt could have eventually amounted to a gradual transformation of the Soviet empire into a commonwealth of nations, one that would have been based on mutual advantages, especially economic, for example a huge market, and not on military and police coercion. [10]

The dream of the Czech and Slovak humanist Marxists was, however, the nightmare of the Warsaw Pact bureaucrats. For the Brezhnevites, the very attempt at redefining the goals of socialism and focusing on the issues of human dignity and freedom was an acceptable challenge. They knew that if the reformist temptation were to spread to other countries, the whole edifice of party domination over society would immediately crumble. As for Dubcek and his supporters, they failed to understand the totalitarian nature of the Soviet regime and nourished the illusion that they would be able to convince Brezhnev of their genuine communist beliefs.

The Prague Spring, therefore, was rooted in a set of illusions about the reformability from within of the existing system, the possibility of eliciting Soviet support for such attempts, and the chances for the communists to remain at the helm of the democatization process because of their role in having unleashed it. Even Zdenek Mlynar, who was a Central Committee secretary in charge of ideology under Dubcek, later recognized the limits upon the reformist group's understanding of the political environment they were operating in:

> There was the illusion of the Party leadership about its own possibilities in the Soviet bloc. You had the idea of reform, but under no conditions was a rift envisaged with the Soviet Union, as had happened in Yugoslavia. And with such assumptions one could only do what Kadar was doing in Hungary. In that case there was hardly any point in starting it all. Illusion number two was that, because twenty years of totalitarianism had freed the way to democratization, the Czechoslovak Party leadership enjoyed enormous support, and that this was likely to continue and to guarantee that people would always be satisfied with what the leadership granted. Finally, there was the population's illusion about the leadership: that it can transgress certain limits provided there is sufficient push from below. [11]

In other words, although Dubcek and his comrades were engaged in actions bound to disrupt the existing hegemonic system and undermine Soviet supremacy in the bloc, they did not realize the amplitude of the threat of a Soviet counterreaction. Because they considered themselves good communists (and from a strictly Marxist point of view they really were), the Dubcekites failed to see the chasm between their uplifting dream of socialist renewal and the cynical Soviet approach to both international relations and ideological affairs. For the Soviets, Marxism-Leninism had long ceased to be anything but camouflage for bureaucratic self-perpetuation. The *nomenklatura*—the ruling class in Soviet-style societies—had no interest whatsoever in engaging in dangerous experimentation with political and economic reforms. After all, it was precisely in order to curb such "destabilizing" endeavors that Khrushchev had been ousted in October 1964, and there was little doubt that the Soviet leaders would not tolerate the resumption or radicalization of de-Stalinization in one of the satellite countries. What the Soviet *nomenklatura* expected from local communist elites was to watch over the internal stability and suppress any critical trends. Indeed, as Ivan Svitak, a philosopher who advocated a complete break with the communist system, wrote retrospectively:

> Every bureaucratic dictatorship collapses as a whole whenever any part of the system ceases to function in a repressive way—economics, politics or the media. This is also the reason why in a bureaucratic dictatorship it is impossible just to add constitutional freedoms, human rights or a prosperous economy to the existing dominant function of repression. It is an impossible task to democratize a dictatorship—irrespective of noble motives. The system functions as a whole and collapses as a whole. Since the Czechoslovak communists refused to give in to Soviet *diktat* and muzzle the country's independent media, relations between Moscow and Prague became increasingly tense. Brezhnev knew that truth in the media is a ticking bomb, which the elite must deal with or fall victim to. He did not wait.[12]

In July and August new negotiations took place between the Soviet Politburo and the Czechoslovak Communist Presidium, and agreement was reached to put an end to mutual polemics and criticism. The agreements were followed by a Warsaw Pact summit in Bratislava (again Romania did not attend) where a simulacrum of unity appeared to have been reached. The communiqué of the Bratislava meeting incorporated some of the traditional Soviet formulations about "the subversive actions of imperialism" and insisted that all socialist countries must strictly and consistently abide by "the general laws of construction of socialist society and, primarily, by consolidating the leading role of the working class and its vanguard—the Communist party."[13] In exchange for their perfunctory and certainly hypocritical pledge to respect Czechoslovakia's sovereignty, the Soviets expected Dubcek to behave like a docile communist and immediately engage in a campaign against the democratic groups and media in his country. But in Czechoslovakia the genie of democracy was out of the bottle, and it would have been impossible for the reformist leaders to back down without completely losing their political credibility. Dubcek's status as a national leader hinged precisely on his capacity to resist Soviet pressures to reintroduce censorship and adopt repressive measures against those forces the Kremlin deemed "subversive." In the meantime, Moscow tried to mobilize the dogmatic forces in the Czechoslovak Communist Party in the hope that a split would take place in the Presidium and Dubcek would be eliminated.

But the pro-Soviet forces were weak and disoriented, with very little support within the country. To restore bureaucratic controls, they needed more than symbolic Soviet support. On August 21, 1968, Warsaw Pact troops occupied Czechoslovakia and tried immediately to impose a pro-Soviet government. Party leader Dubcek, Prime Minister Oldrich Cernik, and other reformist leaders were taken hostage and transported to a military unit in the Soviet Union. In order to justify the intervention, *Pravda*, the Soviet party newspaper, published an editorial accusing Dubcek of having created a right-wing, opportunistic faction whose harmful and irresponsible actions necessitated the "internationalist help" provided by the Warsaw Pact. Confronted with President Ludvik Svoboda's stubborn refusal to engage in negotiations in the absence of the country's legal leaders, Brezhnev agreed to bring Dubcek and his comrades to participate in the negotiations. From that moment on, the fate of the Prague Spring was sealed. Hundreds of thousands of Soviet troops controlled all strategic points in Czechoslovakia. There was very little that Dubcek could have expected to save of the experiment in democratization. With monumental arrogance, Brezhnev accused the Czechoslovak leaders of having betrayed the principles of socialist internationalism. In Prague, an underground Fourteenth Congress of the Czechoslovak Party strongly condemned the Soviet intervention and called for the immediate release of the country's kidnapped leaders.

Psychologically crushed and unable to see any way out of the disastrous situation created by the military occupation of their country, Dubcek and his associates (with the exception of the Presidium member

and President of the National Front, Dr. Frantisek Kriegel) finally yielded
to the Soviet demands. The Moscow talks were conducted by Brezhnev
in a most humiliating way: The Soviet leader did not lose any opportunity to disparage Dubcek and make clear that the Kremlin would not
permit any further search for socialism with a human face. Although
Brezhnev was perfectly aware of the revulsion the intervention provoked
among democratic parties and groups worldwide, he made no secret of his
contempt for those who dared to criticize the Soviet decision. As for
Dubcek, he acted like a political sleepwalker, incapable of taking the
measure of the catastrophe and hoping against hope that, once back in
Prague, he would be able to preserve some accomplishments. Quickly he
realized that there was no role for him in Czechoslovak politics: Challenged by the pro-Soviet faction within the Presidium, Dubcek lost the
support of the country's critical intelligentsia and student movement.
Isolated and alienated from any power base, he became a scapegoat for all
those opportunists who wanted to reassure the Kremlin of their unlimited
support for the Soviet action. One such opportunist was Dr. Gustav
Husak, the Slovak communist who had been one of the most active
supporters of the Prague Spring, but who conveniently switched sides
after the invasion. In April 1969 Husak replaced Dubcek as party leader
and unleashed a large-scale purge that led to the expulsion from the party
of more than half a million members, including Dubcek, Smrkovsky,
Kriegel, and Mlynar.

Less bloody, of course, than the suppression of the Hungarian Revolution, the military intervention in Czechoslovakia was nevertheless extremely traumatic. Thousands of the country's brightest intellectuals decided to seek asylum abroad, while others who remained in the country
suffered the effects of Husak's policy of "normalization." The indignation
abroad did nothing to allay the fear that they had been abandoned to a
resurgence of barbarism. Even the French communist poet Louis Aragon,
long known for his slavish support for the Soviets, including his endorsement of the 1956 crushing of the Hungarian Revolution, protested the
intervention and called the massacre of Czechoslovak culture by the
Soviet-appointed "normalizers" a "Biafra of the spirit." Less revolted by
the Czechoslovak tragedy, the French government deplored the infelici-
tous solution of a localized conflict "within the Communist family." In
fact, the issue reached far beyond "the family": The Soviet intervention
amounted to the violent suppression of an attempt to reinsert Czechoslovakia in the European cultural and political space. In the bitter words of
Milan Kundera, the Czech novelist who was himself forced to leave the
country several years later because of political harassment:

What was actually at stake behind the smokescreen of political terminology (revolution, counter-revolution, socialism, imperialism, and so on, and so forth) was nothing less than a shift in the borders between two civilizations: the Russian imperium had once and for all conquered a piece of the West, a piece of Europe, the better to watch it founder, together with the other countries of Central Europe, in its own civilization. . . . That is what Aragon called the "Biafra of the spirit." Some day Russian mythographers will write about it as a new dawn in history. I see it (rightly or wrongly) as the beginning of Europe's end.[14]

Following the invasion, the Soviet propaganda machine went out of its way to justify the right of the Warsaw Pact to intervene whenever the Kremlin felt that the "socialist conquests" were jeopardized. On September 26, 1968, *Pravda* published an article under the signature of Sergei Kovalev, the paper's expert on international affairs, where the doctrine of limited sovereignty was spelled out in full detail. According to Kovalev, "The weakening of any of the links in the world system of socialism directly affects all the socialist countries, which cannot look indifferently upon this. Each Communist party is responsible not only to its own people, but also to all the socialist countries, to the entire Communist movement." Following this self-serving interpretation of the principles of national sovereignty and equality between socialist countries, *Pravda* was able to conclude that, far from aggression, the occupation of Czechoslovakia represented the fulfillment of the country's self-determination. According to the Soviet official statement, the Warsaw Pact troops

> . . . did not interfere in the internal affairs of the country, were fighting for the principle of self-determination of the peoples of Czechoslovakia not in words but in deeds, were fighting for their inalienable right to think out profoundly and decide their fate themselves, without intimidation on the part of counterrevolutionaries, without revisionist and nationalist demagogy.[15]

This Orwellian Newspeak—an outright semantic fraud—presented foreign occupation as internationalist help. For the Czechs and the Slovaks, the demagogic language used by the occupiers and the normalizers was a symbolic counterpart to the general repression and the restoration of the neo-Stalinist police state. It took them years to recover from the shock of the invasion and gradually to take up the struggle for the construction of a civil society outside the official institutions and values.

Following the Soviet occupation of Czechoslovakia and the ruthless suppression of the reform movement in that country, relations between

Warsaw Pact countries were regulated according to Moscow's definition of limited sovereignty. In November 1968 Brezhnev delivered a speech in Warsaw, where he reiterated the basic tenets of this doctrine. According to the Soviet General Secretary, all communist countries had to abide by the "general laws of Marxism-Leninism." Any deviation from Moscow-defined orthodoxy was considered treason against the principles of socialist internationalism, and the Soviets retained the right to correct it—even by military force. Of course, the so-called normalization in Czechoslovakia offered a lesson to all those who may have been tempted to imitate the Dubcek experiment. Following the crushing of the Prague Spring, Moscow unleashed a forceful campaign to suppress any reformist attempts both in the Soviet Union and in the bloc. Corruption was all-pervasive, and the collective ethos lost any sense of optimism. A general state of malaise affected all the bloc countries. Diversity was again denounced, and a political and economic freeze became the hallmark of the neo-Stalinist political culture often described as Brezhnevism.

Despite the widespread return to malaise, many critical intellectuals in Eastern Europe drew an important lesson from the Prague Spring: The idealistic belief, nourished by its initiators, that communism could be reformed from within was demolished. In their naïve conviction that the Kremlin would tolerate the rise of an alternative model of communism, rooted in the cult of the individual rather than worship of the apparatus, the Czechoslovak reformers discovered the real limits of such an approach. They were committed communists who thought that the Soviet leaders were still interested in the image of socialism. They forgot that Brezhnev and his acolytes were nothing but time-servers, whose careers had been secured by their participation in the Stalinist purges and to whom references to human freedom and the rights of the individual were simply anathema. Understanding that the Prague Spring started as a party-induced and party-controlled reform movement whose principle goal was the renewal, not the abolition of communism, helps to explain why many Czech and Slovak intellectuals had misgivings about the authenticity of the democratic beliefs professed by suddenly reconstructed apparatchiks like Dubcek and his comrades.

The hard core of Prague reformers was not made up of people for whom the sovereignty of the people had to be regarded as the only source of political legitimacy. The very idea that the party could ensure the transition to pluralism and had to be accepted as the center of the emerging pluralist system made many people suspicious or hesitant. One of that core was the young playwright and essayist Vaclav Havel, who, unlike Milan Kundera, Ludvik Vaculik, and Pavel Kohout, had never belonged to the communist party and had never shared any illusions about the reformability of the existing system. Years later, Havel gave the following explanation for his reservations about the democratic credentials of the reform communists led by Alexander Dubcek:

> What caused these doubts and hesitations? In my case, it was primarily knowing how embarrassed the country's leadership was in the face of all these developments. Suddenly these people were enjoying spontaneous support and sympathy, something none of them had ever experienced before, because the only kind of support they had ever known was organized from above. Naturally they were pleasantly surprised and even excited by all this. On the other hand, they were afraid of the elemental groundswell of popular good will. Again and again they were caught off guard, because things began to happen and demands began to be made which were sometimes incomprehensible, even terrifying, given how far they overstepped the limits of the "possible" and the "admissable." Let's not forget that these people were all normal party bureaucrats with the right pseudo-education from the party, with all the right illusions and habits and prejudices, with the right curricula vitae, the right social background, and the standard narrow horizon. The only difference was, they were a little more free-thinking and a little more decent than the people whose places they had taken.[16]

That was indeed the paradox of communist reformation: Those who started the struggle for the overhaul of the status quo were themselves the product, the offspring, of the existing conditions. Their revolt against the irrationality and the injustice of Stalinism was not a rebellion against the Marxist pretense to establish "the best society" but rather an effort to correct what they diagnosed as distortions of an initially humanist and rational program. They were the faithful children of the system. Their opposition to the previous leadership did not challenge the moral and theoretical legitimacy of Soviet-style socialism. Even a radical reformer like Ota Sik, the chief economist of the Prague Spring, could not cross the boundaries of the dominant logic and envision the need for a complete renunciation of the central plan.

Milovan Djilas, the Yugoslav heretic, has often pointed to the dangers contained in the communist conviction that the system could be adjusted and made to work if only some of the parts were fixed and corruption eliminated. The truth was that in all the Soviet-bloc countries the population was deeply hostile to the existing model and resented the idea of perpetuating it. Unlike Dubcek and his idealistic friends, the corrupt manipulators in the Kremlin knew better: They realized that any concession made to the mounting social forces from below would eventually result in more and more radical demands that in turn would force upon the reformers the need to accept new concessions. As a matter of fact, it was Brezhnev who was right. Revising the concept of socialism and depriving it of the Stalinist veneer necessarily results in the complete breakdown of the existing system.

The preservation of the established institutions and power relations were predicated on the impregnability and unquestionability of the official dogma. Any weakening of the communist party's claim to infallibility, even if that claim was simply a forcible repetition of a hollow ritual stripped of its once mystical overtones, would immediately bring about catastrophic side effects. To keep the system in place and going, the authority of the ruling class, the *nomenklatura*, could not be the subject of negotiation. Individuals had to be treated as subjects, not as citizens endowed with human rights. They had to be kept in a perpetual state of insecurity, anguish, and fear, so that there would be no way for them to organize collective forms of protest and civic disobedience. Thus, the secret police had to watch over the maintenance of dictatorial controls and consistently marginalize any form of dissent both inside and outside the ruling party. Although Brezhnevism certainly attenuated the harshness of Stalin's methodology of terror, it continued to rely upon the same institutions and techniques that prevented any form of coagulation of popular discontent into genuine political movements. Analyzing the nature of the Soviet political culture under Brezhnev, Robert Conquest reached the following conclusion:

> Power is in the hands of a self-appointed bureaucracy, and all institutional arrangements are designed with one of two purposes—to perpetuate and to conceal this fact. There are therefore two sets of institutions in the country: those through which power is genuinely transmitted, and those which provide the shadow, though never the substance, of popular sovereignty. Both systems were fully developed in Stalin's times. Both operate essentially the same way to this day.[17]

REVOLTS AND CRACKDOWNS IN POLAND

Brezhnev's updated version of mature Stalinism became the characteristic pattern of the Soviet-style regimes in Eastern Europe. Again, because of its special relationship with the Kremlin and the margin of autonomy acquired during the conflict with the Cominform, Tito's Yugoslavia was the exception. In the other East European countries, however, the rejection of reforms and the hardening of ideological and political controls led to widespread popular diasarray, demoralization of the critical intellectuals, and a general feeling of powerlessness among the opponents of the regimes. It seemed that Eastern Europe would vegetate indefinitely in this state of semiparalysis, with corrupt and blatantly incompetent elites imposing conformity on increasingly disaffected societies. The 1970s were years of apparent slumber in the region, when the rulers enjoyed their monopoly of power without serious challenges from below. The "pacification" of Eastern Europe, which was one of the principal objectives of Brezhnev's foreign policy, seemed to have been accomplished. But by the end of the 1970s Poland again became the troublemaker in the bloc. True, the Poles had never been completely tamed. In 1968 major clashes had taken place between radical students and the repressive apparatus. Although the Polish communists went out of their way to prevent the development of initiatives from below and the construction of a coalition between workers and intellectuals, the rise of an independent, self-governing trade union could not be prevented. Despite extensive police efforts to disband any movement toward such a coalition, Polish civic activists managed to break through the official repression and inaugurate a new antitotalitarian wave that eventually would sweep away the communist regimes in Eastern Europe.

The prelude to the historic piercing of the totalitarian carcass in Poland was the intellectual revolt that took place in that country at the end of the 1960s. Wladyslaw Gomulka, the leader who came to power in October 1956 as an exponent of a liberal trend within Polish communism, had slowly abandoned his initial anti-Stalinist program. Instead of furthering the long-promised reforms, Gomulka started to champion a Brezhnev-style conservatism, organizing the persecution of critical intellectuals. The communist leadership was divided between Gomulka's supporters and a mounting radical-nationalist faction headed by General Mieczyslaw Moczar, Minister of the Interior and chairman of the union of former communist partisans during World War II. In his bid for power, Moczar made use of xenophobic arguments, charging Gomulka with leniency in his dealings with an alleged "imperialist-Zionist conspiracy." At the same time the Moczarites were targeting proponents of political and economic reforms, whom they accused of trying to rock the boat of socialism. Moczar's ideology consisted of rabid anti-Semitism combined with intense hatred of liberalism and democracy. Those themes borrowed heavily from the traditional anti-Semitic literature produced during the interwar period by supporters of *Endecjia*, the ultra-nationalist, extremely

chauvinistic National Democratic Party. As critical intellectuals symbolized the nation's search for an open society, no slander was spared in
Moczar's campaign against the Polish liberal intelligentsia.[18] Professor
Jerzy Holzer, a liberal Catholic intellectual, noted that the intent of the
anti-Semitic campaign was to manipulate public opinion by exploiting
widespread xenophobic superstitions:

> March [1968] represented a powerful manipulation of the consciousness of
> large segments of the population. Anti-Semitism played an essential role
> in this manipulation. From time immemorial the hidden Zionist enemy of
> Poland's welfare was allegedly responsible for all Polish misfortunes. At-
> tempts to ascribe to ourselves all our successes and to people of Jewish
> origin all the possible offenses were an outrage not [only] against the Jews
> but against the entire Polish nation.[19]

Another faction within the communist elite tried to advocate technocratic adjustments aimed at a managerial improvement of the existing
system. One of the leaders of that group was Edward Gierek, then the
party leader in the industrial region of Silesia. Caught in the middle
among the dwindling liberal faction, the technocratic group, and the
increasingly strident nationalist elements, Gomulka tried to maintain a
centrist approach and relied more and more on his personal contacts with
the Soviet leaders. The same man who had so strongly denounced the
"personality cult" in 1956 was now resorting to a decision-making pattern
directly inspired by Stalin: extremely personalist, abusive and con-
temptous of others' opinions. The result was a spreading malaise, which
further accelerated political disintegration and decay.[20]

The worsening of economic conditions and the lack of popular confidence in the rulers were conducive to the outbreak of a new crisis in
Poland. The social turmoil in 1968 expedited the collapse of Gomulka's
strategy of stabilization. Inspired by changes in Czechoslovakia and by
the general European wave of civic activism characteristic of the period,
a powerful student movement had taken shape in Poland after 1967.
Among the moral sources of the movement were the critical writings of a
number of Catholic and neo-Marxist intellectuals who had long highlighted the insuperable contradictions of the prevailing order. For instance, in early 1965 two young critical Marxists, Jacek Kuron and Karol
Modzelewski, addressed an open letter to the United Polish Workers'
Party—the communist party—calling for a revolutionary overthrow of
the existing bureaucratic dictatorship. Reminiscent of Trotsky's criticism
of Stalinism, the letter provoked Gomulka's anger and led to the impris-

North Sea

Baltic Sea

Estonia

Latvia

Lithuania

Memel-territory under League
of Nations control 1919-23

Danzig
Germany
(East Prussia)

Germany

Poland

Soviet
Union

Saar-autonomous
territory until returned
to Germany in 1935

Elbe

Oder

Rhine

Danube

Czechoslovakia

Austria

Hungary

Romania

Black Sea

Yugoslavia

Bulgaria

Albania

Greece

Turkey

Mediterranean Sea

1919–37: Central Europe and the Balkans between the World Wars.

After 1938, Josip Broz, a Croatian communist who became famous under the pseudonym Tito, was entrusted to lead the clandestine Yugoslav Communist Party. Although definitely full of love and admiration for Joseph Stalin, Tito wanted to become his counterpart in the Balkans—an ambition which eventually forced Stalin to excommunicate him from the world communist movement. He is seen here seated with Dr. Ivar Ribar, during activities of the Yugoslav communist resistance in the mountains of northern Montenegro in 1943. *Eastfoto*

A former railroad worker who had spent more than ten years in jails and labor camps, hardliner Gheorghe Gheorghiu-Dej led the Romanian Communist Party against anti-Stalinist elements from the late forties through the early sixties. His protegé, Nicolae Ceausescu, succeeded him upon his death in 1965. Here he is seen at left, being congratulated on the occasion of the adoption of the Romanian constitution. *Eastfoto*

Rudolf Slansky, second from the left, was appointed after World War II by Stalin as the General Secretary of the Communist Party of Czechoslovakia. He is seen here with fellow communist leaders Antonin Novotny and Machacova saluting the May Day parade. Slansky and other prominent communist leaders of Jewish origin were accused by Stalin of Zionist conspiracy and collusion with Western espionage networks. Slansky was the chief defendant during an October 1952 show trial and was hanged in December 1952. *Eastfoto*

In 1952, Ana Pauker, a veteran communist leader who long had been lionized by international communist propaganda as a prominent defender of the communist ideal, was purged from her position as Romania's minister of foreign affairs and Politburo member and placed under house arrest. Silencing Pauker and others, Romania's communist leader Gheorghiu-Dej capitalized on Stalin's interest in eliminating Jewish leaders. She died in 1960, still faithful to the Soviet cause. *Eastfoto*

March 9, 1953. The coffin of Josef Vissarionovich Stalin being carried out of the house of trade unions in Moscow. Pallbearers, right to left, are G. M. Malenkov, General Vassily Stalin, V. M. Molotov, Marshal N. Bulganin, L. Kaganovich, and N. Shvernik. When Stalin died, his cadre of fiercely loyal supporters in Eastern Europe lost not only their leader, but their very means of political survival. *Tass from Sovfoto*

Soviet premier Nikita Khrushchev confers with Yugoslav leader Marshal Tito during Tito's visit to the USSR in 1956. During the de-Stalinization of the late fifties and early sixties, Khrushchev sought a rapprochement with Tito, who had consistently and effectively defied Stalin's attempts to dominate the whole of Eastern Europe. *Sovfoto*

Wladyslaw Gomulka, General Secretary of the Polish Communist Party, is greeted at the border town of Biala Podalska on his return from the Polish–Soviet conference in Moscow in November 1956. Gomulka's return to power that year, after the death of hardline Muscovite sympathizer Boleslaw Bierut, marked the revival of indigenous Polish communism, but certainly no break with the Soviets, whom Gomulka saw as a necessary ally in counteracting Germany's inevitable influence on his country. Note the loaf of bread and salt he is receiving from admirers. This greeting has been a Polish symbol of hospitality since the 10th century. *Eastfoto*

Imre Nagy, President of the Council of Ministers, addressing a session of the Hungarian parliament beginning on January 21, 1954. Nagy replaced the diehard Stalinist Matyas Rakosi as prime minister upon Khrushchev's ascendancy in 1953. Nagy attempted to lead Hungary out of the Warsaw Pact, provoking, on November 4, 1956, Soviet attacks on garrisons and military units loyal to the Nagy government. He was sentenced to death and executed in June 1958. *Eastfoto*

Abetted by prime minister Imre Nagy's personal decision to embrace popular uprising, the Hungarian revolt of 1956 was the first post–World War II democratic revolution in Eastern Europe. It forged a model and a tradition that was to influence all the antitotalitarian social movements in the region for decades thereafter. Here residents of Budapest look at unburied bodies after the first day of fighting on October 24. *Interfoto MTI + Hungary. Photo by Tamas Munk.*

In January 1968, the plenum of the Czechoslovak Communist Party's Central Committee relieved Antonin Novotny from his position as Party First Secretary and replaced him with the well-known reform-minded leader, Alexander Dubcek. Driven by a vision to liberalize Communist rule and pitted against Brezhnev and other leaders throughout the Warsaw Pact nations, Dubcek was taken hostage and deported during the Soviet crackdown against the reformist "Prague Spring" in August of 1968. Here he is seen outside the Central Committee building the same year. *Eastfoto*

Prague, 1968. Students and other activists take to the streets in protest in August 1968 against the Soviet and Warsaw Pact troops sent into Czechoslovakia to put down the popular reform movement. This generation, refusing to tolerate the corrupt practices of their rulers, proclaimed their commitment to humane socialism and announced their plans to form an organization free of party control. *Eastfoto*

Todor Zhivkov, seen here at center with Alexei N. Kosygin and Leonid I. Brezhnev, was the Eastern European leader most slavishly loyal to the Soviets. Zhivkov led Bulgaria from 1954 to November of 1989 when a coalition of reform-minded apparatchiks led by Peter Mladenov and army generals headed by Minister of Defense Dobri Dzhurov forced him to resign. *Sovfoto*

Seen here in 1966, one year after assuming the leadership of the Romanian Communist Party from his mentor Gheorghe Gheorghiu-Dej, is Nicolae Ceausescu. Ceausescu, who at first relaxed the grip of Stalinist domination in order to consolidate his power, ruled Romania with an iron hand until he was overthrown, tried, and executed with his wife, Elena, in December 1989. *Eastfoto*

onment of the two intellectuals.[21] As part of the same repressive campaign, Poland's most celebrated Marxist philosopher Leszek Kolakowski,
was expelled from the party and denied the right to teach at the University of Warsaw. As a result of this harassment, he left Poland to teach
philosophy in England and the United States.

In the spring of 1968 the conflict between the party and the intellectuals came to be a climax. In March the government decided to ban the
performance of Adam Mickiewicz's classic patriotic play *The Forebears'
Eve*, claiming that such a presentation could lead to heightened anti-
Sovietism. The Writers' Union protested the government's censorship and
accused the rulers of ignorance and moral idiocy. Students at the University of Warsaw organized a protest demonstration, but the regime decided
to strike back with terrorist methods. Secret police thugs and armed vigi-
lantes violated the autonomy of the university with a raid that resulted in
hundreds of students wounded and arrested. Following that action, the
whole educational system went on strike. Stefan Cardinal Wyszynski, the
Primate of Poland, expressed apprehension over the government's brutal-
ity in dealing with the legitimate grievances of the youth. The youth
rebellion was the first large-scale social movement since October 1956.
Among its inspirers and supporters were those intellectuals who had once
hoped that the communist party would be able to effect genuine reforms.
The March 1968 movement was the end of lyrical hopes about the party's
capacity for self-transformation. It was the insurrection of a generation
who could not identify itself with the corrupt and corruptive values of the
ruling class. Although the students took care to proclaim their commitment to humane socialism, they announced their intention to form an
organization free from party control and supervision.

Both Gierek and Moczar accused Gomulka of "complacency with
revisionism" and asked for an exemplary repression of the democratic
movement. The fight between Gomulka and Moczar continued for the
next year: The former tried to mobilize the workers on his behalf, while
the latter intensified his vicious anti-intellectual and anti-Semitic activities. Those conflicts at the top prevented the formulation of a coherent
strategy. A new specter was invented by the chauvinist neo-Stalinists,
always obsessed with the "internal enemy." Instead of recognizing the
political causes of the students' protest, they preferred to blame a mythological "Zionist-revisionist plot" for having fomented the unrest. Rampant nationalism overflowed the offical media, which did not refrain
from using Nazi-like clichés in their attacks on critical intellectuals and
students. For all its heroism, the 1968 protest movement had little
chance to succeed. Its main weakness arose from its exclusively intellec-

tual nature. There were almost no ties between the leaders of the student protest and the workers, who did not understand that the new repressive campaign would eventually affect them as well.

The workers understood the students' rebellion better once the economic situation worsened, and they started to realize that the leadership could not live up to its soothing populist promises. Gomulka's autocratic behavior and his complete isolation from the party's rank-and-file resulted in the adoption in December 1970 of a set of extremely unpopular measures, including a 15 to 30 percent increase in the price of food and fuels. Large-scale workers' demonstrations took place in all the industrial cities, primarily in the coastal port of Gdansk. Simultaneously, the fragile balance at the party's top fell apart. Gomulka described the workers' unrest as "counterrevolutionary" and ordered the army and the police to shoot the demonstrators. The man who had come to power as the symbol of the workers' dreams of a better life ended his political career as the cruel oppressor of Poland's rebellious proletariat.

Profiting from Gomulka's dramatic loss of authority, the technocratic faction managed to eliminate him and his supporters. Immediately after his election as First Secretary, Edward Gierek condemned the reprisals and made a solemn pledge to maintain a close bond with the Polish working class. Ironically, ten years later, when workers' unrest broke out anew in Gdansk, Gierek himself ordered the police to fire against the strikers. But this time the party bureaucracy moved too late to stifle the movement from below. The workers and the intellectuals had established the organic links whose absence explains the success of previous repressive actions. Following the workers' strikes in 1976, a Workers' Defense Committee (KOR) had been formed by civic activists and critical intellectuals, including many from the 1968 movement.[22] When a strike started in Gdansk in the summer of 1980, the workers were not alone. They received the necessary political support from KOR activists, who went to Gdansk and became advisers to the Inter-Factory Strike Committee. Among those who played a prominent role in the negotiations between the government and workers were intellectuals like Tadeusz Mazowiecki, Adam Michnik, Jacek Kuron, and Bronislaw Geremek.

The chief causes of the 1980 upheaval in Poland were the growing decline in authority of the communist pary; the worsening of the living standards of the population; the general social malaise; and the fast maturing of the Polish civil society. Long-dormant political aspirations stirred as the result of a conviction that the communist party's pretense to monopolistic power had lost any support—even among professional bureaucrats. The loss of self-confidence on the part of the ruling elite was a precondition for the mounting activism among radicalized elements of the intelligentsia and the working class. Corrupt and inefficient, Gierek's leadership was unable to cope with the country's dramatic social and economic troubles. Disregard for the workers' plight and indulgence in self-righteous professions of good faith offered no remedies for Poland's growing difficulties.[23]

FOUR

A Glorious Resurrection
The Rise of Civil Society

It was a glorious resurrection, from the
tomb of slavery, to the heaven of freedom. My long crushed spirit rose, cow-
ardice departed, bold defiance took its
place; and I now resolved that, however
long I might remain a slave in form, the
day had passed forever when I could be
a slave in fact.

— *Frederick Douglass*

After the crushing of the Prague Spring, few residents of the East European countries retained illusions that communism could be reformed through benign experiments initiated by a liberal wing of the party elite. It became clear that the Soviet Union would not permit any new experimentation with the subversive idea of socialism with a human face. The Soviet leaders maintained their monopoly of the interpretation of Marxism-Leninism and jealously weeded out any new form of "deviation" from their dogma, while the critical intellectuals throughout the East European countries understood that the real demands of society, of the genuine independent life of the people, could not be limited to the restrictive program formulated by the communist party's liberals. In 1978 Adam Michnik characterized the principal weakness of intraparty reformism as the opposition's identification with the linguistic and even metaphysical underpinnings of the established order. Although disgusted with bureaucratic excesses, critical intellectuals remained loyal to the ultimate values of socialism. Their belief system was not radically distinct from what the official ideology was preaching. For the dissatisfied masses, the obsessive revisionist reference to the pristine nature of socialism, adulterated by abominable Stalinist practices, sounded uninspiring and even suspicious. Michnik compared the experiences of the Polish October and the Prague Spring and concluded:

> Although it was the absence of a stimulus from Moscow that made the Prague Spring different from the Polish October, one important similarity lay in the intraparty inspiration for the "movement of renewal." In both cases the strengths and the weaknesses of the movement were determined by the character of this inspiration. Its strength was due to the system's splitting from within—the plague was bred in the very heart of Grenada, so to speak, sparing neither the top layers of the party apparatus, the security apparatus, nor the army. But such a movement was unable to perceive its true historic identity or correctly to define its goals, and that was the source of its weakness. Its leaders used the general term *democratization* in such a manner that its connotations were almost purely negative; the term hardly had any positive meaning, and even then a different one for different people. The leaders themselves, in their call to the people for realism and moderation, failed to appreciate the geopolitical situation (Czechoslovakia) and the real aspirations of the people (Poland); they restored the monoparty system whose human face smiled only at party notables. In both cases, the result was confusion.[1]

The Prague Spring was a delayed offshoot of Khrushchevism, and as a trend within world communism Khrushchevism had quickly exhausted its magnetic appeal. A different approach, a strategy attuned to the times of Brezhnevite political conservatism, which did not represent merely a restoration of Stalinism but rather a new stage in the decomposition of the communist regimes, was needed. The new strategy had to take into account the growing obsolescence of the founding mythology of the existing system, the passing of the first generation of Stalinist crusaders, and the rise of political elites interested in the simple preservation of their advantages. The system had lost its initial absolutist drive: Stagnation and immobility were its main characteristics. The increasingly routinized mechanization of ideology laid open the cracks in the system's edifice for easier exploitation by the opposition.

In the 1970s there were no charismatic leaders in East European communist countries, no ideological rhetorical devices capable of mobilizing large sectors of the population, and no real zealots ready to defend the system because they considered it morally superior to its capitalist opponents. Almost imperceptibly, the classic totalitarian system had been replaced by a combination of technocracy, bureaucracy, and inertial authoritarianism. More significant, the main psychological element that made Stalinism possible, the universalized sense of helplessness of the individual, had vanished almost completely. The regimes, of course, could still resort to violent means to suppress the opposition, and few in the opposition envisioned the development of alternative political parties. But it was clear that for the first time dissent was possible, and that it could have a real social impact. As the regimes declined under the burden of their own ineffectiveness, as the elites lost their sense of historical predestination and showed signs of nervousness, it became possible for the long-silent civil society to reorganize itself and to launch a battle for the reconstitution of the public sphere.

The main battlefield in the 1970s and 1980s was the restoration of hope for social change—people became convinced that the rules of the game were not eternal, that it was worth fighting for human dignity, and that success in fighting such a fight had a real chance. In all the East-Central European countries—East Germany, Poland, Hungary, and Czechoslovakia—as well as Romania, social movements and groups emerged to challenge the powers-that-be and to announce their intention to create networks of informal grassroots initiatives. The degree of development of these actions of activists for social change was directly proportional to the erosion of the ruling apparatus and, as a corollary, the permissiveness of the existing regimes in their dealings with the opposition.

All five countries witnessed attempts to smash the social change initiatives, but they led to different results. In Poland, all the efforts of the Gierek regime to disband the civic initiatives were met by an increasingly radicalized response on the part of the emerging civil society. In the GDR, the huge police apparatus and the ruling SED weeded out any form of dissent; most of the critics were either imprisoned or forced to emigrate.

In Hungary, even the enlightened Kadar regime was far from ready to accept the rise of oppositional movements. The Kadarist politics of compromise granted the opposition more room to maneuver: Critics were not necessarily arrested, but they suffered other forms of harassment. For instance, the Budapest School philosophers (Ferenc Feher, Agnes Heller, György and Maria Markus, Janos Kis, Mihaly Vajda, György Bence) were stripped of their rights to teach and to publish in their own country. Some of them were forced to emigrate. Others, like Kis, remained in Hungary, where in the 1980s they founded the *samizdat* opposition. The term samizdat, a Russian abbreviation of the phrase *samstvennoye izdatelstvo* (self-publication), has become the symbolic designation of all clandestinely published materials in communist regimes. Similar interdictions to publishing were applied to other well-known Hungarian dissidents like Miklos Haraszti and the celebrated novelist György Konrad.

In the scope of its antidissident reaction, Gustav Husak's Czechoslovakia differed dramatically from Kadar's Hungary. In Czechoslovakia members of the human rights underground movement Charter 77 were consistently interrogated by the police, prevented from practicing their professions, and even jailed.

The worst persecution of social critics took place in Nicolae Ceausescu's Romania. There the despotic regime criminalized any form of opposition. Criticism of Ceausescu by those under his Stalin-like rule was perceived as the undermining of the foundations of the system. Ceausescu resented and crushed not only intellectual dissent but also timid attempts by fellow party leaders to advocate a collective leadership. In such conditions, the very idea of a collective challenge to the regime was suicidal. The best-known case of intraparty dissent took place in 1979, when the veteran party leader Constantin Pirvulescu took the floor at the Eleventh RCP Congress and accused Ceausescu of having established a personal dictatorship. Pirvulescu was immediately silenced and assigned to forced residence. Two years earlier, the democratic movement initiated by the writer Paul Goma (a former political prisoner in Stalinist jails), in solidarity with Charter 77, had been violently smashed, and Goma had been forced to emigrate to France. In the summer of 1977 coal miners in the Jiu Valley had organized a strike demanding, among other things, the liberalization of the political system. The strike had been defeated and the miners' leaders had disappeared without any trace.

Dissent in countries like Romania and Bulgaria had to confine itself to individual forms of protest. The case of the Romanian mathematician and human rights activist Mihai Botez is illustrative. Between 1977 and 1987 he engaged in unequivocal criticism of the Ceausescu regime. He granted interviews to the foreign press and addressed the government in countless memoranda showing that the country was moving toward a catastrophe. Botez did not challenge the existing social order but emphasized the regime's failure to observe its own demagogical promises. In 1987, following numerous threats and the government's decision assigning him to internal exile to a provincial town, Botez left Romania for the United States. Not long after Botez's departure, even in Romania, under the impact of changes in the whole bloc and the visible deterioration of

the structure of power represented by the Ceausescu clan, dissent de-
oped in 1988 and 1989.

Despite the rise of individual and collective forms of dissent in Romania and all the Warsaw Pact countries, although corruption, demoralization, and even despair were endemic, the *nomenklaturas*, or ruling
groups, were determined to hang on to power at all costs. The leaders of
the Warsaw Pact countries tried to marginalize the nascent forms of
political activism. In those circumstances, the birth of Solidarity in Poland represented a real watershed. Its creation, preceded by the activities
of the KOR, showed that even under the Brezhnevite regimes stalemate
and paralysis were not inevitable, that there were still ways of lessening
the system's hold on society's life. For an understanding of the development of civil society initiatives, one should be aware of the role of the
lingering independent institutions in Poland, primarily the Catholic
Church and the circles of lay Catholic intellectuals. Other elements that
mattered were the increased links between Polish civic activists and West
European and American sources of support and information, including
the Paris-based magazine *Kultura,* which ensured the bridge between
critical intellectuals inside and outside Poland.[2]

PREMISES FOR A CIVIL SOCIETY

Solidarity opened a new chapter in the history of Eastern Europe by
showing that possibilities existed for waking the long-dormant social
trends and that the cracks in the apparently monolithic totalitarian edifice could be exploited in an imaginative way to restore the civil society.
In Poland, the precondition for the resurrection of the civil society was
the decline, or rather the loss, of the ruling party's authority combined
with a growing decrease in self-confidence among the elites. Add to that
an international factor that played a prominent role in the development
of citizens' movements in East-Central Europe: the signing of the Helsinki Agreements in 1975 by representatives of the the Warsaw Pact,
including their recognition of the international covenants on human
rights.

It did not matter whether or not Brezhnev, Gierek, Husak, or Kadar
really believed in human rights or even whether they were prepared to
live up to their international pledges. What really mattered for the civic
activists was that those leaders had officially recognized principles that
transcended the frozen party dogmas and acknowledged—even if only
hypocritically—the readiness of their governments to behave in accor-

nal documents regarding the rights of humans and
nent on, when those regimes had recognized the
for informal groups to form in the communist
individuals unjustly prosecuted. In their eagerness
respectable members of the international community,
nist leaders provided their domestic critics with unprece-
ammunition: the opportunity to question their policies in reference to their own promises. The applying of the leaders' own words to
their regimes' practices was the new strategy adopted by the mounting
civil society groups in Eastern Europe. Solidarity with victims of human
rights abuses became one of the chief rallying points for the opposition.

POLAND: THE REBIRTH OF THE CIVIL SOCIETY

By the late 1970s Polish society was torn by social and political tensions.
Instead of confronting them, recognizing the failure of the command
economy, and initiating bold reforms, the communist bureaucracy resorted to demagogy and used corruption as the last resort for preserving
the status quo. The emergence of the independent, self-governed union
Solidarity as an alternative organization able to articulate social demands
for rapid political and economic change altered the whole equation of the
political game in East-Central Europe, which had held that all change
would start from the center in Moscow. Peaceful and self-contained, the
Polish revolution of 1980–81 questioned the dogma of the communist
party's power monopoly and advanced a program for the pluralization of a
Soviet-bloc society. The thrust of Solidarity's search for renewal was to
release citizens from the suffocating burden of bureaucratic institutions
through the rehabilitation of the civil society. The efforts of the new
social movement created an autonomous counterpart to governmental
power and eventually ensured the development of what Max Weber
called a national citizen class.[3] The development of such a movement,
with its combination of spontaneous and institutional dimensions, would
have been unthinkable under mature Stalinism. The birth and then the
recognition of Solidarity was predicated on the public's awareness of the
dominant power's loss of authority. Both ideologically and politically, the
Gierek regime had ceased to be a traditional form of totalitarianism.
Although the repressive institutions were still there, their functions had
been curtailed seriously. As for the communist party, its claim to legitimacy was widely questioned by the majority of the population, who felt
that "35 years of political misrule had brought the nation to the point of

economic, as well as political and social bankruptcy, and that any real solution to Poland's problems would require not merely changes in economic policy, but a change in the relationship between the political authority and the civil community as well."[4]

Within Poland, the Solidarity revolutionary movement of 1980–81 revealed that the party's domination was illegitimate and discovered in the nation's popular will a genuine principle of political legitimation. Although the Polish government contemplated the full use of military force to thwart the new protest movement in August 1980, the communist party found itself powerless in the face of an irresistible social movement. The agreement signed on August 31, 1980, by representatives of the government and the strike committee stipulated the party's leading role as the ultimate limit of the negotiable issues, but the communist leadership resigned itself to an increasingly defensive position. Solidarity legally registered itself as an independent trade union several months later, in November: The very fact that the communist government was compelled to admit the right of an independent union to exist showed that its whole ideological pretense to rule was a hoax. Far from holding a historical mandate to rule society, the communists stayed in power by virtue of mere inertia and force. That the communist party itself could not avoid the impact of the societal resurrection became clear at a party congress in July 1981, when the struggle intensified between partisans of democratization and the traditionalists who deplored the concessions made to Solidarity.

Factors outside the Polish crisis, in particular pressure from abroad, especially from the Soviet Union and the German Democratic Republic, added drama. In the autumn of 1980 Solidarity had already become a powerful social movement, incorporating into its ranks not only workers but also intellectuals, students, and peasants. The conflict between the party bureaucracy and the popular challenge represented by the independent union could not be postponed. Without directly interfering in the political struggle, the Catholic Church, with its immense prestige and influence, supported the union's social demands. At the same time the Catholic hierarchy tried to moderate the most hotheaded Solidarity activists and sought to find a bridge between the government and the opposition. Actually, for the whole year of 1981 Polish political life was dominated by those three major actors: the communist party, the Catholic Church, and the ever expanding Solidarity movement. In a matter of months Solidarity had acquired an offensive nature: Its agenda had exceeded the self-limiting social issues and aimed at a renegotiation of the constitutional basis of the Polish state. At the same time, while the

Soviets were lambasting Solidarity for its alleged conspiratorial goals, Western media focused on the movement's innovative strategy, including its espousal of nonviolent means of political change. The special interest shown by Western media in Solidarity's struggle for social and political emancipation provided the movement with much-needed moral support during the exacerbation of its polemic with the orthodox communists in Poland and abroad. Confrontation between the government and Solidarity seemed inevitable when, in October 1981, General Jaruzelski, who had been appointed Prime Minister in February of that year, also became the communist party's First Secretary, a unique situation in the Soviet bloc that foreshadowed a military coup in Poland.

Frightened by the increasingly bold demands spelled out by the Solidarity movement and perhaps genuinely seeking to avoid direct Soviet intervention, the army proclaimed martial law on December 13, 1981. Solidarity was then banned, and its leading activists were jailed. But even military action could not save the system. While the military regime did attempt to establish its patriotic credentials and to disband the popular base of Solidarity altogether, when the Soviet Union itself undertook a new de-Stalinization effort after 1985 under Mikhail Gorbachev, the rationale for Solidarity's interdiction appeared increasingly flawed. The threat of Soviet aggression was minimal; as Gorbachev's policies evolved, it became nonexistent. Recognizing the changes in the Soviet Union and prompted by the failure of his economic and social plans, Jaruzelski granted amnesty to political prisoners, lifted martial law, and tried to embark on a reformist course. He fully endorsed Gorbachev's perestroika and became a close supporter of the Soviet leader in the Warsaw Pact, where Gorbachev faced an embittered coalition of the antireformist Romanian, East German, Bulgarian, and Czechoslovak leaders. All Jaruzelski's conciliatory efforts were not enough to persuade the Polish society of his political credibility.

The Polish government's refusal to relegalize Solidarity and the smearing of prominent civic activists convinced the Poles that the Jaruzelski regime was not really intent upon renouncing its shameful legacy of repression. The outbreak of a new crisis was thus unavoidable, particularly in light of the nation's persistent economic problems. The chasm between the official power and the ever growing civil society continued to widen. Before the 1989 breakup of the Polish equilibrium, that chasm was explained by J. F. Brown, a veteran observer of the East European scene:

> Indeed, the picture Poland now presented was one of two societies—the "official" and the "alternative." The "official" consisted of the regime estab-

lishment and the large number of people who, willingly or unwillingly, cooperated with the regime to some degree. The "alternative" society, in which youth played a disproportionately large role, had its own media, literature, and cultural and educational activities. It avoided contact with the "official" society as far as was ever possible. In a sense two societies had always existed in communist Eastern Europe. But never had the chasm between the two been as wide as it was now in Poland, and never had the "alternative" society been so well-organized and so self-sufficient.[5]

The imminence of a new crisis was conditioned by the very artificiality of the existing societal system. Despite the uninterrupted efforts of successive communist elites to implant Soviet-style regimes in Eastern Europe, and to make them look like home-grown products, those regimes never gained true popular approval. In Poland, more than in any other communist country, the loss of legitimacy of the communist leadership was conspicuous. In 1956 it still had been possible for certain groups within the party to believe that the solution could come from within the communist elite, from some "enlightened" wing of the apparatus, but after the crushing of the Prague Spring and the 1968 anti-intellectual repression in Poland such illusions were simply untenable. Since its beginnings in Eastern Europe, communism had been in a permanent crisis—a crisis of authority and legitimacy, a crisis of morality, and, of course, a crisis of economic effectiveness. But the distinction must be made between latent and manifest crises. Only when the ruling group loses its self-confidence and alternative political actors emerge do latent crises turn into revolutionary situations. According to classic Leninist formulation, in order for a revolution to occur it is necessary for the rulers to cease being able to rule in the old ways and for the ruled to cease accepting the old methods of domination. The spurious, unconvincing political symbolism of the old regime is abandoned, all political taboos are abolished, and the barrier against political experimentation is suddenly removed. The whole principle of political reality is turned upside down in such conditions, and those who had long been pilloried as "public enemies" emerge as the embodiment of the national hope for "salvation." The transformation usually includes a modification of the matrix of power and permits the rise of new social and political groups into political prominence.

Remodeling the public sphere through the restoration of civic dignity becomes the highest priority. Because Stalinist pedagogy annihilated society's civic dimension and forcibly infantilized individuals, for such changes to take place society must reach a degree of self-awareness. The mental habits instilled by Stalinism included a fear of human beings engaged in political activities that might be labeled subversive, and for a totalitarian state any form of criticism, any form of individual self-assertion means an attack on the state's pretense to omniscience and omnipotence. Jacek Kuron, the Polish civic activist, has pointed out that once a mass social movement has emerged in a communist country, its consequences are more powerful than the attempt of the regime to neutralize it. Such a development cannot take place without a maturing of the opposition and a weakening of the Leninist system of control and manipulation:

> It goes back to 1956. We had not yet abandoned Communism but we were already of the opinion that social movements should be independent of the Party and the government. 1968 and 1970 were crucial times for the relationship between the intellectuals and the workers. In 1968 the intellectuals realized that they must ally themselves with the workers. After 1970 the workers reached a similar conclusion about the need for an alliance with the intellectuals. KOR (the Workers' Defense Committee) was born from this experience, and its attempts to foster the self-organization of social movements eventually bore splendid fruits in 1980.[6]

Kuron, one of the KOR founders and a strategist of the Polish opposition after martial law, added:

> True, Solidarity has been crushed and driven underground, but this cannot change the fact that the foundations of the totalitarian system had been broken. We have created and sustained freedom of expression so that the authorities had to open up the official media. Because of the pressure of the Solidarity underground, even all those dummy social movements which they created now cease to be dummies. There is only one road: from totalitarianism to democracy, and we have covered a great length of it.[7]

Solidarity's survival in Poland under martial law conditions and its ability to create a counterculture, including publishing houses, film-making, myriad journals and newspapers, flying universities, and other forms of autonomous social activism, demonstrates how a system can lose its traditional repressive potential. In Poland's case, it was a country ruled by an ailing dictatorship, based primarily on conformity, social inertia, and manipulation of the specter of a potential Soviet intervention. That was not the old-fashioned, brutal despotism that made even the thought of opposition sound quixotic. Even in the harshest conditions imposed by the military regime, Poles enjoyed more elbow room for autonomous activities than Romanians ever had under Ceausescu's personalistic dictatorship. The difference between the two regimes came down to the impact of the Polish social movements on the body politic: Even if temporarily defeated, Solidarity had created a sense of political community and mutual trust that could not exist in the atomized space of a traditional totalitarian polity. Actually, it was during the martial law period that a new generation of oppositional fighters came of age and ensured the continuation of the struggle even though the historical leaders were in jail. The underground Solidarity newspaper *Tygodnik Mazowsze* came out uninterruptedly with a press run of about 50,000. Unofficial committees were formed to collect money for the families of imprisoned activists and other victims of repression. On the one hand, the state appeared to be in full control. On the other, society's independent life continued and even thrived. "If martial law was a setback for the independent society, it was a disaster for the totalitarian state."[8] Thus did Adam Michnik, after his release from prison, explain this paradox of the ruling power's failure to arouse the minimal popular support necessary for it to govern.

For Solidarity to emerge in August 1980 and acquire prominent status in national affairs in a short period, certain conditions had to exist in Poland. Among the the most important was the presence of a politically active nucleus, primarily composed of human and civil rights activists who had long established their *bona fides* in the eyes of the radicalized workers. That was indeed the great achievement of of the KOR. Its main area of activity was social rather than political. The committee monitored the civil rights abuses and indicated the names of those involved in such actions. The ethos of the KOR, as Jan Josef Lipski called the normative code of this embryo of the Polish civil society, was based on categorical rejection of the official lie:

> One important ethical principle adopted by KOR was that KOR did not lie. This principle also had a pragmatic basis and justification, to a greater extent even than the principle of renouncing violence and hatred: in a struggle with authorities who had especially compromised themselves when it came to telling the truth, it was better to renounce falsehood completely and gain confidence in this manner than to lay oneself open to the possibility that every departure from the truth could be blown up by the mass media.[9]

When it was formed in 1976, KOR numbered only fifty-nine members. One year later the group changed its name to the Social Self-Defense

Committee and embarked on underground publishing. Jacek Kuron and other veterans of opposition struggles in Poland knew that without organization the civil society can easily be drawn into violent clashes and smashed by the sophisticated police forces of the regime. In 1970, when strikers in Gdansk tried to burn down the communist party local headquarters, Kuron told them: "Don't burn down committees; found your own."[10]

Another element that added to the uniqueness of the Polish situation was the presence of the Catholic Church, an institution that had succeeded in resisting the Stalinist attempts at regimentation and had remained, as Leszek Kolakowski rightly pointed out, "the only independent source of moral authority in a sick society."[11] Gradually, by the end of the 1970s, as the regime showed its blatant ineptitude and failed to undertake sweeping reforms, a coalition of opposition forces began taking shape in Poland. This time, thanks to the relentless activities of the KOR as well as of those Catholic intellectual groups Michnik once described as "neopositivists," it was possible to create a symbiotic relationship among the critical intelligentsia, the Church, and the workers. It took the extraordinary efforts of the civic activists grouped in KOR and the development of a nationwide communication network to make possible the successful eruption of 1980. The workers in Poland, as it has been so often argued, revolted not only against economic hardships but also against the whole pyramid of injustice created in the name of their own alleged "dictatorship." Perhaps more than the intellectuals, who rationalized the moral abdications of the regime, the workers realized the colossal gap between the government's claim to embody the interests of the proletariat and its true oligarchic-bureaucratic nature. As Kolakowski noted:

> One could see from the very beginning of the 1980 summer strikes that the workers were perfectly aware of the fact that the fight for cultural liberties was an essential part of their cause, and that this cause would be lost if they did not list among their grievances a number of specific political demands: freedom of speech and print, an end to the party's monopoly of the mass media, abrogation of various restrictions imposed on the Church, and release of the political prisoners. It was obvious from the outset that the workers' revolt was not only against poverty and wretched work conditions; it was essentially a revolt against the rule of lies.[12]

What strategic framework ensured the success of Solidarity's revolt? How did the political and intellectual approach adopted by Polish civic activists diminish the impact of the government crackdown? One can understand these fundamental issues through Michnik's pathbreaking political essays, in which he articulates the values and goals of the Polish civil society. In his essay "A New Evolutionism," written in 1976, Michnik analyzed the political traditions of the antitotalitarian struggle in Poland. According to him, all attempts to change the system that followed the denunciation of Stalinism in 1956 partook of the same illusion: that the regime could be changed from within. The revisionists were convinced that the rise of a liberal group to the party's leadership would make possible the humanization of socialism. The "neopositivists," in turn, who were not prisoners of the "intraparty perspective," believed in the possibility of influencing the government through what can be termed "critical cooperation." The revisionists challenged the party's subservience to the Kremlin and found the source of their opposition in the original Marxist humanism. For them Soviet-style socialism was an aberration and even a betrayal of the genuine promises of historical materialism. The neopositivists, most of whom were Catholic intellectuals, distrusted any version of Marxism but considered the friendly relationship with Soviet Russia a pillar for the Polish state's survival. In Michnik's apt metaphor, "If one considers the state organization of the Soviet Union as the Church and the Marxist ideological doctrine as the Bible, then revisionism was faithful to the Bible while developing its own interpretations, whereas neopositivism adhered to the Church but with the hope that the Church would sooner or later disappear."[13]

The bankruptcy of revisionism, especially in the 1960s, could not and should not conceal its importance as a learning experience needed in the formation of a critical intelligentsia in Poland. In countries like Poland, Czechoslovakia, and Hungary, the defeat of revisionism meant the end of the illusions about the reformability of the existing system. With all its tragic moments, this disenchantment was also a needed awakening. In countries where a revisionist experience was absent or severely restricted—for instance, Bulgaria and Romania—the dissolution of the power structure and the rise of alternative intellectual currents was much more difficult than in Poland or Hungary, where the revisionist humanist eschatologies inspired strong criticism of the ruling elites and contributed to the education of young activists who would later completely abandon the Marxist paradigm. At a certain historical juncture, it appears essential to challenge the system in terms of its own ambitions and promises, to show the contrast between the official ideology and the reality of socialism. With all its naïveté and inconsistencies, revisionism irrigated the East European political culture and contributed to the formation of political and intellectual counter-elites. For instance, knowledge of the ideological battles surrounding the attempt to restore the humanist dimension of Marxism furthers an understanding of works by Milan Kundera or Kazimierz Brandys. That is not to say that those writers simply echoed the political polemics, but ultimate values were involved in the struggle between the ideological reactionaries and the exponents of revisionism. Among other things, revisionism rehabilitated the concept of man, denied by the party dogmas. More than that, revisionism showed it was possible and even necessary to engage in criticism of the status quo, that the system was not impregnable, and the ruling elite was less unified and cohesive than it appeared to an external observer.

With all their delusions, including the counterproductive belief in the possibility of a dialogue with the seasoned Leninists that were running the show, the revisionists left a legacy of activism that was to flourish later in the non-Marxist or even anti-Marxist movements of the 1970s and 1980s. Their main weakness, however, was the idealization of the powers-that-be, the firm belief that there were redeemable features in the existing system and that therefore there was no justification for an out-and-out repudiation of the Marxist social design. In all communist countries where revisionist schools managed to come to life, their representatives failed to offer genuine political alternatives to the existing powers. What they were aiming at was at the most an improvement of the system, not its disbandment. In Michnik's words:

> I think that the revisionists' greatest sin lay not in their defeat in the intraparty struggle for power (where they could not win) but in the character of that defeat. It was the defeat of individuals being eliminated from positions of power and influence, not a setback for a broadly based leftist and democratic political platform. The revisionists never created such a platform.[14]

The final blows against the revisionist illusions came with the March 1968 events in Poland, when the Communist Party showed its real chauvinistic, fascist nature, and even more shockingly with the military invasion of Czechoslovakia and the suppression of the reform movement in that country in August 1968. Indeed, one can say that events in 1968 put the final nail in the coffin of revisionism. For those who recognized the amplitude of the drama that took place in that year, it was clear the the exit from Sovietism meant a resolute break with all Marxist illusions. Leszek Kolakowski, a former revisionist Marxist himself, gave full expression to the newly acquired understanding of the intimate connection between the Marxist world view and the practice of communism in the twentieth century:

> It would be absurd to maintain that Marxism was, so to speak, the efficient cause of the present-day Communism; on the other hand, Communism is not a mere "degeneration" of Marxism but a possible interpretation of it and even a well-founded one, though primitive and partial in some respects. . . . The self-deification of mankind, to which Marxism gave philosophical expression, has ended in the same way as all such attempts: it has revealed itself as the farcical aspect of human bondage.[15]

But how could one engage in such a struggle against an enormous repressive apparatus, armed to the teeth with the most sophisticated devices and ready to resort to any means in order to defend its privileges? While revisionists were despairing over the collapse of their dreams, neopositivists were seeking to expand the realm of civil liberties. To accomplish that limited goal, they were ready to pay lip service to the party's leading role and to accept its hegemony. As the situation grew increasingly tense, both the revisionists and the neopositivists discovered that their options were strikingly out of touch with Poland's political realities of the 1970s:

> The conflicts between the public and the authorities showed the illusory character of the hopes held by both the revisionists and the neopositivists, and placed them in a situation in which they had to make a dramatic choice. When there is open conflict, one must clearly state a position and declare whose side one is on—that of those being beaten up or that of those doing the beating. Where the conflict is open, consistent revisionism as well as consistent neopositivism both inevitably lead to unity with the powers-that-be and assumption of their point of view. To offer solidarity with striking workers, with students holding a mass meeting, or with protesting intellectuals is to challenge the intraparty strategy of the revisionist and neopositivist policies of compromise.[16]

Michnik proposed an evolutionary path to change the rules of the game, which at that time made the existing system in the Soviet Union the chief deterrent to bold antiregime activities. However, he saw a possibility for a struggle for the expansion of civil liberties within the existing conditions. The "new evolutionism" was thus closer to the Spanish rather than the Portuguese model of transition from dictatorship to democracy. In other words, Michnik insisted on the need for gradual and piecemeal change, rather than a violent upheaval and the abrupt destruction of the existing system. The most important distinction between the previous attempts at change and Michnik's strategy was that the latter was addressed to the independent society and not to the rulers. That was not a romantic rejection of geopolitical realities but rather the adjustment of the oppositional demands to the existence of a conservative, or even reactionary, imperial center. The new evolutionism was based on the assumption that society could recover from the totalitarian anesthesia, that individuals gradually could become citizens, even without a direct confrontation between the powerful and the powerless. The penetration of the existing structures and the creation of parallel networks of action and communication seemed to be the best means to advance such an agenda. Unlike previous experiments, the new evolutionism saw the working class as the pivotal agent in such a political transition:

> "New evolutionism" is based on the faith in the power of the working class, which, with a steady and unyielding stand, has on several occasions forced the government to make spectacular concessions. It is difficult to foresee developments in the working class, but there is no question that the power elite fears this social group most. Pressure from the working classes is a necessary condition for the evolution of public life toward a democracy.[17]

The philosophy of the new evolutionism became the theoretical axis for the formation of a democratic opposition in Poland and the other East-Central European countries. Anticipating events that were to take place in Poland four years later, Michnik wrote presciently:

> The democratic opposition must formulate its own political goals and only then, with those goals in hand, reach political compromises. Take, for example, a situation in which the workers revolt and the government declares that "it wants to consult with the working class" instead of organizing a bloody massacre. The people of the democratic opposition should treat this reaction neither as a sufficient concession ("but they are not shooting") nor as a meaningless fiction. On the contrary, the democratic opposition must be constantly and incessantly visible in public life, must create political facts by organizing mass actions, must formulate alternative programs. Everything else is an illusion.[18]

It was precisely in accordance with this approach that Solidarity was able to overcome its limited trade union identity and become the center of Poland's emerging civil society. The movement's antibureaucratic nature and its adoption of a comprehensive social agenda contributed to its transformation into the nerve center of the country's awakening: "The essence of the spontaneously growing Independent and Self-Governing Labor Union Solidarity lay in the restoration of social ties, self-organization aimed at guaranteeing the defense of labor, civil and national rights. For the first time in the history of communist rule in Poland 'civil society' was being restored, it was reaching a compromise with the state."[19]

The whole strategy of the new evolutionism was based on a certain definition of socialism by the Soviet Union. More clearly, it was based on the recognition by the civil societies that the ultimate limit of their actions was represented by the Soviet margin of tolerance of political change in any of the former satellite countries. In addition, those struggles were taking place in a Soviet Union dominated by the Brezhnevite clique of gerontocrats, suspicious of any change that would jeopardize Soviet interests. In his autobiography, Lech Walesa, the electrician from the Lenin Shipyard in Gdansk who became the chairman of Solidarity, justified the politics of "self-limitation of the revolution" by quoting a text by Adam Michnik, who for many years had played the role of an adviser to the independent union's leadership. Walesa's autobiography provides a detailed perspective on the strategic and philosophical dilemmas of the East European opposition in the pre-Gorbachev era:

The truth is that without agreement between the government and the people, this country cannot be governed. The truth is also that, in spite of official pronouncements at national functions, this country is not a sovereign country. This is the truth: Poles should admit the fact that their sovereignty is limited by the national and ideological interests of the USSR. In the last analysis, the truth is that the only Polish government acceptable to the leaders of the USSR is one controlled by communists; there is no reason to think that this state of affairs is going to change overnight, if ever.

What follows from this? It follows that every attempt to govern against the people's will leads inevitably to catastrophe, but it also follows that every attempt to overthrow the government of Poland strikes a direct blow at the interests of the USSR. This is our reality. One doesn't have to like it, but one must recognize it.

I realize that many of my colleagues openly reproach me with the charge that I have abandoned our aspirations to independence and democracy. To them, I reply frankly: in our present geopolitical situation, I don't believe that access to independence and parliamentarism is possible. I believe that we can organize our independence from within, in other words, that in becoming an increasingly better-organized society, increasingly efficient, we will enrich Europe and the rest of the world, in turn,

with what we have to offer; at the same time we can offer an alternative
choice, demonstrating our tolerance and humanity. When we accomplish
this we will be on the road to independence and democracy.

Pluralism in all areas of life is possible, the abolition of advance
censorship is possible, a rational economic reform is possible and a just
social policy are possible, press and television subject to the rules of competition and relaying the truth are possible, the independence of science and
the autonomy of universities are possible, as are social controls of prices
and a network of consumers' councils, along with independent courts of
law and police stations where people aren't beaten up.

If we have to obtain all this by force, to wrest it from the government,
since no nation has ever received its rights as a gift, let us be careful in
resorting to this necessary violence not to tear to shreds the Polish state,
deprived of its sovereignty as it already is.[20]

This long quotation is just the opposite of an invitation to passivity.
Michnik's own political career, which started during the student protest
movement at the University of Warsaw in the 1960s, included the formation of KOR, participation in Lech Walesa's team of advisers, and a new
series of prison terms following the proclamation of martial law in December 1981, is testimony against such an interpretation. The philosophy of
the new evolutionism was the attempt to discover a way out of the
stalemate created by the post-totalitarian order. It was a realization,
especially in light of the tragic end of the Prague Spring, that as long as
fundamental changes did not occur in the center of the empire itself, as
long as the Kremlin perceived the East European countries as a mere
extension of its inner empire, any attempt to challenge and modify the
established form of authority was bound to engender Soviet intervention.
But even in those extremely limiting conditions, there was enough to be
done. First and foremost, as civic activists in all the East-Central European countries discovered, it was possible to create a parallel structure of
institutions. The emergence of Solidarity was precisely the result of that
approach. The new union was not simply a movement restricted to the
defense of the workers' interests. As Walesa himself noted, Solidarity
meant the rise of a new form of politics, one opposed to the duplicitous
rituals practiced by the rulers. Later on, Vaclav Havel would speak about
the politics of truth. And that of course was the deeper meaning of the
appearance of Solidarity and of its victory over the principles of self-
serving Realpolitik: It was the dissident's dream turned into a mass movement, the triumph of the humanist creed over bureaucratic pragmatism.

In the preface to his memoir, Walesa describes the experience of
Solidarity as the beginning of a new form of politics, one that would take

into account the ultimate dangers confronting mankind and the right of the individual to reject any ideological imperatives. The new politics involves the defanaticization of the public realm, the affirmation of the right to be different and of the right to civil disobedience. The significance of Solidarity transcended the Polish borders. Its birth was one of those world-historical developments that not only announce a new chapter in a country's national history but also usher in a new order of things on the global scale. In Walesa's words:

> Solidarity is a further sign that a new era is beginning. The burden of the past was weighing us down and forcing us to look for new solutions; it was forcing us to confront problems of impossible complexity. We Poles are exposed to influences from all sides and life requires us to choose, to verify, to experience for ourselves, and then to assert ourselves and draw from within ourselves the necessary moral strength to effect change. Though we are caught in the vise of a fossilized system, a product of an outdated partition of our planet, in August 1980 we overthrew an all-powerful taboo and proclaimed the dawning of a new era. The Polish nation achieved this as a force before the eyes of the world without threats, without violence or a drop of the opponent's blood being shed; no ideology was advanced, no economic or institutional theory: we were simply seeking human dignity. In both camps, free and unfree, this episode has been regarded as a revolutionary act. But we saw nothing revolutionary in what happened. We merely felt that after so many years of living upside down, we were at least beginning to walk on our feet. [21]

Indeed, the strategic outlook represented by the new evolutionism ensured the development and flourishing of an alternative political culture in Poland without producing a direct clash with the ruling elite.

When the Polish government decided to crack down on Solidarity in 1981, it was not only because of its own concerns about the future of the political system and the union's transformation into a rival political force, but also because of pressure from the Soviet Union. One can imagine the reaction of Brezhnev, Suslov, and other orthodox Leninists to the rise of an autonomous, self-governing union in neighboring Poland. They definitely feared that Solidarity's example would become contagious and would inspire similar movements in Eastern Europe and even in the Soviet Union. Yet not all of Jaruzelski's motivations in proclaiming martial law were related to the danger of direct Soviet intervention. Clear evidence of the long-planned nature of the 1981 crackdown appeared in the Polish media during the presidential campaign in December 1990, when Jaruzelski left the political scene and

Lech Walesa was elected President. Plans for a military takeover and a ban on the activities of Solidarity had been initiated immediately after the signing of the Gdansk agreements in August 1980, well before the first recorded instances of Soviet pressure.[22] Later on, when the whole Soviet vision of intrabloc relations changed and the Kremlin decided to let each country follow its own political course, a new approach was needed. The determining and compelling geopolitical limitations that had historically operated to produce a deadlock were replaced by new possibilities for experimentation.

In Poland the regime failed to introduce economic reform, social discontent soared, and industry was paralyzed by working-class unrest. It was clear that far from having been smashed, Solidarity had thrived underground. The huge network of independent press and other activities permitted the sudden revival of the union and helped reconstitute a credible political actor at the moment of the roundtable negotiations. By 1988 the issue was the nature of the political system itself and the regime's monopoly of political power in Poland. The new evolutionism had led to a revolutionary situation where simple intrasystemic reforms were counterproductive. They had been tested, and they had failed. The transcendence of the status quo through the organization of free elections was the only alternative to the prolongation of this agony. As the British political essayist Timothy Garton Ash insightfully commented, what was happening in the first months of 1989 in Poland and Hungary was not traditional tinkering with the system, or adjustment of the opposition to the old-fashioned rules of the game, but rather the combination of reform and revolution in a unique strategic chemistry that included mutual trust and the acceptance by the government of a partner—the democratic opposition—it had long considered intractable. For the opposition, that meant that for the first time its leaders were engaged in a historical deal that could bring them to power.

The dichotomy "reform or revolution" turned out to be irrelevant in Poland and Hungary at the beginning of 1989:

> [W]hat is happening just now is a singular mixture of both reform and revolution: a "revorm," if you will, or perhaps a "refolution." There is, in both places, a strong and essential element of voluntary, deliberate reform led by an enlightened minority (but only a minority) in the still ruling Communist parties, and in the Polish case, at the top of the military and the police. Their advance consists of an unprecedented retreat: undertaking to share power, and even—*mirabile dictu*—talk of giving up altogether, if they lose an election.[23]

But this did happen in the revolutionary year 1989, when all the previous considerations of tactical pragmatism and prudence were reassessed in the light of a new Soviet margin of tolerance.

During the 1970s and 1980s, before Gorbachev came to power and affirmed his new philosophy of international relations based on the supremacy of universal human values, it was unthinkable that the continuum of domination in each East European country could be broken in such a radical way. The opposition strategy had to count on a long and patient construction of another social reality, one different from the official institutional framework based on coercion and lies.

THE POLITICS OF ANTIPOLITICS: HOW CIVIL SOCIETY EMERGES

Nobody better expressed the commitment to a politics of truth than the Czech playwright and human rights activist Vaclav Havel. During the Prague Spring Havel belonged among those independent intellectuals who criticized the party reformers for their timidity in breaking with the Soviet-style system. As a young man, born to a bourgeois family, Havel was denied the right to attend university. He thus experienced the discriminations introduced by an order that claimed to express the interests of all the working people. He discovered that there was no connection between the regime's self-serving demagogy and the social reality of Czechoslovakia. His plays described the predicament of the human being in systems inimical to truth and dignity. Following the Soviet invasion of his country, Havel refused to emigrate and continued to fight in defense of civil rights. He was a founding member of and one of the first spokesmen for Charter 77. For his uncompromising struggle, he was imprisoned on various occasions. In 1979 a group of Czechoslovak and Polish dissidents decided to organize and publish a samizdat collection of essays called *On Freedom and Power*. Because of the political situation in the two countries, the volume that emerged contained only the Czechoslovak contributions, but the Poles had read them and were highly appreciative of their quality. Referring to Havel's contribution to the volume, Zbigniew Bujak, the Warsaw Solidarity leader, noted in 1981 that this essay, entitled "The Power of the Powerless," gave the Polish opposition "theoretical backing, a theoretical basis for our actions."[24] Havel's merit was to synthesize, in a most poignant way, ideas, expectations, and even emotions that had existed mostly in a spontaneous, unarticulated, subliminal form. The new movements in Eastern Europe needed a convincing theoretical explanation of their political legitimacy. Each essay in this pathbreaking multi-author volume deserves special discussion, but Havel's offers a concentrated, comprehensive analysis of the nature of power, dissent, and opposition in post-totalitarian societies.

"The Power of the Powerless" addresses the great moral dilemmas of the individual in a society where terror has become more insidious and almost invisible, and where the mechanisms of repression have been internalized to an unprecedented degree. Havel's essay offers a strategy of self-emancipation for the individual, an alternative to the philosophy of historical abandonment and impotence. His thesis is that it is possible to defeat the logic of conformity, that freedom is a subjective variable that cannot be completely suppressed.

One should bear in mind that the essay describes the political and moral situation in Husak's "normalized" Czechoslovakia, a country where forgetting had been turned into an official state policy. One should recall also that in a totalitarian society dissent is impossible. For critical ideas to be able to come to the fore and to have a social impact, the system must undergo a minimal opening. Havel's essay deals precisely with the sociological and psychological premises for dissent and captures the defining characteristics of the post-totalitarian society. Compared with the Stalinist conditions, when all forms of real or potential critique were ruthlessly suppressed, the post-totalitarian society allows fledgling forms of disobedience. In countries like Albania and Romania, such collective efforts for liberation were impossible, because the regimes had preserved all their coercive powers. In Czechoslovakia, Hungary, and Poland, the erosion of communist authority was accompanied by limited toleration of critical actions. Two features symbolize the nature of such a post-totalitarian regime. First, this is an authoritarian order that reproduces itself by virtue of automatism rather than through traditional mobilizing forms of integration and control. Second, the system's main ally, the individual's conviction that nothing can be changed in the given circumstances, that cooperation with the powers-that-be is the only route to tranquility, has lost its intimidating, self-paralyzing force. Everybody, the powerful and the powerless, is aware of the extinction of the old myths, but very few dare to say so openly. The beleaguered minority of truth-tellers, another post-totalitarian feature, is the alternative to the established order:

> A spectre is haunting Eastern Europe: the spectre of what in the West is called "dissent." This spectre has not appeared out of thin air. It is a natural and inevitable consequence of the present historical phase of the

system it is haunting. It was born at a time when this system, for a thousand reasons, can no longer base itself on the unadulterated, brutal, and arbitrary application of power, eliminating all expressions of nonconformity. What is more, the system has become so ossified politically that there is practically no way for such nonconformity to be implemented within its official structures.[25]

The principal feature of that system is a change in the function and influence of the ruling ideology. Whereas under mature Stalinism ideology imbued life in a monopolistic manner, forcing the individual to participate in collective rituals of "revolutionary excitement, heroism, dedication, and boisterous violence," in the post-totalitarian order the dominant structures appear to be exhausted. There is a general fatigue in the functioning of all institutions.

Of course, ideology still exists in a post-totalitarian society, but it is a residual construct, with no chance to stir responsive chords among the populace or to create deep emotional attachments. To illustrate the situation in which ideology is both omnipotent and irrelevant, Havel resorts to a parable. He describes the behavior of a manager of a fruit and vegetable shop who places in his window, among the onions and the carrots, the slogan: "Workers of the World, Unite!" To be sure, the greengrocer couldn't care less whether or not the world proletariat closes ranks. Besides, he realizes that his placing this slogan in the window does not promote the cause of proletarian internationalism. Nothing is more remote from his everyday concerns than the Marxist call for global workers' solidarity. The question to ask is, If the greengrocer is indifferent to the content of this slogan, why does he act this way? Havel's answer is that by performing the ritual the greengrocer sends a signal to the authorities, who had provided him with the poster and who expect him to behave as a disciplined fragment of the social body.

If he refuses to display the poster, the greengrocer ruins a certain cohesion, he breaks the rules of obedient conformity and jeopardizes his status. At least that is the way he rationalizes his conduct. After all, the greengrocer might ask, what's wrong with the workers of the world uniting? And what's wrong with his placing this poster among the apples and carrots? Havel shows that the hidden meaning behind the greengrocer's gesture is directly related to his ideological conformity: "The slogan is really a *sign*, and as such it contains a subliminal but very definite message. Verbally, it might be expressed this way: 'I, the greengrocer XY, live here and I know what I must do. I behave in the manner expected of me. I can be depended upon and am beyond reproach. I am obedient and therefore I have the right to be left in peace."[26] If the greengrocer refuses to comply with the ritual, he violates the socially sanctioned forms of normalcy.

Under post-totalitarian conditions, the individual is not expected to be an enthusiastic worshipper of the supreme leader. It is enough for him or her to endorse, by practicing them, the rules of systemic self-reproduction. With each greengrocer who abides by those rules, the system adds to its chance to endure. Certainly, if the greengrocer were asked to admit his subservient behavior publicly, to acknowledge that he is just bowing to the dictates of an anonymous power, he would consider such a demand unfair. He would argue that by simply displaying an innocuous slogan he is not adding to the suffering in the world. After all, the slogan has long since lost any uplifting meaning, and nobody takes it seriously any more. Its mere presence in the window guarantees the greengrocer's self-esteem: He does what the power wants him to do, but without publicly confessing his moral capitulation. He does not say: "I am weak and scared and terrified, and therefore I lie." He says: "I am just adhering, even in an abstract way, to a harmless cause. I do what I am supposed to do because it is not up to me to change the world."

The ideological camouflage of serfdom is the main underpinning of the post-totalitarian order.

> Thus the sign helps the greengrocer to conceal from himself the low foundations of his obedience, at the same time concealing the low foundations of power. It hides them behind the façade of something high. And that something is *ideology*. Ideology is a specious way of relating to the world. It offers human beings the illusion of an identity, of dignity, and of morality while making it easier to *part* with them. As the repository of something "supra-personal" and objective, it enables people to deceive their conscience and conceal their true position and their inglorious *modus vivendi*, both from the world and from themselves. It is a very pragmatic, but at the same time an apparently dignified, way of legitimizing what is above, below, and on either side. It is directed towards people and towards God. It is a veil behind which human beings can hide their own "fallen existence," their trivialization, and their adaptation to the status quo. It is an excuse that everyone can use, from the greengrocer, who conceals his fear of losing his job behind an alleged interest in the unification of the workers of the world, to the highest functionary, whose interest in staying in power can be cloaked in phrases about service to the working class. The primary excusatory function of ideology, therefore, is to provide people, both as victims and pillars of the post-totalitarian system, with the illusion that the system is in harmony with the human order and the order of the universe.[27]

Ideology is the substitute for naked terror, the pabulum offered by the system to its subjects in order to placate their doubts and convince them that theirs is the only rational behavior. With its contempt for the values of life, ideology can sanctify moral defeats and criminalize moral heroism. The creation of civil society in Eastern Europe included a rebellion against the mortifying role of ideology.

Civil society was an attempt to de-ideologize the public sphere, to wrest it from the pseudo-political form of manipulation that prevented the free exercise of the individual's basic rights. By defending the "real aims of life," civil society reconstructs the genuine sense of human solidarity and rejects a political system's universalistic pretense. In all the East European countries, the struggle for society's self-emancipation was waged in the name of the right to think and act differently. Whereas the system stakes its life on conformity, regimentation, and uniformity, civil society springs from creativity, originality, and singularity.

To expose the intrinsic mendacity at the foundation of the post-totalitarian system, of the "blind automatism" that ensures its self-reproduction, is one of the main purposes of an emerging civil society. Before offering an alternative to the existing order, it is necessary to understand the characteristics and the essence of the post-totalitarian order: It must be obvious that the times of show trials, of naked terror, are over; the system lacks authentic popular support—its ideology cannot arouse any form of mass fervor; and the system—based on inefficiency, waste of human energy, and immense corruption—still continues to exist, in spite of what common sense would suggest. Everyone is aware that the system is bankrupt, but few will openly break with it. According to Havel, the source of this systemic perpetuation lies in its ability to manipulate signs and symbols. The system is based, more than anything else, on semantic abuse:

> The post-totalitarian system touches people at every step, but is does so with its ideological gloves on. This is why life in the system is so thoroughly permeated with hypocrisy and lies: government by bureaucracy is called popular government; the working class is enslaved in the name of the working class; the complete degradation of the individual is presented as his or her ultimate liberation; depriving people of information is called making it available; the use of power to manipulate is called the public control of power, and the arbitrary abuse of power is called its development; the expansion of imperial influence is presented as support for the oppressed; the lack of free expression becomes the highest form of freedom; farcical elections become the highest form of democracy; banning indepen-

dent thought becomes the most scientific world view; military occupation becomes fraternal assistance. Because the regime is captive to its own lies, it must falsify everything. It falsifies the past. It falsifies the present, and it falsifies the future. It falsifies statistics. It pretends not to possess an omnipotent and unprincipled police apparatus. It pretends to respect human rights. It pretends to fear nothing. It pretends to pretend nothing.[28]

Havel's masterful analysis of the post-totalitarian era offers a clear, insightful explanation of the way the Brezhnevite system operated. The Brezhnevite system did not attack the individual in the traditional, brutal way. It made suffering less visible and tried to annihilate the distinction between victims and torturers. The distance between those two categories almost completely vanishes in a system where everybody is made to participate in the universal lie. It is precisely for that reason, because the lie is embedded in the very core of the established order, because it is its unique source of vitality, that the system must stick to the official doctrine regardless of its absolute and widely understood fallacies. The more absurd the ideological claims, the more important they are for the self-confidence of the power elite.

It is ideology that justifies the command economy, the limitation of individual rights, and the communist party's "predestined role." Without the ideological matrix, the system would simply fall apart. And indeed, at the moment ideological zeal ceased to be fortified by the irradiating power of the Soviet center, the East European regimes collapsed like so many houses of cards. Havel called the system of ideological norms, prohibitions, and limitations that ensured the prolongation of the post-totalitarian system a "metaphysical order":

> This metaphysical order is fundamental to, and standard throughout, the entire power structure; it integrates its communication system and makes possible the internal exchange and transfer of information and instructions. This metaphysical order guarantees the inner coherence of the totalitarian power structure. It is the glue holding it together, its binding principle, the instrument of its discipline. Without this glue the structure as a totalitarian structure would vanish; it would disintegrate into individual atoms chaotically colliding with one another in their unregulated particular interests and inclinations. The entire pyramid of totalitarian power, deprived of the element that binds it together, would collapse in upon itself, as it were, in a kind of material implosion.[29]

Such ideological fetishism is not based on any form of conviction. The symbols that justify the system must be endorsed through the practical behavior of individuals. They are not supposed to believe in these pseudo-values, and everyone knows that nobody is speaking the truth. Precisely this is the key to the post-totalitarian technique of domination: the make-believe, the simulation of conviction, the *as if* transformed into an all-embracing mechanism of self-delusion:

> Individuals need not believe all these mystifications, but they must behave as though they did, or they must at least tolerate them in silence, or get along well with those who work with them. For this reason, however, they must live *within a lie*. They need not accept the lie. It is enough for them to have accepted their life with it and in it. For by this very fact, individuals confirm the system, fulfill the system, make the system, *are* the system.[30]

The moral numbness of the population is the most important ally of post-totalitarian power. The system works as long as the prevailing lie is accepted and tolerated by the individual, as long as the average citizen, the greengrocer, continues to endorse the ideological nonsense although aware that all this verbiage is nothing but a collection of lies. The problem, therefore, is not simply to identify the source of oppression in the government but also to realize how each individual is tied to the power structure. Some are directly responsible for repressive measures, while others consecrate the status quo through their obedience and refusal to state the truth. According to Havel, the system's ability to turn its victims into accomplices makes post-totalitarianism different from classical dictatorships. The very idea of change has vanished, and the individuals try to come to terms with what appears to them to be the only possible form of life. They accept the system's demagogy; they repeat it and thereby strengthen it. This complicity is not rooted only in moral weakness, or careerism, or indifference, but also in despair about the chances of getting out of the existing order.

The schizophrenic post-totalitarian order has penetrated not only the institutional and sociological levels but also the psycho-emotional infrastructure of individuals. When the greengrocer displays the laughable slogan about proletarian unity, he is also sending a signal to the world that he does not see another way to have a normal life without this, after all, innocuous genuflection to official behests. But liberation starts at the individual level, as self-emancipation from the empire of lies and in the decision to live in truth. Emancipation, the birth of an alternative to the all-pervasive lie, comes not as an exogenous benefit bestowed by others, but at the moment when the individual, our friend the greengrocer, decides to put an end to what he sees as a grotesque form of self-denial.

The individual decides that he or she wants to live in accordance with his or her genuine beliefs and sentiments. He decides that he wants to live in truth. To be sure, at the moment the greengrocer ceases to put the slogan in the window, or later, when he opens his mouth and criticizes the rulers for their abuses, he antagonizes those who have not made up their minds and who are still hostage to the official lies. They spurn him and attack him for breaking the rules. He is the dissident who has dared to show that one is not doomed to be a slave forever, that it is up to the human being to assert his or her human qualities, even if this can lead to diminished status or other forms of marginalization.

The significance of the greengrocer's rebellion goes beyond the individual, and the system reacts accordingly, sensing the contagious impact of such behavior:

> The greengrocer has not committed a simple, individual offense, isolated in its own uniqueness, but something incomparably more serious. By breaking the rules of the game, he has disrupted the game as such. He has exposed it as a mere game. He has shattered the world of appearances, the fundamental pillar of the system. He has upset the power structure by tearing apart what holds it together. He has demonstrated that living a lie is living a lie. He has broken through the exalted façade of the system and exposed the real, base foundation of power. He has said that the emperor is naked. And because the emperor is in fact naked, something extremely dangerous has happened: by his action, the greengrocer has addressed the world. He has enabled everyone to peer behind the curtain. He has shown everyone that it *is* possible to live within the truth. Living within the lie can constitute the system only if it is universal. The principle must embrace and permeate everything. There are no terms whatsoever on which it can coexist with living within the truth, and therefore everyone who steps out of line *denies it in principle and threatens it in its entirety.*[31]

The greengrocer's awakening signifies a direct, unmistakable challenge to the system. Post-totalitarianism is based on the generalization of hypocrisy. Again, everybody knows that the system is rooted in a blatant, routinized lie, but saying so publicly is considered sheer madness. The greengrocer's gesture defies the taboos of the city; it institutes a different form of behavior that allows the individual to live in truth, which, for all intents and purposes, should simply mean to live. Because living within the lie means to mutilate life, to force oneself constantly to be at odds with one's own conscience, to be perpetually ashamed of one's self-deprecation.

The greengrocer's revolt represents, therefore, a seditious act. It undermines the most important pillar of the established order, its confidence that its subjects would be forced to lie forever:

> In the post-totalitarian system, therefore, living within the truth has more than a mere existential dimension (returning humanity to its inherent nature), or a noetic dimension (revealing reality as it is), or a moral dimension (setting an example for others). It also has an unambiguous *political* dimension. If the main pillar of the system is living a lie, then it is not surprising that the fundamental threat to it is living the truth. This is why it must be suppressed more severely than anything else."[32]

The decision by an individual to break the enchanted circle of complicity with the powers-that-be and to utter his own truth is the premise for the civil society to resurrect itself. Every single individual who takes that path adds to the possibility for the independent life of society to reorganize, to take shape in various forms and modalities. The system will of course try to slander him, to convince others that such behavior cannot be dictated by noble motives but is rather the expression of either a deranged mind or unfulfilled ambitions. The conflict between the repressive machine and the individual is of course unequal, and not many people are able to endure the hardships associated with the dissident's condition. The signatories of Charter 77, for instance, spent long years in prison, were assigned to menial jobs, and were systematically smeared and abused in the official media. But becoming politically active, being member of an unofficial civic initiative, is a further step that involves the crystallization of a political option. Although Charter 77 from the very outset made a point of its pluralist nature and refused to endorse a particular political philosophy, by its very existence it represented a political gesture. At the same time, as Havel insisted, living within the truth does not necessarily mean direct political commitment. The social impact of individual refusals to cooperate with the regime cannot be exaggerated. The starting point for such a divorce from the logic of conformity is the decision to stop lying. Expressing one's vision of reality, refusing to glorify the status quo and its mythological justification, and asserting one's spiritual freedom are forms of living within the truth that eventually collide with the monopolistic thrust of the system. Living within the truth does not have to be spectacular and does not necessarily include the dimension of martyrdom. Havel points out:

> When I speak of living within the truth, I naturally do not have in mind only products of conceptual thought, such as a protest or a letter written by a

group of intellectuals. It can be any means by which a person or a group revolts against manipulation: anything from a letter by intellectuals to a workers' strike, from a rock concert to a student demonstration, from refusing to vote in the farcical elections, to making an open speech at some official congress, or even a hunger strike, for instance. If the suppression of the aims of life is a complex process, and if it is based on the multifaceted manipulation of all expressions of life, then, by the same token, every free expression of life indirectly threatens the post-totalitarian system politically, including forms of expression to which, in other social systems, no one would attribute any potential political significance, not to mention explosive power.[33]

The authorities' response to the challenges of the burgeoning civil societies in the 1970s and 1980s differed from country to country. The chances for grassroots initiatives to develop were greater in Janos Kadar's Hungary or in Edward Gierek's Poland than in Gustav Husak's Czechoslovakia or Nicolae Ceausescu's Romania. Furthermore, after Gorbachev started his policies of glasnost and perestroika, civic activists in the Warsaw Pact countries saw the Soviet renewal movement as a great chance to advance change in their own countries. When the Soviet leader visited the GDR in 1987, young East Germans acclaimed him not only because they happened to admire his politics but also as a way of expressing their discontent with the conservative line followed by Erich Honecker and his comrades in the SED leadership. In Romania, where Ceausescu made being different from the Soviets a mark of honor, Gorbachev's reforms were officially criticized and the communist party tightened its grip on all strata of society. Opposition in that country had to be individual because of the ubiquitous security police presence and Ceausescu's morbid reaction to the slightest form of criticism. But even in such a country living within the truth was not impossible. Activists like Radu Filipescu (a young engineer in Bucharest who disseminated anti-Ceausescu leaflets) and Doina Cornea (a university lecturer in Cluj who sent Ceausescu countless memoranda protesting his disastrous course) showed that even in the most unfavorable circumstances one could still act like a human being. Those who engaged in such defiant acts in Romania or Bulgaria were of course subjected to harsher treatment than their peers in more tolerant Soviet-style regimes. The absence in Romania of organic movements like Solidarity or even of intellectual initiatives like Charter 77 should not lead to the conclusion that the independent life of society had been completely suppressed. Such an absolute destruction is, after all, impossible.

Even in Albania, the most secluded Stalinist fortress in Eastern Europe, once the totalitarian terror subsided in 1989–90, student protests and other forms of activism exploded.

When discussing the odyssey of civil society in Eastern Europe, it is important to consider the concrete political circumstances under which those efforts to create independent communities had to be undertaken: from a Kadar-like "enlightened despotism" to a Ceausescu-like ethnocentric and paranoid dictatorship. Havel correctly points out that in dealing with the development of civil society in different countries, two criteria must be kept in mind. First, when assessing the impact of the independent activities, do not approach them in a strictly comparative way (how one country fares compared to another one) but in light of the existing conditions in the given country:

> What may appear, from another country, as a very modest, limited, and cautious kind of independence may not necessarily seem that way on the spot. An example: if a Romanian publicly criticizes conditions in his country, the measure of his independence may appear rather low and insignificant from the point of view of the Hungarian situation and its possibilities, whereas in Romania it may be endowed with an almost explosive power. Thus an expression of activity that in one country or at a given moment in time could easily go unnoticed among many analogous and more thoroughgoing expressions or actions, may in another country and at another moment practically shake society at its roots.[34]

Second, the social significance of such activities is not necessarily reflected in the numbers of people involved in them:

> The point is that around these activities there always exists a field of hidden influence, the potential significance of which cannot always necessarily flow from the size of the phenomenon that produced it. It is true that there are not many Chartists, but a large part of society knows about their work (or at least a large part of that part of society that continues to be interested in public affairs and which may therefore be said to "make history", at the very least they know about it from foreign radio broadcasts.)[35]

Commitment to the cause of moral regeneration of society is not motivated by expectations of immediate effects. On the contrary, the idea of social self-organization involves a long-term strategy, the "long march" against the official structures, the building of parallel ones, first at low levels of informal communication, and later through the increasing expansion of these initiatives from below into a genuine social movement.

That has happened in Poland, for instance, where the KOR initially comprised a tiny group of civic-minded activists who managed to capture the expectations, hopes, and aspirations of society at large.

When the social explosion of August 1980 occurred, KOR, with its moral authority, could provide the Solidarity movement with strategic concepts and political expertise. One cannot underestimate the pedagogical value of such nuclei of people who decide to live within the truth. It is not that they are absolutely independent from official society. As long as the state is the only employer and all forms of social behavior, from shopping to education, are state-controlled, it is impossible to be absolutely independent. But what is possible is to fight for the expansion of the margin of autonomy for the individual, or, better said, the reduction of his or her subservience to the state. As Havel put it:

> [I]t is probably not true that there is a small enclave of "completely independent" people here in an ocean of "completely dependent people" with no interaction between them. There is an enclave of "relatively independent" ones who persistently, gradually and inconspicuously enrich their "relatively dependent" surroundings through the spiritually liberating and morally challenging meaning of their own independence, thus strengthening in those surroundings that small sphere of independence that remains or that it has been able to preserve.[36]

Indeed, when the political situation of 1989 evolved in Czechoslovakia and the power elite started increasingly to show signs of disarray, Charter 77 became the magnet for those individuals who had postponed their break with the system.

The existence of Charter 77 was more important in Czechoslovakia's "velvet revolution" than the reformist dreams of the former leaders of the Prague Spring. After all, the ultimate limit upon Dubcekism (and of Gorbachevism, for that matter) was the failure to abandon the rusty Leninist paradigm and to transfer power from the party elite to society. After more than forty years of fanaticism and indoctrination, when people had been saturated with ideological lies, there is a general distrust in the entire region regarding any salvationist creed. In Czechoslovakia in 1989 it became clear that there was no social pressure for the resumption of the experiment with socialism with a human face and that the direction of the revolution had to transcend the mere desire for liberalization. Through its transideological nature, Charter 77 anticipated a new form of politics, characteristic of the postcommunist order: the civil society. If nothing else, Charter 77 embodied the idea of tolerance, and it was this opening to the spirit of dialogue, so salient in Havel's writings and public activities, that made Charter 77 both credible and instrumental in the peaceful transition to pluralism. Like KOR in Poland, the Initiative for Peace and Human Rights in the GDR (a movement that developed in the mid-1980s), the Moscow Trust Group in the Soviet Union, or the Democratic Opposition in Hungary, Charter 77 symbolized the politics of trust, hope, and human solidarity. Elevating the defense of human rights to their chief concern, those movements subverted the system at its weakest spot. They showed that it was possible to hold the rulers account-able for their misdeeds and that such monitoring could have an impact on the government's behavior (if for no other reason, because of interna-tional pressure).

With the benefit of hindsight, activities like those of KOR and Charter 77 appear strategically coherent and historically effective. They led to extraordinary transformations in those societies and created the embryo of the counterpower that was to replace the crumbling commu-nist regimes during the 1989 upheaval. For in its strategy, the civil society rejects the communist party's claim to a leading role and aims to promote genuine pluralism. But at the beginnings of the civil society saga in Eastern Europe, at the moment people like Havel and Michnik started their activities, there was very little reason to expect those regimes to collapse in the foreseeable future. Even such an astute observer of the East European situation as Timothy Garton Ash supposed that the most likely scenario for the future of the region would be further decay and decomposition of the regimes in the form of "Ottomanization." Others, like Milan Kundera, had completely written off the historical signifi-cance of Eastern Europe for the world. Yet civic activists in the region understood that their gestures were bound to irritate the power and that by simply rejecting the official form of politics, by denouncing it as a fraud, they were embarking on a new form of politics. Their moral protest had an explosive political implication, in that it articulated the strategy of nonviolent resistance to the system's attempt to reduce the individual to a submissive, totally pliable entity.

Charter 77 demonstrated that the issues to be advocated by the new movements did not necessarily have to be political. It is not the goal of an informal association of people who have decided to live within the truth to challenge a dictatorship directly. Their opposition is first and foremost moral: They expose the immorality of the government, the discrepancy between its rhetoric and the reality of everyday life. The first act of Charter 77 was to protest the trial organized by the Husak regime against a group of young rock musicians called "The Plastic People of the

Universe." It became clear that defending the young musicians who simply wanted to live within their own truth (which was of course different from the officially dictated truth) was already a politically charged action. Taking the side of the rock musicians had nothing to do with any aesthetic preference. It was a way of denying the system its right to determine the limits of human freedom. In sending people to jail simply because of artistic heresy, the system proclaimed its right to interfere at any time and without any hesitation in individuals' lives. It was a public declaration of war against human freedom. Consequently, defending the young rock musicians meant defending the very idea of human freedom and dignity. The same can be said about the defense of pacifists or ecological activists persecuted because of their opposition to official militarism and irrational destruction of the environment. As Havel said, the revolt of the powerless does not have an explicit political dimension. The politics of antipolitics consists precisely in this discreet, unobtrusive attempt to restore the dignity of the individual:

> [I]n the post-totalitarian system, the real background of the movements that gradually assume political significance does not usually consist of overtly political events of confrontations between different forces or concepts that are openly political. These movements for the most part originate elsewhere, in the far broader area of the "pre-political," where "living within a lie" confronts "living within the truth," that is, where the demands of the post-totalitarian system conflict with the real aims of life. . . . Such a conflict acquires a political character, then, not because of the elementary political nature of the aims demanding to be heard but simply because, given the complex system of manipulation on which the post-totalitarian system is founded and on which it is also dependent, every free human act or expression, every attempt to live within the truth, must necessarily appear as a threat to the system and, thus, as something which is political par excellence.[37]

The ritualization of politics in the official sphere, its bastardization through the continuous deformation of facts, and the imposition of pseudo-elites whose rise to prominence is guaranteed by criteria linked to docility, conformity, and obedience rather than to imagination, intelligence, and honor contribute to the fall into disrepute of the very term politics.

In post-totalitarian systems politics is widely seen as as the profession for lackeys. Those who value human freedoms would engage in any other activity, from music to occultism, from Zen Budhism to ikebana, from jazz to transcendental meditation. The general sentiment seems to be that politics has been forever annexed by evil forces, that there is nothing good to be expected from professional politicians, while the leaders of the dissident movement are writers, poets, physicists, or philosophers. The reinvention of politics must therefore take place outside the officially drawn boundaries of politics. This ethical insurrection takes place in what Havel calls "the real sphere of potential politics in the post-totalitarian system." It is outside the perverse and perverting circle of power that politics acquires its new figures, stripped of ideological blinders.

The antipolitics advocated by East European dissidents repudiates the dominant principle of reality as a mere mystification. In the words of the Hungarian writer György Konrad, author of a number of excellent novels including *The Loser* and *The Case Worker* and a provocative essay significantly entitled *Antipolitics:*

> Antipolitics is the political activity of those who don't want to be politicians and who refuse to share in power. Antipolitics is the emergence of independent forums that can be appealed to against political power; it is a counter-power that cannot take power and does not wish to. Power it has already, here and now, by reason of its moral and cultural weight. . . . Antipolitics and government work in two different dimensions, two separate spheres. Antipolitics neither supports nor opposes the government; it is something different. Its people are fine right where they are; they form a network that keeps watch on political power, exerting pressure on the basis of their cultural and moral stature alone, not through an electoral legitimacy. That is their right and their obligation, but above all it is their self-defense.[38]

Konrad's statement carries to an extreme the widespread East European disgust with what can be called the imperialism of politics, or the politicization of all spheres of life. In his view, the practice of antipolitics, the art of democratic opposition, must be conducted to limit the government's interference in the individual's private affairs. So civil society is also a strategy for restoring the forms of human cooperation and communication that exist outside the state's controls:

> Because politics has flooded nearly every nook and cranny of our lives, I would like to see the flood recede. We ought to depoliticize our lives, free them from politics as from some contagious infection. We ought to free our simple everyday affairs from considerations of politics. I ask that the state do what it's supposed to do, and do it well. But it should not do things that are society's business, not the state's. So I would describe the democratic opposition as not a political but an antipolitical opposition, since its essential activity is to work for destatification.[39]

Antipolitics becomes a galvanizing principle, a collective effort to limit the state's grip on society and to restore the individual's rights as the ultimate and absolutely nonnegotiable value:

> The ideology of the democratic opposition shares with religion a belief that the dignity of the individual personality (in both oneself and the other person) is a fundamental value not requiring any further demonstration. The autonomy and solidarity of human beings are the two basic and mutually complementary values to which the democratic movement relates other values. . . . The culture of autonomy protests against making any human institution superior to the dignity of individual human beings. Whenever the state, or some power bloc, or the world market comes to be regarded as an absolute value, this opposition will appear, invoking the European tradition in order to demonstrate that this allegedly supreme value is really far from universal, and is in fact only the special interest of a certain group of people. It is precisely this critique of ideology that offers the Eastern European democratic opposition a way to contribute to the culture of self-determination for the individuals, for groups, for the nation, and for the continent as a whole.[40]

DISSENT IN POST-TOTALITARIAN SOCIETIES

If opposition to the state that has become the absolute value is inevitable, who are these dissidents who dare to challenge the system and propose a different set of values rooted in respect for truth and human dignity? The term dissident was coined by Western journalists, and many critics of the Soviet-bloc societies had expressed reservations about its relevance. If people like Vaclav Havel or Jan Patocka in Czechoslovakia, György Konrad or Miklos Haraszti in Hungary, Paul Goma or Dorin Tudoran in Romania, Robert Havemann or Wolf Biermann in the GDR, or somebody like Milovan Djilas in Yugoslavia, who anticipated the emergence of dissent as an international movement, are the paradigms, it is clear that more often than not dissidents are critical intellectuals who have reached the conclusion that silence means complicity with the system. According to Havel, dissidents can be identified in the light of the following criteria:

> First, they voice their critical views in a consistent and systematic way, "within the very strict limits available to them, and because of this, they are known in the West." Second, because of their moral stances and precisely because of being denied basic human rights, the dissidents enjoy

a special form of public esteem. Although this respect is rarely manifested in spectacular gestures, the authorities are aware of the popularity of the dissidents and avoid to engage in savage repression against them (or, if they do this, they can expect political complications to follow, including in the international relations). And third, as we have seen dissidents are people inclined to articulate their ideas in a written form: They are people who lean toward intellectual pursuits, that is, they are "writing" people, people for whom the written word is the primary—and often the only— political medium they command, and that gains them attention, particularly from abroad.[41]

In his book *The Velvet Prison*, Miklos Haraszti, one of Hungary's foremost dissident thinkers, explained the ways intellectuals can become dissidents. His book is particularly important in that it deals with the Kadar experiment of "benign dictatorship." The essence of the Kadarist compromise was a silent pact between the power and the society. The regime offered material benefits and a limited range of autonomy so long as society did not dispute the paternalist privileges of the regime, including its right to confiscate memory, slander the 1956 Revolution, and consider any discussion on the nature of Soviet– Hungarian relations unacceptable. Ironically adopting the viewpoint of the co-opted artist, Haraszti's book sounds extremely skeptical. He seems to say that only incurable romantics can engage in direct opposition to a regime that, because of its politics of soft repression, has almost completely annihilated the source of critical activism. Dissidents appear therefore as alien elements in a continuum dominated by conformity and resignation:

> These rare birds are in fact the intellectual progeny of a vanquished civilization whose promise of democracy, individualism and critical thought has left a lingering, though fading, trace. Natives of the new culture, they can only have heard of the old one in a muted fashion. Their fealty to the old—and obstinacy in the face of the new—betrays their real origins. . . . These picturesque orphans herald nothing but their own demise; they are representatives of a dying species, unable to reproduce themselves in the new world that is rapidly rendering them extinct.[42]

Written before the rise of Solidarity, Haraszti's book gave voice to the sense of isolation and even hopelessness experienced by the beleaguered dissident minorities in Eastern Europe. In its melancholy one can detect the author's fear that simulated obedience to the all-embracing official

ideology, with its hypocrisy and self-serving rhetoric, had managed to
become second nature:

> Our ideological conformism does not, of course, prevent us from smiling
> when encountering the dogma. Often, bureaucrats and artists laugh to-
> gether. Enlightened as we are, we consider the liturgy to be sign of narrow-
> mindedness—an idolatry, a childish extremism when compared with our
> natural, simple discipline imbibed since infancy. But our cynicism is a
> conceit that has no effect on our behavior. Marxism is still the foundation-
> myth of our notion of civic responsibility. It is the legend that legitimates
> our ideas of service to the people. It is a comfortable euphemism, like the
> ever-popular story of the stork told to the children. [43]

Haraszti's state artist is the embodiment of the closed universe: There
is no mobility there, no sense of transcendence. All is happening as if the
party has established its domination forever and any opposition is a form
of quixotic (or irresponsible) daydreaming. Kadar's simulated tolerance
did not affect the ultimate reality of the system. Power still lay with the
communist *nomenklatura*, who, in this particular case, had learned to
cajole the intellectuals and cultivate their narcissism. But, as the party
ideologue György Aczel once put it: "The formulation of the rules of the
game, of the essential conditions, and legal supervisory powers (use of the
veto in certain matters) naturally continue to be within the competence
of the socialist state."[44] In such circumstances of ostensible universal
integration, when all opposition nuclei seem to be extinct, how can an
individual maintain autonomy? According to Haraszti's imaginary state
artist, ready to justify his own compromises by denying the meaning of
alternative forms of conduct: "In our civilization there are only two kinds
of dissidents: Naïve Heroes and Maverick Artists. Both are doomed to
irrelevance."[45] Yet Haraszti's sad comments are not a dismissal of dissident
behavior. The author confessed several years after the book was written:

> I hope that I don't have to defend my treatment of dissent in this book. I
> intended the very existence of this book to be a denial of its deliberate
> exaggerations. I hope that its publication is a proof that refutes the despair
> that darkens its sentences. For this reason I chose to speak mostly in the
> third person, in the voice of a state artist, rather than joining the chorus of
> my own natural compatriots in the ghetto of romantic individualism. [46]

The fate of the dissidents is to be continuously mocked at by the self-
satisfied state intellectuals, perfectly adjusted to the existing order and
enjoying the benefits flowing from their subservience.

From the viewpoint of the institutional monolith represented by a state's culture, dissidents are troublemakers sticking to anachronistic ideas of individual freedoms. They must exist at the margin of society, the state artist thinks, because the new civilization cannot, and does not wish to, incorporate them. Some of their ideas can be integrated in the official dogma, but certainly deprived of their explosive meaning. An example is the appropriation by the party ideology in the Soviet Union of the term *glasnost,* long the slogan of the samizdat democratic movement. Likewise, the Kadar-like reformist regimes knew how to appropriate and thereby emasculate terms like pluralism, dialogue, openness, and other lofty ideals championed by the dissidents.

> According to one Hungarian saying, if Solzhenitsyn had lived in Hungary, he would have been appointed president of the Writer's Union . . . given time. And then no one would have written *The Gulag Archipelago*; and if someone had, Solzhenitsyn would have voted for his expulsion. This is the climate of opinion in the culture of "progressive censorship." We consider as unacceptable extremes both the state that is unable to reform and the artist that is unable to conform.[47]

Haraszti's mordant irony deconstructs the rationalizations of the cultural bureaucrat, the intellectual turned into a servant of the state. For him, the nobility of the dissident's refusal to accept humiliation is indicative of a fatal psychological deformity. But, as marginalized as they are by the cultural industry of state socialism, dissidents are still denied the right to be totally different. The state reserves for itself not only the right to punish them but also the right to "reconsider" them once a change in the "party line" has occurred and a new leader comes to power with a different set of promises. Haraszti's character—whose thoughts are not the author's—regards the dissidents as "necessary" for the completeness of the new look of post-totalitarian communism:

> An era of greater generosity is about to dawn. Just as in ancient, long-enduring empires, renegade mandarins might establish taoist monasteries. Similarly, the modern socialist state regards its diehard dissidents as members of a monstrous, weird, misanthropic sect, disenchanted with educating the people . . . but nonetheless essentially innocent and, indeed, not without their uses. . . . Later, of course, some of them will be "rediscovered" and "rehabilitated." Such decisions will be reached by the central authorities. Amnesties are issued when a new ruler is installed. Almost all dissidents can count on becoming part of the official curricu-

lum when the time has come to denounce the failures of the previous dynasty.[48]

When Haraszti wrote his book in the early 1980s, Hungary appeared to be the most advanced country in the Soviet bloc in terms of domestic liberalization. Compared with Romania, East Germany, and Czechoslovakia, dissidents were treated with kid gloves, although the state machine did not spare efforts to thwart their efforts to get out of the political ghetto and establish contacts with the larger society. The underground presses were systematically ransacked by the police, dissidents were interrogated and even beaten up. The regime avoided, however, massive organized crackdowns. As the economic situation deteriorated and the changes in the USSR spurred higher political expectations, Kadar's Hungary ceased to be "the most joyful barrack in the socialist camp." Its youth were radicalized, and the democratic opposition became a national political force. Far from being assigned to eternal marginality, dissidents, Haraszti included, became the architects of the transition to postcommunism. Actually, in the postscript to his book, written in 1987, Haraszti admitted that the changes introduced by Gorbachev in the functioning of the Soviet system and the new wave of de-Stalinization made some of his gloomy predictions invalid. But, at the same time, he insisted that Gorbachevism represented an adoption by the Soviet elite of the same techniques that had ensured the partial success of the "velvet prison" experiment undertaken by Hungary under Kadar:

> I have called this model the "post-Stalinist" or "soft" or "civilian" version of Communist rule, in contradistinction to the "Stalinist" or "hard" or "military" style. . . . Indeed, the Hungarian model might well represent a more rational, more normative, and more enduring version of directed culture. Mr. Gorbachev understands that in order to have a truly successful society with a modern economy he must boost the intelligentsia's sagging morale by giving it a stake in administering the future.[49]

FIVE

The Ethos of Civil Society

> Antipolitics strives to put politics in its
> place and make sure that it stays there,
> never overstepping its proper office of
> defending and refining the rules of the
> game of civil society. Antipolitics is the
> ethos of civil society, and civil society is
> the antithesis of military society.
>
> —*György Konrad*

The development of civil societies in the states of the Soviet bloc cannot be separated from the existence of autonomous centers of independent thought. Living within the truth, although often seen as a gesture of moral idealism with little social significance, has turned out to be the driving force behind the creation of alternative ways of thinking and acting. It is thus clear that the foundation stone of the countersociety is the individual's decision to proclaim his or her mental independence. In Havel's words: "What is this independent life of society? The spectrum of its expressions and activities is naturally very wide. It includes everything from self-education and thinking about the world, through free creative activity and its communication to others, to the most varied free, civic initiatives, including instances of independent social self-organization."[1] The new politics, which relies on informal citizens' initiatives as an antidote to the paralyzing pressure of the bureaucratic Leviathan, which encourages the emergence of multifaceted experiments in grassroots activism, and which maintains that change comes from spontaneous movements from below rather than from munificent concessions from above, resulted in the development of civil societies in Poland, Hungary, and Czechoslovakia.

Initially, it seemed that there was no reason to believe that the governing colossus could be removed or forced to change, but as the situation evolved and more people embarked on such independent initiatives, it appeared that society had become a legitimate actor on the political stage. To the surprise of the communist bureaucrats, societies had found their spokesmen in precisely those long-harassed dissidents who had turned down the system's offer to cooperate. Because the whole strategy of the civil society is rooted in the belief that only the restoration of the independent life of society can guarantee the peaceful transition to a democratic order, such a strategy goes beyond the simplistic pragmatism of those who advocate the supremacy of traditional politics.

> There are times when we must sink to the bottom of our misery to understand truth, just as we must descend to the bottom of a well to see the stars in broad daylight. It seems to me that today, this "provisional," "minimal," and "negative" programme—the "simple" defense of people—is in a particular sense (and not only in the circumstances in which we live) an optimal and most positive programme because it forces politics to return to its only proper starting point, proper that is, if all the old mistakes are to be avoided: individual people.[2]

In countries like Hungary, Poland, Czechoslovakia, and even the more repressive GDR, dissident nuclei started as tiny communities of like-minded individuals. They included people who resented and decided to resist the system's encroachment on a citizen's inner life and protest any form of infringement on the universally recognized human rights. In Havel's words:

> In the "dissident movements" of the Soviet bloc, the defense of human beings usually takes the form of a defense of human and civil rights as they are entrenched in various official documents such as the Universal Declaration of Human Rights, the International Covenants on Human Rights, the Final Act of the Helsinki Conference, and the constitutions of individual states. These movements set out to defend anyone who is being prosecuted for acting in the spirit of those rights, and they in turn act in the same spirit in their work, by insisting over and over again that the regime recognize and respect human and civil rights, and by drawing attention to the areas of life where this is not the case.[3]

The dissident movements made a clear point of their opposition to violence. They realized that the reconstruction of the independent life could not take place in the name of resentment and revenge, but precisely by emphasizing the values of human solidarity the system held in deep contempt. As Adam Michnik pointed out in an essay he wrote while in jail in 1982: "The essence of the programs put forward by the opposition groups . . . lay in the attempt to reconstruct society, to restore social bonds outside official institutions."[4] The ethos of the dissident movements rejected the cult of violence as counterproductive and morally incompatible with the idealistic goals of those initiatives from below.

While the system contained violence in its own structure and in all its modalities of functioning, the opposition argued that its own moral superiority stemmed precisely from its refusal to share the same exclusive, militaristic logic with the rulers. Michnik luminously explained this concept in an essay he wrote in the Gdansk prison in 1985:

> People who claim that the use of force in the struggle for freedom is necessary must first prove that, in a given situation, it will be effective, and that force, when it is used, will not transform the idea of liberty into its opposite. No one in Poland is able to prove today that violence will help us to dislodge Soviet troops from Poland and to remove the communists from power. The USSR has such enormous military power that confrontation is simply unthinkable. In other words: we have no guns. . . . In our reasoning, pragmatism is inseparably intertwined with idealism. Taught by history, we suspect that by using force to storm the existing Bastilles we shall unwittingly build new ones. It is true that social change is almost always accompanied by force. But it is not true that social change is merely a result of the violent collision of various forces. Above all, social changes follow from a confrontation of different moralities and visions of social order. Before the violence of rulers clashes with the violence of their subjects, values and systems of ethics clash inside human minds.[5]

The civil society is strategically opposed to any dictatorial temptations. It is suspicious of those who claim to have ultimate answers to all human dilemmas and regards traditional ideological distinctions between right and left as irrelevant under the existing circumstances. Rereading Michnik's statement on this issue, especially in the light of post-1989 developments in Eastern Europe, one sees that the idealist ardor of the dissident movements included more than a grain of wishful thinking.

Totalitarian dictatorship suspended rather than annulled ideological divisions. Liberals and conservatives, secular humanists and radical nationalists had to freeze their disagreements because they had a common enemy in the communist regime. That did not mean they had abandoned their creeds. But in 1985, when the system seemed more determined than ever to cling to its power, Michnik's thesis sounded quite convincing:

> I think that in Poland the conflict between the right and the left belongs to the past. It used to divide a society that was torn by struggles for bourgeois freedoms, universal voting rights, land reform, secularization, the eight-hour workday, welfare, universal schooling, or the democratization of culture. A different distinction comes to the fore in the era of totalitarian dictatorships: one between the proponents of an open society and the proponents of a closed society. In the former, social order is based on self-government and collective agreements; in the latter, order is achieved through repression and discipline.[6]

Charter 77 in Czechoslovakia symbolized that attempt to overcome ideological segregation through a new approach rooted in the consideration of human rights as the most important foundation of a free society. In its founding document, the Chartists declared that the responsibility for preserving civil rights rests not only with the governments but also "with each and every individual." Precisely because they believed in the sharing of responsibility, the Chartists constituted themselves into an open association whose commitment to the defense of human rights transcended any ideological, religious, or political differences among the signatories:

> Charter 77 is a free, informal, and open community in which various convictions, religions, and professions coexist. Its members are linked by the desire to work individually and collectively for human and civil rights in Czechoslovakia and the whole world. These rights are guaranteed by the final agreements of the 1975 Helsinki Conference and other international treaties against war, violence, and repression. Thus Charter 77 is based on the solidarity and friendship of all people who share a concern for certain ideals.[7]

The Charter's deliberate loose structure indicated the antihierarchical and anti-authoritarian orientation of the group. The founding document insisted that Charter was not an organization: "It has no statutes, permanent organs, or registered membership. Everyone who agrees with its ideas and works to realize them belongs to it."[8]

Charter made clear that it did not constitute itself as an alternative to the existing power, as a political party interested in power and the pursuit of its own strategies. The denial of its political character was, of course, linked to the regime's obsession with any form of criticism. In the conditions of "normalized socialism" in Czechoslovakia, any form of independent political activism could be labeled "subversive" and could land its practitioners in jail. At the same time, the statement indicated Charter's broader understanding of the realm of politics as the sphere where citizens work together in the construction of the public good. It was a way of announcing to the rulers that, while the new movement would not interfere with the vitiated, deformed area of official politics, it would do its best to restore the dignity of autonomous initiatives. This statement is therefore emblematic for the philosophy of antipolitics, which should not be confused with escapism but should rather be understood as a reassertion of civic rights and a form of resistance to the degradation of politics in the post-totalitarian state:

> Charter 77 does not constitute an organized political opposition. It only supports the common good, as do many similar organizations that promote civic initiative in both the East and the West. It has no intention of outlining specific and radical programs for political and social reform but tries instead to initiate a constructive dialogue with political and state authorities, particularly by drawing attention to specific violations of civil and human rights—by documenting them, suggesting solutions, submitting general proposals to ensure that these rights are respected in the future, and acting as a mediator in disputes between citizens and the state.[9]

Like the KOR or the Hungarian samizdat opposition, Charter 77 viewed violent opposition to the communist regime as a political dead end. Those movements considered that, hypocritical as they certainly were, the legal systems of the post-totalitarian regimes had to be exploited to further the cause of human rights. The civil society reemerged by using the loopholes in the system's structure by challenging the rulers to abide by their own promises and pledges. In the struggle new forms of association and new types of communities emerge, including the independent peace and ecological groups, the underground publishing houses, the flying universities, and all other expressions of what the Czechoslovak human rights activist called the "second culture." That those attempts met the repressive response of the system was not surprising. At the same time, those engaged in such activities knew that their efforts would not have any social meaning unless the parallel structures communicated, penetrated, and influenced the "official" ones. Havel warned against any elitism on the part of the emerging informal communities:

> [I]t would be quite wrong to understand the parallel structures and the parallel *polis* as a retreat into a ghetto and as an act of isolation, addressing

itself only to the welfare of those who had decided on such a course, and who are indifferent to the rest. . . . [E]ven the most highly mature form of the parallel *polis* can only exist—at least in post-totalitarian circumstances—when the individual is at the same time lodged in the "first," official structure by a thousand different relationships, even though it may only be the fact that one buys what one needs in their stores, uses their money and obeys their laws.[10]

The dissident, by the very fact that he or she challenged the prevailing universe of norms, habits, taboos, and prejudices, proposed a sense of human identity rooted in the notion of responsibility. If the system aimed to convince the individual that the existing reality was the only possible one, the new movements argued that there was nothing absolutely foreordained in human destiny, and that no mechanical determinism could compel the individual to accept the status quo slavishly. In one of the letters he sent from prison to his wife Olga, Vaclav Havel wrote:

The problem of human identity remains at the center of my thinking about human affairs. If I use the word "identity," it is not because I believe it explains anything about the secret of human existence; I began using it when I was developing my plays, or thinking about them later, because it helped me clarify the ramifications of the theme that most attracted me: "the crisis of human identity." All my plays in fact are variations on this theme, the disintegration of one's oneness with himself and the loss of everything that gives human existence a meaningful order, continuity, and its unique solution. At the same time . . . the importance of the notion of human responsibility has grown in my meditations. It has begun to appear, with increasing clarity, as the fundamental point from which all identity grows and by which it stands or falls; it is the foundation, the root, the center of gravity, the constructional principle or axis of identity, something like the "idea" that determines its degree and type. It is the mortar binding it together, and when the mortar dries out, identity too begins irreversibly to crumble and fall apart.

From this rediscovery of the relationship between the integrity of personality and the ethos of civic duty, Havel could draw the following memorable conclusion: The "secret of man is the secret of his responsibility."[11]

Likewise, the new movements were exactly the opposite of the official vision of politics: While the communist elites were exclusive and intolerant, the civil society championed openness, dialogue, and tolerance. In 1986, responding to questions sent to him by the exiled Czech journalist Karel Hvizdala, Havel offered extensive answers pondering the

meaning of his artistic and political experiences. The result of that exchange was a fascinating memoir, a book that shed revealing light on the
significance of dissent as the first step in the reconstruction of a public
sphere based on trust and solidarity. Referring to the deliberately nonideo-
logical nature of Charter 77, Havel wrote:

> Perhaps I should say something more about plurality within the Charter. It
> was not easy for everyone—many had to suppress or overcome their an-
> cient inner aversions—but everyone was able to do it, because we all felt
> that it was in a common cause, and because something had taken shape
> here that was historically quite new: the embryo of a genuine social toler-
> ance (and not simply an agreement among some to exclude others, as was
> the case with the National Front government after the Second World
> War), a phenomenon which—no matter how the Charter turned out—
> would be impossible to wipe out the national memory. It would remain in
> that memory as a challenge that, at any time and in any new situation,
> could be responded to and drawn on.[12]

The role of the new movements is to convince the average citizen, the
greengrocers who support the system in an inertial way because they
cannot envision any alternative to it, that change is indeed possible even
under such abysmal conditions as those of the post-totalitarian state.

That hope should not be abandoned is the message conveyed by all
people engaged in the rebuilding of civil societies in Eastern Europe:

> Hope, in this deep and powerful sense, is not the same as joy that things
> are going well, or willingness to invest in enterprises that are obviously
> headed for early success, but, rather, an ability to work for something
> because it is good, not just because it stands a chance to succeed. The
> more unpropitious the situation in which we demonstrate hope, the deeper
> that hope is. Hope is definitely not the same thing as optimism. It is not
> the conviction that something will turn out well, but the certainty that
> something makes sense, regardless of how it turns out. In short, I think
> that the deepest and the most important form of hope, the only one that
> can keep us above water and urge us to do good works, and the only true
> source of the breathtaking dimension of the human spirit and its efforts, is
> something we get, as it were, from "elsewhere." It is also this hope, above
> all, which gives us the strength to live and continually to try new things,
> even in conditions that seem as hopeless as ours do, here and now.[13]

One should recollect the conditions in Eastern Europe in the first years
after Gorbachev's coming to power, when there were no indications that

the new Soviet leader could engage in anything but a streamlining of the existing system. Most analysts of Soviet affairs could not predict the dramatic changes in the Soviet concept of intrabloc solidarity. The signals coming from Moscow were generally indicative of the Kremlin's interest in replacing the old East European leaders with new ones, recruited from the same communist elites. The most people could expect in terms of Soviet benevolence was support for communist reformers. [14]

People like Adam Michnik in Poland, Janos Kis in Hungary, and Havel in Czechoslovakia admitted that the changes in the Soviet Union and their impact on the local situation in each East European country were critically important. Yet those thinkers refused to pin all their hopes on the good will of an enlightened czar. Changes, if they were to be fundamental, had to go beyond the visible locus of power. Their source had to be in the reawakening of society, in the collective pressure exerted by autonomous groups and movements, including even certain wings within the ruling elite, on the power-holders to get out of the obsolete system and allow social innovation. Responding to those who pinned all their hopes on Gorbachev's intention to modernize the system and allow genuine reforms, Havel insisted that for the changes to be authentic, for them to result in the detotalization of society, society itself had to be involved in their initiation. More clearly, to those who saw the struggle between doves and hawks, or between liberals and conservatives in the communist Politburos as the generator of political pluralism, Havel and other East European thinkers counterposed the vision of the civil society and its slow but uncontainable growth. The good will of the best general secretary cannot replace the system—it can only make it more bearable. For politics to rediscover its emancipatory dimension, for the individual to cease being treated as a means by those who think they have been designated by history to rule and oppress others without any accountability, a resurrection of the society as a mature and conscious partner in the exercise of government was needed:

> I leave to those more qualified to decide what can be expected from Gorbachev and, in general, "from above"—that is, from what is happening in the sphere of power. I have never fixed my hopes there; I've always been more interested in what was happening "below," in what could be expected "from below," what could be won there, and what defended. All power is power over someone, and it always somehow responds, usually unwittingly rather than deliberately, to the state of mind and the behavior of those it rules over. One can always find in the behavior of power a reflection of what is going on "below." No one can govern in a vacuum. [15]

Civil society, although encountering the resistance of the entrenched apparatus, fills the vacuum and is the place where this new understanding of politics takes place. For example, in Czechoslovakia, where Husak and Jakes had gone out of their way to erase the memory of the Prague Spring and instill in the population the feeling of complete dereliction, the example of the Charter and civic actions contributed to society's reawakening. Not only dissidents, with their "islands of self-awareness and self-liberation," but also groups and associations that were not directly opposed to the system, the "gray area" between the government and the opposition, expressed the rise of the barely perceptible but extremely significant undercurrent of social activism: "Again and again, we were astonished at all the new things that were going on, the greater risks people were taking, how much more freely they were behaving, how much greater and less hidden was their hunger for truth, for a truthful word, for genuine values."[16] The myriad unauthorized publications, the formation of rock and jazz groups in defiance of official bans, the mass demonstrations in defense of religious freedoms—events characteristic of the second part of the 1980s—showed the erosion of the post-totalitarian state's capability to contain the increasing pressure from below. When an unofficial group called VONS (Committee for the Defense of the Unjustly Persecuted) was created, the government labeled it an "antistate organization" and arrested its leaders, Havel included. The mushrooming independent activities demonstrated that the pseudo-consensus based on fear and desperation had exhausted its paralyzing power. All those forms of civil disobedience were showing that deep-seated social discontent smoldered underneath the apparent tranquility of the post-totalitarian state:

> To outside observers, these changes may seem insignificant. Where are your ten-million-strong trade unions? Why does Husak not negotiate with you? Why is the government not considering your proposals and acting on them? But for someone from here who is not completely indifferent, these are far from insignificant changes; they are the main promise of the future, since he has long ago learned not to expect it from anywhere else.[17]

The civil society advanced faster and farther in Hungary and Poland than in countries like the GDR and Czechoslovakia. The case of East Germany, with its bureaucratic police state and rigid orthodoxy, deserves special attention. After all, one can barely understand the collapse of the Honecker regime in the fall of 1989 without reference to the history of democratic dissent and opposition in that country. Formed with Stalin's blessing in October 1949, the German Democratic Republic claimed to be the first German state of the workers and peasants. It was the only European country whose very existence was based on an ideological assumption, namely that a class principle could justify the separation of a nation into two states. In August 1961, to prevent a catastrophic demographic hemorrhage, Honecker's predecessor, the Stalinist hard-liner Walter Ulbricht, decided to erect the Berlin Wall. Following that action, the ruling Socialist Unity Party (SED) pursued a policy of *Abgrenzung* (demarcation) to preserve and enhance the differences between the two German states. To foster its legitimacy, the Communist state claimed to inherit the humanist ("progressive") traditions of German culture. The official propaganda insisted that the GDR was committed to the defense of peace, but that self-serving rhetoric failed to convince the people in the GDR. They could see with their own eyes that the regime was actually engaged in a militaristic course. At the same time, the rigid ideological stances favored by the party leaders resulted in continuous and systematic harassment of those critics who tried to offer an alternative to the official line. In their adamant opposition to reforms, the East German leaders were unmatched by any other Warsaw Pact leader, with the exception of Romania's Nicolae Ceausescu. During his first years in power, after he succeeded Ulbricht in 1973, Erich Honecker seemed to embody a more flexible approach to social and international affairs. He even expressed interest in a dialogue with the party intellectuals, increasingly disaffected with the regime's dogmatism. Later, however, especially after 1980, Honecker rejected any tolerance for the opposition. East Germany party leaders had not forgotten the June 1953 working-class uprising.

To counter the proliferation of reformist-democratic ideas, the regime intensified its commitment to an utterly conservative vision of socialism. When Gorbachev came to power and launched his de-Stalinization campaign, the GDR leaders did not conceal their displeasure with what they perceived as a dangerous "adventurist" course. Ironically, for a country where almost 400,000 Soviet troops were stationed, the government banned certain Soviet publications that were outspokenly advocating the reformation of socialism. Relations between the Soviet and East German leaders grew increasingly sour and tense, especially after the Soviets made clear their intention to renounce the class approach in international relations. The Yakovlev–Shevardnadze doctrine of the preeminence of universal values like peace and human rights in international relations was particularly resented by the seasoned Stalinists within the East German Politburo. For example, speaking at a festive event to mark the seventieth anniversary of the founding of the KPD (Communist Party of Germany) in December 1988, Erich Honecker turned down suggestions to modify SED policies in accordance with the winds of change then blowing from Moscow:

> [W]e have no reason to copy the practice of this or that fraternal country, apart from the fact that this would be a gross contradiction of the funda-mental teachings of Marxism. Peace . . . is served by our foreign policy, it is served by our military policy, it is served by the education of the younger generation, and it is served by the all-round strengthening of our socialist fatherland.[18]

In its efforts to insert itself into national life, the regime desperately tried to emphasize the East German national identity. First, it tried to gain popular prestige through the incorporation into the official ideology of certain symbols and ideas associated with important moments in the history of the German nation. Second, it insisted that the GDR repre-sented a major pillar of the world communist system and insisted on the paramount significance of "socialist internationalism." That second argu-ment tended to lose its significance after 1987, when Honecker and his associates looked increasingly askance at Gorbachev's new policies.

For a long time the SED managed to eradicate the shoots of political dissent, but, especially after 1980, it was confronted with growing autono-mous, grassroots collective efforts to oppose its militaristic course. Ini-tially apolitical, the East German independent peace movement— definitely the largest and most articulate in what used to be the Soviet bloc—realized that the totalitarian state would not enter into dialogue with the alternative forces. The new groups found a source of support and encouragement among members of the Evangelical Church. Because of its special, suprapolitical status, the church was able to provide the emerging independent movement with a powerful protective shield. Al-though the relations between church officials and the representatives of the independent and human rights groups were not always smooth, the religious institutions turned out to be a significant ally for the persecuted activists.

The new groups tried to channel the energies of those who believed in the reformability of the GDR. That was precisely the reason for their failure to attract more people among those who simply regarded the system as alien, unnatural, and inherently illegitimate. Later on, the commitment to the existence of an East Geman state would become the principal liability of the anti-authoritarian groups that headed the struggle against the Honecker regime in the fall of 1989. They seemed impervious to messages from below, to the voices of the younger generation, which found the whole ideological edifice of East German socialism a blatant lie. The poet and songwriter Sascha Anderson emigrated to the Federal Republic in August 1986. Born in 1953 into an intellectual family, he was typical of a generation that refused to consider the GDR a "motherland." Anderson did not nourish any lyrical illusions about the humanist virtues of communism. In that respect, his views differed radically from those held by idealist Marxists like the late physics professor Robert Havemann, a former anti-Nazi resistance fighter who had become increasingly disappointed with the bureaucratic despotism practiced by the SED or even with those spelled out by the nonconformist balladeer Wolf Biermann, who had been expelled by the regime in the late 1970s. Anderson belonged to a deradicalized and totally disenchanted generation of critics. For them, the regime was just a fraud, an opportunity for political scoundrels to take advantage and exert unlimited power over their humiliated subjects. For Anderson and his peers, trying to improve the system looked like a sheer waste of time, or even an aberration. Their attitude was therefore bluntly and unequivocally system-rejective: "I have never taken an interest in the system. . . . I never had an interest in undermining the system from inside. I did not even want to set myself in accordance with the demands of the system."[19]

Most of the dissidents, however, questioned not the existing social order but rather the "distortion" of Marxist principles in the SED's behavior. In that respect the East German opposition was definitely lagging behind similar movements in Poland and Hungary, which had long since abandoned the revisionist hopes of intrasystemic change. The case of Havemann was emblematic. A resolute opponent of police dictatorship, he was convinced that Marxist criticism could decisively affect the politics of the totalitarian system. For Havemann and his supporters in the fledgling democratic opposition, the solution was to reassert the humanist potential of socialism. He identified imagining a communist Utopia based on real equality between citizens as a major task of our times: "There must be no privileged people, classes, or groups of any description, but everybody, every person must have exactly the same opportunities, the same chances, and must be equal with regard to each other."[20] The regime reacted in a draconian way to the humanist challenge championed by intellectuals like Havemann. Dissident authors were harassed, prevented from publishing their books, kept under permanent police surveillance, and often forced to emigrate.

In those circumstances, a new opposition strategy had to be devised to take advantage of those areas not entirely permeated with the dominant ideas and values. A reconstruction of the critical discourse was required, and also a rethinking of the possibilities for autonomous social movements in a strongly authoritarian context. The only solution for those who wished to do something inside the GDR appeared to be to go beyond the merely intellectual opposition, altruistic and heroic but fatally marginal and isolated as it was, and address urgent public issues in accordance with public aspirations, expectations, and needs. In the view of East German critical intellectuals, vital issues included the state's manipulation of the notion of peace and its blatant indifference to environmental degradation. In January 1982 Robert Havemann endorsed the "Berlin Appeal," a document that marked the birth of the unofficial East German peace movement. The statement, whose main author was Reiner Eppelmann, an East Berlin Lutheran minister involved in youth work, was eventually signed by more than two thousand people.[21] The main objective of the "Berlin Appeal" was to challenge the regime's militaristic propaganda. A slogan frequently reproduced on official East German posters read: "The stronger the socialism, the more secure the peace." To this, the signatories of the "Berlin Appeal" replied: "We propose holding a great debate on the questions of peace, in an atmosphere of tolerance and recognition of the right of free speech, and to permit and encourage every spontaneous public expression of the desire for peace." The authors suggested a broad range of topics to be discussed in such a dialogue. Denying the moral validity of the militaristic course, they asked:

(a) Oughtn't we to stop producing, selling, and importing so-called war toys?
(b) Oughtn't we to introduce peace studies in our schools in place of military instruction?
(c) Oughtn't we to allow social work for peace instead of the present alternative service for conscientious objectors?
(d) Oughtn't we to stop all public displays of military might and instead use our ceremonies of state to give expression to the nation's desire for peace?
(e) Oughtn't we to stop the so-called civil-defense exercises? As no worthwhile civil defense is possible in nuclear war, these exercises merely make nuclear war seem more serious. Does it not perhaps amount to a kind of psychological preparation for war?[22]

Apparently the GDR was a state immune to profound challenges from below: The morale of the population was not very high, to be

sure, but there was more dissatisfaction among the students and intellectuals than among the workers. The latter were not inclined toward
labor unrest and preferred to accept the government's offer of better
living standards in exchange for social peace. On the other hand, as
events were to show during 1989 and 1990, there was very little knowledge among GDR citizens of the extent of corruption among the ruling
elite. Whatever people may have thought about such leaders as the
party General Secretary Erich Honecker, the trade union chief Harry
Tisch, and the security police boss Erich Mielke, no one would have
suspected that the Spartan-looking, austerity-preaching East German
communists, many of whom were survivors of Hitler's jails and concentration camps, did not differ in their taste for luxury cars, sumptuous
hunting lodges, and swimming pools from the Soviet leadership under
Brezhnev. In the early 1980s those who dared to criticize the SED for its
lack of concern for the real citizens were few and quite isolated. Had it
not been for church support, they could have been more easily disbanded, and the movement could have been thwarted. The church's
support, however, was motivated by the widespread conviction that
unless a social movement from below emerged to express the concerns
and expectations of large strata of the population, there would be spontaneous eruptions of violence and rage. The church and the peace
movement shared worries about the brutal interference of the state in
private affairs. For young East German pacifists, the idea of turning
"Swords into Plowshares" (*Schwerter zu Pflugscharen*) was more than a
prophetic metaphor. It was the symbol of their decision to rebel against
militarism, censorship, ideological manipulation, and police repression.
It was the only way to resist the system's attempt to integrate and
deflect any form of idealistic behavior. The independent peace movement in the GDR was first and foremost an effect of the all-pervading
moral crisis that affected large strata of East German youth, who were
looking for stable values and were acutely dissatisfied with the government's revolutionary demagogy.

The political changes in the Soviet Union and other East European
countries after Gorbachev's coming to power in 1985 further radicalized
the independent peace and human rights activists in the GDR. Instead of
deterring the pacifists, the official repression convinced them that a
broader agenda was needed. Early in 1985 they decided to address the
relation between peace and human rights in a systematic way. A group of
leading activists, including such veterans of the unofficial peace movements as Reiner Eppelmann, Ralf Hirsch, and Wolfgang Templin,
launched a human rights initiative. More than three hundred people

signed a letter addressed to Honecker calling for the full implementation of the United Nations' Universal Declaration of Human Rights. The letter called for the demilitarization of public life and the creation of an alternative civil service for conscientious objectors. It also condemned travel restrictions and demanded freedom of expression and the abolition of censorship. The government preferred to feign ignorance of the memorandum. In July 1985 a new appeal sent to the official youth organization declared a leading objective of the independent peace movement to be the revival of the civil society. Peaceful assembly and the founding of initiatives, organizations, associations, clubs and political parties, it stated, should not be dependent on political parties. The unrestricted work of independent groups would protect society from "petrifying in an inflexible administrative order that inhibits creativity among its citizens."[23] In this formulation, one recognizes the philosophy of the new evolutionism that inspired the struggles of the Polish opposition and became the common ideology of the democratic activists in East-Central Europe. At the same time, insistence on the organic relationship between peace and human rights was also part of the moral and intellectual treasury of the antitotalitarian movements that had developed in other Soviet-bloc countries. In this regard, mention should be made of Vaclav Havel's celebrated essay "An Anatomy of Reticence," written in April 1985. The Czech dissident discussed the principal disagreements between East European human rights activists and the representatives of the antinuclear movements in Western Europe and the United States. According to Havel, the cause of the arms race and wars was not the existence of weapons but their use for expansionist purposes. East Europeans do not deal with peace and human rights as two distinct, separate issues. They know from their own experience that governments that disparage the rights of their citizens cannot be trusted when it comes to their international commitments:

> Without free, self-respecting, and autonomous citizens there can be no free and independent nations. Without internal peace, that is peace among citizens and between the citizens and the state, there can be no guarantee of external peace: a state that ignores the will and the rights of its citizens can offer no guarantee that it will respect the will and the rights of other peoples, nations, and states. A state that refuses its citizens their right to public supervision of the exercise of power will not be susceptible to international supervision. A state that denies its citizens their basic rights becomes a danger to its neighbors as well: internal arbitrary rule will be reflected in arbitrary external relations. . . . Unreliability in some areas arouses justifiable fear of unreliability in everything. A state that does not

hesitate to lie to its own people will not hesitate to lie to other states. All of this leads to the conclusion that respect for human rights is the fundamental condition and the sole, genuine guarantee of true peace. Suppressing the natural rights of citizens and peoples does not secure peace—quite the contrary, it endangers it.[24]

Havel's views were actually a response to muted criticism and misunderstanding prevailing among Western pacifists about the skeptical attitudes of dissidents regarding international antiwar campaigns.

The new philosophy of the inseparability of peace and human rights had a strong impact on the Western antinuclear groups, which became increasingly involved in activities to support the cause of antitotalitarian movements in the Soviet bloc. Havel was right to state:

> It has become evident that reflection on the bitter daily experience of the citizen in a totalitarian state always leads quite logically to the same point—a new appreciation of the importance of human rights, human dignity and civic freedom. This is the focus of my remarks, and the focus, with good reason, of all reflections about peace as well. It may be that this understanding of the fundamental preconditions of peace, purchased at a high price and marked by a new vehemence, is the most important contribution that independently thinking people in our part of the world can make to our common awareness today.[25]

The inextricable connection between peace and human rights became a leitmotif in the appeals of the mounting East German independent peace movement. It became obvious that its most articulate spokespersons had realized the need to transcend the self-limited peace agenda and to tackle the issue of political change. That did not mean the East German pacifists had abandoned their original project, but rather that internal peace could not be attained without a genuine dialogue between the rulers and the citizens of different political persuasions. Political freedoms, particularly the right to free expression and association, had to be legally guaranteed. Emboldened by the changes in the Soviet Union and the new margins of political activism created by the policy of glasnost, East German oppositionists decided to join other East European dissidents and in October 1986 signed a "Joint Declaration from Eastern Europe" commemorating the thirtieth anniversary of the Hungarian Revolution. The document, signed by 123 activists from four Soviet-bloc countries—Czechoslovakia, East Germany, Hungary, and Poland—proclaimed the traditions and experiences of the Hungarian Revolution of 1956 to be the common heritage and inspiration for their present efforts: "We proclaim our common determination to struggle for political democracy in our countries, for their independence, for pluralism founded on the principles of self-government, for the peaceful unification of a united Europe and for its democratic integration, as well as for the rights of minorities."[26]

The tremendous significance of the joint declaration—a watershed in the development of dissident cross-frontier cooperation—was not missed by the East German authorities. They resorted to threats and abuse against the signatories from their country. The official propagandists clung to the description of the Hungarian Revolution as a "fascist rebellion." But instead of declining, the pacifist and human rights activism continued to gather momentum. In November 1987 the government organized a police raid on the Church of Zion in East Berlin, where *Grenzfall* (borderline), a bulletin of the unofficial peace and human rights movement, was produced. In January 1988 new reprisals were organized against those who were calling for immediate reforms. Some of the most articulate critics, including the painter Barbel Böhley and the singer Stefan Krawczyk, were expelled, although the former was allowed to return after six months.

During the 1989 upheaval that overthrew the Honecker regime, Böhley emerged as one of the leaders of the New Forum, a political association dedicated to the defense of the civil society in East Germany. With their extremely insensitive and unimaginative treatment of reform-oriented groups, the authorities contributed to the disbandment of any potential force for the preservation of an East German state identity in case of genuine political opening. In a way, it was as if Honecker wanted to make sure that the GDR could not exist without him and his clique of pigheaded Stalinists. Prominent members of the independent peace and human rights movement acknowledged the disconcerting impact of the official assault on their nascent structures. By the end of 1988 most East Germans realized that no changes could be expected to come from the stiff and extremely conservative leadership headed by Erich Honecker. The brutal clampdown on dissent and the lack of prospects for the growth of an organic movement like Solidarity in Poland deepened the sense of political despair, especially among the youth. That explains the lack of popularity, after November 1989, of groups and parties that insisted on the preservation of a separate East German entity. One can say, however, that fragile and incipient as it was, the civil society contributed even in the GDR to the erosion of the pseudo-consensus imposed by authoritarian measures. Based on an ideological fiction, the East German state could not outlive the abandoning of naked physical terror. Once its citizens were allowed to choose between their homes in the GDR, with the minimal social protection offered by the state, and the opportunity to leave, they massively opted for the second choice. The East German pacifist and human rights groups were the outgrowth of a certain stage in the decomposition of the East German regime. They contributed to the decline of the regime's spurious authority and became the principal mouthpiece for long-muted national and political grievances. Although they had a limited agenda, once the regime started to fall apart those groups enlarged their set of goals and eventually incorporated the calls for national reunification.

FROM CIVIL SOCIETY TO POLITICAL PLURALISM

This chapter cannot conclude without an attempt to define the role of civil society in the self-destruction of communist societies. Civil society emerges during a certain stage of decomposition of the bureaucratic-authoritarian system in all the countries of the Soviet bloc, including the Soviet Union itself. In some countries, because of political traditions and lack of permissiveness on the part of the ruling elites, the growth of the civil society proceeded more slowly than in others. In all these countries, however, the process of social differentiation and the formation of various interest groups have contributed decisively to the creation of a public sphere autonomous or semi-autonomous in its relation to the government. To be sure, the bureaucratic regimes did not welcome those developments and tried to arrest them, but their attempts were doomed to failure. What the historian Moshe Lewin wrote with regard to the Soviet system applies *a fortiori* to the East European states:

> The political façade of monolithic uniformity can no longer be taken seriously by anyone. Complex urban networks shape individuals, filter official views, and create an infinite welter of spontaneities. Baffled, the conservative leaders were left with the choice of trying to control the uncontrollable or disregarding, and thereby mishandling, the spontaneous. Either recourse would inevitably produce great downturns and put the entire state system under crippling pressure. The coalescence of a civil society capable of extracurricular action and opinion making, independent of the wishes of the state, marks the start of a new age, from which there is no turning back.[27]

Civil society can thus be defined as the ensemble of grassroots, spontaneous, nongovernmental (although not necessarily antigovernmental) initiatives from below that emerge in the post-totalitarian order as a result of a loosening of state controls and the decline of the ideological constraints imposed by the ruling parties. KOR or, more recently, the "Orange Alternative" semi-anarchist group in Poland; Charter 77 in Czechoslovakia; various forms of dissident activities in the Soviet Union; the "Peace and Human Rights Initiative" in the GDR; and all the independent peace and human rights activities, including the underground presses, samizdat publications, and the flying universities as they existed especially in Hungary and Czechoslovakia in the 1980s, can be considered components of the growing civil society. By channeling and catalyzing long-repressed social aspirations, civil society undermines the party-state's monopoly on power. To be sure, in a country like Poland, where the Catholic Church represented a viable alternative to the state's ideological pretense, civil society continued to exist, although in a limited form, even during the heyday of Stalinism. Later, after Stalin's death and the beginning of liberalization, clubs and discussion circles mushroomed in Poland and Hungary and led to the political and cultural ferment of 1956. The reaction against ecological degradation and the movements for the protection of historical monuments were also part of this rising phenomenon that we call civil society. Civil society should not be considered the opposite of state power, but rather an effort to control it and to limit its expansionist drive. Moshe Lewin is therefore right in describing it as "the aggregate of networks and institutions that either exist and act independently of the state or are official organizations capable of developing their own spontaneous views on national or local issues and then impressing these views on their members, on small groups and, finally, on the authorities."[28] The flexibility of official institutions, their readiness to embrace public demands and to criticize government decisions, no doubt depends on the degree of tolerance shown by the authorities. But even in the case of hyper-Stalinist Romania under Nicolae Ceausescu, there were forms of opposition within the existing institutions. For instance, the Writers' Union, created as an instrument of party control over the literary community, became increasingly critical of the leadership's interference and protested the official chauvinism. As a result of the unrest within that association, Romanian writers were unable to organize any national congress after a turbulent gathering in the spring of 1981. Similar actions took place in 1989 within the Czechoslovak official Union of Actors and Drama Writers, whose members decided to support the mounting criticism of the Jakes regime expressed by Charter 77 and other dissident groups.

The creation of civil society proceeded in several stages. Initially, under mature Stalinism, the very idea of autonomous initiatives from below was unthinkable. The very point of Stalinism was to annihilate such unofficial nuclei of resistance. All the propaganda and secret police systems operated in high gear to create the uniformity that would allow the party to establish what the Hungarian political philosophers Agnes Heller, Ferenc Feher, and György Markus aptly called the "dictatorship over needs."[29] The failure of the communist regimes to secure mass support once the open terror started to subside, as well as the erosion of their ideological foundations, shows the limits of the totalitarian paradigm. Indeed, it is now clear that even in the most oppressive conditions there remained forms of resistance to what Carl Friedrich and Zbigniew Brzezinski called "the totalitarian claim to all-inclusiveness."[30] For those who invoke the potential nuclei of autonomy as an argument against the original relevance of the totalitarian model, it is important to say that the model deals with what the rulers were trying to achieve rather than with their actual performances. As Robert C. Tucker has shown, they were regime-movements aimed at completely reconstructing human nature in the name of a universalistic ideology. Once the elites started to question some of the ideological dogmas, it was impossible for the regimes to maintain their missionary zeal. The ideological crisis contributed to what Tucker aptly called the "de-radicalization of Marxist regimes," indeed their gradual secularization.[31] After all, even one of the most pessimistic interpretations of totalitarianism did not exclude the possibility of transcending what claimed to be eternal subjugation. But the sources of the antitotalitarian revolt, according to Hannah Arendt, coincided with precisely those premises that made possible the ascent of totalitarianism in modern society: fear, loneliness, and despair. Ideological manipulation cannot forever triumph over the human quest for individual dignity:

> Totalitarian domination, like tyranny, bears the germs of its own destruction. Just as fear and the impotence from which fear springs are antipolitical principles and throw men into a situation contrary to political action, so loneliness and the logical-ideological deducing the worst that comes from it represent an antisocial situation and harbor a principle destructive for all human living-together.[32]

Indeed, if the experience of reconstructing the civil society in East European communist states has taught us something, it is that no police state and no ideological universalism can forever annihilate the human need for autonomy and self-assertion.

The rise of the civil society cannot be separated from the decline of the authoritarian-ideological state. Since communist regimes are based on the fallacy of the ruling party's omniscience, once the belief system that underlies them is shattered the regimes enter a stage of deep crisis. They try to adjust their dogmas to reality but refuse to go beyond limited changes in the institutional system. Reforms are half-hearted and inconsistent. The paradigm for such experiments is presented by Khrushchevism in the Soviet Union, with its most crystallized East European version, Kadarism in Hungary.[33] The Hungarian writer Miklos Haraszti, who is now one of the leaders of the Alliance of Free Democrats and a member of Hungary's Parliament, offered an interesting classification of the stages in the evolution of civil society. The first phase coincides with the liberalization of the party-state and the beginning of isolated forms of dissident activities. In that stage the opposition remains inchoate, without an alternative platform to express the society's demands. Haraszti calls this phase post-Stalinist and sees its essential quality in the struggle against fear and the rise of independent initiatives, independent opinion, and social activity free from the party-state.

It is only during the second stage, which Haraszti calls post-totalitarian, that civil society in the full meaning of the term, as a collective effort to reduce the impositions and prerogatives of the authoritarian state, emerges. This phase was analyzed by Havel and Michnik in their writings about the creation of parallel structures and the "new evolutionism." The system has lost its self-confidence; the elites are demoralized, unable to cope with the growing popular dissatisfaction; and the economy is a shambles. The old political model is obviously falling apart, and the search for a new one starts at the level of the autonomous enclaves of social initiative. Ideology, the main underpinning of communist authoritarianism, is nothing but an empty ritual, and the prevailing symbols are not trusted by either rulers or ruled:

> Democratization replaces liberalization as the central issue of politics; and while the latter was dictated by the will and the timetable of the party-state, democratization takes place under the pressure of the emerging public opinion. The regime is on the defensive. There is an attempt to put the economy on a pragmatic foundation, and therefore there is a struggle against the old structure even within the establishment. . . . The life of society is characterized by legal and other battles—by conflicts in the areas of democratization of everyday life, individualism, pluralism, the principles of popular representation and minority rights. The fear of our own actions dissipates and large masses acquire the ability to accept conflict openly and also to manifest self-limitation in regard to these conflicts.[34]

The third stage, which Haraszti defines as postcommunist, is marked by the complete breakdown of the party-state and the creation of a multiparty system. At the moment the Hungarian author wrote his essay in 1988, that was still a hypothesis, but one with strong justification in the developments taking place in countries where the civil society had evolved and reached a higher degree of maturity:

> Having lost its rationale, the party-state must collapse in its macro-structure. True democracy emerges, which builds on the forms, energies, experiences and pluralization that were already given shape in civil society. It is a secondary issue whether this process takes place along the lines of Juan Carlos's Spain, as an orderly transition, or through smaller or larger revolutionary shocks. It is also immaterial whether this transition occurs in the context of a European reorganization or prior to it in a more hasty manner. What is significant is that without the evolution of civil society in the preceding two phases, this transition cannot be successful.[35]

Indeed, in countries like Poland, Hungary, and Czechoslovakia, where the civil society had developed to a greater extent, the disintegration of the communist state proceeded in a smoother way than in Bulgaria and Romania, with their periodic flareups of violence even after the elimination of the old-style dictators Zhivkov and Ceausescu at the end of 1989.

For the countries of the "southern tier" the challenge of creating a lawful state based on the accountability of the government and the separation of powers is further aggravated by the relative weakness of political traditions of independent activism during the phase of the civil society. After the December 1989 revolution, Romanians often complained that their country was missing a historic personality like Vaclav Havel to embody national consensus. But the real issue is not the role of exceptional individuals but the absence of a political infrastructure comparable to that erected in Czechoslovakia on the basis of Charter 77. In other words, Romania under Ceausescu experienced not the transition to a post-totalitarian stage, but rather, especially after 1971, the strengthening of party-state controls and the return to a traditional version of totalitarianism, which included and carried to an extreme the cult of the leader and reprisals against any form of criticism and opposition. Romanians did not experience the luxury of Kadarist enlightened authoritarianism or even Jaruzelski's militaristic regime's experimentation with economic reforms. The strategy of civil society is predicated on gradualism, nonviolence, and social education through participation in nonregulated activities.

S I X

c&

The Triumph of the Powerless
Origins and Dynamics of the
East European Upheaval

> I had come to the conclusion—and it
> may seem overly dramatic to put it like
> this, but I swear I mean it—that it is
> better not to live at all than to live
> without honor.
>
> —*Vaclav Havel*

The causes of the East European upheaval and the collapse of the Soviet bloc cannot be reduced to one unique factor. For such a world-historical process to take place a multitude of causes had to interact and create a set of circumstances that made change both urgent and inevitable. One element was the disappearance of the Soviet scarecrow. For many years the clear and present danger of Soviet intervention to quell domestic unrest in the satellite countries was a serious obstacle to the rise of powerful mass movements. The widespread psychology of resignation to what many referred to as the legacy of Yalta—a feeling that the 1945 international arrangement between the superpowers had made any resistance movement in the Soviet bloc a quixotic struggle doomed to inevitable failure—stunted and made fragile the growth of a mass base for opposition movements. The Soviets' realization that they could no longer dominate the East Europeans by using the obsolete Stalinist forms of intrabloc discipline led to a reassessment, during the Gorbachev era, of the

very legitimacy of externally imposed communist regimes in the so-
called outer empire. On various occasions, supporters of glasnost,
including such influential members of Gorbachev's entourage as
Georgy Shakhnazarov, the head of the CPSU international department
and currently one of the Soviet President's closest advisers, made
clear that the old concept of socialism, based on coercion and monopolistic rule by a tiny bureaucratic group, had lost any moral or
political justification. That was the theoretical premise for the renunciation of the Brezhnev doctrine and the adoption of a new course in
Soviet relations with their former satellites. Once the use of force and
violence was condemned by the highest authority in the Kremlin,
there was no reason for the Soviets to stick by the legends of the
popular revolutions that allegedly had brought the East European
communist parties to power in the aftermath of World War II. Once
the Soviets announced their decision to overhaul their strategic as-
sumptions and to reconsider the ideological underpinnings of their
so-called world socialist system, the obstacle of fear among citizens of
the bloc began to dissipate.

Under the new Soviet interpretation of socialism proposed by
Gorbachev and his closest allies, including Aleksandr Yakovlev, a
Politburo member and chief ideologue of perestroika, the crushing of the
Prague Spring by the Warsaw Pact tanks would have been unthinkable.
Indeed, many in Eastern Europe realized that the Prague reformers had
anticipated the search for humane socialism as advocated by the partisans
of perestroika in Moscow. The self-propelling dynamics of reform in the
Soviet Union placed the East European communist leaders in the unenvi-
able position of lagging behind their Soviet patrons in terms of systemic
opening. Ideological orthodoxy at that moment was simply a relic of the
Stalinist past:

> Always before, whatever the Soviets called "socialist" had been defined as
> efficient; now the Soviets were saying that practical efficiency, how things
> actually worked, would be the criterion for viable socialism. This in turn
> removed the fixed Soviet reference point for domestic debate on what was
> efficient and what was needed to be conserved. Indeed, to the extent the
> Soviet Union was still a model, it was becoming a model for the political
> reform needed to make economic reform work; for *glasnost*; for democratiza-
> tion; for legitimate public roles for intellectuals and for hitherto repressed
> groups, including national groups; for experimentation with new forms of
> political debate and political action. To the extent that late Stalinism was
> no longer a model, its inefficiencies and tyrannies became all the harder to

justify, and they had to be justified increasingly on grounds of national specifics.[1]

Although necessary, the transformation of the Soviet variable from a deterrent into a catalyst of change was not sufficient for determining the rapid disintegration of the communist regimes in the bloc countries.

The transition to postcommunism was linked to the deterioration of the communist elites' self-confidence, which was itself a reflection of the moral and ideological crisis of those regimes. Also significant for the success of the transition was the existence of political groups and movements that could articulate the social grievances and propose economic and political alternatives to the prevailing bankrupt policies. In Hungary, Poland, and Czechoslovakia, and to lesser extent in the GDR, the opposition had long reflected on the main elements and challenges involved in the dismemberment of the communist regimes. In Hungary and Poland, reform-oriented groups had emerged within the top leaderships to champion views similar to those promoted by Gorbachev and his team in the Soviet Union. Even in Yugoslavia, a country that had not been formally integrated into the Soviet bloc, the changes occurring in the Soviet Union and the East European states prompted democratic forces in Croatia and Slovenia to launch daring campaigns for reform and the assertion of their national identities. In Romania and Bulgaria, where repression had been more systematic and the opposition less organized, such premises associated with the existence of a developing civil society were only in the infant stage. In those countries, civil societies that had long been subjected to systematic attacks had been left crippled and fearful. Albania, the most isolated of the East European countries, appeared to stick stubbornly to the legacy of Enver Hoxha's radical Stalinism. Hoxha's successor as party General Secretary, Ramiz Alia, who had spent his whole career as a loyal apparatchik, continued to keep the late leader's widow, Nexmije, as a chairperson of the National Front, and the cult of the departed leader seemed to be intact. But as events in 1990, when opposition parties were formed in Albania with the approval of the ruling communists, show, even that country could not completely escape contamination by the reformist movement spreading through the whole of communist Eastern Europe.

In addition to the reshaping of Soviet attitudes toward the bloc countries and the diminishing fear among the East Europeans, a structural crisis affected each country's society with the growing realization, among both regime supporters and regime opponents, that no intra-systemic reforms would be able to resolve the growing tensions. There was a general awareness that socialism, in its Soviet-style version, had exhausted any internal resources for self-regeneration and had become completely hackneyed. Any effort to keep the system going was only a recipe for the prolongation of society's terminal agony. No society can function in the absence of at least a limited consensus among its members about common goals and values. In Soviet-dominated Eastern Europe, especially after 1988, such a consensus vanished. The same thing applied to Yugoslavia—a country not directly integrated in the bloc structure— where the speed of Soviet reforms and their contagious impact in Eastern Europe accelerated the drive toward sweeping reforms and exacerbated the conflicts between conservatives and liberals, often disguised as tensions between the more pluralistic Croatian and Slovenian elites and the more authoritarian Serbian leaders.

The last key element, the Western pressures on these regimes—both governmental and nongovernmental—to live up to their international pledges, especially in the field of human rights, played an important part in strengthening domestic opposition. Especially after 1975, when the Helsinki Agreements were signed, but even more significantly after 1980, the West continually pressed the Soviet Union to relinquish its imperialist strategy. Capital mobility and the growing Soviet need for Western assistance also played significant roles in the dislocation of the foundations of communist regimes. The politics of cultural and political isolationism traditionally practiced by the communist governments, the systematic censorship on correspondence, and the jamming of Western radio stations all were intended to cut the links between the emerging human rights groups in the Soviet bloc and their potential supporters in the West. The feeling that there were people outside the borders of the Soviet bloc who cared about the fate of those who defended the rights of the individuals in the bloc, that the West was not silent when infringements of those rights took place, was extremely important for the development of civil societies. In order to understand the reinvention of politics in Eastern Europe, the role that the West played in the East European upheaval cannot be ignored. In other words, the impact of the West on the scope and speed of changes in Eastern Europe was no less important than the Gorbachev-led Soviet Union's influence. They both concurred on creating an international environment in which the fossilized communist bureaucracies of Eastern Europe looked like vestiges of an embarrassing past. But whereas the West encouraged the rise of pluralist, democratic forces interested in a systemic seachange, the Kremlin staked its hopes on local communist reformers whose agenda would be to streamline rather than disband the existing economic and political mechanisms.

GORBACHEV THE REVISIONIST

When Mikhail Gorbachev came to power in March 1985, he was the embodiment of the successful apparatchik. Nothing in his previous career indicated serious liberal propensities. True, he had been a protégé of the former General Secretary, Yury Andropov, but like his patron he seemed committed to the basic Leninist tenets, including the sacrosanct principle of the party's leading role in society. Like Andropov's, his rejection of Brezhnevism was inspired not by liberalism but by his belief that socialism could be regenerated through a return to the true Bolshevik values tainted by the nepotism and corruption rampant in the apparatus throughout the 1970s and early 1980s. All Gorbachev's public pronouncements and actions were suggestive of a pragmatic, disciplined, and party-minded communist. During his first two years in power, the new leader directly challenged no entrenched ideological dogmas. His anti-Stalin campaign proceeded quite slowly, with numerous setbacks. Gorbachev initially avoided offering any direct support to the proponents of genuine liberalization. Andrei Sakharov, the celebrated physicist and human rights activist, continued to live in internal exile in the city of Gorky. But from the very beginning keen observers could detect some flexibility in Gorbachev's approach to theoretical and cultural issues. There were indications that many in the General Secretary's entourage were committed to a resumption of Khrushchev's aborted attempts at de-Stalinization.

Confronted with bureaucratic inertia, Gorbachev's ruling team realized that only structural reforms, affecting the very foundations of the existing system, could lead to a breakout from the ongoing decay and unleash long-repressed social energies. The attack on the existing institutions started in the form of de-Brezhnevization. At the Twenty-seventh Party Congress, which took place in February 1986 (exactly thirty years after the historic Twentieth, when Khrushchev had denounced Stalin's cult of personality), Gorbachev attacked the "command-administrative system" and called for daring reforms in both the social and economic areas. In unleashing his campaign, Gorbachev expressed the political interests of the middle-aged Soviet bureaucracy and of a certain group of party-linked intellectuals who had come to resent the corruption and incompetence of the Brezhnev era. He championed the values of a generation of the Soviet elite that had internalized the values of the Twentieth Congress, including the ideas of political and economic reforms, peaceful coexistence with the West, and the general deradicalization of the Marxist utopian blueprint. In the initial stage, the thrust of Gorbachev's criticism was the routinized corruption and lack of political imagination in the decision-making process. At the same time Gorbachev insisted on the role of the masses as a reservoir of political inventiveness and allowed the formation of thousands of informal organizations in the Soviet Union.

The new leadership's attempt to modernize was primarily inspired by Lenin's late political and economic writings. In accordance with Lenin's views on the New Economic Policy, Gorbachev favored decentralization and a reduction of the party's controls over society. Reform had to be initiated from above, and the communist party had to preserve its leading role in society. That strategy was criticized by certain Soviet intellectuals who advocated a radical break with the past. Liberalization was seen as merely a continuation of the old system. Their recommendation was to democratize all institutions in order to permit individuals to express their political views fully. Giving voice to the discontent with party-controlled reforms, the well-known playwright Aleksandr Gelman, a strong proponent of restructuring, declared at a meeting of the party organization of the Cinematographers' Union:

> Democratization provides for the redistribution of power, rights, and freedoms, the creation of a number of independent structures of management and information. And liberalization is the conservation of all the foundations of the administrative system but in a milder form. Liberalization is an unclenched fist, but the hand is the same, and at any moment it could be clenched again into a fist. Only outwardly is liberalization sometimes reminiscent of democratization, but in actual fact it is a fundamental and intolerable usurpation.[2]

It took time for Gorbachev to realize that he could not avoid a full-fledged assault on the legacy of Stalinism. The ruling team at first thought it would be able to mend the system by renouncing only some of its features and remedying the others. That period, called acceleration, did not last long. Gorbachev and his supporters realized that without bringing large social groups into the political struggle and without revising the ossified party dogmas there was no way to solve the country's problems. The Gorbachevites, among whom influential economists, political scientists, and sociologists were to be found, insisted that without political reforms there was no way to implement genuine changes in the economy. The vested interests of the military-industrial complex and of other powerful lobbies like the KGB and the party bureaucracy functioned as a main obstacle to any endeavor to modernize the economic system. As a result of the growing awareness of the intractability of the existing contradictions within the old system, the policy of perestroika was born.

The means for perestroika to succeed by allowing the masses to participate in the changes and make them real was the policy of glasnost (openness or publicity). To his credit Gorbachev was quick to accept the need for a dramatic change of the whole vision of socialism. He recognized the need to reorganize the whole political system, limit the communist party prerogatives, and diminish the powers of the repressive apparatus. The search for a rule of law and the creation of a checks-and-balances system in the Soviet Union became priorities on the leadership's agenda. The litmus test, and the most difficult challenge for the Gorbachevites, has been to renounce the communist party's monopoly on power. To accept the emergence of parallel centers of initiative and to engage in dialogue with opponents of the existing system already went beyond the boundaries of Leninism. But while the Gorbachevites were ready to deplore the heritage of Stalinism, they were reluctant to embark on an adventurous criticism of Leninism. In many respects they echoed the Khrushchevite illusions about the reformability of the system without major convulsions. The talk was of course about revolutionary changes, but whenever they were confronted with dramatic challenges, Gorbachev and his team preferred to go only halfway.

The General Secretary's speeches vacillated between the commitment to radical reform and a fear that such reforms would fundamentally destabilize the system. But it was most important that Gorbachev had the willingness to reconsider the basic dogmas and to engage in a redefinition of the very concept of socialism. Despite all his hesitations, he was increasingly drawn to espousal of the revisionist concept of socialism with a human face. Like his predecessors, Imre Nagy in Hungary and Alexander Dubcek in Czechoslovakia, Gorbachev came to emphasize the intimate, indestructible link between socialism and democracy. Especially after the Communist Party's Nineteenth National Conference in June 1988, he moved toward a reconsideration of the historical legacy of socialism in this century. He agreed that there were universal human values that prevailed over limited, class-defined interests. He also agreed that imperial *diktat* was morally condemnable and that the Soviet foreign policy had to be dramatically restructured. Yet Gorbachev's strategy included an element of desperation. He could not ignore that the Soviet system was confronted with insoluble contradictions, but he tried to manage the crisis without completely abandoning the official tenets. As in the case of the Prague Spring reformers, the Soviet leader wanted to square the circle and went out of his way to postpone a complete repudiation of Leninism.

In the meantime, his reformation had contributed to the awakening of both social and ethnic forces that could barely be controlled without the use of violence. But the whole philosophy of perestroika was opposed to dictatorial arbitrariness and called for legal means of solving political and national crises. The basic dilemma of Gorbachev's leadership was convincingly summed up by Zbigniew Brzezinski, who showed that the ultimate obstacle to democratization was the Soviet leadership's failure to renounce the Leninist ideological mythology completely:

> The political obstacles to a real *perestroika* are thus not only formidable but also insurmountable. A break with the Leninist legacy would require nothing short of a basic redefinition of the nature of the ruling party, of its historical role, and of its legitimacy. In fact, a real break would require a repudiation of the grand oversimplification's central premise, namely that a perfect social system can be shaped by political fiat through which society is subordinated to the supreme state acting as history's all-knowing agent. It would require an acceptance of the notion that much of the social change is contingent, ambiguous and often spontaneous, with the result that social complexity cannot be fitted into an ideological straitjacket.[3]

The meaning of Gorbachev's early efforts to rescue the system through the elimination of its most obnoxious features was described by Adam Michnik in 1987 as a self-styled version of "counterreformation." Michnik referred to Leszek Kolakowski's application of the notion of "counterreformation" as a political and ideological movement that not only rejects reformist (heretical) criticism but also incorporates and assimilates some reformist themes in order to ensure the adaptation of the existing structures to changed circumstances. In other words, this view sees the counterreformation as an attempt to change the values and institutions from within the system. It is an effort to integrate critical ideas into the functioning mechanism of the established order so that they cease to be antagonistic and subversive: "So if we accept that Solidarity was a great reformist movement within the boundaries of the communist world, then Gorbachev must, therefore, earn the title of the 'Great Counter-Reformer.' This is the meaning of his 'reforms from above.' This is the counter-reformation which is to rescue the communist system."[4]

Recognizing Gorbachev's intentions of reforming the system without abolishing its ideological foundations, primarily the Leninist principle of the communist party's hegemonic role, was not to say that perestroika was simply window dressing, a propagandistic farce. On the contrary, to understand the true meaning of the Soviet transformations initiated by

Gorbachev, one must take into account all the economic, social, cultural, and strategic constraints that had made such a dramatic overhaul indispensable for the very survival of the system:

> Mikhail Gorbachev's policy is the result of the generational conflict within the Soviet *nomenklatura*; it is the result of technological backwardness and several years of the Afghanistan war; it is, finally, the result of the fear of military confrontation and the uncompromising stance of President Reagan. Gorbachev is not a play-actor—he is a counter-reformer.[5]

In those conditions, when the center was undergoing such tremendous mutations, when the language of the dissidents was being appropriated by the ideological apparatus and turned into official party doctrine, when socialism was defined in terms of its ability to create a state of law, the margin of activism for East European independent movements widened significantly.

> The counter-reformation in Moscow can open the way to new thinking on the philosophy of political compromise. It can teach us to use compromise to regulate international conflicts or social conflicts within the countries of actually existing communism. It is worth relying on this form of compromise today, even if one must not forget that the totalitarian foundation of Soviet institutions has remained unchanged.[6]

Later, after 1988, the self-imposed limits of the democratic movements in Eastern Europe would increasingly lose their basic rationale. As the Soviet Union became more tolerant of autonomous, unofficial domestic activism, there was little reason to believe that Gorbachev would automatically side with the besieged communist elites in Eastern Europe at the moment of serious political and social unrest. The Soviet counter-reformation opened the way for a real revolution in Eastern Europe.

The break with Stalinism in Moscow was the green light for a break with Leninism for those in Warsaw, Budapest, and East Berlin. As for Gorbachev himself, he increasingly realized that simple liberalization would lead him and his supporters into Khrushchev's predicament: Hated and subverted by the party apparatus, he did not have a popular base to rely upon. That explains the decision to open up the political system, to create a genuine parliament, and to reduce the party's power drastically after 1988. Forced by the logic of political struggle and encountering the overt or covert sabotage of the bureaucracy, the General Secretary had to admit that only democratization could ensure his political survival. In 1989, despite all his hesitations and doubts, Gorbachev recognized the role of the civil society as a counterpart to a rigid political system in desperate need of change. That need was obsessively stressed also by Gorbachev's main critic within the party (until his resignation from the CPSU at the Twenty-eighth Congress in 1990), Boris Yeltsin.

As the political struggle intensified at the top of the Soviet bureaucracy, Gorbachev himself seemed to understand the imperative to rip off the ideological straitjacket. The same man who in November 1987 was still ready to praise the virtues of Marxist-Leninist doctrine boldly moved toward a redefinition of the fundamental values of the Soviet political culture. The historical and theoretical debate advanced to an unprecedented level. Advocates of perestroika like Alexander Tsipko and Yury Afanasyev directly questioned the whole legacy of Soviet-style socialism. After 1988 the very notion of the enemy changed in official Soviet doctrine. The West ceased to be demonized as a perpetual fomentor of anti-Soviet conspiracies; socialism stopped being considered tantamount to the rule of inept bureaucracies over demoralized masses; and the Soviet national interest was reconsidered in the light of a "common European home." The entire philosophy of communism, as it had existed for more than seven decades, suffered a rapid decline as a result of the Soviets' official recognition of the historical failure of the existing system. The triumph of the philosophy of revisionism in the Kremlin affected not only the inner empire but also the outer empire, the whole community of nations long known as the Soviet bloc. The margin of Soviet tolerance for political experimentation in Eastern Europe widened considerably. What used to be anathema from the Soviet viewpoint under Brezhnev— the idea of socialism with a human face—had become, especially after 1988, the official Soviet line. In Brzezinski's words:

> The implications of a revisionist General Secretary in the Kremlin were momentous. It was not only bound to fuel a bitter and intense debate within the Soviet Union over almost all aspects of Soviet life. It was also bound to revive and intensify the more far-reaching East European revisionism, while depriving the Kremlin of the ideological cathedral from which to excommunicate the heretics. It posed the particularly grave danger of dissolving the common core of Marxist-Leninist tenets of world communism. In brief, even modest revisionism in Moscow had to accelerate the political disintegration and the doctrinal eclipse of communism as a distinctive historical phenomenon.[7]

Remember how initially Gorbachev tried to keep both the internal and external empires together? During his first years in power he preferred to streamline relations with the East European countries, to establish closer ties with the CMEA, and to coordinate international actions. While engaged in the new approach within the Soviet Union, he wanted Eastern Europe to remain calm, and it was in his interest to deal with younger, reform-oriented leaders in those countries. He did not encourage immediate changes. Seweryn Bialer characterized Gorbachev's early attitude toward Eastern Europe as an all-out hard-line policy that included "a much stronger insistence on political orthodoxy, particularly in Poland and Hungary; crackdowns on dissent; encouragement of a siege mentality and of crude anti-Western propaganda; greater pressure against economic experimentation; and rapid reaction to social and political unrest or to signs of attempted greater independence of satellite leaderships."[8] But that restrictive and imperialistic attitude did not last long. Gorbachev could not separate the developments in the Soviet Union from those in the satellite countries.

The shock waves of glasnost galvanized political opposition in all East European countries. For instance, East German peace and human rights activists made glasnost one of their slogans with which to challenge directly the conservative leadership under Erich Honecker. In Poland Solidarity gathered momentum, and in Hungary the Democratic Opposition started to organize itself as a political party, particularly during 1988. Both those in power and the oppositionists in Eastern Europe realized that Gorbachev's new definition of socialism inaugurated a new stage in Soviet–East European relations. The image of the Soviet Union as international gendarme, always watching over the orthodoxy of local leaderships, dissolved at the moment the Soviet leader proclaimed at the Nineteenth Party Conference in June 1988 that his country was renouncing "everything which deformed socialism in the thirties and which led it into stagnation in the seventies."[9]

Later on, in December 1988, Gorbachev elaborated further on his new philosophy of international relations. Addressing a United Nation session, the General Secretary endorsed the rights of nations to engage in struggles for democratization. His frankness in renouncing the traditional Soviet claims about the need to continue ideological competition with the West indicated that he was not merely indulging in rhetoric. Although he did not abandon the Leninist veil of his language, Gorbachev recognized the non-Leninist thesis that the relations between states should not be subordinated to ideological considerations:

> Today the preservation of any kind of "closed" society is hardly possible. This calls for a radical review of approaches to the totality of the problems

of international cooperation as a major element of international security. . . . The new phase also requires de-ideologizing relations among states. We are not abandoning our convictions, our philosophy or traditions, nor do we urge anyone to abandon theirs. [10]

This statement, although paying lip service to the fears of dogmatic hardliners, was unequivocal in its determination to relinquish the logic of the Cold War.

The idea that the world was divided along ideological lines, a leftover of Stalin's or even Lenin's approach to international affairs, was yielding to a new conception that allowed for each nation to decide its own fate. To his credit, Gorbachev understood that the Soviet presence in Eastern Europe was strategically less important in the age of *European integration*. The nations of Western Europe, already united against the Soviet Union militarily, were moving steadily to overcome their political differences to create an economic power bloc never before seen in Europe. With living standards in Western Europe already surpassing those in the Soviet Union, if the Soviet Union was to modernize, avoid further isolation, and rival an integrated Europe, it had to reduce its imperial burden. There was no reason to continue to protect local communist bureaucracies against growing social movements from below. On the contrary, it was in Moscow's best interest to appear as the ally of change and progress rather than the stereotype (based on history) of "Big Brother," always ready to use his troops to restore the privileges of local despots.

The new attitude toward political change in Eastern Europe stemmed from the realization that the cost of the outer empire, including the psychological cost, had been too high for its benefits. Stalin's obsession with the western border had led the Russians to an overextension that sowed the seeds for popular uprisings. In November 1988 the imminence of such a series of revolts was already obvious:

[M]ost people in most of those eight countries in communised Eastern Europe do not want to be run by communist governments, and do not like being told by Russians that they have got to be. Forty years of this double arrogance from Moscow—Marx knows best, and Russia knows what Marx really meant—have created the makings of an East European rebellion. [11]

The new Soviet approach to Eastern Europe was actually the result of long discussions within Soviet think tanks. One should also keep in mind that among Gorbachev's advisers were a number of former editors of the Prague-based *World Marxist Review*, who had empathized with Dubcek's renewal movement in 1968 and deplored the Soviet intervention that put an end to that reformist experiment. As the Soviet Union's Foreign Minister and one of Gorbachev's closest allies within the Politburo, Eduard Shevardnadze had great influence in the decision-making process that led to the disbandment of the bloc. Actually, after his resignation as Foreign Minister in 1990, Shevardnadze was singled out by conservative critics for his "deleterious" role in the collapse of Soviet international power.

Then in July 1988, at a Soviet–American scholarly conference in Alexandria, Virginia, the Soviets presented a paper representing the collective work of the staff of the influential Institute of Economics of the World Socialist System, headed by Academician Oleg Bogomolov. Although only semi-official, the paper indicated clearly that there were substantive changes in the Soviet approach to Eastern Europe. It recognized that far from having eliminated the diversity of the cultural, ethnic, political, and economic traditions in Eastern Europe, the externally-imposed Soviet model of socialism "had not withstood the test of time, thereby showing its sociopolitical and economic inefficiency." According to the paper, a pressing need had arisen for those countries to engage in radical reforms that would result in the creation of a new model of socialism that would be truly humane in nature. The paper offered a vivid analysis of the main features of Sovietism as a militaristic-bureaucratic system based on uniformity and coercion:

> In many countries of Eastern Europe, perestroika of the system of political power has begun. The model of the existing system was created in the Soviet Union during the 1930's and 1940's. This model was profoundly influenced by Stalin's perverted concepts of the character of political mechanisms in socialism, as well as by the insufficient political maturity on the part of Soviet society and the lack of democratic traditions and political culture. The administrative-command system started in the USSR was replicated in other socialist countries. It was characterized by hyper-centralism, an absolute monopoly on the decision-making, monolithic thinking, a disdain for the masses (who were seen as "small crews" and as objects of management), and isolation from the outside world. Political institutions aimed at securing political stability primarily through suppression and the leveling of diversity. This system, which demanded servile obedience, undermined the foundations of societal dynamism and viability.[12]

For any reader familiar with Imre Nagy's writings of 1955–56 or with the Action Program of the Czechoslovak Communist Party adopted in April

1968, the revisionist flavor of this analysis was unmistakable. The Soviet scholars shared the revisionist illusions that changes in Eastern Europe could be kept within the systemic boundaries. The issue for them was to construct a new model of socialism. They did not address the most disturbing question: whether the nations in that region were interested in testing such a new model.

At least during 1988, the Soviets partook of the traditional revisionist fallacy that socialism still had a future in Eastern Europe, if it could be stripped of its bureaucratic outgrowth and allowed to arouse the social energies and imagination suppressed during the Stalinist age. The solution for them, as for the revisionists of 1956 or 1968, was a return to the genuine Marxist paradigm. The systemic roots of the deplored aberrations were thus obfuscated by the ultimately mystical belief in the redeeming virtues of socialism.

> The essence of the new model of power can be defined as the delegation of considerable responsibility to the local level, to labor and territorial collectives; the expansion of pluralism in public life; and the democratization of institutions, including the vanguard party. The aim is to create more effective guarantees against the power monopoly of the layer of managers and professional politicians—against the bureaucratic apparatus.[13]

In the summer of 1989 Gorbachev addressed the parliamentary assembly of the Council of Europe in Strasbourg. On that occasion he went farther than ever in his repudiation of the Brezhnev doctrine of limited sovereignty. He admitted that there was no immutable social system and hinted that such transformations could take place in Eastern Europe as well. Gorbachev's statement in Strasbourg was widely interpreted as a green light to reformers in Eastern Europe in their efforts to move toward a multiparty system and a market-oriented economy. According to Gorbachev,

> The fact that the states of Europe belong to different social systems is a reality. The recognition of this historical fact and respect for the sovereign right of each people to choose their social system at their own discretion are the most important prerequisite for a normal European process. The social and political order in some particular countries did change in the past, and it can change in the future as well, but this is exclusively a matter for the people themselves and of their choice. Any interference in the internal affairs, any attempts to limit the sovereignty of states—both friends and allies or anybody else—are inadmissible.[14]

The meaning of the Strasbourg address did not go unnoticed by the East European political actors, both rulers and oppositionists. The possible excuse for the communist governments to organize new crackdowns on dissent in order to avoid Soviet intervention had lost its deterrent effect.

In the months preceding that address, tremendous changes had already taken place in Eastern Europe. In February Hungary's ruling communists had agreed to move toward a multiparty system, a decision that no one had anticipated one year earlier. In Poland the government and the opposition organized a roundtable that led to the signing of an agreement in April. The agreement provided for the legalization of the banned Solidarity trade union, for one-third of the the seats in the lower house of the parliament to be reserved for the communists, and for free elections to a new upper house. The Polish changes also ensured the communist government's control over the military and the security apparatus, and the powerful presidency remained in the hands of General Jaruzelski.

The reform movements in Eastern Europe could hardly be contained. The logic of change within authoritarian systems shows that whenever concessions are made by those in power, new demands are formulated by the opposition as an expression of the growing expectations of the masses. If those demands are not met by the government, social unrest heightens and the rulers have to grant new concessions. Gorbachev watched those changes and did not show any irritation with them. In April 1989 he met the Hungarian communist leader, Karoly Grosz, and, after having discussed the experiences of 1956 and 1968, when the Soviets had crushed attempts at democratization in Hungary and in Czechoslovakia, respectively, he told his guest that "all possible safeguards should be provided so that no external force could interfere in the domestic affairs of socialist countries."[15]

The new Soviet approach had an enormous impact in Eastern Europe. It weakened the conservative forces, primarily in the Romanian, East German, Czechoslovak, and Bulgarian communist leaderships. For one, those hard-liners found Moscow unwilling to endorse their neo-Stalinist policies. In July 1989 a Warsaw Pact summit took place in Bucharest. On that occasion Gorbachev challenged the hard-line coalition within the bloc by advocating the transformation of the alliance from a military and political one into a political and military one. The final communiqué of the meeting denied the existence of a universal socialist model. Following the summit, Hungary's Foreign Minister Gyula Horn declared that it was high time for the practice of socialism to be updated in order to meet the challenges of the modern world. Expressing the position of the reformist trend within the bloc, he said: "We also stated in this respect, and I find it highly important, that the times are past for a number of states or the alliance to interfere by any means with the internal affairs of another member. As we set it down: the period of enforcing the so-called Brezhnev doctrine is over once and for all."[16] To sum up, after the first attempts to establish a new cohesion within the bloc, Gorbachev moved radically toward an increasingly tolerant approach to unity within the bloc. Not only was diversity now permitted, but it was actually encouraged.

The modification in the Soviet policy toward Eastern Europe was defintely linked to domestic struggles in Moscow. One should not forget that even during the Nineteenth Party Conference, but primarily earlier, in March 1988, when Nina Andreyeva's notorious letter was published, the Soviet conservatives had criticized what they perceived as a policy of unjustified concessions to the West. There was a direct relationship of mutual determination between domestic democratization and disengagement from external adventurism (usually presented as defense of "proletarian" conquests, as in the case of the invasions of Hungary and Czechoslovakia). In her indictment of perestroika, Andreyeva, a lecturer from Leningrad whose views spelled out the frustrations of the emerging coalition of Stalinists and Russian nationalists, took the Gorbachevites to task for their championing of what she saw as an extremely dangerous course in international relations:

> I was puzzled recently by the revelation by one of my students that the class struggle is supposedly an obsolete term, just like the leading role of the proletariat. It would be fine if she were the only one to claim this. A furious argument was generated, for example, by a respected academician's recent assertion that the present-day relations between states from the two socio-economic systems apparently lack any class content. I assume that the academician did not deem it necessary to explain why it was that, for several decades, he wrote exactly the opposite—namely that peaceful coexistence is nothing but a form of class struggle in the international arena. It seems that the philosopher has now rejected this view. Never mind, people can change their minds. It does seem to me, however, that duty would nevertheless command a leading philosopher to explain at least to those who have studied and are studying his books: What is happening today, does the international working class no longer oppose world capital as embodied in its state and political organs?[17]

Indeed, Andreyeva was not alone in lamenting the end of the ideological age of conformity, fanaticism, and blind regimentation. Even some of Gorbachev's Politburo colleagues, primarily his longtime nemesis Yegor

Ligachev, saw the new thinking in foreign policy as a "capitulation" to Western pressure.

Far from giving in to the admonitions of his critics, Gorbachev continued to push for further changes in the structure of the bloc. What he was aiming at, in this stage, was to help reformers within the ruling communist parties get the upper hand and get rid of the Stalinist hacks. One can assume that Gorbachev's strategic calculation was that in all East European countries revisionist leaders would come to power who would embrace his political vision of a socialism based on law and respect for the individual. Addressing the Soviet Congress of Peoples' Deputies on October 23, 1989, Foreign Minister Eduard Shevardnadze insisted that "historic, qualitative changes" were taking place in Europe, and they required a complete divorce from the old ready-made recipes: "New, alternative forces are entering the political arena in some of these countries. No one is bringing them in. They arise because the people want them."[18] It was obvious that, as the Soviet spokesman Gennady Gerasimov put it bluntly, the Brezhnev Doctrine had been replaced by a new perspective, respectful of each country's right to have "its own way."[19] Some might even say that a "Sinatra Doctrine" was thus born.

The shift in the Soviet approach to changes in the political and economic system and the encouragement of reforms in the Warsaw Pact countries contributed to the revival of long-suppressed revisionist trends within the ruling elites in those countries, as well as to the radicalization of the social movements from below. That was particularly evident in Poland and Hungary, the two countries that had advanced the farthest in past experimentation with liberal policies. Gorbachev's initial strategy, between 1986 and 1988, was to encourage the liberal factions within the ruling parties to take over and initiate rapid economic reforms, open up the political system, and allow more social activism, including the formation of independent associations and groups. The first testing ground for the new strategy, radically different from Brezhnev's stubborn rejection of any liberalization in the Soviet bloc, was Poland.

SOLIDARITY REDUX AND THE COLLAPSE OF POLISH COMMUNISM

The nonviolent exit from an authoritarian regime based on the ideological dictatorship of the communist party was possible in Poland because there were groups within both the power elite and the opposition who understood the need for compromise. The maturing of such an attitude, especially among those who had run the country without any accountability for decades, came with the understanding of the intensity of the social and economic crisis and the realization that without bringing society into the governing process the situation could only worsen. Although the Jaruzelski regime had long tried to win national legitimacy, it was identified by large strata of society with the martial law repression. In 1988, as a gesture of opening and good will, Jaruzelski appointed Mieczyslaw Rakowski, an astute politician and journalist, as Prime Minister. In 1989 Jaruzelski stepped down as party leader and ensured that Rakowski, whose Gorbachevism was beyond question, would be his successor. But it was too late for modest reforms in Poland.

Two waves of strikes in April and August 1988 compelled the Jaruzelski regime to recognize that it could not govern in defiance of society. The mounting social unrest could not be suppressed without a new recourse to force. But that was precisely what the Gorbachevites sought to avoid. The military solution had been tried in the early 1980s and had failed lamentably. All the regime's attempts to co-opt prominent intellectuals into the power structure and to eliminate the risk of a revival of the Solidarity movement had been met with categorical refusals.

Engaging in dialogue with representatives of Solidarity and admitting the need for power sharing in times of dramatic social and economic crisis appeared to be the only alternative to prolonging the chaos. It was true that for many communist hard-liners the very idea of a compromise with those whom they had long seen as mortal enemies looked like capitulation. So strong was the resistance of the dogmatics in the party leadership to the relegalization of the independent union in January 1989, that Jaruzelski and three of his closest advisers threatened to resign if the party failed to accept a dialogue with Solidarity.[20] In spite of mutual resentments, rooted in the memories of repression and the underground struggle against the police state, both sides, the government and Solidarity, admitted that only a roundtable discussion could take the country out of the stalemate. The talks began in February 1989 and resulted in a political agreement on April 5. The compromise provided for the relegalization of Solidarity, the farmers' Rural Solidarity, the Independent Students' Association, and other components of the Polish civil society. The institutional framework of the government was restructured, with a new state presidency enjoying limited powers; a new, freely elected Senate; and a lower house, the Sejm, that would need a two-thirds majority vote to override a Senate veto of its bills. The communist coalition (the Polish

United Workers Party and its allies) was guaranteed, at least during the first elections, 65 percent of the seats in the lower house. The communists continued to hold the key ministries, Defense and Internal Affairs, but the opposition was allowed to publish its own newspapers and would have limited access to government-controlled radio and television.

Compared with the other Eastern-bloc countries, Poland had entered a new era. The once persecuted activists emerged from political hiding and were acclaimed as national figures. With regard to economic reforms and control, the agreement provided for a transition to a market economy without offering a clear indication of the strategies to be pursued. Conflicts between the government and the independent trade unions over wage indexation continued in the following months. Lech Walesa, chairman of the Solidarity union, praised the accords as the beginning of the road to a democratic and free Poland. Walesa insisted that compromise was the only solution to ensure the country's nonviolent transition to a democratic system: "Our representatives in the Sejm and Senate can create a platform from which we will jump into freedom and independence."[21]

In the first round of elections in June 1989, the Poles overwhelmingly supported Solidarity candidates and denied even unopposed communist candidates victory. The elections, the first free ones in the history of the Soviet bloc, sanctioned the historical defeat of the Polish communists and the rise of Solidarity as the country's decisive political force. The Polish situation was indeed unprecedented in the annals of communism: a parliament in which the anticommunist opposition had 99 of the 100 seats in the upper house and an increasingly active political life that included not only Solidarity and the communists, but also the suddenly revitalized former allies of the communist party who strove to assert their autonomy and ceased to support the communists automatically. Based on those parliamentary arrangements, unthinkable only several months earlier, Solidarity ensured its domination in the legislature. While Solidarity had accepted the continuation of communist control over government, its calculation turned out to be correct: As events unfolded in Eastern Europe during the revolutionary year 1989, the Polish communists continued their political retreat. The whole approach to the compromise was based on the awareness that Polish communism had come to a political and intellectual end—it was basically exhausted, and it could not mobilize any serious social support.

In August 1989 a new threshold was passed in Poland when Jaruzelski, who had been re-elected president with the support of Solidarity, decided to appoint Tadeusz Mazowiecki, a prominent Catholic intellectual and a key Solidarity adviser, as the country's new Prime Minister.

It is known that the decision had been preceded by a phone call from Mikhail Gorbachev to the communist leader Mieczyslaw Rakowski, in which Moscow presumably expressed its readiness (or even willingness) to accept a Solidarity-run government with a communist minority.[22] The communists had no other choice but to accept this deal. Otherwise, there would be a return to the previous ungovernable situation, with more social unrest, strikes, and even street violence. For the communists, a coalition government in which Solidarity representatives were responsible for economic management and social affairs could even be turned into an advantage. After all, they were placing the burden of economic recovery and the unpopular decisions associated with drastic reforms on Solidarity, while they retained the levers for controlling society through the ministries of Defense and Internal affairs. So on September 12, Tadeusz Mazowiecki became the first noncommunist Prime Minister in a Warsaw Pact country.

Poland's revolution had taken place over ten years of heroic battles, romantic dreams, brutal repression, and miraculous resurrection of an extraordinarily imaginative and resilient society. One year earlier, no analyst anticipated the speed or the depth of the changes that were to take place in that country and that brought to power, as a result of painful negotiation, those whom Jaruzelski had jailed as public enemies after the proclamation of martial law. Now the public enemies were ruling the country's economy and were preparing for the next round of the struggle for the complete conquest of political power. With the benefit of hindsight, and by comparison with the changes that would happen in the next months in the other bloc countries, the Polish compromise seemed too limited, too moderate, and maybe too rational. But at the moment of its achievement, in the early autumn of 1989, it was a revolutionary alteration in the logic of power within the communist world. One should remember that Leninism, as a doctrine, rejects power sharing and sees the communist party's leading role, that is, its monopoly on power, as a sacrosanct dogma. What happened in Poland was the public and unequivocal recognition by the communists that they had lost the struggle with society. Later there would be many voices to reproach the Solidarity negotiators' acceptance of a communist president and tolerance of communists in crucial government positions. That reproach, however, did not take into account the complexity of the Polish and international situation in the summer of 1989, when the Soviets were only beginning to reconsider their commitment to the existence of the GDR. The Polish communists were still ready to engage in the life-or-death struggle to preserve their positions in the army and police. Writing in May 1989,

Timothy Garton Ash noted that in countries like Poland and Hungary the difficulties of peaceful transition arose from the need for the rulers to get accustomed to the sentiment of their political defeat:

> Prediction is now, more than ever, impossible. The best and the brightest people on both sides in Poland and Hungary have engaged in a great and perilous adventure. "You know," one of the most intelligent Polish Party leaders said to one of the most intelligent of the Polish opposition leaders during a coffee break at the Roundtable, "all the textbooks tell us how difficult it is to seize power. But no one has described how difficult it is to relinquish power."[23]

The decision to relinquish power cannot be dissociated from the moral and ideological crisis of the communist elites. The Polish communists were forced to recognize the historical failure of the political and social model they had imposed on their society. The unreconstructed Leninists had lost the game, and the reformers desperately tried to rescue whatever could be salvaged of the leftist heritage. In January 1990, when the Polish United Workers Party held its Congress, it decided to rename itself the Party of Social Democracy, under a new leader, Aleksander Kwasniewski. A splinter group of this new party emerged bearing the name the Social Democratic Union, under the leadership of the reform communist, former Politburo member, and Gdansk party leader Tadeusz Fiszbach. To comprehend the collapse of communism in Poland, one should compare the membership of the PUWP in 1986, when it had more than 2 million members, with the combined membership of the two neocommunist formations in March 1990, which did not exceed 67,000.[24] The reshaped party admitted its responsibility for the crimes perpetrated during the Stalin years and recognized its role in engineering Poland's economic disaster. The self-criticism was, however, insufficient to restore the party's image.

Polish communism can be considered to have ended in incurable moral and political discredit. To those who were still promising experiments with different versions of socialism, the overwhelming majority of the Poles would have responded that socialism for them had amounted to the degradation of the individual, the mistreatment of the environment, the persecution of free thought, and the spiritual impoverishment of society. There was no constituency in Poland even for a reconstructed communist party. Poles wanted not to revitalize socialism, but to get rid of it. The most important cause of the breakdown of communism in Poland was the general realization that after martial law the rulers did not have any weapon left with which to keep the system going. At the moment they started to make concessions and accepted the dialogue with society, even if initially in a self-serving and certainly Machiavellian way, the Polish communists ruined the principal underpinning of their dictatorship: the population's sense that the system was immutable and that any form of opposition would automatically result in the marginalization and persecution of the dissenters.

The proclamation of martial law in Poland was actually the beginning of the ultimate and complete erosion of communism in Eastern Europe. The moment the communists admitted that they had to use naked violence against 10 million people organized in an independent union, they acknowledged that the real nature of their power had nothing to do with government by the working class. It was a striking exposure of the system as a bureaucratic, antiproletarian dictatorship. Because of the succession crises in the Kremlin and the already disconcerted Soviet reaction to challenges coming from Eastern Europe, there was no hope that external intervention could save the system. Jaruzelski and his associates clung to power in contempt of their own ideological pretenses and thus admitted that the whole ideology was nothing but a rhetorical mirage, a semantic usurpation meant to legitimize the control exerted by a tiny, sectarian minority over the whole of society. The long decade that started with the foundation of Solidarity in August 1980 culminated in the end of the communist monopoly on power in Poland in the summer of 1989. The strategy of the "new evolutionism" had provoked the slow but irresistible erosion of government power and the rise of a counterpower in the shape of the unofficial groups and movements that had mushroomed in the 1980s despite the regime's repressive measures.

Poland's failed totalitarianism had become an ailing authoritarian regime whose rulers came to the conclusion that the stalemate could not continue forever. At the same time, the Roundtable strategy required a willingness on the part of both the moderate groups within the opposition and the reformers within the government to accept a deal best described by Adam Michnik, the dissident historian, as "your president, our prime minister." From that moment on, the transition to postcommunism was a possibility, even though key positions in the government were still held by the partisans of martial law. Actually, with the benefit of hindsight, one can observe that the military regime imposed in December 1981 had almost annihilated the communist party as the center of decision-making and had transferred power to a technocratic coterie utterly devoid of ideological commitment. Of course, the party continued to exist and to perform its ritualistic functions, but it had lost the impetus that had made possible its domination over society for so many

years. Mihaly Vajda, a Hungarian social philosopher, explained the collapse as the fading away of the myth about the system's infallibility and
omnipotence:

> [T]he strength of the system rested on the demonstration of its omnipo-
> tence—on demonstrating that any kind of disobedience would be regis-
> tered and retaliated against, that there was simply no chance of initiating
> anything from below. As soon as the regime proved unable to observe
> this principle, when it started to show a degree of responsiveness to
> society's demands, its magic power was over. And, against appearances,
> it was already over in 1981. Martial law in Poland was actually a sort of
> unadmitted compromise. The "normal" solution would have been a So-
> viet intervention, or better the intervention of the allied armies of the
> Warsaw Pact. But since the Russians were no longer able to take the risk
> of civil war in the middle of Europe, they accepted martial law as a
> solution, even though it must have been clear to them that the Polish
> army would not suppress society with the ruthlessness and regardlessness
> which had always been proof of the system's strength. So, from the point
> of view of the system, martial law was a failure and a fatal blow to its
> identity.[25]

To make his point even more poignant, Vajda mentioned that it was
precisely on December 13, 1981, the day when Martial Law was proclaimed in Poland, that the Hungarian democratic opposition launched
its samizdat journal *Beszelö*. "On that day it became clear that the system
was vulnerable, that it was not imperishable. After 13 December 1981
there was no other way out for the regime than to follow a line which at
least had something in common with European rationality—thus ceasing
to be the same system."[26]

The Polish opening in 1988 and 1989 had a substantial impact on the
whole region: Hopes were uplifted not only in Hungary, where the political system had begun to relax in previous years, but also in Czechoslovakia, where people started to organize public protests against official repression of dissident activities. The revolutionary meaning of the changes in
Poland was not lost on Romania's Nicolae Ceausescu, who tried, in a
desperate way, to convince other Warsaw Pact leaders that the formation
of a Solidarity-led government had to be halted by all means, including
military intervention. There is irony in the fact that the man who in
August 1968 had protested the crushing of the Prague reform movement
was calling in 1989 for immediate suppression of the Polish experiment in
democratization. But Ceausescu's rabid outbursts of neo-Stalinist conservatism could not convince anyone. The movement toward radical re-

forms in Eastern Europe had acquired a dynamic of its own. As long as
the Soviets refrained from direct intervention, there was no way to stop
it. After having been pronounced dead in the early 1980s, at the end of
the decade Solidarity emerged as a truly national movement that took
upon itself the building of a pluralist society and launched dramatic
reforms in the hope of solving Poland's economic predicament rapidly.

From the moment the Solidarity-run government was formed, it was
clear that the movement could not continue to deny its inherently political nature. It was also clear that it had to structure itself as an organized
political party, or, even more likely, several political parties could emerge
as a result of the inevitable fragmentation dictated by both ideological
and personality-related factors. Solidarity had acted as a united body as
long as it confronted a common enemy represented by the communist
party-state with its immense repressive apparatus. Now that the state had
acknowledged its failure and Solidarity was charged with the country's
social and economic recovery, the long-denied differences among the
movement's various groups and factions came to the surface. The age of
undifferentiated brotherhood had to come to an end.

The saga of anticommunist resistance was succeeded by the reconstruction of a heterogeneous and extremely colorful political spectrum.
Lech Walesa, who initially kept a low profile, staying away from the
mainstream of the new politics, was still the towering figure within
Solidarity. Meanwhile, many of his former advisers and other prominent
Solidarity activists became involved in parliamentary and governmental
activities and soon were perceived as a new political class.

THE HUNGARIAN BREAKTHROUGH

As previously discussed, the logic of Kadarism was based on the neutraliza-
tion of political opposition and the conservation of the established order
with its increased tolerance for criticism as the best deal under the existing circumstances. Kadarism represented a political stalemate, and it
could last only as long as the economic conditions permitted relative
prosperity—at least compared with the standard of living in other communist countries.

In 1968 the Hungarians had initiated a daring economic experiment
in the direction of decentralization. It included limitation of the imperative role of central planning, increased autonomy for enterprises, the
formation of a managerial class free of ideological illusions, and encouragement of private initiative. Had those reforms been pursued in a consis-

tent manner, they would have released the market forces and might have ensured propitious conditions for Western investment. But dogmatic elements in the Hungarian communist leadership, supported by Moscow, eventually prevailed over the reformers, and the New Economic Mechanism was abandoned. Janos Kadar himself, a seasoned apparatchik with limited political imagination, was reluctant to engage in reforms that could undermine the foundations of the system he considered to be the best from the viewpoint of the working class. The Leninists, obsessed with the specter of unemployment, argued that economic reforms would generate explosive social tensions. They preferred to keep the system in its existing form and accused the liberals of irresponsibility.

One thing should be made clear: The Hungarian dogmatics were of a different mold from their Romanian, East German, and Czechoslovak counterparts. For them, the principle of government was consensus based on a tacit compromise between rulers and ruled. Neither Kadar nor his Prime Minister, Jenö Fock, not even the chief ideologue, György Aczel, conceived of socialism in such a restrictive and rigid way as Ceausescu, Honecker, or Husak. At the same time, those people were not ready to espouse a radical break with the traditional rules of the game. They saw the communist party as the center of political life, the embodiment of a superior understanding of historical rationality. It was therefore normal for them to resent the attempts of the liberals to open the system and encourage the emergence of pluralist forces in economic life. Rezsö Nyers and Bela Biszku, two party leaders well known for their reformist views, were dropped from the Politburo in the early 1970s.

The restoration of Leninist dogmas in the economy did not mean, however, a relapse into political terror. Even during the 1970s and early 1980s Hungary remained the least repressive of the Warsaw Pact countries. That tolerance was based on a fragile articulation of basically incompatible social interests, as would become strikingly clear in the 1980s, when the country's economic collapse would create a state of general unrest and widespread discontent with the government's ineptitude. The once acclaimed Kadar, the man who had been credited with a sense of political adjustment in the unfavorable circumstances that had permitted him to turn Hungary into the most livable barrack of the communist camp, had lost his maverick image. Instead, he was widely seen as the patron of a corrupt and blatantly inefficient bureaucracy. Far from being the guarantor of the country's progress, Kadar was increasingly perceived as the main obstacle to his own party's renewal.

The political and social situation worsened in the 1980s, when large social groups started to question the validity of the Kadar policies. The old leader's astute manueverings had ceased to pay off. Once Gorbachev gave the signal for a new liberalization and encouraged the search for reforms in the countries of the bloc, Kadar found himself increasingly out of touch with the new trends. The challenge to his authority came not only from opposition groups outside the communist party but also from within the communist elite itself. His political instincts, which had proved remark-ably realistic during Brezhnev's period, did not help him under Gorbachev. It was clear that Hungary was moving fast in the direction of political democratization, and Kadar was not the man to allow such a course to develop. He had been the one to preside over the post-1956 repression, and as the economic situation deteriorated, people began to remember Kadar's role in the suppression of the Budapest uprising.

In a political document published by the Democratic Opposition in 1987 and symbolically entitled "The Social Contract," the failure of Kadarism was explained in light of the irreversible economic decline of the system and the refusal of the old leadership to recognize the magni-tude of the social crisis that was already shaking the Hungarian system. According to the authors of that political platform, published in the samizdat journal *Beszelö*, the evolution of society in the thirty years that followed the suppression of the revolutionary upheaval of 1956 had made impossible the continuation of a compromise based on half-truths and self-delusions. The consensus personified by Kadarism had ceased to in-spire confidence and support among the population. The document stated:

> Janos Kadar has been the symbol of the golden middle road in Hungary. He, in contrast with Rakosi, has not attempted to force on the people grandiose programs for society's transformation. And unlike Imre Nagy, he has been unwilling to accept curbs on the Communist Party's rule. Hold-ing a monopoly of power, he has avoided encroachment of his interests by any group capable of voicing discontent. And he has allowed everyone to find compensation for one's losses, wherever possible. The country . . . approved of Kadar's policy of consolidation, longing for a secure and peaceful life. In exchange, it accepted that the party rules in the name of the people, and the apparatus rules in the name of the party's rank and file. This was the so-called consensus.[27]

Kadarism had led the country into a political and social dead end. The Democratic Opposition began calling for the immediate departure of the man whose name was inextricably linked to that system. But Kadar's political elimination was not enough. Instead of the patronizing policies practiced by Kadar and his associates, the ruling party had to reassess its relationship with society dramatically.

The policy of false consensus had to be supplanted by a strategy of national compromise. For such a compromise to be reached, society had to wake up immediately from its long-induced torpor and start to organize itself. It was not enough for a circle of heroic intellectuals to challenge the communist party's domination. Criticism from below had to engage large social strata, including some within the reformist wing of the party, on whom pressure from the rank-and-file could be a catalyst to radicalize their stances in opposition to bureaucratic conformity. According to the Democratic Opposition, the power structure could enter into a dialogue only if it found that the intellectuals were not the only ones with whom it had to negotiate. Intellectual narcissism had to be abandoned in favor of a systematic building of grassroots nuclei of civic activism. Those nuclei, the backbone of the emerging civil society, would make demands for the radical transformation of the system. Their demands would include a long-term and a short-term agenda.

In the long run, they would resume the legacy of October 1956 by advocating political pluralism and representative democracy in government; self-management in the workplace; local government in the settlements; and national self-determination and neutrality in foreign policy. Because those demands appeared too radical for the circumstances of 1987, the Democratic Opposition offered a compromise that would rapidly modify the relationship between the power structure and society. The principal slogans suggested by *Beszelö* for the coming stage of political revival were: constitutional checks on party rule; a sovereign national Assemby; an accountable government; freedom of the press guaranteed by law; legal protection for employees; representation of interests; freedom of association; social security and an equitable social welfare policy; and, as an all-embracing demand, civil rights.[28] Written during the first stage of Gorbachevism, when the Kremlin had not yet made clear its new approach to East European political realities, the "Social Contract," like Michnik's new evolutionism, went on the assumption that the communist party's leading role could not be successfully challenged. The purpose, therefore, became to limit it, to place it under popular control and to create the institutional guarantees that would prevent communist bureaucrats from perpetuating their abuses. But events continued to gather momentum, and several months after the publication of this path-breaking document it appeared that there were significant groups within the communist elite who envisioned a redefinition of the party's role in society. The factional struggle within the leadership and the meteoric rise of Imre Pozsgay as the symbol of a Hungarian version of Gorbachevism accelerated the erosion of Kadarism.

The Kadar era came to an end in May 1988, when a national party conference replaced the old General Secretary with a four-member presidium chaired by Rezsö Nyers, the driving force behind the aborted economic reform of the late 1960s. The new General Secretary, in charge of everyday party operation, was Karoly Grosz, a colorless apparatchik whom Kadar had groomed for succession. The other two members of the foursome were the flamboyant reformer Imre Pozsgay and the dogmatic ideologue Janos Berecz, who had suddenly converted to pluralism. Initially, Grosz appeared to bid for control over the party apparatus and tried to keep the situation under control. But he could not exert real power; like Kadar he had been associated with the antirevolutionary repression after 1956 and had climbed the career ladder as an obedient party bureaucrat. Grosz was increasingly challenged by members of the radical reformist wing within the Hungarian communist party, headed by Rezsö Nyers and Imre Pozsgay. Pozsgay criticized the party leadership for its procrastination in restoring the truth about the 1956 revolution and rehabilitating Nagy and other victims of the Kadarist terror. He insisted that the communists come to terms with their role in the various phases of repression, if they wanted to continue to participate in a pluralistic Hungarian political system. He continued to defend the ideals of socialism that, according to him, had been viciously disfigured in the practice of Stalinism.

Like Gorbachev, Pozsgay continued to stick to his Marxist beliefs while drawing a drastic line of demarcation between humane socialism and Stalinist totalitarianism. But his indictment of the existing system was more radical than anything the Soviet leader had ever said about systemic changes:

> This is a crisis of Stalinism. It has become absolutely certain that this system cannot be reformed because it has failed and has proven inadequate to give the experience and feeling of freedom to people. This system is unable to create internal driving forces in the individuals and citizens to accept something noble, and this system destroyed solidarity among people and cooperation among producers. Under such circumstances, the only decision we could make was that this entire Stalinist system should be discarded, complete with its ideology. I do not see the essence of this ideology in Marxism or in distorting Marxism, because it has nothing to do with Marxism.[29]

Less than one year after Kadar's dismissal Nyers, a former social democrat widely perceived as a man of decency and lucidity, replaced

Grosz as party leader. In October 1989 a Congress of the Hungarian communist party (the official name was the Hungarian Socialist Workers' Party) took place. The party decided to change its name to the Hungarian Socialist Party and renounced its Bolshevik ideology, including the claim to a constitutionally guaranteed leading role in society. A splinter group headed by Grosz and Berecz refused to accept that change and stuck to the old party name, while Pozsgay, Nyers, and Prime Minister Miklos Nemeth went out of their way to persuade public opinion that they had indeed internalized the principles of pluralism.[30]

In the meantime the opposition organized itself. Several major political parties emerged in Hungary during 1988 and 1989. The Democratic Forum, a conservative populist group, was primarily concerned with the tragic degradation of the Hungarian countryside under communism, the decline in moral values, and the communist neglect of the fate of Hungarian minorities abroad. The Free Democrats were basically an intellectual party championing the values of a free economy and liberal society. They originated in the Democratic Opposition of the late 1970s and 1980s. The leaders of the Free Democrats were brilliant intellectuals who had organized the samizdat counterculture during the decades of social torpor and political apathy under Kadarism. Among their leaders was Laszlo Rajk, an architect and civil rights activist whose father had been hanged after the Budapest show trial in 1949; Janos Kis, a philosopher who had written a number of seminal essays on opposition strategies in Soviet-style societies; Miklos Haraszti, the author of such works as A Worker in a Workers' State and The Velvet Prison; and Gaspar Miklos Tamas, a philosopher born in Transylvania, who had emigrated to Hungary in 1978 and had joined the samizdat opposition. For years these people had published the small independent journal Beszelö.

In the summer of 1989 the Hungarian opposition organized a roundtable to engage in talks with the government, which was controlled by the communist reformers. During those negotiations between the Opposition Roundtable and the government an agreement was reached to organize free elections in 1990. The transition to a pluralistic order was accepted as inevitable by both the opposition and the dominant Socialist Party, but the relationship between the opposition parties was not always smooth. Actually, the Free Democrats resented the fact that representatives of the Democratic Forum had held earlier and separate negotiations with Pozsgay and his associates without inviting other political groups. For instance, a meeting took place in Monor where Pozsgay and the leaders of the emerging Democratic Forum analyzed possibilities for a future dialogue.

In the summer of 1989 the political spectrum in Hungary was already diversified, ranging from the dogmatic communists rallying around Karoly Grosz, through the reformers who had adopted the language if not the ideology of social democracy (Nyers and Pozsgay), to the Free Democrats and the Democratic Forum. A uniquely Hungarian political party, with a flavor of anarchism in its rejection of the status quo and proud rebellion against the accomodationist values of the adult generation, was FIDESZ (Federation of Young Democrats), a political formation founded in the spring of 1988, which held its congress in the fall of that year. During its First Congress, FIDESZ fixed an age limit for membership that made possible entry into the party only for those between twenty-six and thirty-five. In its "Declaration of a Political Program," adopted in 1988, FIDESZ proclaimed the need to fight for Hungary's rapid reintegration into the European community. As it took an increasingly active role in Hungarian civil society, FIDESZ rejected any sectarian or conspiratorial activity. The movement was therefore part of the mounting East European wave of civil rights activism that refused to reduce the struggle to the strictly political dimension:

> FIDESZ distances itself from the idea that the seizure of state power is enough to create democracy. We do not believe that the fact of any new organization gaining power will of itself make the realization of human and civil rights possible. The safeguard of democracy, its ultimate guarantee, is not state power but a society with a democratic political culture. The existence of parties competing for the control of state life is a necessary but not a sufficient condition. We must not seize power, but should have the objective of fostering self-organization in the hope that the reborn society, built up from its communities, will be capable of electing its own government.

Emphasizing its commitment to the idea of developing grassroots structures, FIDESZ made a clear point of its rejection of any form of violence or Jacobin dictatorial methods of coercion:

> We have reached the point where we must organize our defense quickly and without delay against policies of the authorities that are hostile to society. We profess that the most effective tools against the mistaken and self-interested policies of the authorities are a democratic way of thinking and organization. In our work for a society capable of building itself and of creating its own state power, the two most feared weapons, inner independence and moral convictions, as well as an invincible solidarity with each other, stand at our command.

Echoing the moral philosophy of the Polish and Czechoslovak opposition movements, FIDESZ professed its belief that "no social objective is of greater value than the guarantee of citizens' peaceful, free and independent lives."[31]

During Imre Nagy's reburial ceremony in Budapest, FIDESZ representatives had outshone other political figures with their unabashed anticommunist stance. According to Ferenc Köszeg, a sociologist who had been an editor for *Beszelö* and had become a member of the nine-member leadership of the Alliance of Free Democrats, this party could not be considered a mere intellectual club. Interviewed in June 1989, Köszeg declared:

> It is true that some of the best-known intellectuals are among our founding members, but we are able increasingly to recruit other people: qualified workers, for example. . . . Our membership is still only about 3,000, but it has been increasing during the last few months since we began to publicly discuss our programme. The Free Democrats are the main successors to the democratic opposition, which was highly respected by people who were really critical of the regime. I would say that the Free Democrats is both the party of radical intellectuals and the party of the angry people, those who really wish to see the implementation of some far-reaching radical changes.[32]

According to Köszeg, the Democratic Forum recruited primarily among the disaffected middle class of the provincial cities, especially among those who had been denied social promotion because of their refusal to join the communist party, but who were nonetheless part of the establishment.

THE COLLAPSE OF THE GDR: SETTING THE STAGE FOR THE COLLAPSE OF CZECHOSLOVAK COMMUNISM

In the fall of 1989 the Hungarian government took the unprecedented step of allowing East German tourists to cross into Austria on their way home. In so doing, the Hungarian regime reneged on its treaty obligation to East Germany not to allow GDR citizens to leave Hungary for a Western country and thus opened the way for a demographic hemorrhage that would ruin the East German economy. With about 100,000 East German tourists on Hungarian territory, it was clear that the decision of the Nemeth government to remove the barbed-wire barriers at the crossing point with Austria was an extraordinary blow to the East German regime's policy of denying its population the right to emigrate.

The situation turned even more complex when mostly young East German tourists flooded the West German Embassy in Prague. Because Czechoslovakia was one of the few countries where the East Germans could travel without passports, Prague became a magnet for the increasingly disaffected young East Germans, who saw no hope for reform in their own country. Unlike the Hungarians, the Jakes regime was sympathetic to the plight of the East German government but could do nothing to stop the massive wave of East Germans flocking to the West German Embassy in Prague. Special trains were organized to transport the East Germans through the GDR to the Federal Republic, which was faced with an unexpected flood of new settlers. According to the West German constitution, the newcomers were fellow Germans eligible for the benefits and privileges of West German citizenship.

Ironically, that crisis coincided with the the Honecker regime's preparations to celebrate the fortieth anniversary of the GDR. It was obvious that the regime was experiencing a deep crisis. The frictions with the Soviet Union and the reluctance to engage even in limited reforms had undermined the leadership's power base. For Honecker and his associates, the changes in Moscow were more difficult to deal with than for any other communist leadership in Eastern Europe because of the GDR's direct dependence on Soviet military and economic support. Perhaps the only comparable situation was that of the Husak–Jakes team in Czechoslovakia, whose coming to power had been the direct consequence of the Soviet invasion of that country in August 1968.

Once the Soviets changed their assessment of the Prague Spring, the Czechoslovak communists too found themselves politically isolated and deprived of both internal and external support. It then became possible for the deposed leaders of the reform movement to reemerge as champions of the strategy of socialism with a human face. For instance, after years of internal exile and refusal to join underground civil rights movements, Alexander Dubcek granted an interview in January 1988 to the Italian communist daily L'Unitá, in which he reaffirmed the basic principles of the Soviet-suppressed reform movement and openly endorsed Gorbachev's policy of glasnost. He insisted on the similarity between the fundamental sources of inspiration between the two reform movements and contended that had a Gorbachevite leadership been in charge in 1968, the Soviet intervention would have been unthinkable.[33] In April 1989 another symptomatic event took place, suggesting that a reconsideration of the 1968 invasion was imminent: The government-run Hungarian television broadcast an interview with Dubcek, officially a nonperson in his own country, who argued again that the origin of the 1968

Following the Soviet invasion of Czechoslovakia in 1968, playwright and human rights activist Vaclav Havel refused to emigrate and continued to fight in defense of civil rights. His essay "The Power of the Powerless," published in a samizdat collection in 1979, offered a strategy of self-emancipation for individuals living in societies where the mechanisms of repression are both insidious and invisible. Now president of his country, he is seen here working in a brewery in the 1970s. *Ivan Barta*

The independent Polish labor union, Solidarity, opened a new chapter in the history of Eastern Europe by showing in 1980 that the cracks in the apparently monolithic totalitarian edifice could be exploited in an imaginative way. Lech Walesa, an electrician from the Lenin shipyard in Gdansk, its original leader— elected president of Poland in 1991—is seen here in 1989 celebrating after his reelection as president of Solidarity. *Photo © Marek Swiezewski/Delta*

Adam Michnik's political career started during the student protest movement at the University of Warsaw in the 1960s, included participation on Lech Walesa's team of advisors, and was punctuated by a series of prison terms. Michnik has distinguished himself as a dissident, philosopher, newspaper editor, and senator.
East European Reporter

Among those involved in the grassroots activism directed against Bulgarian dictator Todor Zhivkov was Zhelyu Zhelev, a philosopher who had been expelled from the Communist Party in the 1960s because of his opposition to totalitarianism. In 1988 Zhelev had been a co-founder of the "Club for the Support of Glasnost and Perestroika," and in December 1989 he was elected president of the coordinating committee of the union of democratic forces. *East European Reporter*

Among the leaders of the Free Democrats in Hungary is Janos Kis, a philosopher who has written a number of seminal essays on opposition strategies in Soviet-style societies. The Free Democrats, active in the reorganization of Hungary's political system since 1989, are a political party whose origins lie in the samizdat counterculture during the decades of social torpor and political apathy under Kadar. *East European Reporter*

On June 16, 1989, a solemn ceremony took place in Budapest. For more than 30 years, Imre Nagy and the other martyrs of the 1956 revolution had been besmirched as fomenters of counterrevolutionary conspiracy. Now, the leaders of Hungary's 1956 uprising were finally granted a proper burial. *Nagy Piroska*

Freedom and democracy came more quickly to Poland than to any other Eastern European country. Seen here are some campaign posters outside Solidarity's Warsaw headquarters in June of 1989 just as the first round of national elections was getting underway. Poles overwhelmingly supported Solidarity candidates and denied even unopposed communist candidates victory. *East European Reporter*

In August 1989 a new threshold was passed in Poland when Communist leader General Jaruzelski appointed Tadeusz Mazowiecki, a prominent Catholic intellectual and a key Solidarity advisor, as the country's new prime minister. It is known that the decision had been preceded by a phone call from Mikhail Gorbachev to the communist leader Mieczyslaw Rakowski, in which Moscow presumably expressed its readiness to accept a Solidarity-run coalition government, with communists maintaining a number of key ministries (defense and security police). *Juliusz Sokolowski/Delta*

On November 29, 1989, the Czechoslovak federal assembly abolished the Constitutional clauses guaranteeing the Communist Party's leading role. The way was thus open for the complete disbandment of the artificial power structure imposed by Soviet tanks in August 1968. Vaclav Havel was elected Czechoslovakia's president on December 29. On the right, he is seen with Alexander Dubcek, upon hearing of the resignation of the Politburo. *East European Reporter*

The Romanian Revolution began in the city of Timisoara, sparked by the courage of one man, the Reverend Laszlo Tökes. On December 15,1989, when secret police tried to evict Tökes forcibly from his parish house, thousands of people formed a human chain and unleashed a massive anti-Ceausescu demonstration. By Christmas Day, the Communist Party had been swept out of office and Nicolae and Elena Ceausescu tried and executed. Pictured here are scenes from the revolution: (Top) Tanks stand outside the Central University in Bucharest. (Above) Democrats remove the letters from a plaque on a government office building. *Radek Sikorski (both photos)*

(Above) Todor Zhivkov's expulsion from power as leader of Bulgaria's Communist Party (he is seen here on his way to his trial in February 1991) opened the way for large street demonstrations in Sofia and other Bulgarian cities. Popular discontent forced the Communist party to renounce its monopoly on political power and eventually to change its name to the Bulgarian Socialist Party as a symbolic departure from Leninist dogmas. (Right) A helicopter is seen removing the communist red star from the party headquarters in Sofia. *Credit: Above: Michaela Prancheva. Right: East European Reporter*

crisis lay in the dogmatism of Brezhnev and of his associates in the other Warsaw Pact countries.

The significance of the Dubcek interview broadcast by Budapest Television lay in the fact that Hungary had participated in the military action against the legal Czechoslovak government in August 1968. Dubcek challenged the official line of the Husak—Jakes regime, which claimed that the foreign intervention had been made indispensable by the rise of counterrevolutionary forces protected by the lenient Dubcek leadership:

> Not only were there no counterrevolutionary forces within the country, there were also no such forces that could endanger socialism whatsoever. If there were, then we know what it was only too well: the dogmatism of Brezhnev. This is what endangered socialism and weakened the party's stands, the international communist movement, social democracy, and the left-wing socialist parties. And why? To serve a political line which is not in harmony with the interests of democracy, socialism, and the people.[34]

The reactivation of the Prague Spring reformers was considered ominous, and rightly so, by the beneficiaries of the Soviet occupation of Czechoslovakia in 1968. Dubcek's attempt at a political comeback was ridiculed in the official Czechoslovak media, where he was described as a bankrupt politician, an adventurer, and a political renegade.

Terrified at the prospect of a Soviet reconsideration of the 1968 decision to use military force against a reform movement essentially similar to the one launched by Gorbachev himself, the dogmatics in Prague attacked Dubcek with special ardor. For instance, *Rude Pravo*, the official party daily, chose to see Dubcek's political resurrection as the megalomaniacal illusion of a failed politician rather than as a signal that times were changing and that the Soviets themselves had abandoned the internationalist mythology that justified the brutal end of the Prague Spring:

> Dubcek obviously still thinks that he is indelibly written into the history books of our country as an enlightened reformer of socialism who was wrongfully expelled from the party. He expects that the time will come when this "wrong" will be righted. However, it is possible to falsely interpret history, but not to change it. His era in history will remain chronicled as a warning of where the policy of a man that denounces Marxist-Leninist maxims, who casts aside socialist principles, and who betrayed the interests of the people leads. He will forever remain simply the man who led our party and country to the brink of catastrophe.[35]

Despite the adamant tone of these warnings, the conservatives in Prague did not fail to realize that their time had passed. The consensus within the Czechoslovak top elite had evaporated as a result of the confusing signals coming from Moscow. Even the former Prime Minister, Lubomir Strougal, who had been one of the architects of the post-1968 politics of "normalization," started to advocate reforms. His successor, Ladislav Adamec, hinted at the need to rejuvenate the party leadership and to recognize the faults of the past.

So in October 1989 the East German regime could count only on the wholehearted support of one like-minded communist leader: Romania' Nicolae Ceausescu, who actually participated in the ceremonies organized in East Berlin to glorify the achievements of the Honecker regime. The Czechoslovak leaders were confronted with an increasingly vocal opposition. In Bulgaria Todor Zhivkov desperately tried to stay in power while his colleagues were already fomenting a Byzantine plot that was to remove him ingloriously one month later. As for Gorbachev himself, he went to East Berlin only to tell Honecker that those who lag behind in reforms would pay dearly for their conservatism.

Despite the carefully orchestrated marches and parades, it was clear that the SED was challenged by a growing movement of despair and discontent. Its driving force comprised the unofficial peace, ecological, and human rights groups, long persecuted by the government, who managed nevertheless to survive under the protective shield of the East German Lutheran Church. The regime could still use force against growing street protests. In June 1989 Erich Honecker and Nicolae Ceausescu had been the only East European leaders to congratulate the Chinese communists for their crackdown on the Tienanmen Square demonstration. Knowing Honecker's fierce intransigence, the risk of bloodshed loomed in the GDR. In East Berlin, Leipzig, and Dresden, protesters clashed with police forces. The police used truncheons to beat up the demonstrators and menaced them with water cannons. Far from intimidated by the regime's tough reaction, the demonstrators continued to voice their protest against the communist dictatorship. The crowds were spurred by Gorbachev's presence in the official celebrations and often mingled their calls for freedom with chants of "Gorby, Gorby!" Enormous rallies were organized, and the police stood by surprisingly passive as the public anger mounted. The New Forum, a political movement headed by former dissidents, was created to express the people's main demands. Since the Soviets discouraged the use of violence to quell the unrest, it was clear that the ruling party had no alternative but to sacrifice the hard-liners and to promise the immediate launching of sweeping reforms.

The public demands for human rights and the complete overhaul of the political system continued to gather momentum. An era came to an end on October 18, when the SED Central Committee ousted the Stalinist Erich Honecker and elected Egon Krenz, a fifty-two-year-old party bureaucrat and Honecker's former right-hand man, to replace him. It was a clumsy and unconvincing choice, since many people knew that Krenz had been directly responsible for the antidissident campaigns of previous years. He was also associated with the fraud in the May 1989 local elections. Initially, Krenz tried to assuage public anger by placing the blame for the ongoing crisis on the previous leadership's failure to engage in reforms. In his first public address as the new SED General Secretary, Krenz declared:

> It is clear that we have not realistically appraised the social developments in our country in recent months, and we have not drawn the right conclusions quickly enough. We see the seriousness of the situation. But we also sense and recognize the major opportunity we have opened for ourselves to define the policies in dialogue with our citizens, policies that will bring us to the verge of the next century. [36]

But Krenz's soothing remarks came too late and sounded utterly hypocritical. Society's awakening proceeded much faster and more radically than any communist reformer could have expected. Dismayed and disoriented, the SED leaders could not cope with the lightning radicalization of the masses.

What was happening in the GDR was indeed spectacular. Only a few months earlier, it seemed that the country was politically paralyzed, with very few centers of opposition able to challenge the regime's huge police apparatus. A Western journalist noted an August 1989, at the beginning of the exodus that inaugurated the ultimate crisis of the GDR:

> In a curious way the existence of West Germany helps prop up the outdated regime. It has always been easy for East Germans to bundle dissidents and troublemakers out to the West to eliminate protest at home. Thus there is virtually no active internal opposition in East Germany. The only public criticisms, albeit cautious, are voiced by the Protestant church, which also gives shelter to a handful of tiny groups in the bigger cities, but it would not dream of challenging the system. [37]

The country's very existence indeed had been built upon an ideological fiction, and any endeavor to change that foundation would ruin its future. If Hungary, Poland, Romania, and Czecholslovakia reformed themselves to the point of abandoning socialism completely, they would still be Hungary, Poland, Romania, and Czechoslovakia. For the GDR to embrace such reforms would result in the very end of its statehood. The country's existence derived from the division of the world into two rival blocs.

Once the logic of the Cold War was recognized as obsolete, the GDR lost its reason to exist. That peculiar situation had been acknowledged in no uncertain terms by one of the regime's top ideologues, Otto Reinhold. In August 1989 he granted an interview to an East German radio station in which he made clear that the issue of socialist identity was essential for the very existence of the GDR as a separate state in the heart of Europe. For him, as for the whole SED elite, the GDR was conceivable "only as an antifascist, socialist alternative to the Federal Republic."[38] Until the beginning of the October crisis, the SED elite appeared to be united in its defiance to Moscow's injunctions to embark on a reformist path. In December 1988 Erich Honecker adamantly rejected suggestions that his party emulate the Soviet policy of glasnost and denied the need for any perestroika in the GDR. Speaking at a plenum of his party's Central Committee, the increasingly embittered leader turned down the invitations "to deviate from our course and march into a anarchy."[39] In a widely publicized speech, the SED's chief ideologue, Kurt Hager, had dismissed the Soviet reforms as a model: "Just because your neighbor puts up new wallpaper doesn't mean that you have to also."[40] In April 1989 Hager, who had served for decades as the watchdog of Leninist orthodoxy, elaborated before a gathering of party historians and social scientists on the need to emphasize the peculiarities of the East German model of socialism.

Hager's statement was an unmistakable criticism of the Soviet "new thinking" in foreign policy and a passionate plea for the preservation of the established East German system:

> The history of socialism in the GDR confirms that the socialist social system is marked by significant advantages. If we speak of "socialism in GDR colors," this means that we have pursued our own unique path, that we have applied Marxism-Leninism to our conditions, and that socialism in the GDR has developed characteristics that are in harmony with our traditions, preconditions, experiences and possibilities. Being a bastion of socialism at the dividing line of the imperialist system, and confronted with an imperialist state of German nationality, we are in a unique combat position.[41]

In the same vein, Margot Honecker, the General Secretary's wife and Minister of Public Education, did not conceal her resentment of

Gorbachev's new course, which she saw as a direct threat to the future of socialism. For the SED elite it was vitally important to maintain a climate of national alarm against attempts by both the East and the West to destabilize the status quo. Giving voice to the growing anxiety among the higher strata of the GDR *nomenklatura,* in a highly inflammatory (and comminatory) speech at a pedagogical congress in East Berlin in June 1989, Margot Honecker stated:

> The fact that all forces inimical to socialism have again turned up—and they will do so again and again—to stop socialism on its path and to damage it, can, should, and must be understood by the young people. We have to open their eyes to this so that they realize: It is not yet time to fold one's arms; our time is a time full of struggle, it needs young people who can fight, who help to strengthen socialism, who work for it, who defend it with word and deed, and, if necessary, with weapons. [42]

Krenz himself had been directly involved in all the antireformist campaigns that preceded and had tried to preclude the rise of a mass movement for democracy. Now he postured as a born-again reformer and a sworn enemy of the corruption and conservatism of the former leadership. He promised immediate liberalization but emphatically declared that socialism was "not negotiable."

For Krenz, and for the whole SED leadership, it was clear that fundamental concessions that would allow free elections would immediately result in the end of the established regime and of the GDR as as a separate state. Indeed, as a West German journalist wrote: "Only Prussosocialism buttresses East Berlin's claim to separate statehood. Let it go, and out goes East Germany's reason for being. Allow for free elections today, and you might just as well celebrate anschluss with West Germany tomorrow." [43] Krenz was caught in a political maelstrom that he could not arrest. The forces set in motion by Gorbachev's reforms, the changes in the Soviet international strategy and the renunciation of the Brezhnev Doctrine, had left the East German leaders with only one alternative to pursue: surrender to the pressure of the masses and recognition of society's right to participate in government. Thus the more the government accepted the demands of the protesters, the bolder and more radical the demonstrations became.

On October 23, 1989, hundreds of thousands took to the streets in Leipzig calling for democratic changes, including the legalization of opposition movements and independent labor unions and the separation of powers between the communist party and the state. On November 4 a half-million East Berliners demonstrated peacefully demanding free speech, free elections, an end to the "leading role" of the communist party, and the disbandment of the *Stasi,* the hated security police. The march in East Berlin was organized by the official Union of Actors, who insisted on the need to maintain calm and order. Günther Schabowski, a Politburo member and the SED chief in East Berlin, was whistled and jeered at when he tried to address the demonstrators. What had started in October as a spontaneous mass revolt against tyranny and injustice was turning into a political revolution. The movement was nonviolent, but its demands pointed clearly toward the complete destruction of the existing system.

East Germany's outburst of anger and desperation could not be contained. On November 7 the whole Politburo resigned, and on November 9 an extraordinary event took place: The Berlin Wall was breached, and people were allowed to celebrate freely the end of an era of fear, suspicion, and terror. The mood was ecstatic at the moment Chancellor Helmut Kohl addressed an immense crowd of East and West Berliners gathered outside the West Berlin city hall in highly emotional terms: "I want to call out to all in the German Democratic Republic: We're on your side, we were and we remain one nation. We belong together."[44] Following the opening of the border and the elimination of the SED old guard, Krenz tried to capitalize on his role in those sea-change decisions and announced major reforms. A Plenum of the Central Committee announced the party's new program, which included free, democratic, and secret-ballot elections; the orientation of the economy toward market conditions; separation of party and state; parliamentary supervision of state security; freedom of assembly; and a new law for the media.[45] New associations and groups had started to form, and East German political life entered a stage of tremendous ferment. The long-controlled Christian Democratic and Liberal Democratic token parties got rid of their collaborationist leaders and started to assert their independence from the SED. At the same time, the few reformers within the SED gathered around the Dresden party chief, Hans Modrow, and pushed for a reshuffling of both party and government leaderships.

On November 13 Modrow became the new Prime Minister in a desperate attempt by the SED to restore its credibility and to launch a comprehensive reform program. But the demonstrations continued, this time heightened by revelations about the luxurious living conditions of the Honecker team and the corruption of a political class that had long preached the virtues of socialist asceticism to the population. Extensive coverage was given in the suddenly liberated East German media to the opulent life-styles of Erich Honecker and the other former leaders. The shock experienced by the East Germans was all the greater because they had believed the self-serving propaganda of the old regime regarding its commitment to the values of collectivism and equality. True, it was widely known that the SED leaders were enemies of freedom, but the population was totally ignorant of the colossal privileges accumulated by the members of the SED *nomenklatura*. Disclosures were made about Wandlitz, the heavily guarded compound of twenty-three houses where the former leaders had enjoyed swimming pools, consumer goods unavailable to the general public, and other luxuries their subjects could only dream of. Information was published about the hunting lodge of the former trade union chief Harry Tisch and about the involvement of the former Politburo member Günther Mittag in murky financial arrangements that had milked hard currency earnings from East German companies that exported valuable antiquities to the West.[46] The image of the communist leadership that had terrorized the East Germans for decades took on hues of cynicism and cruelty, which evoked hatred, horror, and disgust among the population.

On December 3, under the impact of those traumatic revelations, Krenz and the whole SED Politburo resigned. Two weeks later the SED's moral and political crises were recognized during an extraordinary Congress at which delegates engaged in recriminations and devastating criticism of the deposed leadership. On that occasion a report was presented by professor Michael Schumann, a proponent of reform and a member of the Academy of Science, who accused the former leaders of having betrayed the confidence of the party: "The Politbureaucrats denounced the uprising of the people as a counterrevolution and wanted to repress it with violence, but in reality they were the counterrevolutionaries."[47] As the general mood in the GDR increasingly favored reunification, the communists found themselves at a loss. Even if they had championed the most dramatic reforms, they had no constituency for their strategies. With its corruption and despotism, the previous leadership had dramatically compromised the ideal of socialism even in the eyes of those who had believed in Marxism-Leninism and had fought for the preservation of the GDR. The only solution for the party was to rename itself and to undertake a complete cleansing of its apparatus. The party's new name was the Socialist Unity Party of Germany–Party of Democratic Socialism, a clear indication that the values of socialism with a human face had finally been embraced by the East German communists. The new name was the late and spasmodic triumph of revisionism within a political formation that had most consistently opposed any form of democratization. Its Congress elected Gregor Gysi, a forty-one-year-old lawyer, as the party's new chairman. Gysi had started his political career in early December, when he was chosen to head the commission set up by SED reformers to investigate the abuses perpetrated by the former leaders. His background, however, would have recommended him for a leading position in the country's emerging democratic parties. During the Honecker regime Gysi, the son of a party veteran who had served in the 1960s as Minister of Culture, was well known for his long-standing support for the opposition. Indeed, he had been involved in the defense in court of dissidents and conscientious objectors and had represented the opposition group New Forum when the group was seeking official recognition in September and October. At that time the authorities had labeled the New Forum "an enemy of the state." Gysi brought all his prestige as an advocate of pluralism and human rights to bear in an effort to refurbish the party's battered image. Why Gysi accepted the suicidal mission as the captain of the sinking ship of East German socialism remains a mystery. The only explanation is that he himself was a leftist idealist who hoped against hope that something could be rescued from the moral rubble associated with the SED rule.

In the month that followed the breach of the Berlin Wall, the SED membership decreased from 2,300,000 to 1,800,000, and the overall trend was definitely toward dissolution. Gysi's position was that the SED had to be actually refounded by breaking with the Stalinist legacy and committing itself to the values of pluralism and democracy. Gysi called for a genuine change in the party's identity so that it could become "the natural home of democratic socialists and not a class party or a party of the masses." That new philosophy was the exact opposite of the Bolshevik conception of the communist party as an enlightened vanguard that dictates to the masses its own ideological choices without any concern for their real needs and grievances. Gysi also accepted the principle of competition with other political parties as a natural component of an open society.[48] As a result of those fundamental concessions, the SED hoped to burnish its image and to remain a significant political force even in the aftermath of free elections.

The discontent of the population however, was so powerful that in a matter of months the calls for reunification became national, and the opposition parties advocated acceleration of the process. With his halfhearted reforms and lack of inspiring political vision, Hans Modrow, the communist Prime Minister, could not convince the East Germans that a separate socialist state had any reason to exist. Even alternative groups like the New Forum, which preferred a gradual rapprochement between the two German states to a rapid reunification, lost their political appeal.

The anger of the masses grew in direct proportion to the procrastinations of the Modrow government in purging the secret police. There were explosions of popular wrath that led to the storming of *Stasi* headquarters. Communism in East Germany collapsed ingloriously and unlamented. As for Erich Honecker, he and most of his acolytes were placed under house arrest to await trial for their involvement in political and economic crimes.

CZECHOSLOVAKIA'S VELVET REVOLUTION

The breakdown of the East German police state exhilarated the unofficial groups and movements in neighboring Czechoslovakia. The radicalization of the opposition had been visible since January 1989, when demonstrations were organized to commemorate the self-immolation twenty years earlier of the student leader Jan Palach. The playwright Vaclav Havel and dozens of other civil rights activists were imprisoned in the regime's attempt to stifle the growing dissent. In June 1989 Havel and other opposition figures issued a petition entitled "Just a Few Sentences," which called for the country's immediate democratization. Increasingly alienated from the population, the Husak—Jakes regime promised limited economic reforms but refused to enter a dialogue with the mushrooming opposition groups. The uniqueness of the Czechoslovak situation was that there was no reformist group in the leadership to engage in immediate negotiations with the opposition. Because the authority of the ruling party had fallen apart, the prospects for further social unrest were high. On November 17 the government used police violence to quell a student demonstration. That brutal response to an absolutely nonviolent form of civic protest was the spark that ignited a public explosion. Strikes and protest meetings spread across the country.

Stripped of Soviet support and even sympathy, the communist leaders in Czechoslovakia backed down and renounced the only option— taking up the military high command's offer to intervene—they had for remaining in power. Short-sighted and arrogant as they were, the bureaucrats realized nonetheless that such a solution would have resulted in immense bloodshed that would have horrified the world. They lacked the Ceausescu-like fanaticism that operated one month later in Romania, when the army and the police were used against unarmed demonstrators in Timisoara and Bucharest. It was not, of course, because of humanism that the Czechoslovak leaders renounced the use of violence, but because they knew that such a course would have contradicted Soviet interests.

Brought to power in the name of the Brezhnev Doctrine, the Husak–
Jakes team of collaborationists lost power as an effect of the "Sinatra
Doctrine," the Soviet decision to allow each East European country to
pursue its own variety of reform. Battered and humiliated, the communist leadership resigned en masse on November 25. The hard-liner Milos
Jakes was replaced by Karel Urbanek, a forty-eight-year-old former party
boss in Bohemia. Immediately thereafter Prime Minister Ladislav Adamec, who had engaged in negotiations with representatives of the opposition, announced his intention to resign as well. The cosmetic changes in
the party elite convinced no one, and hundreds of thousands gathered
again in Wenceslas Square, a long pedestrian plaza, to listen to Vaclav
Havel and Alexander Dubcek denounce the attempts of the neo-
Stalinists to preserve power: "The new leadership is a trick that was
meant to confuse."[49] As a further expression of the maturation of the
civil society, in the days that followed the ruthless suppression of the
student demonstration the opposition formed two alliances: the Civic
Forum in Prague and the Slovakian Public Against Violence in Bratislava. A prominent role in the formation of the Civic Forum was played
not only be such celebrated leaders of Charter 77 as Vaclav Havel and Jiri
Dienstbier but also by intellectuals belonging to the official culture. In its
programmatic document issued on November 26, the Civic Forum called
for the reconstruction of the Czechoslovak political and economic system, a separation of powers, the development of a market economy free
of bureaucratic intervention, environmental protection, and a foreign
policy that would allow Czechoslovakia to resume its honorable position
within Europe and the world:

> We demand fundamental and permanent changes in the political system in
> our society. We must establish or renew democratic institutions and mecha-
> nisms which will allow the real participation of all citizens in public affairs
> and at the same time become effective barriers against the abuse of politi-
> cal and economic power. All existing and newly founded political parties
> and other political and social associations should have the right of equal
> participation in free elections for all levels of government. This assumes
> however that the Communist Party abandons its constitutionally guaran-
> teed leading role within our society, as well as its monopoly control of the
> media. There is nothing to prevent it from doing so tomorrow.[50]

A general strike on November 27 paralyzed the whole country and
showed that the government had no choice but to accept the demands of
the opposition. The pressure from below had become unbearable for the

increasingly beleaguered Czechoslovak communist leaders. As an indication of the disintegration of the ruling group's cohesion, the official daily *Rude Pravo* deplored the paralysis of the Central Committee and of the "political mummies" who were preventing the opening of the political system. The newspaper struck a Gorbachevite note when it urged the party to recognize the principle of pluralism and to prepare for "free democratic elections." On November 29 the Federal Assembly abolished the constitutional clause guaranteeing the communist party's leading role. The way was thus open for the complete disbandment of the artificial power structure imposed by Soviet tanks in August 1968. With his remarkable self-control and strategic acumen, Havel emerged as a national leader. The nation recognized itself in the idealistic, self-effacing playwright and ex-prisoner whom the tide of history had brought to the forefront of a revolutionary upheaval. The same man who had served jail sentences for having advocated respect for human rights and had defended those unjustly persecuted was now a leading partner in negotiations with those who had sent him to prison. After two reshuffles, on December 10 a coalition government was formed that included a noncommunist majority. On December 29 Vaclav Havel, the founder of the Civic Forum and the architect of the "velvet revolution," was elected Czechoslovakia's President.

In the meantime, a Warsaw Pact summit had taken place in Moscow on December 4. The Kremlin and its allies had formally acknowledged that the invasion of Czechoslovakia in August 1968 had been illegal. The joint statement published at the end of the summit meant the final solemn repudiation of the Brezhnev Doctrine and constituted a green light for the revolutionary forces in the former satellite countries. The issue for Czechoslovakia and the other Sovietized societies was to get rid of the vestiges of a political and economic system that had imposed an immense toll on the individual. In his New Year's Day address, Havel poignantly emphasized that democracy had to be rebuilt on a social ground devastated by corruption, incompetence, and cynicism. It was not only the economic decay that Havel deplored, but first and foremost the destruction of the sense of human trust and solidarity and the debasement of society's moral fabric. Those ailments were seen as communism's most unfortunate legacy:

> We have become morally sick because we have become accustomed to saying one thing and thinking something else. Concepts such as love, friendship, compassion, humility and forgiveness have lost their depth and their dimensions. For many of us, these qualities are now little more than

mere psychological peculiarities or lost greetings from times long past, somewhat laughable in an age of spaceships and computers. Only a handful of us were strong enough to cry loud that those in power should not be all-powerful, that the special farms growing ecologically pure quality food for the rulers should send their produce to the schools, childrens' homes and hospitals, since thus far, our agriculture was unable to offer this kind of produce to everyone. The previous regime—armed with an arrogant and intolerant ideology—reduced Man to a force of production and the natural world to an implement of production. In so doing, it assaulted their very essence as well as their relationship. The regime reduced a gifted and self-determining people, capable of skillfully managing their country, to cogs in some monstruously large, noisy and evil-smelling machine of whose purpose nobody could be quite sure. The machine was capable of little more than slowly and inexorably winding down, wearing itself and all its cogs out in the process. [51]

Drawing upon the theoretical and political legacy of Czechoslovakia's precommunist experiment in democracy, Havel suggested that his country could become the ideal place for trying out a new type of politics. He referred to Tomas Masaryk's ideas about a political life based on mutual respect and even love rather than on petty squabbles and endless bickering:

Masaryk based his politics on morality. Let us attempt in this new era to reaffirm this concept of politics within us. Let us teach ourselves and others that politics should be an expression of the desire to contribute to the well-being of the community rather than of the urge to create or violate the community. Let us teach ourselves and others that politics can be more than the mere art of the possible, especially if this means the art of speculation, calculation, intrigue, secret deals and expediency. Let us teach ourselves and others that politics can even be the art of the impossible, namely the art of improving ourselves and the world. [52]

This uplifting counsel from the philosopher-playwright-turned-president mapped the course for the reinvention of politics in Eastern Europe. From the economic and moral debris of the old regime, the people were advised to reconstruct human nature in accordance with the commandments of solidarity, trust, and hope. It was important to overcome the legacy of suspicion and the widespead mistrust of politics and to recognize that the social space could and should be impregnated with moral values.

The revolution against Sovietism had been waged in the name of a universal conception of human rights, and it was perfectly normal for

Havel to assume that the new politics in Czechoslovakia would be different from the schemings and rivalries characteristic of traditional politics.
The ethicization of politics sounds a bit idealistic, but it is important to
remember that the whole East European upheaval had started in the
name of transpolitical and sacred human rights. Decades earlier, hoping
against hope that the Stalinist glacier would melt down one day, Czeslaw
Milosz presciently wrote that

> . . .these countries seem to be the most important part not only of Europe,
> but of the whole world: if we assume that the New Faith [Marxism-
> Leninism] will spread throughout the earth, then these are the first and the
> most interesting areas of the experiment outside Russia itself. If we assume
> that the Center will lose, then the economic and culture patterns that will
> arise subsequently in these countries will certainly be new, for there is no
> such thing in history as a return to the status quo.[53]

Indeed, as will be discussed in Chapter 7, the break with communism and
the restoration of a free public space did not result in the mere revival of
the precommunist traditions. The new forms were actually syncretic
combinations of nostalgia for the past and bold experiments in society-
building. One could not simply write off more than four decades of
communist domination, including the indoctrination of the population,
the instilling of a sense of fear and insecurity in the individual, and the
suppression of personal autonomy. It is difficult but necessary to embark
on the construction of a state based on the rule of law in a place where
the inhabitants have spent most of their lives under lawless regimes. The
new politics therefore meant not a continuous and ineffective settling of
accounts, but a regeneration of the social space through a rehabilitation
of the moral fiber within the individual citizen. That could be achieved
within the newly created associations, groups, and parties, which would
ensure the limitation of government power and would create an environment conducive to the affirmation of the citizens' rights. Havel gave
expression to the ultimate dream of moral and political emancipation of
the long-subjugated East European nations: "You may ask what kind of
republic I dream of. And I reply: I dream of a republic independent, free
and democratic, of a republic economically prosperous, yet socially just,
in short, of a humane republic which serves the individual and which
therefore holds the hope that the individual will serve it." And to conclude this masterful lesson in civic consciousness, the Czechoslovak President solemnly announced: "People, your Government has returned to
you!"[54]

While Havel was speaking in January 1989 of the return of legitimate government in Czechoslovakia, in Bulgaria three leaders of the emerging human rights movement were arrested while the regime pretended to pay lip service to Soviet-style reforms. The opposition exploited the regime's official support for perestroika to organize informal associations dedicated to promoting glasnost in Bulgaria. But it was in Romania, more than in any other Warsaw Pact country, that repression reached its most appalling and grotesque level. Whether in Bulgaria or Romania or outside the Warsaw Pact in Albania or Yugoslavia, in the long run the efforts of the hard-liners to coordinate their resistance to change could not succeed. They were all exponents of a different political age, Stalinist dinosaurs who could not prevent the development of critical currents within their own societies. The more they refused to accept the need for change, the stronger the reaction of the oppressed population and the weaker the capability of the communist elites to preserve a minimal credibility at the moment of revolutionary explosion.

THE BULGARIAN DOMINO: THE ANTI-ZHIVKOV COUP

For decades the most obedient and trustworthy of Moscow's allies was the Bulgarian leader, Todor Zhivkov. He desperately maneuvered to avoid opening the political system and to preserve his monopoly on power. On various occasions, especially after 1987, he engaged in rhetorical attacks on dogmatism and conservatism and promised to emulate the Soviet perestroika. In reality, Zhivkov used those demagogic devices to maintain his hold over the party apparatus and get rid of potential reformers within the leadership.

As a concession to Moscow's growing pressure for liberalization, in August 1987 the Bulgarian Politburo passed a resolution on state symbols that required, among other things, the removal of Zhivkov's portrait from public display and the demolition of his statue in his home town, Pravets. In March 1988 most of the institutions (such as the People's Palace of Culture, the Youth Theater, and the Institute of Balkan Studies) that had been named after Zhivkov's late daughter Lyudmila, a former Minister of Culture and Politburo member, had their original names restored.[55] In December 1988, in another hypocritical gesture designed to placate the Soviets and to deter his domestic opponents, Zhivkov told a Central Committee plenum that the time was ripe for a bottom-up revolution and a complete reform of the political system.

On February 1, 1989, the reformist Prime Minister Georgi Atanasov was forced to resign, and it seemed that Zhivkov had managed to smash the mounting intraparty opposition. In the meantime, the increasingly sclerotic Zhivkov regime began to be challenged by a number of growing civic initiatives from below that called themselves discussion clubs. The emergence of those associations in direct defiance of the authorities signified the end of political passivity and the beginning of the opposition's self-organization. Among those directly involved in the grassroots activism was Zhelyu Zhelev, a philosopher who had been expelled from the communist party in the 1960s because of his heretical ideas and outspoken criticism of totalitarianism. In 1988 Zhelev had been a founding member of the "Club for the Support of Glasnost and Perestroika," an informal association dedicated to the struggle for democratization. Despite the appearance of civic activists, the prevailing feeling among Bulgarians was that the Zhivkov regime still had enough strength to disarm the opposition and to curb any genuine reformist efforts. The public's fear resulted in an increased level of cynicism and "a sense among many Bulgarians that any changes sweeping other corners of the Eastern bloc would not be touching them soon."[56]

The impression of Bulgarian immobility, however, was not exactly accurate, because underneath the apparently cohesive party leadership strong tensions were smoldering. In early November about five thousand people marched on the National Assembly building in Sofia to protest environmental pollution, but the thrust of the demonstration was political. The marchers questioned the competence of the government to run the country's economy. Then, suddenly, on November 10 a coalition of reform-minded apparatchiks led by Petar Mladenov and army generals headed by the veteran Politburo member and Minister of Defense Dobri Dzhurov forced Todor Zhivkov, the man who had run Bulgaria's communist party since April 1954, to resign. What happpened in Bulgaria was very different from the revolutionary changes in Hungary, Poland, and East Germany, where the communist elites had to relinquish their hold on power after more or less dramatic confrontations with the opposition. The Bulgarian communists tried to preempt such a denouement by ridding themselves of Zhivkov and taking the credit for the launching of radical reforms. Knowing General Dzhurov's intimate ties with Moscow, one could assume that his critical role in the conspiracy had something to do with the Kremlin's increasing dissatisfaction with Zhivkov's sluggishness and ineptitude.

Zhivkov's short-lived successor as party leader was the fifty-three-year-old Petar Mladenov, who had served during the previous eighteen years as the country's Foreign Minister. Because Mladenov did not come from the highest echelons of the party bureaucracy, it appeared that a traditional succession pattern was broken. Mladenov announced that sweeping reforms could be postponed no longer and pledged that under the new leadership Bulgaria would become "a modern, democratic and lawful country."[57] The new government abolished the law proscribing unauthorized political activity, and control over the media was relaxed. As for Zhivkov himself, he hoped to save face (and at least part of his privileges) by yielding to the Politburo's verdict and formally admitting his own responsibility for the failure to revitalize the system.

Following Zhivkov's downfall, large street demonstrations took place in Sofia and other Bulgarian cities. Vigils were organized to protest the preservation of the communists' dictatorship, and demands were made for the immediate establishment of a multiparty system. On December 13 the communist party's Central Committee decided to expel Todor Zhivkov from its ranks. According to Andrei Lukanov, a Politburo member who was the head of a commission investigating the power abuses perpetrated by Zhivkov and his cronies, Zhivkov's expulsion from the party meant a resolute break with the corrupt practices of the past. "[W]e are not only saying goodbye to a person, we are saying goodbye to a policy," Lukanov declared. As in the GDR, exposés about Zhivkov's luxurious life-style enraged the already discontented masses, who increasingly demanded his immediate arrest for gross violations of laws and abuse of power.[58] At the same meeting, the Central Committee gave in to popular pressure and supported Mladenov's call for the communist party to renounce its guaranteed monopoly on political power. In early December the opposition formed its own umbrella organization, called the Union of Democratic Forces (UDF), and Zhelyu Zhelev was elected the president of its Coordinating Committee. On December 29, 1989, following mass demonstrations by ethnic Turks, the new government and the Bulgarian communist party's Central Committee pledged to renounce Zhivkov's assimilationist policies. But the seeds of nationalism had been implanted deeply over preceding decades, and immediately after the Turks demonstrated thousands of ethnic Bulgars took to the streets in the southern town of Kurdjali calling for a referendum on the assimilation issue. After the passage of decrees to allow members of the Turkish minority to recover their original names and to reopen mosques, Bulgarian nationalists formed the "Committee for the Defense of National Interests," which championed opposition to Turkish representation in the parliament.

Following Zhivkov's ouster, the communist party was dominated by a triumvirate made up of the General Secretary Petar Mladenov and the

Politburo members Andrei Lukanov and Alexander Lilov. In January 1990 Zhivkov was placed under house arrest on charges of having incited ethnic hostilities between Bulgarians and the country's Turkish minority and having misused government property and money.[59] The Bulgarian communist party held a stormy Congress from January 30 to February 2, 1990. On that occasion, Alexander Lilov succeeded Petar Mladenov as the party's leader. Lilov's election to the top of the communist party's hierachy meant that the old *nomenklatura* was not ready to accept defeat passively. Although marginalized by Zhivkov after 1983, Lilov had made his career as a faithful party ideologue and had enjoyed a close relationship with Zhivkov's daughter Lyudmila.[60] As for Zhivkov's personal fate, in July he addressed a letter to the parliament in which he refused to face the legislative body, arguing that he did not want to be used as an instrument for the political ambitions of certain groups and personalities. Furthermore, Zhivkov insisted, there was no judicial base for charging him with criminal offenses: "I have made many mistakes, but I haven't committed any crime against my nation. So I assume only political responsibility for the mistakes."[61] In disarray and frustration, the Bulgarian communists tried to dissociate themselves from the excesses of the Zhivkov regime and to reassert their party's precommunist traditions. In 1990 the party changed its name into the Bulgarian Socialist Party as a symbolic departure from the Leninist dogmas.

THE SIEGE OF THE ROMANIAN FORTRESS

In the case of Romania, the situation was the most dramatic and enigmatic. Nicolae Ceausescu's policy had amounted to the unrestricted monopolization of political power in his hands. When he was elected General Secretary of the Romanian Communist Party in March 1965, Ceausescu embodied the promise of liberalization. He loosened party controls over cultural life and developed further the independent foreign policy inaugurated by his predecessor, Gheorghe Gheorghiu-Dej. During the first stage of his rule, between 1965 and 1971, Ceausescu advocated collective leadership, criticized the repression of the Stalinist years, and opposed the Soviet integrationist policy within the CMEA. He appeared to be a supporter of the national communist line as formulated by Tito in Yugoslavia. As a member of the Warsaw Pact, Ceausescu resisted Soviet demands for joint military maneuvers and insisted that each national army be subordinated to the domestic leadership. He challenged the Soviet interpretation of socialist internationalism and refused to walk in

Moscow's footsteps during the 1967 Middle East crisis—Romania was the
only Warsaw Pact country to maintain diplomatic relations with the
State of Israel. In 1967 and 1968 Ceausescu publicly criticized the abuses
of the *Securitate* (the secret police) during the Stalinist years and pledged
that such atrocities would never be repeated. In April 1968 a plenum of
the Romanian Central Committee rehabilitated Lucretiu Patrascanu, the
former Minister of Justice and Politburo member who had been executed
on trumped-up charges in April 1954. Meanwhile, Romania continued
to maintain a neutral stance in the conflict between China and the
Soviet Union. In August 1968 Ceausescu reached the apex of his domestic popularity when he publicly and vehemently condemned the Soviet
invasion of Czechoslovakia. But it was precisely at that moment that he
decided to convert his popular support for launching an autonomous
course into a personal asset for the expansion of his personal power and
the construction of a despotism second to none in the post-Stalin Soviet
bloc.

Ceausescu's displeasure with Brezhnev's interventionist policy in Eastern Europe was not motivated by reformist proclivities. On the contrary,
when the Romanian leader realized that domestic relaxation had contributed to the awakening of limited but increasingly vocal critical orienta-
tions, he decided to put an end to the liberal interlude. In June 1971 he
visited China and North Korea and was fascinated with the mobilization
techniques of the personality cults surrounding Mao Zedong and Kim Il-
Sung. During that trip he was accompanied by his wife Elena, whose
influence on her husband and on Romanian political life was to grow in
direct proportion to the deterioration of the social climate and the development of a uniquely extravagant cult of personality. In 1974 Elena
became a full member of the Communist Party's ruling body, the Political
Executive Committee.

During the 1970s Romania also continued to pursue a foreign policy
slightly different from Moscow's, which made Ceausescu look like an
opponent of Soviet imperialism and earned him praise from Western
media and chancelleries. At the same time, Ceausescu restored the
power of the secret police and transformed the communist party bureaucracy into an instrument for the implementation of his increasingly erratic decisions. He lost touch with the political group within the party
apparatus that had helped him to consolidate his power during the early
stage of his rule. Any form of criticism within the top elite was considered seditious, and those who dared to question Ceausescu's authority
were immediately eliminated from the leadership. One of those who
expressed reservations regarding the wisdom of the neo-Stalinist offen-

sive launched by Ceausescu in the summer of 1971, when he returned from his Asian trip, was Ion Iliescu, then a Central Committee Secretary in charge of ideology and widely regarded as the President's protégé and even heir-apparent. During a Central Committee plenum, Iliescu was singled out by Ceausescu and censured for alleged liberalism and intellectualism. After that Iliescu served as a secretary in charge of propaganda in the Timis County party committee and then as first secretary of the Iasi County party committee. In the early 1980s he became Chairman of the State Committee for Water, and later, until the December 1989 revolt, he held the directorship of the Technical Publishing House in Bucharest.

From the 1970s onward Ceausescu seemed increasingly intent upon establishing a dynastic version of socialism. Elena's role grew to incredible proportions, as she became the *de facto* number two person in the party hierarchy. As a chairperson of the Central Committee Commission in charge of personnel appointments and a First Deputy Prime Minister who effectively controlled all government operations, Elena came to dominate the Romanian political scene. She controlled all her husband's interviews and managed his schedule. It was she who encouraged the President's morbid vanity and surrounded him with a wall of adulation and pseudo-mystical devotion. That is not to say that without Elena Nicolae Ceausescu would have been a liberal. He had grown up in the underground Romanian communist party, which never resolved its legitimacy complex and thus had a strong sense of fanaticism characteristic of tiny conspiratorial sects. Besides, Ceausescu had been directly involved in the repression against the peasants and intellectuals in the 1950s. With Elena as the second-in-command and other members of the Ceausescu clan, including the couple's youngest son Nicu as first as leader of the Communist Youth Union and then as head of the Sibiu County party committee and an alternate Political Executive Committee member, the success of the dynastic design seemed to be ensured.

The type of personalist leadership that developed in Romania after 1971 made impossible even minimal constraints upon the ruler's behavior by his close entourage. There was no opposition either within the higher ranks of the *nomenklatura*. An atmosphere of unequaled servility stifled the slightest critical initiative.[62] Ceausescu's psychology also played a large part in the unfolding disaster. Writing in 1988, a perceptive observer of Romanian communism noted:

> The greatest single factor in Romania's internal debacle has been Ceausescu's capriciousness. No European leader in the second half of the twentieth century has personified the debilitating effects of power more than he has.

An intelligent man; an extraordinarily hard worker; a patriot; not personally cruel (in the sense that, say, Matyas Rakosi of Hungary or Stalin was); once well intentioned—he has probably remained so in a perverted way— his name has yet become synonymous with historic tyranny.[63]

After Gorbachev came to power, Ceausescu found himself extremely isolated. Once the Soviet Union changed and the Warsaw Pact lost its bellicosity, the long-praised Romanian domesticism ceased to excite the West. Ceausescu's anti-Sovietism was finally recognized as rooted in his unreconstructed Stalinism rather than in any reformist temptation. Unlike Yugoslavia under Tito, where external autonomy had been accompanied by limited domestic liberalization, Ceausescu had used the international recognition of his semi-independent course in foreign policy to foster a Draconian authoritarian regime based on the unabashed exaltation of nationalism and the preservation of the basic Stalinist institutions, including the ubiquitous secret police. All forms of opposition had been smashed. For instance, in the summer of 1977 the Jiu Valley coal miners went on strike, but they were disbanded and their strike leaders were jailed or simply disappeared. Dissidents like the writer Paul Goma, the historian Vlad Georgescu, and the poet Dorin Tudoran were forced to leave the country after countless harassments. The same happened to the mathematician Mihai Botez, who had criticized the regime from the viewpoint of its own pledges to respect human rights. Others, like the poet Mircea Dinescu, the literary critic Dan Petrescu, and the university lecturer Doina Cornea, were kept under strict police surveillance. There was little hope that anything could come out of the higher echelons of the communist party, where Ceausescu's domination was totally undisputed.

Frightened by any form of potential external pressure, Ceausescu engaged in a breakneck effort to pay his country's foreign debt of more than $12 billion. That resulted in an almost complete ban on imports, including vitally important spare parts for Romania's industry. At the same time agricultural output was used for exports in order to expand the country's reserves of foreign exchange. The hardships imposed on the population, especially after the winter of 1984, were beyond the imagination. People were forced to freeze in their apartments because of the government's decision to cut off energy supplies for domestic consumption. With their bitter sense of gallows humor, Romanians used to say that the difference between Hitler and Ceausescu was that the former killed people by turning on gas, and the latter did the same by turning it off. Romania, the country that gave birth to Eugène Ionesco, the French author of absurd plays, looked like a land where absurdity ruled supreme.

As if all those measures were not enough to excite anger and outrage among an increasingly humiliated population, Ceausescu ordered the razing of the historical center of the country's capital city, Bucharest. In its place, construction started on a megalomaniacal new administrative center, including a "House of the Republic" bigger than the Versailles Palace in France. The communist monarchy needed symbols to eternalize itself, and Ceausescu did not hesitate to spend huge amounts of money and to use forced labor in building monuments to his own glory. Since the regime continued to play the nationalist card in its propaganda, ethnic minorities were seen as dangerous carriers of alien values. Among Romania's minorities, the 2 million Hungarians were Ceausescu's particular obsession. He saw them as dangerous foreigners, a Trojan horse that threatened the cohesion of the Romanian nation. The *conducator* (leader) delivered harangues against those who did not understand the imperative of creating a totally homogeneous nation. Eventually thousands of Hungarians decided to leave their homes and illegally cross the border into Hungary. Ironically, they were joined by numerous Romanians, who chose to leave their homeland rather than suffer the effects of Ceausescu's ruling delirium. Ceausescu also initiated the forced resettlement of populations from villages to urban shanty towns to demonstrate the country's rapid progression to communism. With his primitive Stalinist mind, the *conducator* wanted to erase all differences between urban and rural areas by simply bulldozing more than seven thousand villages. That action, which Romanian propaganda tried to present as a "civilizing" step, aroused enormous international outrage. All over the country, Romanians were quietly seething.

The first visible fissure in the apparently impregnable Romanian Stalinist fortress was a popular demonstration in Brasov, Romania's second industrial center, on November 15, 1987. Although the regime tried to play down the meaning of that public explosion of discontent, Western radio stations informed the population about the repression taking place in Brasov. People learned that the workers from the Red Flag truck factory had not only demonstrated for economic goals but also chanted antidictatorial slogans. The Brasov rebellion—the protesters ransacked the local party headquarters and burned the portraits of Nicolae and Elena Ceausescu—was the first act of the Romanian revolution. But even at the last moment, in 1989, the lethargic Romanian political class did not react to prevent a violent denouement of the crisis.

As the reformist movements were gathering momentum in the other communist countries, Ceausescu grew increasingly nervous. He started to criticize Gorbachev publicly for having abandoned the essential principles of Marxism-Leninism. The regime's propaganda combined its commitment to hard-line communism with a growing insistence that its national (Romanian) roots were threatened by foreign conspiracies and infiltrating agents recruited among the ethnic minorities. In this extreme nationalist campaign, Ceausescu was not unique. In neighboring Bulgaria Todor Zhivkov, another potential victim of an expanded perestroika, was intensifying his campaign against the Turkish ethnic minority. Faced with the danger of a reform movement encouraged by the revisionist Moscow leadership, the Romanian and Bulgarian communist leaderships resorted to the traditional technique of scapegoating. The marked xenophobia of the antireformist communist leaders took overt or covert forms, depending on the degree of autonomy the regime enjoyed in relations with Moscow. The desperate attempt by Stalinist elites to preserve their power through manipulation of ethnic passions and frustrations was described as "xenophobic communism." It was an attempt to avoid modernization and reforms by creating a general sense of national danger and resorting to patriotic fundamentalism rather than traditional Marxist universalism:

> "Xenophobic communism" is besieged communism in quest of the lowest *national* common denominator. Its purpose is to mobilize society, a need that it strives to achieve by appealing to national resentment. And while this appeal is by no means novel in communist annals, what makes the ideal-type of "xenophobic communism" *sui generis* is the fact that its ideological enemies are indistinguishable from its national enemies.[64]

Indeed, for xenophobic communists, any call for reform is perceived as a betrayal of the national interests. Ceausescu's hysterical fixation with foreign infiltration, which was to culminate in his final speech on December 21, 1989, represented an extreme version of this baroque combination of intense nationalism and unrepentant Stalinism.

Despite the xenophobic appeals, even within isolated Romania there were calls for a break with the dictatorial methods of leadership and an opening of the political system. At the beginning of March 1989 six former top figures in the Romanian Communist Party addressed an open letter to President Nicolae Ceausescu. The document represented both a scathing indictment of Ceausescu's disastrous policies and an alternative political platform for the democratization of political life in Romania. Undoubtedly stimulated by Gorbachev's policy of glasnost, the signatories, among whom were two former General Secretaries of the Romanian Communist Party, attacked Ceausescu for having discredited the image of socialism. Without directly criticizing the monopolization of power by the presidential clan, the six prominent members of the party's "Old Guard" advocated the establishment of a lawful state through the strict observance of the constitution. They considered the Ceausescu-ordered "systematization" campaign an insult against all Romanian citizens and decried their country's alarming isolation from both East and West. The first paragraph of the letter summarizes the atmosphere of terror in Ceausescu's Romania: "At a time when the very idea of socialism, for which we fought, is discredited by your policy, and when our country is isolated in Europe, we have decided to speak out. We are perfectly aware that by doing so we are risking our liberty and even our lives, but we feel duty bound to appeal to you to reverse the present course before it is too late."[65] Immediately after the letter was broadcast by the BBC World Service, the six communist veterans were placed under house arrest and subjected to secret police interrogations. But their arrest did not suppress the growing discontent in Romania.

In March 1989 the French daily *Libération* published an interview with Mircea Dinescu, a thirty-eight-year-old poet widely regarded as one of the country's most prominent writers. After he likened the hopelessness of the Romanians to that of guinea pigs used for the experiments of a paranoid dictator, Dinescu outlined the heightened expectations among Romanians and other East Europeans created by Gorbachev's policies of glasnost and perestroika:

> In the first place, Romania has always looked to the East with fear, which is historically understandable in the case of a people situated on the edge of an empire. In the second place, Stalinism didn't land on us from Honolulu, but from ideological missile silos imported from the Kremlin. For years we've been told—sometimes in a whisper, sometimes through veiled hints—that the "Eastern Bear" was preventing the system from becoming more liberal. And our people believed it. "Soviet troops are conducting maneuvers on the Romanian border": that was the refrain the authorities trotted out every time we tried to speak our minds. I don't know whether or not Gorbachev is considered a good tsar by the peoples of the Soviet Union; but in Poland, Hungary, Bulgaria, Czechoslovakia, East Germany and Romania, the millions who kept quiet and endured humiliation for dozens of years see him as a preacher of "good news," a messiah of "socialism with a human face."[66]

Confronted with both external pressure and potential domestic unrest, the *conducator* became increasingly vociferous in his repudiation of any reform. He claimed that Romania had long since inaugurated a reformist policy and that the political system in his country did not need any significant adjustment. Actually, Ceausescu was the most outspoken of all the Warsaw Pact leaders in his refusal to emulate Gorbachev's initiatives. On various occasions he suggested that Gorbachevism amounted to the rise of a right-wing deviation within world communism and maintained that the "building of socialism could not be achieved through reformism." In that respect there was no difference between Ceausescu's stances and the Stalinist views voiced by Ramiz Alia, the leader of isolationist Albania, who lamented the reformist drive in the Soviet Union, Hungary, and Poland for having opened the way to private property and other evils associated with capitalism.[67] In October 1989 *Scinteia*, the official newspaper of the Romanian Communist Party, bluntly rejected the calls for a multiparty system as attempts to undermine the socialist system:

> The RCP considers that the thesis regarding a return to the multiparty system in socialism is completely wrong and harmful as it paves the way for a comeback to the anachronistic forms of the capitalist political system. As the Theses for the RCP 14 Party Congress underline, in the new conditions created after the disappearance of the exploiting classes, the existence of a single party of the working class and the consolidation of the people's unity around the party is an objective historical demand.[68]

On November 17, a week before the opening of the Fourteenth RCP Congress, and with the other Soviet-bloc countries in full turmoil, *Scinteia* found it convenient to reprint an interview with the Soviet hardliner Yegor Ligachev in which he endorsed views similar to those expressed by Ceausescu with regard to the need to preserve the one-party system. At the Party Congress Ceausescu again displayed his rhetorical arsenal to convince an increasingly disaffected population that Romania would be able to resist change. Well-orchestrated hosannahs were rhythmically chanted by a totally controlled and obedient party audience. Ceausescu railed against alleged international plots against the independence of small states. Referring to the announced Malta summit between President Bush and General Secretary Gorbachev, Ceausescu gave vent to his fear that it could lead to a superpower condominium of the world. At the end of the Congress he solemnly pledged to remain in charge for the foreseeable future, a guardian of the purity of Marxism-Leninism and of Romania's autarchic socialism: "Almost 60 years ago I first joined the party and in the future I will always be a soldier in the ranks of the Romanian Communist Party."[69]

During the Party Congress Romania's isolation was made clear by the absence of delegations of "brotherly" parties from Hungary, Italy, and, to Ceausescu's dismay, the GDR. Less than two months before, East Germany had been Ceausescu's closest supporter in his adamant refusal to accept reforms. In the meantime, the Honecker leadership had been replaced as a result of a mounting wave of popular protest. In the GDR the long-repressed civil rights and pacifist groups spearheaded the revolt and ensured its nonviolent nature. For Ceausescu the end of the Honecker regime was a very serious blow. With Zhivkov under attack within the Bulgarian party, with hundreds of thousands taking to the streets in Prague and Bratislava, and with the East German government giving in to pressure from below, the Romanian leader found himself totally isolated within the Warsaw Pact. That isolation was accentuated further by the boycott of the RCP Congress on the part of foreign guests as well as by the vitriolic criticism heaped on Ceausescu by the foreign media, including the ones in the allied countries. The East German news agency ADN explained the decision of a number of communist parties to call off their attendance at the RCP Congress by referring to "continued human rights violations, the personality cult surrounding Nicolae Ceausescu and serious violations of socialist democracy."[70]

Even in the face of such disdain and isolation, Ceausescu managed to use the propaganda machine of his regime to create the impression that Romanian communists would be able to avoid the fate of their peers in the other Soviet-bloc countries. Less than one week before the beginning of the anti-Ceausescu rebellion in Timisoara, the Western media reported:

> In the short run, Ceausescu's grip on power appears firm. Not only was he unanimously reelected at the recent Communist Party congress, but the tyrant vehemently denied the possibility of reforms. Sending a signal to reformist Hungary, Ceausescu even sealed the border with his Warsaw Pact neighbor. For all his despotism, Nicolae Ceausescu is a shrewd and far-sighted politician. Events in Eastern Europe may have caught the West unprepared, but Romania's present stability indicates that Ceausescu has been ready for quite some time.[71]

The reality, however, was that neither Ceausescu nor his allies in the rejectionist front had been well prepared for such an upheaval. They reacted erratically and, the moment Moscow ceased to play the protective role it used to play in the past, behaved like political orphans. All over Eastern Europe the communist parties collapsed ingloriously. In some countries, such as Hungary and Poland, the reformist groups within the party elite managed to engage in face-saving negotiations and hoped to be able to preserve some power. In Romania there was no reformist faction within the leadership that could unseat Ceausescu and his clique and engage in sweeping liberalization. The conditions were therefore ripe for a spontaneous popular explosion.

The Romanian revolution began in Timisoara, sparked by the courage of one man, the Reverend Laszlo Tökes, a pastor of the Reformed (Calvinist) Church and a member of the Hungarian ethnic minority. Despite repeated harassment by the Romanian secret police, the *Securitate*, Tökes had been an adamant champion of human and religious rights. On December 15, 1989, when secret police agents tried to evict Tökes forcibly from his parish house, thousands of people—Romanians as well as Hungarians—formed a human chain and unleashed a massive anti-Ceausescu demonstration. During the night of December 16 the city was virtually taken over by anti-Ceausescu and anticommunist protesters. The religiously inspired act of civil disobedience triggered a full-blown mass rebellion against one of the most tightly controlled authoritarian regimes in the world.

On December 17, on orders from Ceausescu, security forces cracked down on the Timisoara demonstrators with lethal force. It became clear that the Romanian dictator would not follow the East German pattern of self-restraint and would use any means to preserve his power. On the same day, news of the Timisoara uprising and its bloody repression reached Budapest, Belgrade, and Western capitals. Western radio stations beamed the story back to Romania. Although the dictator did not seem to recognize it, as he left on December 18 for Teheran, from that moment on the fate of the Ceausescu regime was sealed. How could Ceausescu have been so blind to the myriad signals announcing the imminent reaction against his Draconian rule? Why did he ignore the dissatisfaction that was rampant even among the party, military, and police bureaucracies? The Timisoara uprising came in a period when Ceausescu's closest allies in the Warsaw pact—Todor Zhivkov, Erich Honecker, and Milos Jakes—had been overthrown. Isolated in the grip of his delusions, the hostage of an unbounded personality cult and a subservient entourage, Ceausescu preferred to neglect reality and to believe the fantasies codified in the party documents, including slogans about the monolithic unity between the Romanian nation and its *conducator*.

Upon returning to Bucharest, Ceausescu made a colossal blunder: On December 20 he addressed the nation on radio and television, blaming the events in Timisoara on "hooligans," "fascists," and instigators from abroad. "On the basis of data available so far," he stated, "one can say with full conviction that these actions of a terrorist nature were organized and unleashed in close connection with reactionary, imperialist, irredentist, chauvinist circles, and foreign espionage circles in various countries."[72] The General Secretary praised the army and the *Securitate* for their "utmost forbearance" before having taken action, and in so speaking, he took personal responsibility—as supreme commander of the Romanian armed forces—for the savage massacre. His stern warning that demonstrators in other places would be fired on was seen as both a confirmation of the horrifying news about the Timisoara bloodbath and a humiliating challenge to a restless, edgy, deeply frustrated population. That was perhaps the magic moment when, in the consciousness of many Romanians, the threshold of fear was crossed: Revulsion, moral indignation, outrage, and contempt suddenly became stronger than fear.[73] Romania's revolution was born out of absolute desperation: The youths who took to the streets knew that they would be murdered, but they refused to accept the prolongation of oppression.

Ceausescu's second, even more astonishing blunder was his decision to organize a huge demonstration of popular support for his rule similar to the one staged only a month before, after the carefully orchestrated pageants of the Fourteenth RCP Congress. The tens of thousands of people herded by the *Securitate* and assorted party bosses into the Palace Square on the morning of December 21 were a highly volatile crowd, people on the brink of rebellion. Romanian television, and soon world television, captured the tyrant's incredulity and anger as the cheering multitude suddenly began to boo him, and ritual chants of "*Ceausescu si poporul!*" (Ceausescu and the people!) changed to "*Ceausescu dictatorul!*" (Ceausescu the dictator!). Whether, as some later would claim, the switch from simulated praise to sincere and contagious abuse was triggered by members of the *Securitate* acting under instructions from their superiors, who had secretly decided to get rid of Ceausescu, we may never know. At any rate, millions of viewers witnessed large numbers of people screaming against the dictator on live TV. The skillfully constructed edifice of allegedly impregnable and immutable power fell apart with that spontaneous outburst of popular hatred. The image of the dictator waving his arms in bewilderment was then extinguished—though Elena Ceausescu's voice could still be heard for a few seconds, urging her husband to stay calm—and the broadcast was interrupted for three long minutes. When live transmission resumed, Ceausescu was seen making demagogic promises—such as a rise in the minimum wage—in a last attempt to calm the furious crowd. But power had already slipped from the balcony of the Central Committee building to the street.

A sequence of revolutionary events followed: a string of student demonstrations in University Square, which went through December 22, in spite of bloody repression; spontaneous anti-Ceausescu marches through the streets of Bucharest, in which hundreds of thousands participated; the seizure of the TV station with the help of the army, which had switched sides and was supporting the popular uprising. As the party headquarters were attacked by the demonstrators, Nicolae Ceausescu and his wife fled the building by helicopter, but they soon were captured by the army, which kept them incommunicado in a secret location. The same day a National Salvation Front Council was formed. It proclaimed its commitment to political pluralism and abolished all the institutions of the old regime. The Romanian Communist Party seemed to disappear as if it had never existed. The resistance put up by isolated units of the secret police between December 22 and Christmas Day, when Ceausescu and his wife were executed, provided a dramatic backdrop to the popular euphoria and did not essentially affect the near-universal sense of relief, enthusiasm, and hope sweeping the country. Despite the violence—less widespread than at first thought—the revolutionary feast lasted well into the first days of 1990, when disappointment in the new government, the self-appointed National Salvation Front (NSF), started to set in.

The December revolution generated a number of questions, particularly about the circumstances of the death of Nicolae and Elena Ceausescu and the provenance of the NSF. An observer far removed from the events might have fathomed a good bit regarding the intentions of the NSF by exploring the circumstances surrounding the reported trial and execution of the former leading couple. Although an NSF spokesman had promised a public trial when the Ceausescus were captured on the morning of December 22, three days later it was announced that a secret military tribunal had sentenced the two Ceausescus to death and that they had been executed immediately. The rapid trial and the execution by firing squad of the Ceausescus, the NSF argument went, saved many lives by causing *Securitate* "terrorists" loyal to Ceausescu to stop fighting for a lost cause and surrender. In hindsight, however, one can see that such resistance was much more sporadic and less intense than had been suggested in some spectacular footage shown on television, which concentrated on the burning of the central university library in Bucharest and extensive damage to the art museum housed on the second floor of the old Royal Palace. When no "terrorists" were brought to justice or otherwise heard of, the public began to doubt their very existence. For many in Romania, it seemed that the hard-core communist nucleus of the NSF had deliberately exaggerated the "terrorist" threat in order to contain the anticommunist revolution from below. In a sense, the good news of the tyrant's death was clouded by the circumstances surrounding it. Instead of a pure revolutionary tyrannicide, the people of Romania were witness to what appears to have been a case of pseudo-judicial murder, with the defense lawyers as vehement and sarcastic as the prosecutor in their attempt to humiliate the deposed leader and his wife. Ceausescu had to be liquidated as soon as possible in order to silence him and ensure a smooth transition from an unreconstructed Stalinist autocracy to a Romanian version of reformed communism. The new leaders took great care to stigmatize the former dictator and his coterie as chiefly responsible for all the country's disasters. Instead of a genuine trial of Romanian communism, the population was provided with a simulacrum of justice intended to demonize the former leader and exonerate the huge apparatus that had made possible the aberrations of Ceausescu's rule.

A mystery as profound as that attending the Ceausescu trial surrounds the origins of the NSF itself. If in Czechoslovakia the Civic Forum originated in the long-banned and systematically harassed Charter 77, the new ruling formation in Romania had no domestic dissident or opposition movement with which to identify. Who appointed the original members of the Front or selected Ion Iliescu, a former Central Committee Secretary, as President and the young Polytechnical School Professor Petre Roman as Prime Minister? What criteria were used to select the leadership? Initially, the NSF Council included a number of genuine noncommunist dissidents ready to endorse its original platform promising free elections, the establishment of a democratic system, and, more broadly, the development of a civil society in Romania. But as the chasm between the Front's rhetoric and its Leninist practices became evident, celebrated dissidents such as the human rights activist Doina Cornea and the poet Ana Blandiana resigned. Romanians began to realize that the new structure of power was in many ways a continuation of the old. From that moment on, the rapidly emerging civic groups and associations, as well as the resurrected democratic parties that had been suppressed by the communists, engaged in direct criticism of what they called the NSF's "neo-communism." The conflict between power and society in Romania intensified further when the Front announced its intention to field candidates for the forthcoming elections, thereby renouncing its promise to be only a transitional government. When the opposition protested the resurgence of authoritarian methods, the Front mobilized workers to protect their rule through intimidation. But the intimidation did not work, and the opposition continued to gather momentum. The traditional Romanian parties—the National Peasants, the National Liberals, and the Social Democrats—formed their own structures and participated in the provisional parliament. Extraparliamentary opposition developed primarily among the increasingly radicalized student population and the intelligentsia. The Hungarian minority, long subjected to outrageous discrimination, formed its own political party, called the Hungarian Democratic Union. In turn, Romanian nationalists organized their own political movement named *Vatra Romaneasca* (the Romanian Hearth), whose statements were reminiscent of the worst excesses of the interwar chauvinist groups.[74] Although the NSF used its immense state machine to discourage and neutralize the opposition, there was a widespread sense that the clock of history could not be reversed and that Romania would join the other East European countries in the difficult but inevitable transition to democracy.

POPULISM AND REFORMS IN YUGOSLAVIA

In Yugoslavia, after Tito's death, a process of continuous diversification and fragmentation contributed to growing discrepancies between the more civic-oriented republics of Slovenia and Croatia and the ethnically dominated cultures of Serbia, Montenegro, and Bosnia. The rise to prominence of the strongman party leader Slobodan Milosevic, a dyed-in-the-wool nationalist in Serbia, threatened the prospects for keeping the country together, because the Croatians and Slovenes resented Milosevic's populist and radically antireformist stances. At the same time, many Serbs, including some intellectuals long known for their opposition to nationalism, placed their bets on the likelihood of Milosevic's becoming a true champion of what they perceived as their republic's threatened existence. For instance, many thought that "Slobo," as the Serbian leader was popularly called, had repaired many of the wrongs inflicted on their nation since Yugoslavia's creation in the wake of World War I. Professor Kosta Mihailovic, an economist and member of the Serbian Academy of Sciences in Belgrade, gave voice to this widespread sentiment of wounded national pride: "Serbia was politically and economically dominated in Yugoslavia. An anti-Serbian coalition existed for a long time. We occupied a vassal position in Yugoslavia. This was totally changed by the appearance of Slobodan Milosevic."[75] Milosevic's swift ascent was indicative of the emerging mixture of nationalism, authoritarianism, and egalitarian populism, an ideological hybrid that seemed appealing to large social strata in the post-totalitarian cultures. Born in

1941, Milosevic, the rising star of Serbian political life, was an active communist at the University of Belgrade, where he graduated with a law degree in 1964. After having worked in the economic bureaucracy, he joined the Serbian party apparatus in 1984 as head of the Belgrade organization. Three years later he was elected Chairman of the Serbian Communist Politburo, and in May 1989 he became the President of Serbia. The secret of his rise to prominence lay in his skillful use of populist and nationalist slogans. To those who were afraid of marketization, Milosevic promised the preservation of government control over economic resources. To Serbs irritated by the rise of nationalist movements in the other republics, he promised that he would defend what he called Serbian dignity. Convinced that he had to perform a mission equal to Tito's pioneering effort to found a viable federation, Milosevic pushed hard for the restoration of a permanent presidential office that would replace the existing system, in which the presidency was rotated among the leaders of the country's six republics.

The conflict between Belgrade and the economically more advanced republics of Croatia and Slovenia has deep historical and cultural roots. Milosevic's passionate identification of Serbian interests with pan-Yugoslav ones was deeply resented by the mounting autonomist and even separatist movements in the other republics. Added to that was the further deterioration of the situation in the explosive Kosovo region, where the Serbs resorted to violence to smash the increasingly radical Albanian nationalists. The uneasy Yugoslav state construct, a legacy of Tito's attempt to blur national antagonisms and unify the country on a basis of communist ideology, could not resist the rise of ethnic passions. As we have seen, the ideology was dead in all the East European communist states, but its collapse was perhaps most obvious in Yugoslavia, because of the realization that Marxism-Leninism, instead of diminishing ethnic conflicts, had suppressed them only temporarily. As soon as the police pressure and the myth of Titoism ceased to be compelling, the breakup of Yugoslavia became, if not imminent, at least a realistic possibility. The Yugoslav League of Communists, once cohesive thanks to Tito's charismatic presence, became a powerless umbrella that included six diverging republic parties, each championing local interests and defying the central authority. By the end of 1989 the army remained the only national institution, although the overwhelming Serbian component (about 70 percent) made it a potential instrument for the fulfillment of Milosevic's hegemonic plans. Understandably, the danger of a military crackdown on the centrifugal republics made them nervous and accelerated the disintegrative trends.

THE WARSAW PACT'S REACTION TO GORBACHEV

Gorbachev's opening of the Soviet system contributed to the polarization and disintegration of the Soviet bloc. Two trends coalesced in response to the changes coming from Moscow. Polish and Hungarian communists were apparently prompted by Gorbachev's thaw to pursue their own reforms in a more systematic way, while their fellow bloc members chose to resist reform. In Poland, although General Jaruzelski was associated with the proclamation of Martial Law in December 1981, the communists found in Gorbachev's reforms an opportunity for domestic relaxation and more experimentation in the economy. The catchword used by Jaruzelski and his successor at the helm of the Polish Communist Party, Mieczyslaw Rakowski, was "socialist pluralism." The Hungarian communists evolved in the same direction, first under the leadership of the veteran General Secretary Janos Kadar, then, after Kadar's forced retirement in 1988, under the increasingly disputed guidance of Kadar's former protégé, Karoly Grosz. In both countries, strong factions emerged within the ruling elite and contributed to the growing fragmentation of the once cohesive ruling bodies.

Stimulated by the changes in the USSR, where Gorbachev showed increasing patience with and even encouraged criticism from below, the civil societies in Poland and Hungary too renewed their activities with growing courage and imagination. Contacts were established between radical reformers in Hungary and exponents of the democratic opposition. For instance, the Minister of State, Central Committee member Imre Pozsgay, participated in a meeting with representatives of the unofficial democratic forces in 1987. In 1988 the reformers managed to rid the top leadership of the Hungarian communist party of Janos Kadar. A whole era came to an end once this man, who had presided over the post-1956 "normalization," lost his power. The taboo on historical reassessments imposed by Kadar was lifted, and society engaged in a frantic rediscovery of its own past.

But while Poland's and Hungary's trend toward liberalization proceeded quite rapidly and with apparently little resistance from the ruling bureaucracies, the new wave of de-Stalinization encountered staunch resistance in Romania, Bulgaria, the GDR, and Czechoslovakia. At the level of the Warsaw Pact, the rapid pace of democratization in Hungary and Poland, as well as Gorbachev's policies of glasnost and perestroika, alarmed the entrenched Stalinist groups in the other countries. For Ceausescu, Zhivkov, Honecker, and Jakes, the Soviet pressure to engage in overall reforms amounted to an invitation to subvert their own power base. Each of those communist potentates had run his country with an iron fist for a long time. They had ruthlessly stamped out political dissent and opposition. They had eliminated all rivals who could have championed a reformist line.

The degree of resistance to Soviet-encouraged and even Soviet-suggested reforms varied from country to country. For instance, it was simpler for Ceausescu, with his experience of autonomy from Moscow, to mobilize the party elite's support for a hard political line, including staunch anti-Soviet elements. An unambiguous challenge to Moscow was more problematic for the Czechoslovak leadership headed by President Gustav Husak and General Secretary Milos Jakes. For those two, cutting the umbilical cord with the Soviet Union was practically impossible. Their unique political credentials for staying in power consisted in their active support for the repression that followed the invasion in August 1968. In Bulgaria, Zhivkov's whole political career had been based on slavish subservience to orders coming from Moscow, so now he could not defy the center. As for the East German leaders, they knew that it was the Red Army umbrella that made possible the very existence of their regime. By opposing radical reforms, they would only delay the natural historical process that would lead to German reunification and the disbandment of what many considered the artificial state construct called the GDR. Those nonliberalizing leaders tried to play for time, to simulate support for Gorbachev while secretly hoping that the hawks in the Soviet Politburo would soon get rid of the turbulent General Secretary and restore the only version of socialism they were able to identify with: the Brezhnevite model based on militarism, expansionism, corruption, and social apathy. Jacques Rupnik correctly termed the attitudes of the East European communist leaderships toward Gorbachev's reforms as "a function of the relationships that they had with their respective societies, the degree of acceptance or coolness being correlated with the priority they gave either to social control or to the tacit search for consensus in society."[76]

SEVEN

The Birth Pangs of Democracy

> We can return to the beasts. But if we
> wish to remain human, then there is
> only one way, the way into the open
> society.
>
> —*Karl R. Popper*

> I pray that we do not change from pris-
> oners into prison guards.
>
> —*Adam Michnik*

The upheavals of 1989 and the collapse of the communist parties
demonstrated the precariousness of the governing institutions in
Eastern Europe. Actually, long before those revolutions the erosion of
the authoritarian-bureaucratic regimes had become evident. The prolongation of the communist regimes depended on the use of force and
the perception of a foreign threat that would demolish any attempt to
get rid of the existing order. The memory of Budapest in 1956 and
Prague in 1968 functioned as a powerful deterrent for those who saw
the vital need for reforms. Later, as Soviet pressure loosened and the
local elites found themselves deprived of foreign support, a new wave
of rebellious experimentation could gather momentum.

In 1988 and 1989 the impossible seemed to have come true. With
lightning speed, all the previous taboos were abolished; the opposition
realized that for the first time it was reasonable to think about the radical
overcoming of the power structure that had existed since the satellization
of Eastern Europe in the aftermath of World War II. No barrier was solid
enough to withstand the mounting revolutionary turmoil. The appa-

ratchiks were confused, unable to take the measure of the new challenges. From Honecker to Ceausescu, from Zhivkov to Jakes, they were all dismayed and helpless. The only expedient they could envision to arrest the popular upheaval would have involved violence. But that tactic was definitely the opposite of what Moscow was interested in endorsing. The smiling face of socialism that Gorbachev and his team tried to project in international relations meant a renunciation of traditional repressive methods. Persuasion rather than coercion was the slogan of the day.

Initially, the prevailing feeling in all the former communist countries was that detotalitarianization—that is, the disintegration of the communist institutions and structures—would occur without large-scale conflicts. The mood was euphoric, especially because, with the exception of Romania, the revolutionary changes that had taken place did so in a nonviolent way. Expectations were high regarding how the birth of democratic institutions, including parliaments and political parties, would proceed without convulsions, almost as a natural process. But those were illusions encouraged by the speed of the 1989 events. One of the principal illusions was that communism would necessarily be followed by democratic forms of political and social organization.

Because of the widespread disenchantment with Leninist ideology and practice, it was taken for granted, by political actors in the region and by many foreign analysts, that the long exposure of those nations to the hardships of dictatorship had made them immune to new authoritarian temptations. But, as Kenneth Jowitt has shown, that belief was founded on wishful thinking. Leninism had left its imprint on the collective psyche, generating behavior patterns that, even if only in a residual way, would continue to affect the public sphere. This "old rule" residue has been the main obstacle confronted by all the postcommunist societies. The articulation between public and private interests characteristic of procedural democracy has been lacking: The "Leninist legacy understood as the impact of party organizations, practice, and ethos *and* the initial charismatic ethical opposition to it favors an authoritarian not a liberal capitalist way of life, the obstacles to which are not simply how to privatize and marketize the economy, or organize an electoral campaign, but rather how to institutionalize public virtues."[1] Communism had not run those countries in an orderly and benign way. In all of them the secret police had kept the population under strict surveillance, intellectuals were muzzled, students were indoctrinated, workers were overworked and underpaid. All those societies had been plagued by corruption, cultural despair, economic decay, and, more than anything else, an abysmal decline in the sense of social solidarity. Suspicion was rampant. With its compulsive drive toward conformity and uniformity, communism went out of its way to destroy all intermediate institutions and associations that could become the pillars of a revived civil society. Timothy Garton Ash's insight is thus noteworthy: "Perhaps the beginning of wisdom is to recognize that what communism has left behind is an extraordinary mish-mash, a freagmentation and cacophony of interests, attitudes, views, ideals, traditions."[2] Think of Czechoslovakia, where in March 1991 ten members of the parliament were indicted for their previous links with the secret police. The issue was not their individual guilt, but rather the absence of a procedural framework for dealing with those charges in a dispassionate way. In all those countries, recriminations and settling of accounts tended to obfuscate the in-depth analysis of the real causes of the communist disaster. The politics of hysteria often competed with the clear-minded search for democratic reconstruction. The big losers in the 1989 showdown, the communists, took special pleasure in poisoning the public atmosphere and engaging in social demagogy.

The demise of the communist regimes did not mean the immediate collapse of the communist political cultures—all the habits, mentalities, attitudes, symbols, and values that had permeated social life for decades. The principal dilemmas for the new elites in Eastern Europe can be posed in a series of "how to" questions. How to create a democratic polity in the absence of a culture tolerant of differences or able to integrate conflicting trends without resorting to authoritarian methods of control and coercion? How to instill a sense of common responsibility and overcome the selfish and more often than not immoderate advocacy of particular interests to the detriment of the public good? How to replace the almost total state monopoly of the public realm with a different form of organization in which the exclusive logic of Leninism can be supplanted by the common search for compromise? How to transform the long-dormant or even nonexistent civic virtues into social energies able to contribute to the limitation of government arbitrariness without becoming a perpetual source of unrest, anarchy, and nihilism? Or, in countries where different ethnic groups compete to promote their values and aspirations, how to protect the rights of the minorities threatened by ethnocentric trends within the majority?

The East European dilemma is aggravated by unrealistic expectations about what it means to adopt Western values. The belief that the end of the communist parties' monopoly on power automatically amounted to the end of communism and the birth of democracy contributed to a continuously growing gap between the rising expectations of the populations and the limits of the existing system. In fact, what happened in these countries signified less the establishment of full-fledged democratic regimes—such an occurrence would have been sociologically impossilble after so many years of dictatorship—but rather the gradual reconstruction of the political space. After decades when politics had been seen as the realm of demagogy and duplicity, a perfect springboard for opportunists, it now became possible to approach politics as the domain where the individual could freely exert his or her civil and human rights. New political movements emerged in addition to the former opposition groups that had challenged the communist governments. After the lethargy and desperation of previous years, when it had seemed that history had come to an end in that part of the world, there was a general sense of exhilaration and hope. The first months of 1990 were dominated by enthusiasm and romantic dreams of national solidarity. The new politics emerged as an attempt to restore historical traditions, but in none of those countries did the new formations claim that the nascent political system should be a simple reproduction of the precommunist ones. In all those societies the general trend has been a frantic pursuit of Western models for a rapid transition to democracy.

For many it appeared that the immediate transition to a democracy with a market economy would be a panacea for the evils associated with central planning. There was a kind of intoxication with the virtues of a free market. As privatization proceeds and millions find themselves unemployed, one can predict the rise of populist demagogic movements that will promise everything to everyone in the hope of winning political power. It is therefore critical for those countries to identify what guarantees, institutional and cultural, will diminish the danger of a relapse into a brand of authoritarianism different from the Leninist one only because it does not necessarily incorporate Marxism's ideological mystique. In other words, those nations have to build their civil societies in order to avoid the calamitous slide from oligarchic tyranny to the tyranny of the mob. In the words of Ralf Dahrendorf:

> "We are the people" is a nice slogan, but as a constitutional maxim it is a mirror image of the total state that has just been dislodged. If the monopoly of the party is replaced merely by the victory of the masses, all will be lost before long, for the masses have no structure and no permanence. . . . The key question is how to fill the gap between the state and the people—sometimes, as in Romania, one of frightening dimensions—with activities which by their autonomy create social sources of power.

Before this is achieved, the constitution of liberty and even the market economy, social or otherwise, will remain suspended in midair.[3]

In countries with little experience of democratic procedures, there is a potential for the manipulation of the mass of gullible and often confused individuals by cynical adventurers or irresponsible opportunists who can exploit collective anxieties and frustrations in order to seize power. Communism is dead in Eastern Europe, but its legacy includes a yearning for immediate reward and compensation, and that impatience leaves the door open for oracular political movements rooted in hopelessness and insecurity. Take for instance the overwhelming majority that the National Salvation Front won during the May 1990 elections in Romania. The NSF won by pledging to avoid the shock of a painful transition to a market economy and by playing up the NSF strongman, Ion Iliescu. Another example is the populist overtones employed by Yugoslavia's Slobodan Milosevic in his political performances, which are outmatched by his even more nationalist opponent, Vuk Draskovic, leader of the radical Movement for Serbian Renewal. Draskovic uses the following stereotypes referring to the Croats: "Most Croats have an irrational hatred of Serbs. The only feeling the Croatian people have is hatred."[4] Such movements can win temporary majorities in new parliaments and can impose their intolerant visions on a nation's beleaguered minorities. To understand the nature of those intolerant visions, created by the sudden leap into pluralism without the existence of institutional foundations for an orderly democratic process, one can turn to Alexis de Tocqueville's analysis on the tyranny of the majority and the right of the individual to resist it: "When I refuse to obey an unjust law, I do not contest the right which the majority has of commanding, but I simply appeal from the sovereignty of the people to the sovereignty of mankind."[5]

The risk that the new political formations that emerged from the ashes of communism would be unable to use their authority in a reasonable and cautious way should be neither exaggerated nor underestimated. There remains, however, the real danger that, in order to ensure their electoral success, many of the new groups, with inchoate ideological preferences, will cater to the crowds and indulge in populist fantasies.

It is one thing to vanquish communist bureaucracies and another to construct a world where individuals cease to distrust each other. The restoration of politics, the discovery of the public arena as a place for the competition of values, and the appearance of different interest groups signified the opening of the public space. Democracy, however, with its impersonal procedural culture, had to be built upon a still fragile foundation haunted by the demons of the past. As Karl Marx wrote in *The Eighteenth Brumaire of Louis Bonaparte:* "The traditions of all the dead generations weigh like a nightmare on the brain of the living."[6] Because the past had been suspended for decades, it was now coming back with all the complexes and neuroses that had created the drama of East European history for centuries before the advent of communism.

Although the dominant rhetoric throughout Eastern Europe now included references to ideological preferences, the new parties constituted themselves on the basis of personal affinities and shared experience. The new political elites are made up of different groups that have participated in similar activities and have long-established, strong interpersonal connections. Ideology matters, but it is subordinate to sentiments. For example, to understand the accusations and recriminations in contemporary Hungary and Poland, one has to be familiar with the history of the Democratic Opposition and the KOR. Many of the current senators and ministers in both countries were once involved in the underground actions of the heroic dissident period. Others were among the uncommitted spectators who, without endorsing communist power, did not directly engage in anticommunist activism. Regarding the Hungarian and the Polish political scene, Timothy Garton Ash observed:

> In present-day politics, you have the class of '48, the class of '56, the class of '68, the class of '80, and (largest of all) the class of '89, and both between and within each class there is a complex personal history of friendships and rivalries. You cannot begin to understand the personal alignments of today unless you know who did what to whom over the last forty years. . . . [T]he only serious path to real understanding is a detailed historical and, in the case of the leading actors, biographical narrative.[7]

The transideological nature of those affinities is striking if one considers that a cultural and political conservative like Gaspar Miklos Tamas is one of the leaders of the Alliance of Free Democrats in Hungary, a political formation that is quite liberal in its values. Tamas, however, had been a driving force of the samizdat opposition and a close friend of the *Beszelö* circle headed by the current chairman of the Free Democrats, Janos Kis. At the same time, György Bence, a philosopher who in the past stood together with Kis and was a young member of the Lukacs school of critical Marxism, is now an informal but close adviser to the FIDESZ leadership. One can identify a similar role of personal relations in Polish political life, where the Warsaw and Krakow intellectual elite tended to side with Tadeusz Mazowiecki rather than with Lech Walesa during the presidential elections in December 1990. Unless one pays attention to the "prehistory" of those relations, one can barely understand the bitterness of certain charges and the intensity of what often looks like senseless fratricidal strife.[8]

In most of these countries one of the most important issues has been the fate of the former communist parties. In Romania, for instance, the communist party, as previously mentioned, seemed to vanish without a trace following the spontaneous anticommunist uprising in December 1989. But was that disappearance an accurate perception? Can one seriously believe that a political movement that numbered almost 4 million members before the December 1989 revolution had simply left the historical scene without leaving any legacy? For many, the National Salvation Front, the formation that rose to prominence during the vacuum of power that followed Ceausescu's flight from Bucharest, was simply a reincarnation of the old communist party. Later, in December 1990, a group of former leaders of the vanished but not defunct communist party announced the party's restoration under the name Socialist Labor Party.[9] In other words, even in an anticommunist society institutions, beliefs, and thought patterns characteristic of the old regime do not die out overnight.

In the avalanche of confusing signals coming from Eastern Europe, one can distinguish a number of significant common features of the wondrous upsurge that swept away the corrupt and incompetent communist regimes. The thrust of the 1989 revolutions was anticommunist, anti-authoritarian and anti-ideological. It was precisely because those revolutions defied the communist politicization of the public sphere that most of the new leaders maintained a skeptical attitude toward the formation of political parties in the aftermath of their victory. The tension between institutional obligations and moral apprehensions explains the hesitation expressed not only by Vaclav Havel and the Civic Forum but also by Hungarian activists to solidify their efforts in the form of political parties. Indeed, it took a number of years for the former members of Hungary's samizdat opposition to form first a Network of Free Initiatives and later the Alliance of Free Democrats—a genuine political party, with its statutes, hierachy, and grassroots organizations, including a youth branch. In the past, the opposition had justified its activities by reference to the universalist vision of human and civil rights. Most of its leaders were distinguished intellectuals who had decided to live in truth regardless of the price they had to pay for this East European form of civil disobedience. Since human rights transcend national and social boundaries, for many of those activists it was a great surprise—and not a pleasant one—to discover that underneath the frozen totalitarian monolith the old (and ugly) passions and animosities had lingered and were ready to explode as soon as police pressure ceased to be exerted. Communism had not solved any of the region's problems in terms of social and national injustices. On the contrary, those problems had only been denied, and therefore exacerbated through neglect and symbolic manipulation, as in the case of the chauvinistic populism practiced by Bulgarian, Serbian, and Romanian communist leaders.

The break with the past was dominated by the overarching emphasis, in the programs and statements of the new movements, on the need to restore morality in public life. It was vitally important to debunk the ideological mirage used by the communists to justify their hold on society. It was also important to create a social environment where the individual would cease to feel threatened and humiliated by an omnipotent repressive apparatus. The accountability of public officials had to be enshrined in new constitutions that would guarantee the thoroughness of the ongoing changes. The nature and dynamics of the transition to genuine politics were determined by the maturity of local opposition groups and their aptitude for offering workable alternative strategies for economic and social recovery. In all those countries the issues relating to political justice and the punishment of people responsible for the calamities of the past became of paramount importance for the national healing and the purification of public life. The ghosts of the past had to be exorcised. The public demands for justice had to be met by the new authorities without giving in to the calls for bloody revenge and unruly outbursts of anger that could degenerate in lynchings and massacres of the former apparatchiks and security police cadres and informers. The treatment applied to the former leaders and their tools, who had helped create and maintain a most inhumane system, was one of the most complex and potentially destabilizing problems of the postrevolutionary regimes. It was often almost impossible to find criteria for separating those had been simple pawns from those who took special delight in persecuting the critical thinkers and the independent working-class activists. What should happen to the judges who had passed long prison sentences upon people who were now members of the government? Timothy Garton Ash pointed to that dilemma of the postcommunist power when he described the new sources of anger in Eastern Europe:

> Former censors, former border guards, former apparatchiks, former secret policemen: what is to be done with them? Or rather, what is to be done

with Them—*Oni*—as the Communist power holders, great and small, were universally known. There is the question of justice. At the highest level, this is the Nuremberg question. Should the men at the top be brought to trial for the evil they did, or that was done under them? If so, on what charges and by what laws? At a lower level it becomes almost a question of social justice. Is it fair, people ask, that those who had comfortable office jobs under the communists should still have them today, when ordinary people are having to tighten their belts yet more? Is it fair that members of the *nomenklatura* are exploiting the unclear legal conditions of privatization to take over as capitalists the enterprises they had previously commanded as Communists?[10]

The discontent with the slow pace of national purification and the widespread sentiment that the entrenched bureaucracies continued to retain positions of influence, especially in the economic apparatus, inspired new outbursts of popular anger. The construction of civil societies and the restoration of interpersonal bonds of solidarity turned out to be a much longer and more difficult process than anticipated. It was one thing to fight against an easily identifiable enemy—the communist power—and another to create a culture of trust, dialogue, and tolerance. Institutional and constitutional designs became the most important issues. In Romania and Bulgaria, public dissatisfaction with the gradual dismemberment of the old institutions created new crises. There was thus a growing gap between the East-Central European model of political development, which included a palpable and unequivocal break with the communist past and a strong commitment, on the part of the new political actors, to observe the rules of pluralism, and Southeastern Europe, where the legacy of totalitarianism turned out to be more persistent and stubborn and prevented the rapid opening of the public space. Especially in Bulgaria, Romania, and Serbia, nationalist movements rooted in resentful myths and atavistic phobias tried to inflame collective passions. Ethnocracy rather than democracy threatened to be the future of those societies.

Romanian extremist movements started to attack the Hungarian minority for nourishing "irredentist" hopes with regard to Transylvania. The former collaborators of the Ceausescu regime, the sycophants of the late *conducator*, resurfaced and launched a particularly vicious magazine called *Romania Mare* (Great Romania), in the pages of which no dissident from the time of the dictatorship was spared. Slanders and insults inundated the pages of an increasingly anarchic press. Efforts were made to rehabilitate the military dictator Ion Antonescu, who ran Romania during World War II, and to present him as a defender of national interests. The progovernment media engaged in vicious campaigns against King Michael, who had arrested Antonescu in August 1944 and had established a short-lived democracy before the communists took over. In Serbia, but also in Croatia and Bulgaria, the specter of nationalism loomed ominously. Signs of ethnocentrism were detected as well in Slovakia, where Christian nationalist groups emerged and tried to rehabilitate the pro-Nazi nationalist government headed, during World War II, by Monsignor Tiso. Drawing from that authoritarian-nationalist tradition, a small but vociferous minority advocated an independent Slovak state. In Bulgaria, anti-Turkish nationalism was rampant.

Across the East European countries there was a feeling that it was enormously important to divulge the workings of the police state and to make public identification of former security police collaborators. Those exposures were particularly dramatic in the former GDR, Czechoslovakia, and Romania. President Havel issued a decree calling for the screening of all public officials. It was revealed that even leaders of the reconstituted anticommunist parties had collaborated with the secret police and belonged to the category of "tainted people."[11] Punishment of the human instruments of totalitarianism was part of the necessary coming to terms with those societies' past. It was part of the revival of a political culture ready to assume both its failings and its accomplishments. The learning of democracy had to coincide with the renunciation of the modes of thought and the behavior patterns instilled during more than forty years of Leninist regimes. People had to get rid of their readiness to expect all decisions to be made by an external authority and to realize that no charismatic leader would magically save them from poverty and insecurity. The emergence of new elites, able to perform in a culture based on merit and competition, was thus a barrier to the slide toward new authoritarian experiments.

The main task, therefore, in all those countries was to build up a political culture solid and self-confident enough to counter the rise of new fundamentalist movements. As Karol Modzelewski, the well-known Polish historian, opposition activist, and, after 1989, senator, put it:

> Dictators don't become dictators by themselves; they don't dominate countries simply because they have dictatorial tendencies. People make a dictator—the people who advise him and who take orders from him and especially the people in society at large who support him. In other words, whether a country has a dictator or not depends primarily upon the political culture of the country in cause.[12]

The consolidation of a constitutional framework that would prevent the rise of populist movements supportive of demagogic "strongmen" has to be accompanied by continuous efforts in the field of everyday politics and the "illuminist" struggle with the obscurantist, superstitious, and highly intolerant practices bequeathed on those societies not only by communism but also by the nondemocratic or semidemocratic cultures of the interwar period. Among other things, that includes the recognition and protection of minority rights, a major irritant for those who would like to assert the primacy of the "organic" ethnic community over the individual.

As the shock of modernity is inevitable in all these countries, the risk exists of a coalescence of "movements of disenchantment" driven by fear and despair. Communism is definitely extinct in those countries, but democracy is not necessarily its successor. There is danger of a baroque synthesis between nostalgia for the protective shield of the police state and readiness to accept the promises of social demagogues able to manipulate the symbols of national salvation. In this respect, Ralf Dahrendorf has wisely emphasized the pitfalls of the painful first stage of the transition to an open society: "I hate to think of the combination of military leaders, economic planners and racist ideologists which might be brought to power by dislocated and disenchanted groups. Guard against the beginnings! Fundamentalists are waiting around many corners to collect their contributions from those who have lost their nerve on the road to freedom."[13] Indeed, the reinvention of politics takes place against the background of many immoderate and often unreasonable expectations. As the first stage of triumphant ecstasy fades away, people realize that the next one would be marked by new hardships, especially in terms of economic recovery. It will take the new elites' courage, imagination, and strong commitment to pluralist values to defend the democratic institutions against authoritarian attacks. The precedents of Spain and Portugal, countries ruled by dictators for decades, show, however, that such a transition is feasible. Pointing to the dangers, including the fascist one, should not make us skeptical about democracy's chances to establish itself in Eastern Europe.

BETWEEN EUPHORIA AND RAGE

After the spectacular breakdown of the communist structures of domination, all the countries in Eastern Europe engaged in a feverish search for new political formulae that would facilitate the establishment of demo-

lum when the time has come to denounce the failures of the previous dynasty. [48]

When Haraszti wrote his book in the early 1980s, Hungary appeared to be the most advanced country in the Soviet bloc in terms of domestic liberalization. Compared with Romania, East Germany, and Czechoslovakia, dissidents were treated with kid gloves, although the state machine did not spare efforts to thwart their efforts to get out of the political ghetto and establish contacts with the larger society. The underground presses were systematically ransacked by the police, dissidents were interrogated and even beaten up. The regime avoided, however, massive organized crackdowns. As the economic situation deteriorated and the changes in the USSR spurred higher political expectations, Kadar's Hungary ceased to be "the most joyful barrack in the socialist camp." Its youth were radicalized, and the democratic opposition became a national political force. Far from being assigned to eternal marginality, dissidents, Haraszti included, became the architects of the transition to postcommunism. Actually, in the postscript to his book, written in 1987, Haraszti admitted that the changes introduced by Gorbachev in the functioning of the Soviet system and the new wave of de-Stalinization made some of his gloomy predictions invalid. But, at the same time, he insisted that Gorbachevism represented an adoption by the Soviet elite of the same techniques that had ensured the partial success of the "velvet prison" experiment undertaken by Hungary under Kadar:

> I have called this model the "post-Stalinist" or "soft" or "civilian" version of Communist rule, in contradistinction to the "Stalinist" or "hard" or "military" style. . . . Indeed, the Hungarian model might well represent a more rational, more normative, and more enduring version of directed culture. Mr. Gorbachev understands that in order to have a truly successful society with a modern economy he must boost the intelligentsia's sagging morale by giving it a stake in administering the future. [49]

F I V E

The Ethos of Civil Society

> Antipolitics strives to put politics in its
> place and make sure that it stays there,
> never overstepping its proper office of
> defending and refining the rules of the
> game of civil society. Antipolitics is the
> ethos of civil society, and civil society is
> the antithesis of military society.
>
> —György Konrad

The development of civil societies in the states of the Soviet bloc cannot be separated from the existence of autonomous centers of independent thought. Living within the truth, although often seen as a gesture of moral idealism with little social significance, has turned out to be the driving force behind the creation of alternative ways of thinking and acting. It is thus clear that the foundation stone of the countersociety is the individual's decision to proclaim his or her mental independence. In Havel's words: "What is this independent life of society? The spectrum of its expressions and activities is naturally very wide. It includes everything from self-education and thinking about the world, through free creative activity and its communication to others, to the most varied free, civic initiatives, including instances of independent social self-organization."[1] The new politics, which relies on informal citizens' initiatives as an antidote to the paralyzing pressure of the bureaucratic Leviathan, which encourages the emergence of multifaceted experiments in grassroots activism, and which maintains that change comes from spontaneous move-

intact the sense of obedience and conformity as well as the traditional Prussian militaristic values. In other words, the problem with the East Germans was that they had never experienced either genuine de-Nazification or de-Stalinization. Certainly their integration in the constitutional-pluralistic system of the Federal Republic diminished the dangers of mass outbursts of fanaticism and intolerance. The rise of two varieties of neo-Nazi activities, which provoked the immediate response of the democratic forces, however, was evident. One varietal trend that rose as the political repression disappeared consisted of viciously xenophobic, thuggish gangs that started to disseminate anti-Semitic, racist tracts and even organized assaults on foreign workers, primarily Vietnamese. During demonstrations in East Berlin, Leipzig, and other large cities, anti-Polish and generally anti-Slav slogans were heard. Following the disintegration of the fake consensus of the totalitarian state, the first variety tended to capture the attention of public opinion. The fringe extremist movement of East German neo-Nazis was made up predominantly of male youths. Their activities were often violent, and their targets were those considered alien elements threatening the "purity of the German race": Jews, Poles, and Asians.[15] The second trend arose under the impact of the West German far right, especially that of the Republican Party headed by the former SS member Franz Schönhuber. There was growing support for the political groups inclined to champion the aspirations of the extreme right.

As the Republican Party and other far right formations intensified their campaigning in the GDR, the former communists, grouped in the Socialist Unity Party–Party of Democratic Socialism, made the struggle against fascism a prominent theme of their electoral propaganda. "We didn't fight against Stalinism to make room for neo-Fascists," Gregor Gysi declared. But the communists had lost any credibility, and all their efforts to revamp their image as a Eurosocialist party failed to attract significant popular support. They were actually outflanked by the recently formed Social Democratic Party, which during the March elections won eighty-eight seats in the four-hundred-member parliament. The leader of the Social Democrats, Ibrahim Böhme, himself a former communist, challenged the communists by advocating rapid reunification.[16] As for the New Forum, the anti-authoritarian group that had been in the forefront of the demonstrations in October–November 1989, it lost its appeal because of the reluctance of its leaders to turn it into a real political party and the hostility they expressed toward German unification. For many in the New Forum, the rush of the Eastern Germans to support unification seemed a betrayal of the ideals of the October uprising. For instance, Sebastian Pflugbeil, a dissident physicist and one of the leaders of the New Forum, declared: "We became revolutionaries because we were fed up with party dictatorship and had no chance to influence things around us—we wanted a real democratic state of affairs here."[17]

One of the striking effects of the four decades of communist rule in East Germany was precisely the generally conservative orientation of the electorate and the lack of real appeal of the left-wing formations. Once integrated into a united Germany, the former GDR evolved in a different pattern from that of the other postcommunist states, which had to act on their own in the attempt to reshape the economy and restore the civic sphere. The rest of Eastern Europe had no Western "Big Brother" to invest munificently, and there were no political parties to export their know-how in terms of building a democratic culture. As for the bitter political and moral legacy of forty years of Soviet-style socialism on German soil, one could sum it up in three words: lies, corruption, and terror. As was noted by an editorial in an influential West German newspaper:

> We know now that much in the GDR was far worse than even those people who lived under the dictatorship themselves had sensed and the critics of the regime had ever imagined. The ostensible values that under-lay the socialist society of the GDR have been dissolved into nothing and are now shown to have been a mere fiction. . . . What remains of the policies of peace and disarmament that seemed so crucial to Honecker's claim to legitimacy? What remains of the communist declaration against the use of force and terror now that the links with the West German terrorists, the dead in the concentration camps, and the widespread surveil-lance of citizens have been revealed? What can remain from this legacy even for those who were prepared to look beyond the arbitrary and dictato-rial ways of the party and who ignored the realities of socialism as it was practiced in order to cling to the idea of some purer form of socialism?[18]

Bulgaria: The Impossible Cohabitation

In Bulgaria it seemed at first that the former communist party, renamed socialist, would continue to run the country in an effort to preserve its domination and avoid a radical transition to an open society. Despite internal opposition, the Socialist Party continued to control that country for most of 1990. But even the reformed communists were threatened by factionalism because of the emergence of both liberal and conservative trends. The former accused the party leader Aleksandar Lilov of still nourishing Leninist beliefs, while the latter were critical of his abandoning of the party's monopoly and the tolerance shown to antisocialist forces. After pressure from below forced the party to disband its organizations in workplaces, defections became endemic, and the Bulgarian Socialist Party's membership dwindled from almost 1 million in February 1990 to some 250,000 by mid-December.[19] In January and February roundtable discussions were organized between representatives of the BSP and the opposition. As a result of those negotiations the BSP and the opposition groups signed joint statements regarding the transition to a democratic system and the nature and future of that system. The roundtables culminated in the signing in March of an agreement on draft laws on constitutional changes, the electoral system, and political parties. In the meantime the communists went out of their way to improve their image and to convince the population that they had broken resolutely with the totalitarian past. The party renounced its control over a number of auxiliary organizations, including the trade unions.

The opposition rallied around the Union of Democratic Forces (UDF), an umbrella organization made up of movements and associations committed to pluralism and democracy. After its leader, the philospher and human rights activist Zhelyu Zhelev, was elected the country's President in August, he was replaced by the leader of Ecoglasnost, Petar Beron. In December, Beron had to resign after it was revealed that he had collaborated in the past with the secret police. Opposition parties in the UDF included the "Agrarians-Nikola Petkov", a successor to the party suppressed by the communists in 1947, which refused to merge with the larger Agrarian Union, long a satellite of the communist regime; the Bulgarian Social Democratic Party; and the Radical Democratic Party. The independent union Podkrepa, a founding member of the UDF, left the alliance in order to underline its autonomy but preserved its observer status. Meanwhile the previously harassed Turkish minority— which counted about 1.5 million—found a voice for its grievances in the Movement for Rights and Freedoms. The Movement's leader, Ahmed Dogan, announced his intention to defend human rights regardless of nationality. The Movement won twenty-three seats in the new Parliament, thus becoming the third political force in the country.[20]

The most significant event in Bulgaria was the election that took place in June 1990, during which a polarization of the electorate became visible. Although the BSP obtained the absolute majority in terms of parliamentary seats, it won less than 50 percent of all the votes and was strikingly defeated in Sofia and other big cities. What followed was a continuous deterioration of the political system: The opposition charged the Socialist-controlled government with sabotaging the democratization and eventually compelled the Socialists to accept a renegotiation of the power arrangements. In July President Petar Mladenov, the communist who had engineered Zhivkov's removal in November 1989, was forced to resign after it was disclosed that he had contemplated the use of violent means to quell a protest demonstration. On August 1, after six rounds of voting, the Parliament elected Zhelyu Zhelev as the new President. At that moment the communists still held control, because one of their leaders, Andrei Lukanov, was the Prime Minister.

On August 26 the BSP headquarters in the heart of the Sofia was set afire. All opposition parties condemned the action as a provocation organized by the unreconstructed communist forces interested in destabilizing the fledgling democratic system. While the Socialist leader, Aleksandar Lilov, claimed that the opposition should be held responsible for the incident, the UDF responded by emphasizing that it was precisely the most reactionary wing of the Socialist Party and the security police that had an interest in compromising the opposition and blocking the transition to democracy.[21] As the political and economic situation worsened, there were more outbursts of popular anger, especially over the refusal of the Socialist Party to renounce its domination. Lack of parliamentary support for the Lukanov government and the intensification of social unrest, including a general strike by the students and the two trade union organizations, forced the Socialist Lukanov to resign. His resignation forced the Socialists eventually to realize that there was no hope for them to continue the one-party government system and that the BSP's hegemonic role in Bulgarian politics had come to an end. In December a coalition government was formed under the leadership of Dimitar Popov, a respected jurist with no political or party affiliations. Key ministries were divided equally between the BSP and the UDF. The new government inherited a disastrous economic situation, with unprecedented scarcities and a rapid decline in industrial output. It was therefore vitally urgent to reconsider all economic policy and to engage in rapid and consistent privatization. Cooperation between the government and the presidential institution as well as the appointment of respected civic activists in key positions indicated that Bulgaria had a chance to overcome its economic and political predicament.[22]

Czechoslovakia: A Faltering Consensus

In Czechoslovakia the presence of a charismatic, almost unanimously admired figure like President Vaclav Havel helped to preserve an indispensable national consensus. The country launched an ambitious reform program whose outcome would be the full marketization of the economy. Observers noticed, however, that the euphoric mood of the last months of 1989 had been increasingly replaced by skepticism and apathy. For many it appeared that there was little hope of solving the immense problems amassed during four decades of communist misrule. Ethnic tensions intensified during 1990 and 1991, with the Slovaks criticizing the Czechs for their domineering propensities. At the same time there were attempts in Slovakia to rehabilitate the former Nazi collaborators of the short-lived Slovak national state during the interwar period. Those efforts, it should be said, did not necessarily arise from nostalgia for fascist values. It is a sad paradox that the only time in history that Slovaks managed to achieve statehood coincided with the advent of a Nazi-backed regime under Monsignor Josef Tiso.

Politically, the oustanding events were the elections that took place in June 1990. The Civic Forum and the Public Against Violence, the two umbrella groups that emerged as national forces during the 1989 up-heaval, won a comfortable majority of 170 in the 300-seat Federal Assembly. Although compromised by long years of collaboration with the Soviet occupier, the communists, led by the young bureaucrat Vasil Mohorita, managed to win forty-seven seats and became the second strongest political force in the country. Other parties that became prominent were the Christian Democrats, a coalition grouping the Slovak Christian Democratic Movement, the People's Party, and the Christian Democratic Party—with forty seats—and groups representing regional, ethnic, or nationalist interests.[23]

Havel was reelected President for a second term in July, and Marian Calfa, who had left the communist party in January, continued to head the government. The transition as a whole proceeded far more smoothly than in the other countries. But even in Czechoslovakia, with its more developed tradition of representative democracy, the absence of a clear understanding of the role and mechanism of a party system was evident in the internecine struggle that affected both the Civic Forum and the Public Against Violence. There were many anti-authoritarian trends that simply rejected the idea of turning those large social movements into genuine political parties. In October, however, the Forum held its congress, and Finance Minister Vaclav Klaus, an economist strongly attached to the antistatist views of Friedrich von Hayek, was elected chairman. Klaus pledged to turn the Civic Forum into a dynamic, well-organized party. Upset with what they perceived as a right-wing takeover of the Forum and the formation of an Interparliamentary Group of the Democratic Right, left-wing deputies formed their own interparliamentary faction, called the

Civic Association. It seemed that the differentiation of political trends within the Forum was a prelude to the reconstitution of a national political life that would include parties based on ideological affinities rather than movements committed to advocating abstract ideas. In February 1991 the tension between the left and the right within the Civic Forum reached its climax, and the movement split into two wings. One was dominated by Klaus and supported the idea of forming a "definitely right-of-center party" to contest for the 1992 parliamentary elections. Such a party did indeed emerge in the spring of 1991. The other wing, more diffuse, founded its political arm under the name of the Liberal Club, whose best-known personality was the Deputy Prime Minister, Foreign Minister, and veteran Charter 77 activist Jiri Dienstbier. According to Klaus, the divergence between the two factions caused by their different political and economic philosophies. He criticized the Liberal Club for its commitment to social democratic values and for the influential role played within its ranks by former dissident communists. In order to avoid unnecessary strife over who could legitimately use the name "Civic Forum," the two groups agreed to reserve it for a coordinating committee on which both factions would be equally represented.[24] Meanwhile, Finance Minister Klaus advocated a fast privatization of the economy and managed to persuade the parliament to pass a number of laws regarding the restitution of confiscated property and state encouragement of small-scale businesses. In November 1990 the parliament supported large-scale privatization, and a new system of taxation and capital markets was designed to prevent spiraling inflation and massive social convulsions.

During this evolutionary time for the development of the political parties and a market economy, Slovak national claims continued to gather momentum. A symbolic gesture was made by the Federal Assembly in April, as the country's previous name "the Czechoslovak Federal Republic" was changed to the Czech and Slovak Federal Republic. Decentralization proceeded quickly, with the federal government yielding many of its prerogatives to the two republics. The country was on the verge of a constitutional crisis in December 1990, when the Slovak deputies to the parliament threatened to proclaim the supremacy of Slovak laws over federal ones in protest of parliamentary attempts to change the draft constitutional amendment. Speaking on that occasion, Vaclav Havel deplored the rise of nationalistic passions and asked the Federal Assembly immediately to pass laws providing for the creation of a constitutional court and enlarged presidential powers in the case of a national emergency. Ironically, Vaclav Havel, who had always opposed any concentration of power in the hands of one person, discovered that there are moments when morality and politics reach a collision point. He discovered that ethnic animosities and hostile feelings, including rabid xenophobia, continue to exist and to poison the public atmosphere. The long-denied ethnic tensions were only the beginning of the new political problems. Getting out of the totalitarian heritage of fear, resignation, self-pity, and self-contempt involved a reconstruction of the political subject. It meant, as Vaclav Havel pointed out in his speech on the anniversary of the 1968 Warsaw Pact invasion, a revival of the civic spirit that made possible the great upheaval of 1989:

> In order to change our situation for the better we must act energetically and without delay. We should return to the days of last November at least in spirit in order to recreate the feeling of unity of purpose and desire for change, that civic courage and civic imagination which at that point proved stronger than the totalitarian structures. . . . We must again place the common weal above individual and party political interests. We must again act nonviolently and with tolerance, but decisively and fast, as we acted toward the end of last year when the all-powerful Communist Party obeyed the will of the people and within a few days gave up its "leading role."[25]

Hungary: Disenchantment and Bitterness

In the spring of 1990 Hungarians elected a new parliament, and the former communist party suffered a crushing defeat. The Hungarian Democratic Forum won 42.9 percent of the seats, followed by the Alliance of Free Democrats with 23.83 percent and by other less powerful formations. However, during the local elections that took place in September and October, many former communist officials were reelected, suggesting that although their party had lost the national battle, there were still possibilities for them to maintain influence locally. At the same time the Alliance of Free Democrats managed to win in a number of large cities, including Budapest, where the former samizdat opposition activist Gabor Demszky became mayor. Also very interesting was the electoral success, during the local elections, of FIDESZ, the party of the young professionals and students, which seemed to symbolize the aspirations of many Hungarians for a brand new political spectrum.

Unlike Czechoslovakia, Poland, and Romania, where the presidency retained a strong hold in terms of political authority, in Hungary the new system provided for a decisive role of the government and the Prime Minister. It was a parliamentary rather than a presidential system. Following an agreement between the two most important parties, a Free Democrat writer and former political prisoner, Arpad Göncz, was elected the new President. The task of forming the new government was entrusted to Jozsef Antall, the chairman of the Hungarian Democratic Forum, who established a coalition with two smaller parties, the Smallholders and the Christian Democrats. One could therefore conclude that following the March and April 1990 elections, "Hungary became the only true multiparty democracy in Eastern Europe."[26] At the same time, the government showed no consistency in implementing drastic economic reform and full-fledged marketization of the country's ailing economy. Even when privatization took place, it resulted in the sudden transformation of the former managers into capitalist bosses. That transformation created discontent among social groups that had resented the previous social stratification and who had hoped that the new political system would allow for more social justice. There were, for instance, many who shared the resentful opinion expressed by Laszlo Miklos, an engineer of a food processing firm:

> Until now, we were managed by comrade Ballay, who sat in his office surrounded by statues of Lenin and pictures of comrade Kadar while Comrade Kolosznay, his secretary, brought in his customary Courvoisier to treat the comrades who came to see him. Now, it is Mr. Ballay who owns the firm, and he sits in his office surrounded by pictures of Mr. Bush shaking hands with him while his secretary, Mademoiselle Kolosznay, offers Courvoisier to customers in his office. The products remain the same; only the labels have changed.[27]

The old technocratic bureaucracy continued to manage the bankrupt factories inherited from the communist regime.

Unfortunately, while the old technocratic bureaucracy continued to operate, the differences between the Democratic Forum and the Alliance of Free Democrats continued to deepen as the economic situation deteriorated and a climate of dissatisfaction became all-pervasive. The Forum made a point of championing the interests not only of Hungarians living in Hungary, but of all 15 million Hungarians, including the Magyar minorities living in other countries, primarily Romania and Czechoslovakia. At the same time, during the electoral campaign some intellectuals associated with the Forum engaged in attacks on the Free Democrats that were often reminiscent of the anti-Semitic outbursts characteristic of the interwar period. Although Prime Minister Jozsef Antall and Foreign Minister Geza Jeszensky took great care to emphasize the European orientation of their party, they did not emphatically repudiate such not-so-ambiguous expressions of populist ethnocentrism. The traditional conflicts between populists and urbanists tended to resurrect themselves along the same mythological and counterproductive lines as they had followed before communist rule: on the one hand idealization of Christian and Magyar values of law and order, on the other abhorrence of the cosmopolitan, Westernizing, decadent, and soulless program of the liberal intelligentsia. But that is an exaggerated picture that emphasizes the most radical expressions of their approach. An astute observer of the Hungarian scene noted in 1990 that the parties' ideological polarization took a turn for the worse: "Venomous debates on religious education in schools, abortion, privatization, anti-Semitism, and the control of the media, and clashing assessments of the prewar Horthy regime have shattered the new parties' fragile postelection consensus on national priorities."[28] Nevertheless, the ideological debates of the 1930s could not simply be replayed in the 1990s. The rhetoric might sound the same or very similar, but the constituencies were different. The reason for the conflict between Free Democrats and the Democratic Forum should be sought in the mutual suspicion between Budapest and the rural areas, with each party trying to expand its electoral base as much as possible.[29] As the Forum resuscitated the values of the prewar right, the Free Democrats appeared increasingly as the party of modernity. In their platform they championed rapid privatization and criticized the Forum for its failure to address the nation's most urgent problems. In October 1990 Budapest was paralyzed as a result of a taxi and truck drivers' strike. Despite the palpable positive results of the transition period, the general mood in the country remained pessimistic. A provocative explanation came from the Prime Minister himself: "Everyone thinks our results are better than we do. A Hungarian will always see the worst. It comes in part from a peasant mentality, which will never predict a good harvest."[30] Following frequent expressions of popular anger, Antall promised to reshuffle the government and to bring in more competent people. The economy stagnated, and the general feeling was that the leading team was not prepared to propose any remedy. While Budapest looked increasingly like a prosperous Western capital, the countryside remained dramatically poor. As the economy deteriorated and political fragmentation continued, Hungary's future was fraught with new tensions and strife. But those could occur within a democratic structure, and it seemed that all political parties agreed that a return to dictatorship was unlikely.

Toward a Polish Presidentialism?

Bitter conflict surfaced in Poland in the summer of 1990, when Lech Walesa decided to challenge the government he had helped come to power several months earlier. With harsh words and unsparing energy, Walesa took the government to task for its procrastination in dealing the *coup de grâce* to the communist *nomenklatura*. The rationale behind Walesa's anti-Mazowiecki outburst was that the union leader did not want to accept power sharing with the communists, which was actually the constitutional principle on which the Mazowiecki government had first been formed. For Walesa and his allies, there was no reason for Poland to lag behind the other former communist regimes in ridding the government of the former *nomenklatura*. The presence of General Jaruzelski as the country's President—even if it was primarily a ceremonial job—was for Walesa an anomaly in a time when the Hungarians and the Czechoslovaks had already jettisoned their communists from all positions of authority. Walesa and his supporters perceived the strategy designed by the Solidarity parliamentary caucus headed by the historian Bronislaw Geremek as unjustified: There was no reason to abide by the roundtable agreement when the whole domestic and international equation had so fundamentally changed. The time was ripe for all-out warfare against the holdovers of communism. Those who did not share his view were suspected of having crypto-leftist sympathies. Sometimes, in significant, almost Fruedian, slips of the tongue, Walesa alluded to their "imperfect" Polishness—an oblique way of reminding the electorate that some of Mazowiecki's political friends were Jewish or of Jewish descent. The tensions between the maverick Solidarity leader and Prime Minister Mazowiecki's team cannot be understood only in personal and psychological terms. Still, one cannot ignore Walesa's feeling of having been marginalized by the sophisticated intellectuals of the Warsaw and Kracow circles.

Walesa seemed to be displeased with the conversion of his former allies into government bureaucrats and to dislike the leniency they showed. In order to accelerate the transition to democracy, he used his advisory council, called the Citizens' Committee, a body established in 1987. In 1989 the Committee selected lists of candidates to run under the Solidarity banner for the Sejm and the Senate in every electoral district. In 1990 Walesa reasserted his control over this body by appointing Zdislaw Najder, a literary historian and the former head of Radio Free Europe's Polish Service, as the new chairman. He appointed new members and replaced—by public letter—Henryk Wujek, a former close associate, as the Committee's secretary. He also attempted to oust Adam Michnik from *Gazeta Wyborcza*. Insisting on his popular roots—as opposed to the alienation of the Warsaw intellectuals from the working class—Walesa summoned Prime Minister Mazowiecki to a meeting in front of the workers at the Lenin Shipyard in Gdansk. Incensed at this continuous bashing, close allies of the Prime Minister made public their disagreement with Walesa's authoritarian practices. A sharp debate developed between the daily *Gazeta Wyborcza*, whose editor was Michnik, the well-known historian, and *Tygodnik Solidarnosc*, a paper controlled by Walesa's supporters. As the confrontation intensified between the two newspapers and groups, mutual accusations were raised and Solidarity reached a breaking point. In May 1990 the movement split into two groups, or proto-parties: Walesa's partisans formed the Center Alliance, and in July the pro-Mazowiecki activists formed their own faction called the Citizens' Movement—Democratic Action (Polish Acronym: ROAD).[31] In their first statements, the ROAD activists accused the Center Alliance of using revolutionary methods and suggested that the slogan "acceleration" favored by Walesa and his supporters could destabilize the country and antagonize the West. Walesa was often depicted as an irrational demagogue, a populist adventurer with no sense of political compromise. ROAD chose the self-effacing Tadeusz Mazowiecki as its presidential candidate, thus almost forcing him to run for President. Among the most prominent ROAD supporters were Jerzy Turowicz, the respected editor of the Cracow Catholic weekly *Tygodnik Powszechny*; two veterans of Solidarity's heroic underground stage, Zbigniew Bujak and Wladyslaw Frasyniuk; and Adam Michnik.

The Center Alliance argued that because of the hesitations shown by Mazowiecki and his team Poland had become bogged down in the transitory stage between communism and democracy. The Alliance rejected ROAD's claim that it embodied the "ethos of Solidarity" and made clear that it saw itself as the inheritor of the independent union's best traditions. According to Jacek Maziarski, an editor of *Tygodnik Solidarnosc* and one of the Alliance's foremost partisans, both the program and the activities of this party

> . . . follow from the fundamental tradition of Solidarity, identified neither with the Polish Left (which borders on social democracy and recruits its adherents from among scientists, journalists, artists, *et al.*), nor the Polish Right. The Center Alliance is trying to prevent a head-on collision of left- and right-wing tendencies by establishing a solid political majority located between the two extremes.[32]

The ROAD spokesmen, in turn, rejected the label "leftist" attached to their party by the pro-Walesa spokesmen. ROAD claimed that it drew its inspiration from the East European civic and democratic movements of the 1970s and 1980s. ROAD also took credit for having initiated shock therapy, an economic strategy that could not be suspected of any leftist propensity. On various occasions, ROAD representatives insisted that their party was the true guarantor of Poland's integration in the democratic family of European nations and proclaimed that their group was "West of Center." Asked about the meaning of that slogan, Zbigniew Bujak, a legendary figure who had run the Solidarity underground after the Martial Law, declared: "We are for the rule of law and parliament, for judicial independence, etc., against any methods which might threaten our democratic achievements. . . . One cannot disentangle oneself from totalitarianism by applying undemocratic methods."[33] The conflict between the two trends also had a deeper source, namely a difference over the identity of the main danger to Poland's fragile democracy: The Center Alliance saw communist restoration as a real threat and pushed for an immediate and uncompromising purge of the *nomenklatura* from all the government offices, while ROAD pointed to ethnocentric populism and demagogy as the most serious menace. Adam Michnik, for instance, called Walesa "a danger to the nation" and argued that the Solidarity leader, with all his skills as a popular tribune, did not have the qualifications for being President in a democratic state. According to Michnik, Walesa's "political ideal is a job where he holds all power and bears no responsibility."[34] Bujak echoed those dismissive views of Walesa when he stated that the Center Alliance's "empty populism" had magnetized nationalist emotions: "Because of this nationalist point of view, they [the Center Alliance] aren't able to build a political movement that connects Poland to the West. ROAD will be the party which brings Poland to Europe."[35]

Prime Minister Mazowiecki, a man certainly more popular than his ministers, engaged only halfheartedly in a battle with the energetic and still charismatic Walesa. During the elections in December 1990 Walesa won only 40 percent in the first round and 70 percent in the second runoff. After the first run Mazowiecki withdrew, letting Walesa confront Stanislaw Tyminski, a previously unknown emigré businessman from Canada and Peru, who had pledged to improve Poland's economic situation within a month, and who drew more votes than the incumbent Premier. To the surprise of Polish observers and to the dismay of all the democratic parties, the newcomer with no qualifications for becoming President other than his self-serving and often suspicious braggadoccio, managed even to win about 25 percent of the vote in the runoff election. It was clear that conflict between the two Solidarity factions, with their verbal fireworks and mutual indictments, had contributed to general confusion and widespread disappointment among the voters. Reporting from Warsaw a few days after the first round of the presidential elections in Poland, an Italian journalist who had specialized in East European affairs wrote:

> The atmosphere in Warsaw is now so saturated with hysteria that an outsider might think that the city was recently declared an ecological disaster zone, or that it is in fact a vast insane asylum, an asylum in which each inmate accuses his neighbors of insanity in an effort to appear sane himself. The term "psychopath," by the way, frequently pops up in the statements of intellectuals and politicians here.[36]

This was a alarming sign to both ROAD and the Center Alliance, which realized that popular discontent was smoldering and that unless an improvement in the economic performance happened soon, there was potential for new explosions of social unrest. To achieve such an improvement, Walesa worked to promote national reconciliation and reappointed Leszek Balcerowicz, the Minister of Economy responsible for the shock therapy to the same position in the new government now headed by thirty-nine-year-old Jan Krisztof Bielecki, a Parliament member from Gdansk and an economist turned businessman and politician.

The composition of the new government, as well as Walesa's reassuring stances, confirmed that the flamboyant Solidarity activist actually was able to understand the imperatives of a realistic policy. In an illuminating portrayal of Walesa, Piotr Wierzbicki, one of Poland's most influential journalists, analyzed the plethora of myths surrounding the former Gdansk electrician and demonstrated their fallacy. Wierzbicki concluded:

> Walesa may seem a chameleon because he is an extreme pragmatist. Apart from his rejection of force, his attachment to the Polish Catholic Church, his complete insusceptibility to anti-Semitism, and his avoidance of Solidarityspeak ("ethos," "subjectivity," and so on), Walesa nurtures no doctrinal attachment of any kind. When he says that Solidarity is neither left-wing nor right-wing, he speaks primarily about himself. He is not interested in formulas or concepts. He's interested in what people have to eat and what they say about Solidarity. He's interested in society's mood of which he is an unerring register. He knows that if he fails to stay in touch with the attitudes and feelings of the common people, he'd be nobody. As far as he is concerned, every peaceful road that leads as quickly as possible to a truly free Poland is good.[37]

The breakup of Solidarity and the formation of the two new major parties has contributed to a healthy process of political differentiation. In a democratic society there is no need for a monolithic *esprit de corps* among those who make up the political class. As long as all parties share the same ultimate values, their competition is an indication of social dynamism and contributes to the further development of a civic culture that can prevent the transformation of a strong presidency into a dictatorial experiment.

Fear and Frustration in Romania

In its original platform, Romania's National Salvation Front claimed that it represented the spirit of the anticommunist December revolution. But it took Romanians less than a month to start realizing that the new government was reluctant to engage in a sweeping dissolution of the old institutions. In January 1990 the NSF organized a massive workers' demonstration against the opposition parties accused of serving foreign interests. Populist slogans were chanted by the Front's supporters, and Iliescu, the NSF chairman, was acclaimed as a providential man. In February the NSF renounced its suprapartisan pretense and announced its intention to field candidates for the forthcoming elections. From that moment on, it started to lose credibility among the youth and the intellectuals— precisely the groups that had been most active in the anticommunist uprising. One of the country's influential columnists, Octavian Paler, wrote in *Romania Libera,* the most important independent national daily, that the NSF's ambition was to take advantage of its revolutionary image in order to neutralize the opposition and ensure its victory in the parliamentary and presidential elections due in the spring.

Well before the spring of 1990, at the onset of the Romanian Revolution of 1989, there were many people who held suspicions that the new leaders had known each other before the collapse of the Ceausescu regime and that they had conspired to take power at the moment the dictator was overthrown by a popular insurrection. In other words, far from being a spontaneous emanation of the revolution from below, the NSF was the institutional expression of a conspiracy from above. Because the dissident movement in communist Romania was weak and its political culture backward, then, the revolutionary upheaval failed to result in the formation of a revolutionary government. What happened was actually the abduction of the revolution by a group of seasoned apparatchiks, well versed in palace intrigues and behind-the-scenes maneuvers. It was also likely that their actions had the blessing of the Soviet leadership, who had every reason to favor Ceausescu's replacement with an "enlightened autocrat" in the Gorbachev mold instead of the uncompromising and unpredictable anticommunist forces already manifest in Poland, Hungary, and Czechoslovakia.

To put it bluntly, the NSF sounded quite convincing when it proclaimed its willingness to break with the past. But that intention was merely a rhetorical device. Certainly the *Securitate* was officially abolished, but in March 1990 it resurfaced under the name the Romanian Service of Information. Not a single individual, of those who organized the savage massacre in Bucharest after Ceausescu's flight on December 22, 1989, was brought to trial, and the progovernment media embarked on vicious campaigns to besmirch the opposition and all those who dared to raise the slightest question with regard to the NSF's legitimacy. Actually, the principal source of instability in postrevolutionary Romania has been the attempt of the reform communists to preserve political and economic power in the hands of the same *nomenklatura* class that had administered and ruined the country for more than four decades. As the independent civic groups and media came to recognize the colossal hoax of the NSF as the "emanation" of the revolution, the political spectrum grew increasingly polarized. On the one end was the Front, headed by Ion Iliescu, a personality whose communist convictions were universally known. On the other were the opposition parties, dominated by the three "new old parties" (the National Liberals, the National Peasants, and the Social Democrats). In the meantime, the NSF had created a large number of satellite parties, ready to endorse its policies in hopes of a share in power. During the May 1990 elections more than eighty political parties presented candidates. Out of them, the critics of the NSF argued, about forty were sympathetic to the Front. The opposition had little time to organize, and its political discourse was not accessible to the population because of the obstacles created by the Front-run government. Prime Minister Petre Roman, the son of a top communist ideologue who had spent the war years in Moscow as a Comintern official, had no record as a dissident during the Ceausescu regime. The NSF's Secretary, Dan Martian, had served in the 1970s as the First Secretary of the Communist Youth Union and the Minister for Youth Affairs. As for Iliescu, he never fully and unambiguously abjured his communist past, including his role as a chief ideologue in the late 1960s. Although the NSF was far from a real political party, its often decried neo-Bolshevism was rather a survivalist strategy on the part of the beleaguered *nomenklatura* and an attempt to contain the anticommunist tidal wave from below. More an umbrella movement than an ideologically constituted party, the NSF played upon and stirred fears of instability and chaos. The NSF had to admit its own debility in February, when it invited the other parties to join a peculiar miniparliament called the Provisional Council of National Unity. By co-opting representatives of the opposition into this fragile body, the NSF aimed to put an end to public unrest.

But discontent in Romania had deep social roots and could not be easily mitigated. The Front's indulgence in half-truths and aggressive warnings only further irritated the revolutionary and civic forces. It was perhaps Iliescu's foremost illusion that a Romanian version of perestroika would satisfy the population. To his dismay, the NSF leader saw that instead of decreasing, the radical ferment continued to gather momentum. The widespread sentiment that the NSF's hidden agenda consisted of the preservation of an authoritarian regime was not groundless. Romanians knew that the dreaded *Securitate* continued to exist in spite of official denials. A few of Ceausescu's henchmen were brought to trial, but only for their participation in the December 16–22 slaughter, not for the role they had played in the functioning of one of Europe's most vicious despotisms since Stalin's death. Instead of purging the administrative apparatus of the servants of the old regime, the NSF appointed them to key positions. It was indeed a peculiar Romanian way of simulating the exit from totalitarianism. In all the other former communist countries the opposition either came to power or at least managed to mount a serious challenge to reconstructed Leninist elites. In Romania, however, the former collaborators usurped the revolutionary mantle and rhetoric and unleashed a vicious campaign against the true democrats. Instead of the roundtable approach, which was based on the possibility of a dialogue between the reform communists and the opposition, the "Bucharest syndrome" amounted to the impersonation by party bureaucrats and sycophantic hacks from the old regime of pristine anticommunist revolutionaries and the simultaneous denial of those anticommunist credentials to the people really committed to a political and economic breakthrough.[38] Iliescu and Roman talked about pluralism and marketization, but they did not initiate any genuine reform that would have diminished the power of the state bureaucracy. Private initiative continued to be stifled by countless government decrees and regulations, and foreign investment was discouraged by such Front slogans as "We don't sell our country to Western multinationals." Inflation spiraled and only black-marketeers and government bureaucrats were able to benefit from the liberalized prices.

As conceived by unrepentant Leninists, the NSF strategy backfired. It did so because it neglected the dynamism of society's self-organization, the impetus of collective passions for freedom, and the infectious effect of the democratic advances in the other East European countries. In March 1990 the NSF was challenged by the publication of the "Timisoara Proclamation," a political statement written by several young intellectuals in Timisoara, the first city to rise up and challenge Ceausescu's rule during the revolutionary year of 1989. Article 7 of the "Proclamation" questioned the revolutionary *bona fides* of those who had emerged as the beneficiaries of the upheaval: "Timisoara started the revolution against the entire Communist regime and its entire *nomenklatura,* and certainly not in order to give an opportunity to a group of anti-Ceausescu dissidents within the RCP to take over the reins of political power. Their presence at the head of the country makes the death of our heroes senseless."[39] Of utmost significance in this veritable charter of the Romanian revolution was Article 8, which called for a modification of the electoral law in order to prevent former communist activists and *Securitate* officers from holding government jobs and running for parliamentary seats. Even more emphatically, the document opposed the right of those who had served the communist regime to stand for the office of President. The Proclamation hit its target: The offended *nomenklatura* reacted with its traditional weapons, including slander, innuendo, and intimidation.

The Proclamation's goals were espoused by hundreds of independent groups and associations, including the Group for Social Dialogue, a community of prominent intellectuals well known for their refusal to collaborate in the past with the Ceausescu regime. At the end of April thousands of students, workers, and intellectuals seized University Square in Bucharest, where they proceeded to organize a sit-in to protest the government's refusal to meet the demands formulated in the Proclamation. Although the NSF government sent in police troops to disband the demonstrators camped in the square, the marathon demonstration continued day and night. Confronted with this unwavering defiance, Iliescu lost his temper and called the protesters *golani,* or hoodlums. That proved to be a very costly mistake, as the term was ominously reminiscent of Ceausescu's outbursts against the "hooligans" in Timisoara during the first days of the revolution.

In May 1990 the NSF won the majority of seats in Romania's bicameral parliament, and Iliescu, the Front's presidential candidate, triumphed with more than 85 percent of the national vote. In comparison with other former communist countries, Romania was exceptional. The secret of the NSF's landslide lay in the systematically entertained ambiguities about its true attitude toward communism as well as in the opposition's fragmenation and lack of organization. Clinging to the memory of their bygone splendor, the "historical parties" failed to tap responsive chords among many middle-aged Romanians. Another element in the NSF's victory was its continuous intimidation and harassment of the opposition. For many Romanians, voting for the NSF seemed the only alternative to a slide into anarchy.[40]

Conceding defeat after the May elections, the chief organizers of the University Square sit-in decided to withdraw. By mid-June the dwindling number of protesters, including several hunger strikers, were asking for little more than the establishment of one independent television station. Iliescu need only have waited a bit longer, and the flickering anarchist fire in the heart of Bucharest would have extinguished by itself. But on June 13 the police seized the square and dismantled the tents of the hunger strikers and the platform that the demonstrators had erected for speeches. Protesters were beaten up and forcibly removed during what was the first stage of a massive campaign by the regime to suppress the opposition completely. The police action was followed by a series of provocations, including attacks on the buildings of the Ministry of Internal Affairs and central television. Those explosions of violence were the pretext Iliescu needed to bring in an extralegal force, the coal miners, and give them his presidential blessing to exert unbounded terror in Bucharest on June 14 and 15. The miners rampaged through the headquarters of the most active independent associations, ransacked the headquarters of the opposition parties, and attacked and mutilated hundreds of university and high school students. It was an explosion of reactionary populism, indeed a Stalinist-fascist orgy of hatred and violence.[41] The international outrage resulting from the miners' rampage forced Iliescu and his associates to renounce their initial plan, which aimed at the complete annihilation of Romania's emerging civil society. As for the opposition, despite the traumatic effect of the June crackdown it continued to organize. In September representatives of the most dynamic independent groups participated in a meeting of the Romanian Resistance.[42] In November the Civic Alliance was formed as an expression of the need to bring together the dispersed forms of extraparliamentary opposition. Led by well-known cultural and political figures, the Alliance announced its commitment to building up a democratic political culture in Romania by means of education and dialogue. Although it did not identify itself as a political formation, the Alliance found a source of inspiration in the Czechoslovak Civic Forum. In July 1991 the Civic Alliance held its National Convention. A core of prominent activists decided to form the Civic Alliance Party as its political branch to field candidates for the forthcoming elections. The proposal to create the party was overwhelmingly supported by the delegates. Among those who appeared as key figures in the new political party were such prestigious intellectuals as the literary critic Nicolae Manolescu, the political columnist Stelian Tanase, the Timisoara civic activist and editor Vasile Popovici, and George Navon, a trade union leader from Constanta.

Unable and unwilling to initiate more than cosmetic reforms, the NSF regime resorted to chauvinist campaigns and appealed to the patriotic sentiments of Romanians against an imaginary international scenario intent on destabilizing the country. In that operation, the regime mobilized former communist activists, *Securitate* officers, and xenophobic intellectuals ready to spearhead the government's increasingly egregious anti-Hungarian propaganda. The extremist organization *Vatra Romaneasca* took the lead in this exceptionally vicious campaign, which even outdid the xenophobic efforts of Ceausescu. Because the economic situation in Romania continued to deteriorate, the NSF was losing its mass base, so chauvinism in its most unsavory form became the last demagogic resource for the rulers. Romania's unfinished revolution failed to create a state of law, and the former communists, dressed up as born-again democrats, established a political regime that can be described as a "totalitarian democracy" or "a dictatorship resting on popular enthusiasm."[43]

But enthusiasm is bound to wither away at the moment the masses recognize the scope of the official lies; therefore, it is expected that new cycles of violence in the country will occur, eventually breaking the NSF's hold on power. At that moment, one of the alternatives to chaos might be a return to a precommunist political formula represented by constitutional monarchy. The NSF has already sensed this danger; in December 1990 it expelled Romania's former King Michael, who had come for a short visit to his country, after an exile that started with his forced abdication in December 1947.[44] Again, the Spanish experience is worth a comparative look: One can see the advantages of constitutional monarchy, because it resumes an interrupted tradition and provides a political culture of cleavage with a suprapartisan arbiter capable of presiding over national reconciliation. Indeed, in December 1990 the Civic Alliance issued a statement calling for a nationwide referendum to decide whether Romania should again be a constitutional monarchy. For many in Romania, the King was the symbol of the country's short-lived democratic experiment in the aftermath of World War II, as well as the possible guarantor of a return to a long-denied normalcy in public life. The democratic constitution adopted in 1923 thus has been seen increasingly as the legitimate foundation for the establishment of a pluralist order in that country.

Yugoslavia: Ethnic Strifes, Separatism, and Disintegration

During 1990 the League of Communists of Yugoslavia renounced its monopoly on power and suffered almost complete dissolution. During its
Fourteenth Congress, the party admitted that it could no longer invoke its
constitutional privileges and recognized that in a democratic society no
one can claim to be the holder of absolute historical truth. Those concessions were not sufficient to assuage the radical reformers from Slovenia,
who asked for a complete restructuring of the party. When their demands
were rejected, they walked out of the Congress, thus consecrating the
collapse of the once cohesive federal party. In May the Congress resumed
in an atmosphere of general confusion. Calls were made for the complete
transformation of the party into an umbrella organization for all the leftist
groups in Yugoslavia. The change of heart and the acceptance of a redefinition of its status, however came too late. In the meantime the rebellious
Croatian and Slovenian communist parties had been defeated in multiparty elections, so in two of the country's most developed republics the
communists ceased to be the ruling force. Unable to keep pace with breath-
taking changes, the communists tried to reorganize themselves as a movement committed to the survival of the Yugoslav federation. In other republics the communists continued to lose ground: In November the League of
Communists of Bosnia and Herzegovina was defeated by the Moslem Party
for Democratic Action, and one month later the Macedonian communists
lost in a third round of voting.[45]

Federal Prime Minister Ante Markovic tried to oppose the apparently
invincible centrifugal trends and championed immediate reforms. He
even announced his intention to organize an all-Yugoslav Alliance of
Reformist Forces and enjoyed great popularity among the many citizens
who did not endorse the idea of a complete breakup of the federation.[46]
But political diversity and even incompatibility between the social and
national agendas of the different republics' governments continued to
deepen. As a result of elections in Slovenia and Croatia, those republics
were run by center-right coalitions, while during the December 1990
elections the communists managed to stay in power in Serbia, the country's largest and most powerful republic. As an all-Yugoslav institution,
the army continued to oppose the separatist trends, but for many in
Slovenia and Croatia the military was seen as an instrument of the
Serbian strongman Slobodan Milosevic's domineering appetite. Meanwhile, in Slovenia a reform communist was elected President, but the
parliamentary elections were won by the center-right coalition of five
parties called Demos. In December 1990 Slovenes overwhelmingly voted

in a referendum for their country's independence from Yugoslavia, thus inaugurating a pattern that boded ominously for the federation's future. That did not necessarily mean secession, but rather a gradual process that would permit the Slovenian republic to take control of military, foreign, and monetary policies that had been the prerogative of the federal government in Belgrade. Some Slovene officials sought a formula of confederation similar to that of the European Community, but others contemplated the possibility of complete secession. For instance, the former dissident activist Dimitrij Rupel, who after the elections became Slovenia's Secretary of Foreign Affairs, declared: "This country is disintegrating. There is great instability especially from the point of view of the legal system, se we are forced to search for a new form of coexistence."[47] In Croatia, the former wartime partisan and retired general Franjo Tudjman became the first noncommunist President of a republic in Yugoslavia's history. He had run as a candidate of the nationalist Croatian Democratic Union. His rhetoric was no less inflammatory than Milosevic's bellicose statements about Serbia's possible questioning of the existing interrepublic borders if Yugoslavia were to become a confederation. The preexisting bitterness and suspiciousness between Serbs and Croations was only exacerbated by Milosevic's crusading nationalist activism. Indeed, the Serbian President looked to many in his country, and to foreign observers, like a cynical practitioner of populist authoritarianism, "a late communist-nationalist reactionary who tried to turn back the clock, but succeeded only in hastening an anti-communist Balkanization of Yugoslavia."[48] In June 1991 the Slovene and Croatian parliaments proclaimed the independence of those republics. An ultimatum was sent by the central government in Belgrade to the rebellious Slovene leaders, who proudly refused to accept it. The army intervened and attacked public institutions and private units in Slovenia. For many, the army appeared as a tool for the imposition of Serbian hegemony. The country was caught in turmoil, intense fights opposed the military to the Slovene defense forces, and many were killed and injured. The beginning of a compromise was reached when the Serbs accepted a Croatian politician as President, but the real issues that provoked the crisis remained. Without a thoroughgoing rewriting of the country's constitution and allowance for the component republics' real sovereignty, Yugoslavia cannot survive. At the same time, the intervention of the army in political affairs—actually an undeclared coup—inaugurated a disturbing pattern for postcommunist Eastern Europe.

The collapse of Yugoslav communism, the irreversible political and economic decentralization, and the growth of powerful nationalist movements, including some extreme chauvinist groups, led to an explosive situation where the intervention of the army appeared likely. Albanians in Kosovo persecuted by Serbs, Serbs in Croatia threatened by Croatian fundamentalism, Slovenes increasingly attracted by a dream of a Central European federation, Moslems hating Christians, Christians attacking Moslems, endemic working-class unrest, some 2 million workers faced with the prospect of becoming unemployed as the result of drastic economic reforms—the Yugoslavia of the 1990s was a powderkeg whose explosion and disintegration was likely to be halted only by a drastic, Pinochet-style military coup. But even then, how could such an action prevent the country's further slide into anarchy and even civil war? Nothing but grudges and resentments seems to remain of Marshal Tito's utopia of equal republics united by their ideology and their desire to build the socialism of self-management.

Albania: A Farewell to Stalinism?

As the dominoes of the former Soviet satellites in Eastern Europe were falling one after the other in the revolutionary year 1989, Albania looked like an impregnable fortress, sticking adamantly to its refusal to liberalize and its stubborn defense of Stalinist orthodoxy. Speaking in November 1989, the communist party leader Ramiz Alia insisted that his country was opposed to the changes initiated by Gorbachev and warned against those who were seeking to emulate them. Sounding very much like such diehard enemies of reform as Nicolae Ceausescu and Fidel Castro, Alia said:

> We especially emphasize this when we bear in mind what is happening now in the countries of the East. There, the bourgeoisie and the opportunists have joined forces and unified their tactics and strategy to abolish socialism as a social order. With demagogic slogans about freedom and democratic rights, which ignore the toiling masses in favor of certain antipeople individuals and social strata, and under the pretext of correcting mistakes that they themselves committed, they are reimposing the laws of a capitalist-like society.[49]

To prevent infection with the "revisionist" ideas, harsh security measures were taken in Albania at the beginning of 1990. But to no avail: The impact of the changes in the other countries was more powerful than the communist propaganda machine. In June 1990 thousands of Albanians took refuge in Western embassies in Tirana, and in July, recognizing its weakness, the communist government allowed them to leave the country.[50] In October 1990 the regime suffered another defeat: The country's most prominent writer and a cult figure for young Albanians, Ismail Kadare, applied for political asylum in France. In a letter addressed to Alia, the celebrated intellectual, who in the past had been supportive of Hoxha's break with Khrushchev and had contributed to the building of the late leader's mystique as a nationalist hero, stated:

> Until today I have tried to soften the regime to the extent that it is authorized in Albania. In the course of my meetings and an exchange of letters which I had with the President last spring I expressed very clearly the necessity for a rapid, profound and complete democratization of the country. Because there is no possibility of legal opposition in Albania I have chosen this course which I never wished to take and which I will not recommend to others.[51]

Several months later, noting the start of opening in his country, Kadare declared that in the case of the democratic process in Albania, "the pace of change is a matter of life and death."[52] As if to bear out this reading of Albanian realities, a wave of student demonstrations for democracy led to a dramatic political shift.

As mass unrest developed, Alia showed that he had drawn the necessary lessons from Ceausescu's infamous end: The one-party system was abolished; opposition groups were allowed to form; the widow of Enver Hoxha, Nexhmije, stepped down as leader of the People's Democratic Front; and for the first time in twenty years after Albania had proclaimed itself an atheistic state, Masses were celebrated in Greek Orthodox Churches. The symbolic end of an era of zealotry and fanaticism came on December 21, 1990. The occasion was the 111th anniversary of Stalin's birth. Instead of the traditional pledges of orthodoxy, a crane moved into Tirana's Stalin Boulevard at midnight and loaded the dark bronze statue of the Soviet tyrant onto a truck, its head hanging off the back of the vehicle.[53] Soon thereafter political parties were formed and mass rallies took place in support of democracy. The government allowed multiparty elections to take place in March, but some of the opposition leaders detected the same trick used by Romania's NSF in its rush to exploit the lack of information and confusion among the population. For instance, Genc Pollo, a spokesman for the main opposition Democratic Party, said: "There has been so much indoctrination and political intimidation, the Stalinist legacy is so strong, that we do not think there is enough time for us before the elections to develop an alternative frame of mind among

the majority of the electorate. We are therefore avoiding being exces-
sively optimistic that we can win."[54] All those apprehensions notwithstanding, it was clear that the ruling party had come to the conclusion
that the old methods of terrorist coercion had to be abandoned and that
Albania's leaders had to move away from the uncompromising Stalinist
model they had so jealously guarded in the past. Actually, in the March
elections the opposition managed to win the majority of votes in the
urban areas, while the communists succeeded in the countryside. This
indicated that the transition to pluralism would involve a long process of
civic awakening, especially in the regions less exposed to information.
Another element noticed during the Albanian elections was the government's systematic attempts to intimidate the opposition and the use of
the regime-controlled media to slander the opposition. In this respect,
again, there were similarities between Albania and Romania.

EPILOGUE

Fears, Phobias, Frustrations
Eastern Europe Between Ethnocracy and Democracy

> To be the object of contempt or pa-
> tronising tolerance on the part of proud
> neighbors is one the most traumatic ex-
> periences that individuals or societies
> can suffer. The response, as often as
> not, is pathological exaggeration of
> one's real or imaginary virtues, and re-
> sentment and hostility towards the
> proud, the happy, the successful.
> —*Isaiah Berlin*

From Warsaw to Tirana, and from Bratislava to Sofia, Eastern Europe has moved beyond the communist-led past and entered a new era. The present and future belong now to diverse national actors, and it is up to them to build democratic or authoritarian polities. No one can lay down guidelines for the transition. There is no error-proof blue-print to ensure the smoothness of this huge transformation. It is obvi-ous, however, that in all these societies a struggle is being waged between the partisans of democracy and those of authoritarianism. The triumph of the latter would result in bloody domestic and interna-tional confrontations. On the other hand, one cannot ignore that in all these countries there are strong groups and parties who cherish plural-ist values and who are ready to fight for their assertion.

For many in my generation, communism appeared to be immortal. We grew up in Eastern Europe (in which I also include the Soviet Union) with the belief that the order of things as dictated by the powers-that-be could be challenged, but not radically overthrown. Thanks to the epoch-making events of 1989, that conviction has ceased to have any justification. The spectacle offered to our astonished eyes was almost unbeliev-able. It was the miracle of the sudden breakdown of a formation that had claimed to embody millennial expectations of earthly redemption. At least in its leftist version, radicalism was a shambles and could find no resource (or disguise) to conceal its wreckage. This collapse meant the end of a utopian dream of universal salvation and the rediscovery of the long-despised values of individual freedom. The closed society celebrated by various "engineers of human souls" disbanded under the onslaught of forces fascinated by its opposite, the open society, with its respect for differences, minorities, and nuances.

The process started perhaps with Khrushchev's denunciation of Sta-lin's cult (the "Secret Speech") at the historic closed session of the Twentieth Congress of the CPSU. During that night of February 1956, the myth of the monolithic unity of world communism received a mortal blow. What followed were long periods of exaltation and dereliction, passionate recriminations and frantic polemics. In all East European soci-eties, the holistic mystique of the party as a collective pedagogue met the defiance of new social movements that did not identify themselves with either the traditional right or the left. Communism was perceived as an enormous hypocrisy, an attempt to regiment and control the human mind and human needs in the name of a mortifying ideology devised by a young German philosopher in the mid-nineteenth century. With incredi-ble speed, people realized that it was in their power to get rid of the ideological straitjacket, to tear it off, and to create liberated enclaves of human communication. In this century, when information has become a most powerful weapon, an ardent yearning for transparency and commu-nication exploded the tissue of lies and superstitions that had ensured the persistence of communist tyrannies.

Some four years ago I participated in a conference in New York City on the topic "Will the Communist States Survive? The View From Within." That was in October 1987, and Gorbachev's reforms had gener-ated a widespread state of euphoria. The rise of a revisionist leader in the sanctum sanctorum of the empire seemed to justify high expectations of rapid change. It was obvious that the margin of permissiveness or, rather, the limits of the Kremlin's tolerance of experiment with reform had dramatically changed. What had been absolute heresy under Brezhnev was enshrined as the new party line under Gorbachev. For instance, the slogan of socialism with a human face was embraced by the Soviet General Secretary and designated as one of the main goals of perestroika. But among us there were also some skeptics. I remember that the well-known Soviet dissident writer and logician Alexander Zinoviev ironically titled his contribution "Crocodiles Cannot Fly." Miklos Haraszti, the Hungarian maverick intellectual and human rights activist, sent a paper titled "The Paradigm of the Boots," referring to Stalin's monument in Budapest and maintaining that the totalitarian boots had been internalized to an extent that made any hope of liberation a simple illusion. Ivan Svitak, the Czech philosopher, argued that Gorbachev's reforms were nothing but dust in the eyes, another propaganda exercise bound to save, not to abolish, the system. The Romanian dissident Mihai Botez spoke of the rise of the national-communist state as the most likely development one could foresee even under Gorbachev. At that moment Kadarism, described by Georg Lukacs's students Agnes Heller and Ferenc Feher as an enlightened version of Khrushchevism, appeared to be the best one could expect for Eastern Europe. Others, including myself, thought the new elbow room created by the revisionist czar in the Kremlin had suppressed the barriers that for decades had prevented the triumph of Eastern Europe's "long rebellion against Yalta" (to use the telling formula proposed by these lucid Hungarian philosophers). That approach focused on the rise of the civil society in most of these countries, including such fortresses of Stalinism as East Germany and Bulgaria.

The great rebellion of 1989 shattered many deeply imbedded beliefs and forced us to question much of the conventional wisdom with regard to those regimes. When we refer to the causes of the 1989 convulsions we have to mention the following factors: First, the upheaval was linked to the complete loss of legitimacy of the ruling elites in the region. True, that phenomenon had started in the mid-1950s, but it reached its zenith during the times of profound pessimism and even despair of Brezhnevism, when socialism in its Soviet version appeared to be a hopeless historical *cul de sac.* The communist parties had lost all self-confidence and had suffered irresistible political decay. All attempts to instill new life into the old dogmas, all endeavors to engage in what the Catholics did with the strategy of *aggiornamento,* did not work in Eastern Europe. There was no reservoir of faith for those who believed in the salvation of the existing structures. In other words, the Marxist myth had exhausted its galvanizing power, and there were no social groups interested in perpetuating the matrix of domination as it had functioned for decades. Second, as the communist elites demonstrated their absolute ineptitude, new social forces were coming to the fore and proposing alternative solutions. In a broad sense, those were the segments of the emerging civil societies, that is, collective efforts to create parallel institutions and activities, challenging the government's claim to control the whole of human life. Third, the decline of the Marxist myth and the rise of the civil society were linked to the overall political, social, economic, and moral crises experienced by all those countries. The most palpable catalyst of the imminent collapse was the economic bankruptcy of state socialism and the awareness that only a free market could guarantee economic recovery. The command economies had failed to provide the goods that would have justified the sacrifices ceaselessly imposed on the population. Fourth, the external factor cannot be underestimated: Without the sweeping changes in the Kremlin and the redefinition by the Gorbachev–Yakovlev–Shevardnadze team of Soviet international strategy, including the new doctrine of the de-ideologization of international relations, the changes in Eastern Europe would have been much slower and certainly more disruptive and violent. The threat of foreign intervention had ceased to function as a deterrent, especially after the Soviet withdrawal from Afghanistan. It appeared clear to civic activists in Eastern Europe that the Soviet Union would not be interested in any new adventure that would jeopardize its new image and the relations established by Gorbachev with the West. The "Gang of Four"—Nicolae Ceausescu, Milos Jakes, Erich Honecker, and Todor Zhivkov—opposition to Soviet-inspired reforms was actually counterproductive from the viewpoint of local communist elites, who completely lost any chance to play a significant role in a post-totalitarian transition period.

The nature of the upheaval needs a special analysis, because it also explains the difficulties encountered by these countries during their transition period. First, one must notice that the 1989 revolutions challenged a false principle of authority, based on universally execrated lies and pseudo-legitimacy. The changes were revolutionary because they raplaced one form of political power with another: All those regimes were mythocratic dictatorships whose only reason to stay in power was the ideologically defined predestined role of the working class and its vanguard party. Once that ideological fallacy was exposed as a mere rationalization for the usurpation of power by an incompetent and corrupt bureaucracy, there was no foundation for their survival (except fear, apathy, and inertia). The upheaval was a synthesis of two trends: on the one hand the anticommunist surge and on the other the search for alternative institutional and axiological solutions. What has happened in Eastern Europe since 1989 has been the simultaneous self-destruction of the communist political culture (with its traditions, habits, attitudes, mentalities, values, and behavior patterns) and, on the "positive" side, the reconstitution of civil societies (atomized and almost destroyed by communism) and the structuring of genuinely political forms.

Communist regimes had appropriated the rhetoric of the left, although in reality they were authoritarian dictatorships based on the manipulation of both nationalism and internationalism. Hungary's Kadar was somewhat different, with his old-fashioned indifference to national symbols, which played into the hands of the mounting opposition. With the exception of Albania, Romania, and Yugoslavia, they were all ready to toe the Soviet international line. It was therefore logical that their repudiation had to be *antitotalitarian* (or, in the East European political language, anticommunist). Since communism had turned ideology into a state religion and since Leninist ideology appeared to the people as the name of their oppression, the revolts were also *anti-ideological.* Most of the rebellions originated in widespread frustration with the political cynicism of the ruling elites and therefore acquired *antipolitical* dimensions. That distrust of anything smacking of behind-the-scenes, Machiavellian arrangements explains the current reluctance of people to engage in political activism: Politics is perceived as the market place of social climbers, opportunists, impostors, and adventurers. In all those countries, there was a general suspicion of government attempts to organize personal life and invade any domain of privacy. That explains the *antistatist* and *antihierarchical* dimensions of the upheaval as well as the ongoing difficulties in building up new principles of authority. Although it is not named frequently, there is a current "anarchist" temptation in Eastern Europe that runs parallel to the search for state protection and can be called the *paternalistic temptation.*

In Poland, Hungary, and Czechoslovakia, the long-beleaguered underground groups and movements spearheaded the spontaneous outbursts of discontent and provoked the nonviolent collapse of communist autocracies. The roundtable negotiations and the peaceful transitions to protopluralist forms of government in those countries were guaranteed by the relative maturity of the civil societies and the disintegration of communist elites, symbolized by the inevitable split between the "hawks" (Stalinist conservatives) and the reform-minded (Gorbachevite) liberals. At the same time, it is the tension between moral apprehensions (the antipolitical viewpoint) and institutional obligations that explains certain hesitations and reservations among former opposition groups.

Because the civil society was underdeveloped or frail in Romania and Bulgaria, and because the communist elites were unable to offer any alternative to their disastrous policies, the transitions were significantly different in those two countries. In Romania, the euphoria of the first days of the post-Ceausescu period was followed by the bitter realization that the National Salvation Front, instead of identifying itself with antitotalitarian ideals, had only self-servingly and pragmatically appropriated them. In a speech at a conference in Timisoara on "Power and Opposition in Post-Communist Societies" (March 25–27, 1991), Nicolae Manolescu, one of Romania's prominent intellectuals and currently the chairman of the Civic Alliance Party, a political formation similar to the Czechoslovak Civic Forum, gave the following analysis of the situation in his country as well as an idea of the path to be pursued:

> [W]e had a revolution driving out the dictator, but failing to destroy communism. The old structures were restored with new names. Sometimes, even the same people can be met there. . . . Where East European societies consider themselves to be traveling the road of reform, they should know they are chasing an illusion. For communism is not reformable—it can be only destroyed. And until the last germ of communism has been removed, our societies will have no peace and no chance to establish democracy.[1]

According to Stelian Tanase, another influential Romanian civic activist and editor of the weekly *Acum* (Now), the basic contradiction in post-Ceausescu Romania is the conflict between the embryonic civil society (most of which is represented by the extraparliamentary opposition) and the state, which has inherited the totalitarian structures.[2] As for the Bulgarians, their opposition managed to organize and to overcome internecine strife. However, according to the civic activist and political philosopher Dimitrina Petrova:

> The hope for real political pluralism is rooted in an awareness of fluidity: the whole process has just begun. Opposing interest groups are not yet clearly defined, insofar as the relations of property are not yet constituted and the specific form of market awaiting us in the future is not yet fixed. At the moment we live in an open situation, not in a system of any kind; we experience the responsibility of trying to understand it, while participating in the creation of the political stereotypes of tomorrow.[3]

At this moment, intellectuals from all the postcommunist countries are engaged in a soul-searching investigation of long-obscured social and historical realities. Communists, in spite of their internationalist rhetoric, have always encouraged the nationalists' autarky. It is therefore vitally important for civic activists and critical intellectuals in all the former communist states to embark on an open and uninhibited dialogue. If it is true that Serbia and Romania lag behind the Czech and Slovak Republic in terms of pluralist development (or, some may argue, Slovakia lags behind Bohemia, and Serbia behind Slovenia), it is nevertheless obvious that all these societies have experienced similar torments brought on by similar causes. They were all victimized in the name of a pseudo-univeralistic teleology according to which a classless utopia could and should be constructed, regardless of the people's will. They are all faced now with the enormous challenge of creating the legal framework that would grant the procedural expression of the most important under-pinning of democracy: popular sovereignty. An illuminating statement was made by Agnes Heller, who took issue with Timothy Garton Ash's frequently quoted argument that nothing new (no new idea, institution, or phenomenon) has come out of the antitotalitarian upheaval in Eastern Europe: "Political revolutions happen or take place by the change in sovereignty. In these terms, a political revolution took place in all previous Soviet satellite states in the year 1989, for popular sovereignty has been substituted for party sovereignty in all of them, at least *de jure*, if not necessarily also *de facto.*"[4]

All those societies have been deprived to a greater or lesser extent of civic culture. In all of them the individual has been repressed, regimented, and manipulated as a simple pawn by the powers-that-be. Those countries today are all experiencing the revival of politics as the liberated space where the most humane features of the individual find their natural expression. And, one might add, all have rediscovered the value of the revolutionary experience and, as a corollary, morality as a primary source of political behavior. To those who claim that no new ideas have emerged during the antitotalitarian upheavals in Eastern Europe, one is tempted to answer that it was precisely during those uprisings (revolutions, revolts, insurrections, rebellions—the best term remains to be found) that concepts like popular sovereignty, European consciousness, civil rights, and many others reacquired full semantic justification. During such momentous times people have a chance to become part of the dream for the Great Republic or, to use Hannah Arendt's term, they rehabilitate the "revolutionary tradition and its lost treasury."[5]

Communism cannot be considered completely dead. True, in its traditional form, as a messianic, militaristic, fanatic movement, it has been defeated in the historical sense. With the grotesque exception of those who are incurably possessed, no one takes the communist ideology seriously. On the other hand, recent events in Slovakia and Yugoslavia, as well as the growth of populist-authoritarian movements in most of the countries of Eastern Europe, have shown that democracy is not the inevitable successor to communism. One of the prevailing illusions during the postcommunist euphoric stage was that xenophobia and other outbursts of the tribalist, pseudo-communitarian, and mystical-romantic spirit would remain merely a marginal phenomenon. As the economic situation has continued to deteriorate and the new elites have failed to offer persuasive models for a rapid transition, those movements have gained momentum. They have recruited primarily among the frustrated and disenchanted social groups by stirring responsive chords among those unable to overcome the traumatic effects of a sudden break with the past. In countries with large national minorities, the demagogical movements play upon ethnic resentments and phobias. We sometimes have the disturbing feeling of a historical *déjà vu*: Histrionics and hysteria commingle in explosions of intolerance and exclusiveness. Indeed, the dividing line now seems to separate the pro-European parties, inspired by liberal values, from their counterparts who look for inspiration in the exaltation of collective nouns like fatherland, nation, ancestry, or even blood community. The conflict, if one can say so, is less between communists and anticommunists than between *collectivism* and *liberalism*. The latter is pro-Western, tolerant, interested in dialogue, and supportive of rapid marketization. The former is atavistic, resentful, xenophobic, militaristic, and exclusive. Ralf Dahrendor was not the only one to mention the risk of derailment into new forms of dictatorship, including fascist ones. Adam Michnik wrote:

> Nationalism is reborn, and with it national conflicts, xenophobia and the nightmare of anti-Semitism. The conspiracy theory of history makes its return. . . . Countries with a weak democratic tradition, which are in the midst of regaining their national identity, are rehabilitating their national history. They have rehabilitated that which in the communist period was banned, everything which was supposed to have been removed from the pages of national history and from the collective memory. Today the rehabilitation goes on even when it is least deserved, when there are the most disgraceful crimes on its conscience, including collaboration with the Nazis. Consider the conflict over the future in post-communist states. This conflict, in which one finds the same terms with which we are familiar from debates in the West, is in fact quite different. Its origins lie not in a conflict between left and right, even if there are forces on the political scene which use these terms to denote their direction. Nor is it a conflict between conservatism and liberalism, any more than it is one between radicalism and moderation. What it is is a conflict over the form the new country is to be given: whether it is to imitate European models, or

whether it is to follow its own road by elaborating a radically different kind of model.[6]

Think of the exclusiveness displayed by the Romanian fundamentalists, often linked to the ruling formation in that country (the National Salvation Front), and the appearance of such phenomena as "Party X," under the eccentric Peruvian-Canadian emigré Stanyslaw Tyminski in Poland. Their only ideological ingredient is an ill-defined sense of historical malaise, a rejection of the consequences of modernity, and a celebration of the presumably pristine values of the preindustrial agrarian life. All those who advocate integration in democratic Europe are targets for smear campaigns and are stigmatized as agents of a universal Zionist-plutocratic-Masonic conspiracy.

One should not exaggerate, however, the dark colors in this picture and the difficulties of the ongoing evolution from totalitarianism to a different political order based on the rule of law. Compared to 1987, we can now certainly state that the communist states cannot and, in fact, did not survive—at least in the countries of the former Soviet "external" empire. Leninist regimes did irrevocably fall apart. But the legacy of the Leninist system, including its cultural and moral elements, is much more complex and stubborn than anyone had foreseen. For transitions to occur successfully and to result in the emergence of open societies, some factors are indispensable. First, the emergence of a pluralist political space with genuine political parties. Second, the redefinition of the relationship between power and opposition by understanding that the existence of a powerful and dynamic opposition is essential for the healthy functioning of a democracy. Third, the formation of a political elite (class), which despite all natural divergences would be able to agree on the ultimate values characteristic of an open society, including the role of the market, the protection of the individual, and the indispensable guarantees for minorities.

But while the democratic orientation of the mainstream political discourse seems unquestionable in many of these countries, we should not gloss over the persistence of unavowed fears, phobias, and frustrations, the neurotic syndrome that explains the readiness of many individuals to join ethnocentric, nebulously prophetic movements. As the world sadly knows from the experience of Weimar Germany, democracy is not immune to the attacks of such movements. On the other hand, democratic polities can defend themselves if they get rid of their self-serving illusions and identify the social and psychological motivations of populist extremism. To deny those motivations and to confine oneself to the rhetoric of self-glorification is hardly a way to consolidate or strengthen the victories of the last two years. As these societies have exited the communist morass, their alternatives have ranged from real democracy to fundamentalist ethnocracy.

Hence, in addition to the difficulties created by economic renewal, these societies have inherited the political, social, and cultural crises provoked by communism. To avoid the exploitation of those tensions by movements grounded in resentment and hatred, to prevent the emergence of a combination of extreme right and left "indigenist" radicalism, fledgling democratic institutions need to create a counterbalance at the level of social psychology. Democratic politics is founded not on myths and emotions but on the modest and patient search for those impersonal procedures that foster what totalitarianism wanted to destroy: the accountability of political power and the existence of an independent judiciary and other institutions that aim to protect and not to humiliate the individual. The building of those institutions transcends the will of a political party: It entails the individual in its integrity, because the roots of liberty lie in the awareness that man was born free and that no government has the right to assign to itself the power to limit this freedom.

Notes

In this section, each work cited more than once appears in a full citation at its first mention in each chapter. Subsequent citations within a chapter are rendered in a short form. When a subsequent reference occurs more than ten note numbers after the last previous mention, reference is made to the note where the full citation appears, e.g.: "(note 3 above)."

Chapter 1   Victims and Outsiders

1. Adam Michnik, "The Presence of Liberal Values," *East European Reporter*, 4, no. 4 (London: Spring–Summer 1991): 71.

2. For a splendid account of the spiritual effervescence in Budapest before World War I, see John Lukacs, *Budapest 1900: A Historical Portrait of a City and Its Culture* (New York: Grove Weidenfeld, 1988).

3. Jean-François Revel, "Sortir du communisme, une tâche sans précédent dans l'histoire," *Est-Ouest*, no. 90, (Paris, June 1991), p. 3.

4. Joseph Rothschild, *Return to Diversity: A Political History of East Central Europe Since World War II* (New York: Oxford University Press, 1989), pp. 3–24.

5. Carol Skalnik Leff, *National Conflict in Czechoslovakia: The Making and Remaking of a State, 1918–1987* (Princeton, N.J.: Princeton University Press, 1988), p. 138.

6. Rothschild, *Return to Diversity*, p. 70.

7. Adam Michnik quoted in Jacques Rupnik, *The Other Europe: The Rise and Fall of Communism in East-Central Europe* (New York: Schocken Books, 1989), p. 28.

8. For a clear analysis of Romania's interwar political life, see Vlad Georgescu, *The Romanians: A History* (Columbus: Ohio State University Press, 1991), pp. 189–232.

9. Milan Kundera, "The Tragedy of Central Europe," *The New York Review of Books*, April 26, 1984.

10. Danilo Kis, "Variations on the Theme of Central Europe," *Crosscurrents: A Yearbook of Central European Culture*, no. 6, (Ann Arbor: University of Michigan, 1987), p. 11.

11. Alexander Wat, *My Century: The Odyssey of a Polish Intellectual* (Berkeley: University of California Press, 1988), p. 15.

12. Helmut Gruber, *International Communism in the Era of Lenin: A Documentary History* (Garden City, N.Y.: Anchor Books, 1972), pp. 241–46.

13. For the fate of foreign communists in the Soviet Union during the Great Purge, see Robert C. Tucker, *Stalin in Power: The Revolution from Above, 1928–1941* (New York: Norton, 1990), pp. 504–13.

14. See Kenneth Jowitt's discussion of this issue in his *Revolutionary Breakthroughs and National Development: The Case of Romania, 1944–1965* (Berkeley and Los Angeles: University of California Press, 1971), pp. 175–77.

15. In 1935, at the Comintern's 7th (and last) Congress, Dimitrov delivered the keynote address; in it he formulated the orthodox Stalinist definition of fascism as "the dictatorship of the most reactionary forces of monopolistic capital." After World War II Dimitrov went back to Bulgaria, where he became the country's president until his

sudden and still mysterious death while in the Soviet Union in 1948. In 1990, following the collapse of the communist regime in Bulgaria, Dimitrov's embalmed body was removed from the Soviet-style Mausoleum in Sofia as part of a national campaign for the elimination of communist symbols and iconology. For fascinating details on the Comintern elite, see Branko Lazich in collaboration with Milorad M. Drachkovitch, *Biographical Dictionary of the Comintern: New, Revised and Expanded Edition* (Stanford, Calif.: Hoover Institution Press, 1986).

16. Norman Davies, *Heart of Europe: A Short History of Poland* (Oxford and New York: Oxford University Press, 1986), p. 426, and Anthony Read and David Fisher, *The Deadly Embrace: Hitler, Stalin, and the Nazi-Soviet Pact 1939–1941* (New York: Norton, 1988).

17. See "What Is Central Europe: The Telltale Scar," *The New Republic,* August 7 and 14, 1989, p. 28.

18. For Tito and Titoism, the literature is enormous and very controversial. See Adam Ulam, *Titoism and the Cominform* (Cambridge: Harvard University Press, 1952), and Vladimir Dedijer, *The Battle Stalin Lost: Memoirs of Yugoslavia* (New York: Viking, 1971).

19. Arshi Pipa, "The Political Culture of Albanian Communism," in Tariq Ali, *The Stalinist Legacy: Its Impact on the Twentieth Century World Politics* (Harmondsworth, Middlesex: Penguin Books, 1984), pp. 434–64.

20. See Leszek Kolakowski, *Main Currents of Marxism,* vol. III, *The Breakdown* (Oxford: Oxford University Press, 1978), and Vladimir Tismaneanu, *The Crisis of Marxist Ideology in Eastern Europe: The Poverty of Utopia* (New York and London: Routledge, 1988).

21. Gavriel D. Ra'anan, *International Policy Formation in the USSR: Factional "Debates" During the Zhdanovshchina* (Hamden, Conn.: Archon Books, 1983), and William O. McCagg, Jr., *Stalin Embattled 1943–1948* (Detroit: Wayne State University Press, 1978).

22. The statutes of the Union of Soviet Writers adopted in 1934, as quoted by Abram Tertz (Andrei Sinyavsky), *The Trial Begins and On Socialist Realism* (Berkeley and Los Angeles: University of California Press, 1982), p. 148.

23. Quoted in McCagg, *Stalin Embattled,* pp. 250–51.

24. *Ibid.,* p. 264; the full text of the declaration appears in *For a Lasting Peace, for People's Democracy* no. 1 (Belgrade, 1947), p. 1.

25. Zbigniew Brzezinski, *The Soviet Bloc: Unity and Conflict* (Cambridge: Harvard University Press, 1967), pp. 3–151.

26. Paul Ignotus, "The First Two Communist Takeovers of Hungary: 1919 and 1948," in Thomas T. Hammond, *The Anatomy of Communist Takeovers* (New Haven: Yale University Press, 1975), p. 395.

27. Nissan Oren, "A Revolution Administered: The Sovietization of Bulgaria," in Hammond, *Anatomy,* pp. 321–38.

28. Adam Bromke, *Poland's Politics: Idealism vs. Realism* (Cambridge: Harvard University Press, 1967), pp. 60–61.

29. *Kulturny Noviny,* no. 7 (Prague, 1968), quoted by Pavel Tigrid, "The Prague Coup of 1948: The Elegant Takeover," in Hammond, *Anatomy,* p. 400.

30. Brzezinski, *Soviet Bloc,* p. 65.

31. Kolakowski, *Main Currents* (note 20 above), II:85.

32. Brzezinski, *Soviet Bloc,* p. 52.

33. Quoted by Mikhail Heller, *Cogs in the Wheel: The Formation of the Soviet Man* (New York: Knopf, 1988), p. 6.

34. Czeslaw Milosz, *The Captive Mind* (New York: Vintage Books, 1981), p. 220.

35. Jacek Trznadel, "An Interview with Zbigniew Herbert," *Partisan Review*, no. 4 (1987), pp. 559–60.

36. Brzezinski, *Soviet Bloc*, p. 67.

37. Bertram Wolfe, *Khrushchev and Stalin's Ghost* (New York: Praeger, 1957), p. 10.

38. Nadezhda Mandelstam, *Hope Abandoned* (New York: Atheneum, 1974), pp. 249–50.

Chapter 2   Children in the Fog

1. George H. Hodos, *Show Trials: Stalinist Purges in Eastern Europe, 1948–1954* (New York: Praeger, 1987), pp. 11–12.

2. *Ibid.*, p. xiii.

3. "The Trial of Laszlo Rajk," in Gale Stokes, ed., *From Stalinism to Pluralism: A Documentary History of Eastern Europe since 1945* (New York and Oxford: Oxford University Press, 1991), pp. 69–70.

4. See Louis Rapoport, *Stalin's War Against the Jews: The Doctors' Plot and the Soviet Solution* (New York: The Free Press, 1990).

5. Zbigniew Brzezinski, *The Soviet Bloc: Unity and Conflict* (Cambridge: Harvard University Press, 1967), p. 137.

6. Jacques Rupnik, *The Other Europe: The Rise and Fall of Communism in East-Central Europe* (New York: Schocken Books, 1989) p. 116; on Stalin versus Tito, see Khrushchev's "Secret Speech" in Tariq Ali, *The Stalinist Legacy* (Harmondsworth, Middlesex: Penguin Books, 1984), p. 256.

7. See Ivo Banac, *With Stalin Against Tito: Cominformist Splits in Yugoslav Communism* (Ithaca and London: Cornell University Press, 1988).

8. See Oskar Gruenwald, *The Yugoslav Search for Man: Marxist Humanism in Contemporary Yugoslavia* (South Hadley, Mass.: J. F. Bergin, 1982).

9. See Milovan Djilas, *The New Class: An Analysis of the Communist System* (New York: Harcourt Brace Jovanovich, 1957), and *idem, Of Prisons and Ideas* (Orlando: Harcourt Brace Jovanovich, 1986).

10. Wolfgang Leonhard, *Three Faces of Marxism: The Political Concepts of Soviet Ideology, Maoism, and Humanist Marxism* (New York: Paragon Books, 1979), p. 268.

11. Teresa Toranska, *"Them": Stalin's Polish Puppets* (New York: Harper & Row, 1987), p. 257.

12. *Ibid.*, p. 354. The reader will find an enormous amount of invaluable information in this book about the psychological and moral makeup of the Polish Stalinist elite.

13. For these biographies, see the appropriate entries in Branko Lazich and Milorad M. Drachkovich, *Biographical Dictionary of the Comintern: New, Revised and Expanded Edition* (Stanford, Calif.: Hoover Institution Press, 1986).

14. Brecht as quoted by William Echikson, *Lighting the Night*, (New York: Morrow, 1990), p. 63; Timothy Garton Ash, "Comrade Brecht," in his book *The Uses of Adversity: Essays on the Fate of Central Europe* (New York: Random House, 1989), pp. 28–46.

15. Brzezinski, *Soviet Bloc*, p. 174.

16. Celestine Bohlen, "Warsaw Pact Agrees to Dissolve Its Military Alliance," *New York Times*, February 26, 1991.

17. Leszek Kolakowski, *Main Currents of Marxism* (Oxford: Oxford University Press, 1978), III: 451.

18. Khrushchev's "Secret Report," in Ali, *Stalinist Legacy* (note 6 above), pp. 269–70.

19. Isaac Deutscher, "The Tragedy of Polish Communism," in Isaac Deutscher, *Marxism, Wars and Revolutions: Essays from Four Decades* (London: Verso, 1984), p. 121.

20. For the Polish political traditions, see Marcin Krol, "The Polish Syndrome of Incompetentness," in Stanislaw Gomulka and Antony Polonsky, eds., *Polish Paradoxes* (London and New York: Routledge, 1990), pp. 63–75, and Jan Jozef Lipski, "Two Fatherlands, Two Patriotisms," in Robert Kostrzewa, ed., *Between East and West: Writings from Kultura* (New York: Hill & Wang, 1990), pp. 52–71.

21. Paul Zinner, ed., *National Communism and Popular Revolt in Eastern Europe: A Selection of Documents on Events in Poland and Hungary February–November 1956* (New York: Columbia University Press, 1956), pp. 47–48.

22. Stanislaw Baraczak, "Before the Thaw: The Beginning of Dissent in Postwar Polish Literature (The Case of Adam Wazyk's 'A Poem for Adults')," *East European Politics and Societies*, 3, no. 1 (Winter 1989): 11.

23. Quoted in Irving Howe, *Beyond the New Left* (New York: McCall Publishing Company, 1970), pp. 31–32.

24. "Victor Orban's Speech at the Reburial of Imre Nagy," *Uncaptive Minds*, II, no. 4 (August–October 1989): 26.

25. William E. Griffith, "The Origins and Significance of East European Revisionism," in Leopold Labedz, ed., *Revisionism: Essays in the History of Marxist Ideas* (New York: Praeger, 1962), pp. 223–38.

26. Adam Michnik, *Letters from Prison and Other Essays* (Berkeley and Los Angeles: University of California Press, 1985), p. 135.

27. *Ibid.*, p. 137.

28. See György Aczel and Tibor Meray, *The Revolt of the Mind* (New York: Praeger, 1959).

29. Leonhard, *Three Faces of Marxism* (note 10 above), pp. 282–83.

30. *Ibid.*, p. 283.

31. *Ibid.*, p. 284.

32. *Ibid.*

33. See "Christ and Commissar," an interview with Milovan Djilas, in George Urban, ed., *Stalinism: Its Impact on Russia and the World* (Cambridge, Mass.: Harvard University Press, 1986), pp. 180–245.

34. Ferenc Feher and Agnes Heller, *Hungary 1956 Revisited: The Message of a Revolution— A Quarter of a Century After* (London: George Allen & Unwin, 1983), p. 150.

35. *Ibid.*, p. vii.

36. Quoted by Albert Camus in his preface to *The Truth about the Nagy Affair: Facts, Documents, Comments* (New York: Praeger, 1959), p. vii.

37. Quoted by Melvin Croan in his masterful essay "East German Revisionism: The Spectre and the Reality," in Leopold Labedz, ed., *Revisionism: Essays on the History of the Marxist Ideas* (New York: Praeger, 1962), p. 254.

38. The journal ceased to come out in 1990 as an effect of both the dramatic changes in Eastern Europe and Gorbachev's markedly diminished interest in what used to be called the "world communist movement."

39. See William E. Griffith, *Albania and the Sino-Soviet Rift* (Cambridge, Mass.: MIT Press, 1963).

40. J. F. Brown, *The New Eastern Europe: The Khrushchev Era and After* (New York: Praeger, 1966), p. 206.

Chapter 3   From Thaw to Freeze

1. For excellent insights into the background of the conspiracy that eliminated Khrushchev, see Sergei Khrushchev, *Khrushchev on Khrushchev* (Boston: Little, Brown & Company, 1990).
2. See the interview with Eduard Goldstücker in Antonin Liehm, *Trois générations: Entretiens sur le phénomène culturel tchécoslovaque* (Paris: Gallimard, 1970), p. 212.
3. See the extensive passages of Ludvik Vaculik's speech in Harry Schwartz, *Prague's 200 Days: The Struggle for Democracy in Czechoslovakia* (New York: Praeger, 1969), pp. 47–48.
4. For Dubcek's political background, see William Showcross, *Dubcek: Revised and Updated Edition* (New York: Simon & Schuster/Touchstone, 1990).
5. Vojtech Mastny, *Czechoslovakia: Crisis in World Communism* (New York: Facts on File, 1972), pp. 21–25.
6. For thoughtful contributions to the discussion on Eurocommunism, see George Schwab, ed., *Eurocommunism: The Ideological and Political-Theoretical Foundations* (Westport, Conn.: Greenwood Press, 1981).
7. For the full text of the manifesto, see Mastny, *Czechoslovakia*, pp. 28–34.
8. *Ibid.*, p. 38.
9. Ibid., p. 44.
10. Antonin J. Liehm, "It Was You Who Did It!" in Jiri Pehe, ed., *The Prague Spring: A Mixed Legacy* (New York: Freedom House, 1988), p. 172.
11. Jacques Rupnik, *The Other Europe: The Rise and Fall of Communism in East-Central Europe* (New York: Pantheon Books, 1989), pp. 256–57.
12. Ivan Svitak, "The Premature Perestroika," in Pehe, *Prague Spring*, p. 179. Svitak was the author of an even more radical manifesto for democratization that the Czechoslovak communist leadership chose to suppress in the summer of 1968. After the Soviet invasion he was singled out by the collaborationist media as one of the ideologues of the alleged counterrevolution that the Warsaw Pact intervention succeeded in preventing. After two decades of exile in the United States, professor Svitak returned to Czechoslovakia in 1990, after the collapse of the communist regime.
13. Mastny, *Czechoslovakia*, p. 59.
14. Milan Kundera, *The Joke* (New York: Penguin Books, 1982), "Author's Preface," p. xiv.
15. Mastny, *Czechoslovakia*, pp. 144–45.
16. Vaclav Havel, *Disturbing the Peace: A Conversation with Karel Hvizdala* (New York: Knopf, 1990), p. 95.
17. Robert Conquest, *Russia After Khrushchev* (New York: Praeger, 1965), p. 6. Conquest was not the only one to emphasize the institutional continuity between mature Stalinism and Brezhnevism. Other scholars who shared this view were Zbigniew Brzezinski and Leonard Shapiro, who showed that as long as the Soviet-style regimes maintained their inherent contempt for the rule of law there was little reason to consider that Stalinism had been really abolished. See especially Leonard Shapiro, *The Communist Party of the Soviet Union* (New York: Vintage Books, 1971), pp. 628–29.

18. See Jakub Karpinski, *Countdown: The Polish Upheavals of 1956, 1968, 1970, 1976, 1980 . . .* (New York: Karz-Cohl, 1982), pp. 105–55.

19. Jerzy Holzer quoted in Tadeusz Szafar, "Anti-Semitism: A Trusty Weapon," in Abraham Brumberg, ed., *Poland: The Genesis of a Revolution* (New York: Vintage Books, 1983), p. 120.

20. Jan de Weydenthal, *The Communists of Poland: An Historical Outline* (Stanford, Calif.: Hoover Institution Press, 1986), p. 121; Ray Taras, *Poland: Socialist State, Rebellious Nation* (Boulder, Colo.: Westview, 1986), pp. 103–17.

21. "The Kuron-Modzelewski Open Letter to the Party," in Gale Stokes, ed., *From Stalinism to Pluralism: A Documentary History of Eastern Europe Since 1945* (New York: Oxford University Press, 1991), pp. 108–14.

22. Jan Josef Lipski, *KOR: Workers' Defense Committee in Poland 1976–1981* (Berkeley: University of California Press, 1985).

23. For the birth of Solidarity, see Neal Ascherson, *The Polish August* (New York: Viking Press, 1982).

Chapter 4   A Glorious Resurrection

1. Adam Michnik, *Letters from Prison and Other Essays* (Berkeley and Los Angeles: University of California Press, 1985), p. 157.

2. See Robert Kostrzewa, ed., *Between East and West: Writings from Kultura* (New York: Hill & Wang, 1990).

3. In an illuminating essay on Gorbachev, Kenneth Jowitt used this Weberian term to explain the rise of Solidarity as a resurgence of Poland's long-repressed civic culture. See Daniel Chirot, ed., *The Crisis of Leninism and the Decline of the Left: The Revolutions of 1989* (Seattle: University of Washington Press, 1991), pp. 74–99.

4. Abraham Brumberg, ed., *Poland: The Genesis of a Revolution* (New York: Vintage Books, 1983), p. 10.

5. J. F. Brown, *Eastern Europe and Communist Rule* (Durham, N.C.: Duke University Press, 1988), p. 197.

6. For an excellent analysis of this organization, see Jan Josef Lipski, *KOR: A History of the Workers' Defense Committee in Poland, 1976–1981* (Berkeley: University of California Press, 1985).

7. Jacques Rupnik, *The Other Europe: The Rise and Fall of Communism in East-Central Europe* (New York: Schocken Books, 1989), pp. 258–59.

8. William Echikson, *Lighting the Night: Revolution in Eastern Europe* (New York: Morrow, 1990), p. 161.

9. Lipski, *KOR*, p. 68.

10. Echikson, *Lighting the Night*, p. 160.

11. Leszek Kolakowski, "The Intelligentsia," in Brumberg, *Poland*, p. 65.

12. *Ibid.*, p. 66.

13. Michnik, *Letters from Prison* (note 1 above), p. 136.

14. *Ibid.*, p. 137.

15. Leszek Kolakowski, *Main Currents of Marxism: Its Origins, Growth and Dissolution*, vol. III, *The Breakdown*, (New York: Oxford University Press, 1978), pp. 526, 530.

16. Michnik, *Letters from Prison*, p. 142.

17. *Ibid.*, p. 144.

18. Ibid., p. 147.
19. Michnik, "A Year Has Passed—1981," in *Letters From Prison*, p. 124.
20. Adam Michnik quoted in Lech Walesa, *A Way of Hope: An Autobiography* (New York: Henry Holt, 1987).
21. Ibid., p. 2.
22. See Stephen Engelberg, "As Jaruzelski Leaves Office: A Traitor or Hero to Poles," *New York Times*, December 22, 1990.
23. Timothy Garton Ash, *The Uses of Adversity: Essays on the Fate of Central Europe* (New York: Random House, 1989), p. 309–10.
24. Steven Lukes, "Introduction," in Vaclav Havel et al., *The Power of the Powerless* (Armonk, N.Y.: M. E. Sharpe, 1990), p. 12.
25. Vaclav Havel, "The Power of the Powerless," in *ibid.*, p. 23.
26. Ibid., p. 28.
27. Ibid., pp. 28–29.
28. Ibid., pp. 30–31.
29. Ibid., p. 32.
30. Ibid., p. 31.
31. Ibid., p. 40. Emphasis in original.
32. Ibid.
33. Ibid., p. 43.
34. Havel's contribution in Vaclav Benda, Milan Simecka, Ivan M. Jirous, Jiri Dienstbier, Vaclav Havel, Ladislav Hejdanek, and Jan Simsa, "Parallel Polis, or an Independent Society in Central and Eastern Europe: An Inquiry," *Social Research*, 55, nos. 1–2 (Spring–Summer 1988): 235.
35. Ibid., p. 236.
36. Ibid., p. 237.
37. See Havel, "Power of the Powerless," p. 48.
38. George Konrad, *Antipolitics* (San Diego and New York: Harcourt Brace Jovanovich, 1984), pp. 230–31.
39. Ibid., p. 228.
40. Ibid., pp. 123–24.
41. Havel, "Power of the Powerless," p. 57.
42. Miklos Haraszti, *The Velvet Prison: Artists Under State Socialism* (New York: Basic Books, 1987), p. 10.
43. Ibid., pp. 142–43.
44. Ibid., p. 146.
45. Ibid., p. 150.
46. Ibid., p. 162.
47. Ibid., p. 156.
48. Ibid., p. 158.
49. Ibid., p. 162.

Chapter 5   The Ethos of Civil Society

1. Vaclav Havel, "The Power of the Powerless," in Vaclav Havel et al., *The Power of the Powerless* (Armonk, N.Y.: M. E. Sharpe, 1990), p. 65.
2. Ibid., p. 68.

3. ibidem, p. 69.

4. Adam Michnik, *Letters from Prison and Other Essays* (Berkeley and Los Angeles: University of California Press, 1985), p. 28.

5. *Ibid.*, pp. 86–87.

6. *Ibid.*, p. 91.

7. Hans-Peter Riese, *Since the Prague Spring: Charter '77 and the Struggle for Human Rights in Czechoslovakia* (New York: Vintage Books, 1979), pp. 13–14; for one of the most informative and authoritative analyses of the rise of democratic movements from below in Czechoslovakia, see H. Gordon Skilling, *Charter 77 and Human Rights in Czechoslovakia* (London: George Allen & Unwin, 1981).

8. Riese, *Since the Prague Spring*, p. 14.

9. *Ibid.*

10. Havel, "Power of the Powerless," p. 80.

11. Vaclav Havel, *Letters to Olga* (New York: Knopf, 1988), p. 145.

12. Vaclav Havel, *Disturbing the Peace: A Conversation with Karel Hvizdala* (New York: Knopf, 1990), p. 138.

13. *Ibid.*, p. 182.

14. Seweryn Bialer, Charles Gati, and Karen Dawisha all discussed, with remarkable sophistication, Gorbachev's strategy for the removal of the anachronistic Brezhnev-style elites and the promotion of more imaginative, reform-oriented, and pragmatic, or even technocratic teams. It turned out, however, that a sea change in strategic rethinking took place in the Soviet leadership's vision of the bloc. Not only was domesticism, the old heresy, encouraged, but, especially after 1988, Moscow renounced the Brezhnev doctrine of "limited sovereignty" and overhauled its decades-long definition of the outer empire. In this respect, Gorbachev seemed to recognize, in the other former communist countries, an imperative that he refused to admit for the Soviet Union itself: that the Leninist experiment had failed and the communist party's privileged status had to come to an end. Seweryn Bialer, *The Soviet Paradox: External Expansion, Internal Decline* (New York: Knopf, 1986); Charles Gati, *The Bloc That Failed: Soviet-East European Relations in Transition* (Bloomington, Ind.: Indiana University Press, 1990); Karen Dawisha, *Eastern Europe, Gorbachev, and Reform: The Great Challenge*, 2nd ed. (New York and Cambridge: Cambridge University Press, 1990).

15. Havel, *Disturbing the Peace*, p. 182.

16. *Ibid.*, p. 183.

17. *Ibid.*, pp. 185–86.

18. *Neues Deutschland*, December 30, 1988.

19. *Der Spiegel*, September 1, 1986, quoted in B. V. Flow, "The Literary Avant-Garde Leaves the GDR," *Radio Free Europe Research*, RAD Background Report 132, September 18, 1986.

20. Robert Havemann, *Ein deutscher Kommunist: Rückblicke und Perspektive aus Isolation* (Hamburg: Rowohlt, 1978), pp. 98–103; excerpts from Havemann's book are translated in Roger Woods, *Opposition in the GDR Under Honecker: An Introduction and Documentation* (New York: St. Martin's Press, 1986), pp. 165–69.

21. After the breakdown of the communist regime in the fall of 1989, Eppelmann was active in the newly created political group called "Democratic Awakening" and served, until the reunification in Lothar de Maizière's government as the GDR's Minister of Defense and Disarmament.

22. Woods, *Opposition in GDR*, pp. 195–96.

23. A. Wynton Jackson, "Introduction" to "GDR: Appeal on the Occasion of the UN Peace Year," *East European Reporter*, 2, no. 1 (Spring 1986), p. 61.

24. Vaclav Havel, "An Anatomy of Reticence," in *Crosscurrents: A Yearbook of Central European Culture* (Ann Arbor: University of Michigan Press, 1986), p. 18.

25. Ibid.

26. For the full text of the statement, see Vladimir Tismaneanu, "Dissent in the Gorbachev Era—A Documentation," *ORBIS*, Summer 1987, pp. 234–43.

27. Moshe Lewin, *The Gorbachev Phenomenon: A Historical Interpretation* (Berkeley: University of California Press, 1988), p. 147.

28. *Ibid.*, p. 80.

29. See Ferenc Feher, Agnes Heller, and György Markus, *Dictatorship Over Needs* (New York: St. Martin's Press, 1983).

30. Karl Friedrich and Zbigniew Brzezinski, *Totalitarian Dictatorship and Autocracy* (Cambridge, Mass.: Harvard University Press, 1965), p. 27.

31. Robert C. Tucker, *The Marxian Revolutionary Idea* (New York: Norton, 1969), pp. 172–214.

32. Hannah Arendt, *The Origins of Totalitarianism* (San Diego: Harcourt Brace Jovanovich, 1973), p. 478.

33. "Kadarism as the Model State of 'Khrushchevism'," in Agnes Heller and Ferenc Feher, *From Yalta to Glasnost: The Dismantling of Stalin's Empire* (New York: Basil Blackwell, 1990), pp. 129–45.

34. Miklos Haraszti, "The Beginnings of Civil Society: The Independent Peace Movements and the Danube Movement in Hungary," in Vladimir Tismaneanu, ed., *In Search of Civil Society: Independent Peace Movements in the Soviet Bloc* (New York: Routledge, 1990), pp. 85–86.

35. Ibid., p. 86.

Chapter 6   The Triumph of the Powerless

1. Thomas W. Simons, Jr., *The End of the Cold War?* (New York: St. Martin's Press, 1990), pp. 150–51.

2. *Sovetskaya Kultura*, April 9, 1988.

3. Zbigniew Brzezinski, *The Grand Failure: The Birth and Death of Communism in the Twentieth Century* (New York: Charles Scribner's Sons, 1989), p. 48.

4. Adam Michnik, "The Great Counter-Reformer," *Labour Focus on Eastern Europe*, 9, no. 2, (London, July–October 1987): 23.

5. *Ibid.*

6. *Ibid.*

7. Brzezinski, *Grand Failure*, p. 64.

8. Seweryn Bialer, *The Soviet Paradox: External Expansion, Internal Decline* (New York: Knopf, 1986), p. 206.

9. Baruch Hazan, *Gorbachev's Gamble: The 19th All-Union Party Conference* (Boulder, Colo.: Westview, 1989), p. 156.

10. "Gorbachev's View of Changing World," *Philadelphia Inquirer*, December 11, 1988.

11. "Russia's Surly Empire," *The Economist* (London), November 26, 1988, p. 13.

12. "The Soviet Perspective," *Problems of Communism*, May–August 1988, p. 62.

13. *Ibid.*, p. 63.

14. *Pravda*, July 7, 1989.
15. Henry Kamm, "Gorbachev Said to Reject Soviet Right to Intervene," *New York Times*, April 2, 1989.
16. Vladimir F. Kusin, "Mikhail Gorbachev's Evolving Attitude to Eastern Europe," *Radio Free Europe Research*, RAD Background Report 128 (Eastern Europe), July 20, 1989, p. 4.
17. Nina Andreyeva, "I Cannot Waive Principles," *Sovetskaya Rossiya*, March 13, 1988, translated in FBIS—Soviet Union, March 16, 1988, p. 51.
18. *New York Times*, October 24, 1989.
19. Reuters, October 16, 1989.
20. Charles Gati, *The Bloc That Failed: Soviet–East European Relations in Transition* (Bloomington and Indianapolis: Indiana University Press, 1990), p. 167.
21. Radio Free Europe, *Daily Report*, May 8, 1989.
22. Gati, *The Bloc That Failed*, p. 168.
23. Timothy Garton Ash, *The Uses of Adversity: Essays on the Fate of Central Europe* (New York: Random House, 1989), pp. 321–22.
24. Karen Dawisha, *Eastern Europe, Gorbachev and Reform: The Great Challenge* (Cambridge and New York: Cambridge University Press, 1990), p. 296.
25. Mihaly Vajda, "The Collapse of Socialism: A Theoretical Explanation," *East European Reporter*, 4, no. 3 (Autumn–Winter 1990): 51.
26. *Ibid.*
27. "The Social Contract: Prerequisites for Resolving the Political Crisis," special issue of samizdat journal *Beszelö*, June 10, 1987 (English translation), p. 2. *Beszelö* was run by an editorial staff that included some of the most famous names of the Hungarian Democratic Opposition: Miklos Haraszti, Janos Kis, Ferenc Koszeg, György Petri and Sandor Szilagyi.
28. *Ibid.*, pp. 7–8.
29. "Pozsgay Inteviewed by Radio Free Europe 24 May," *Magyar Nemzet* (Budapest), May 29, 1989, translated in FBIS—Eastern Europe, June 7, 1989, p. 26.
30. Dawisha, *Eastern Europe, Gorbachev and Reform*, p. 179.
31. "The Struggle for Political Pluralism: The First Congress of the Association of Young Democrats," *East European Reporter*, 3, no. 4 (Spring–Summer 1989): 17–18.
32. "Democracy Within the Warsaw Pact: An Interview with Ferenc Köszeg," *EER*, 3:12–14.
33. Vladimir Tismaneanu, "From Prague Spring to Moscow's 'Glasnost'," *Philadelphia Inquirer*, February 17, 1988.
34. Interview with Alexander Dubcek, former General Secretary of the Czechoslovak Communist Party, broadcast by Hungarian television on April 26, 1989, in FBIS—Eastern Europe, April 28, 1989, p. 23, and Vladimir V. Kusin, "Hungarian Television Interviews Alexander Dubcek," *Radio Free Europe Research*, Czechoslovak SR/10, May 5, 1989, pp. 9–15.
35. Karel Horak, "In the Role of the 'Savior' of Socialism: Annotations on Some of A. Dubcek's Statements to Foreign Information Media," *Rude Pravo*, March 29, 1989, translated in FBIS—Eastern Europe, March 31, 1989, p. 21
36. Krenz quoted in Serge Schmemann, "East Germany Removes Honecker and His Protégé Takes His Place," in Bernard Gwertzman and Michael T. Kaufman, eds., *The Collapse of Communism: By the Correspondents of the New York Times* (New York: Random House, 1990), p. 159.

37. Patricia Clough, "Unreal Country Where Reform Depends on the Grim Reaper," *The Independent* (London), August 22, 1989.

38. Barbara Donovan, "Reform and the Existence of the GDR," *RFER*, RAD Background Report/158 (GDR), August 25, 1989, p. 2.

39. Barbara Donovan, "The SED Becoming More Outspoken on Reform," *RFER*, RAD Background Report/6 (GDR), January 12, 1989.

40. Pamela Shemid, "East Germany and the Marxist Malaise," *U.S. News & World Report*, November 14, 1988, pp. 40–41.

41. "Hager Delivers Address at Historians Meeting," *Neues Deutschland* (East Berlin), April 8–9, 1989, translated in FBIS—Eastern Europe, April 11, 1989, pp. 30–32.

42. "Margot Honecker: 'Defend Socialism With Weapons'," *Neues Deutschland*, June 14, 1989, translated in FBIS—Eastern Europe, June 20, 1989, pp. 41–42.

43. Josef Joffe, "Who's Egon Krenz? He's No Gorbachev," *New York Times*, October 19, 1989 (op-ed page).

44. Serge Schmemann, "The Border Is Open—Joyous East Germans Pour Through Wall—Party Pledges Freedoms and City Exults," in Gwertzman and Kaufman, *Collapse of Communism*, pp. 175–80.

45. Barbara Donovan, "The Tenth SED CC Plenum: Moving Toward Reform," *RFER*, RAD Background Report (GDR), November 20, 1989, pp. 6–9.

46. David Binder, "Reports of Corruption in East Berlin Shock Even the Party Rank and File," *New York Times*, November 25, 1989.

47. Craig R. Whitney, "East German Communists Confront Party's Collapse," *New York Times*, December 17, 1989.

48. Barbara Donovan, "The Extraordinary SED Congress: A New Beginning or the Beginning of the End?" RFE, *Report on Eastern Europe*, January 19, 1990, pp. 5–8.

49. R. W. Apple, "Prague Opposition Mounts Huge Protest, Denouncing New Leadership as 'a Trick,' " in Gwertzman and Kaufman, *Collapse of Communism*, p. 238.

50. "What We Want: The Programme Principles Issued by the Czechoslovak Civic Forum," *East European Reporter*, 4, no. 1 (Winter 1989–90): 50–51.

51. "Czechoslovak President Vaclav Havel's New Year's Day Address," *East European Reporter*, 4, no. 1 (Winter 1989–90): 56.

52. *Ibid.*, p. 57.

53. Czeslaw Milosz, *The Captive Mind* (New York: Vintage, 1981), p. 45.

54. "Havel's New Year's Day Address," p. 58.

55. Stephen Ashley, "Can Todor Zhivkov Survive as Bulgaria's Leader?" *RFER*, Bulgarian SR/6, July 14, 1988, p. 4.

56. Clyde Haberman, "Bulgarian Change Barely Plods Along," *New York Times*, October 7, 1989.

57. Clyde Haberman, "Bulgarian Chief Quits After 35 Years of Rigid Rule," *New York Times*, November 11, 1989.

58. Clyde Haberman, "Communists in Bulgarian Expel Zhivkov," *New York Times*, December 14, 1989.

59. "Report on 'Deformations' of the Zhivkov Era," *Rabotnichesko Delo* (Sofia), January 16, 1990, translated in FBIS—Eastern Europe, January 19, 1990, pp. 11–13.

60. For biographical sketches on Bulgaria's new (and not so new) political personalities, see Pavlina Poppisakova, "Who's Who in Bulgarian Politics," *East European Reporter*, 4, no. 3 (Autumn–Winter 1990): 32–33.

61. Chuck Sudetic, "Bulgaria's Ex-Dictator Refuses to Face Parliament," *New York Times,* July 31, 1990.

62. For an analysis of political decay in Romania during the 1980s, see Vladimir Tismaneanu, "Personal Power and Political Crisis in Romania," *Government and Opposition* (London), 24, no. 2 (Spring 1989): 179–98.

63. J. F. Brown, *Eastern Europe and Communist Rule* (Durham, N.C.: Duke University Press, 1988), p. 276.

64. Michael Shafir, "Xenophobic Communism: The Case of Bulgaria and Romania," *RFER,* RAD Background Report/112 (Eastern Europe), June 27, 1989, p. 3.

65. "Letter to President Nicolae Ceausescu" and Vladimir Tismaneanu, "The Rebellion of the Old Guard," both in *East European Reporter,* 3, no. 4 (Spring–Summer 1989): 23–24.

66. Mircea Dinescu, "Where Policemen Outnumber the Pigeons," *Uncaptive Minds* (New York), II, no. 3 (May–July 1989): 34.

67. Michael Shafir, "Eastern Europe's 'Rejectionists'," *RFER,* RAD Background Report/ 121 (Eastern Europe), July 3, 1989, p. 2.

68. "Building a New Social System with the People and For the People," *Scinteia,* October 18, 1989, translated in FBIS, Eastern Europe, October 27, 1989, p. 69.

69. Alan Riding, "In Romania, the Old Order Won't Budge," *New York Times,* November 25, 1989.

70. Kevin Devlin, "Ceausescu's Isolated Internationalism," *RFER,* RAD Background Report/212 (Romania), December 1, 1989.

71. Thomas P. Barnett, "Romania Domino Stays Upright," *Christian Science Monitor,* December 11, 1989.

72. "Speech by President Nicolae Ceausescu on Romanian Radio and Television Stations in Bucharest on 20 December," FBIS Daily Report: East Europe (FBIS—EEU), December 21, 1989, p. 66.

73. For a detailed analysis of the collapse of Romanian communism, see Matei Calinescu and Vladimir Tismaneanu, "The 1989 Revolution and Romania's Future," *Problems of Communism,* January–April 1991, pp. 42–59.

74. Trond Gilberg, "Romania: Will History Repeat Itself?" *Current History* (Philadelphia), December 1990, p. 432.

75. Henry Kamm, "Yugoslavs Astir over Serbian Rise," *New York Times,* August 6, 1989. For Milosevic's career and ideological preferences, see Paul Yankovitch, "Slobodan Milosevic: l'homme fort de la Serbie," *Le Monde* (Paris), October 18, 1988.

76. Jacques Rupnik, "Perestroika and the Empire," *European Journal of International Affairs,* 1, no. 1 (1988): 117.

Chapter 7   The Birth Pangs of Democracy

1. Kenneth Jowitt, "The Leninist Legacy," in Ivo Banac, ed., *Eastern Europe in the 1990's* (Ithaca, N.Y.: Cornell University Press, 1991). I am particularly indebted to Kenneth Jowitt who agreed to share with me his exceptionally insightful ideas on the extinction of Leninism and the authoritarian-tribalistic temptation in Eastern Europe.

2. Timothy Garton Ash, "Eastern Europe: Après le Déluge, Nous," *New York Review of Books,* August 16, 1990, p. 52.

3. Ralf Dahrendorf, *Reflections on the Revolution in Europe* (New York: Random House, 1990), p. 105.

4. Celestine Bohlen, "Double-Headed Eagle Cries to Serbs for Revenge," *New York Times*, September 12, 1990.

5. Alexis de Tocqueville, *On Democracy, Revolution, and Society*, ed. John Stone and Stephen Mennell (Chicago and London: University of Chicago Press, 1980), p. 98.

6. Robert C. Tucker, ed., *The Marx-Engels Reader* (New York: Norton, 1978), p. 595.

7. Ash, "Eastern Europe," pp. 53, 54.

8. See Stephen Engelberg, "Walesa's Victory Now Complicates Poland's Unease," *New York Times*, December 30, 1990.

9. Dan Ionescu, "The Communist Party Re-Emerges Under a New Name," *Report on Eastern Europe*, 1, no. 51 (December 21, 1990): 22–27.

10. Ash, "Eastern Europe," p. 51.

11. See "Reorienting the Security Services," an inteview with Petruska Sustrova, Deputy Minister of Internal Affairs and a longtime opposition activist, in *Uncaptive Minds*, November–December 1990, pp. 38–40.

12. Karol Modzelewski, "Who and What Makes a Leader," *Uncaptive Minds*, November–December 1990, p. 32.

13. Ralf Dahrendorf, *Reflections on the Revolution in Europe*, pp. 115–16.

14. See Charles S. Maier, *The Unmasterable Past: History, Holocaust and the German National Identity* (Cambridge, Mass., and London: Harvard University Press, 1988).

15. Christopher Husbands, "Haunted by the Ghost of Nazism," *The Independent* (London), January 10, 1990.

16. Henry Kamm, "East German Social Democrats Back a Candidate and a Unification Plan," *New York Times*, February 26, 1990.

17. Serge Schmemann, "East Germany's Ballot: Voting Away a Nation," *New York Times*, March 18, 1990.

18. *Frankfurter Allgemeine Zeitung*, June 27, 1990, quoted in Ronald D. Asmus, "An Obituary Without Tears," *Report on Eastern Europe*, January 4, 1991., p. 18.

19. Rada Nikolaev, "Between Hope and Hunger," *Report on Eastern Europe*, 2, no. 1 (January 4, 1991): 5–10.

20. Zlatko Anguelov, "The Leader and His Movement," *East European Reporter*, 4, no. 3 (Autumn–Winter 1990): 27–28.

21. "Bulgaria's Reichstagsbrand?" *EER*, 4, no. 3: 29.

22. For a survey of the Bulgarian changes during 1990, see John D. Bell, " 'Post-Communist' Bulgaria," *Current History* (Philadelphia), December 1990, pp. 417–20, 427–29.

23. Jiri Pehe, "The Instability of Transition," *Report on Eastern Europe*, January 4, 1991, p. 12.

24. Henry Kamm, "Civic Forum, Prague's Leading Party, Splits in Two," *New York Times*, February 12, 1991.

25. "President Havel's Speech on the Anniversary of the 1968 Invasion," *EER*, Autumn–Winter 1990, p. 93.

26. Ivan Volgyes, "For Want of Another Horse: Hungary in 1990," *Current History*, December 1990, p. 423.

27. Ibid., p. 424.

28. Rudolf L. Tökes, "Hungary's New Political Elites: Adaptation and Change, 1989–90," *Problems of Communism*, November–December 1990, p. 64.

29. See the interview with the Hungarian social philosopher Mihaly Vajda in *East European Reporter*, 4, no. 3 (Autumn–Winter 1990): 43.
30. Celestine Bohlen, "Hungarians Are Thriving, Gloomily," *New York Times*, June 24, 1991.
31. For an informative and dispassionate analysis of the split, see Jakub Karpinski, "The Difficult Return to Normality," *Uncaptive Minds* (New York), November–December 1990, pp. 24–26.
32. Jacek Maziarski, "The Goals of the Center Alliance," *East European Reporter*, Autumn–Winter 1990, p. 7.
33. Interview with Zbigniew Bujak, *East European Reporter*, Autumn–Winter 1990, pp. 10–11.
34. Mary Battiata, "The Two Lech Walesas: Solidarity Hero Accused of Demagoguery," *Washington Post*, November 22, 1990.
35. Victoria Pope, "Lech-Luster: Walesa's Personal Transformation," *The New Republic*, December 3, 1990, p. 25.
36. Barbara Spinelli, "The Day After," *La Stampa* (Milan), November 30, 1990; English translation in *Uncaptive Minds*, November–December 1990, p. 35.
37. See Piotr Wierzbicki's masterful essay "Lech Walesa: The Sphinx from Gdansk," *Uncaptive Minds*, November–December 1990, pp. 27–31.
38. Vladimir Tismaneanu, "Sindromul Bucuresti," *Romania Literara* (Bucharest), August 9, 1990.
39. "Proclamatia de la Timisoara," *Romania Libera* (Bucharest), March 20, 1990; English translation in *East European Reporter*, Spring–Summer 1990, pp. 32–35.
40. For the difficulties of Romania's transition to democracy, see Vladimir Tismaneanu, "The Revival of Politics in Romania," in Nils H. Wessell, ed., *The New Europe: Revolution in East–West Relations* (New York: Proceedings of the Academy of Political Science, 1991), pp. 85–99.
41. See Vladimir Tismaneanu, "Homage to Golania," *The New Republic*, July 30–August 6, 1990, pp. 16–18; William McPherson, "In Romania," *Granta*, no. 33, pp. 9–56; Mihnea Berindei, Ariadna Combes, and Anne Planche, *Roumanie, le livre blanc: La réalité d'un pouvoir néo-communiste* (Paris: La Decouverte, 1990).
42. "Romanian Resistance," *East European Reporter*, Autumn–Winter 1990, pp. 89–91.
43. J. L. Talmon, *The Origins of Totalitarian Democracy* (New York: Praeger, 1960), p. 6.
44. David Binder, "Exiled Romanian King Has Hopes of Return," *New York Times*, February 17, 1991.
45. Milan Andrejevich, "The End of an Era, New Beginnings?" *Report on Eastern Europe*, January 4, 1991, p. 39.
46. Robin Alison Remington, "The Federal Dilemma in Yugoslavia," *Current History*, December 1990, p. 408.
47. Brenda Fowler, "Slovenes Vote Decisively for Independence from Yugoslavia," *New York Times*, December 24, 1990.
48. Sabrina P. Ramet, "Serbia's Slobodan Milosevic: A Profile," *Orbis* (Philadelphia), Winter 1991, p. 105.
49. "Alia Speaks on Ideology, Changes in Bloc," *FBIS—Eastern Europe*, November 29, 1989, p. 6.
50. See Simon Jones, "Albanians Cheer for Their New Freedom," *The Independent* (London), July 14, 1990.

51. "Top Albania Writer Seeks Asylum in France, a Blow to His President," *New York Times*, October 26, 1990.

52. David Binder, "Albanian Exile Writer Sees Reform," *New York Times*, December 6, 1990.

53. "Albania Removes Statues of Stalin," *New York Times*, December 22, 1990.

54. Paul Anastasi, "New Albania Barely Conceals a Stalinist Bedrock," *New York Times*, January 20, 1991.

Epilogue   Fears, Phobias, Frustrations

1. Nicolae Manolescu, "How We Have to Destroy Communism," *East European Reporter*, 4, no. 4 (Spring–Summer 1991): 79–80.

2. Stelian Tanase's speech "Romanian Civil Society and Violence," delivered at the Timisoara Conference, March 25–27, 1991.

3. Dimitrina Petrova, "Political Pluralism in Bulgaria," *East European Reporter*, 4, no. 4 (Spring–Summer 1991): 35.

4. Agnes Heller, "Is There Anything New Under the Sun in East-Central Europe?" paper presented at the Timisoara Conference; French translation: *Est-Ouest* (Paris), June 1991, pp. 8–11.

5. Hannah Arendt, *On Revolution* (Harmondsworth, Middlesex: Penguin Books, 1985), pp. 215–81.

6. Adam Michnik, "The Presence of Liberal Values," *East European Reporter*, 4, no. 4 (Spring–Summer 1991): 71, and Ralf Dahrendorf, *Reflections on the Revolution in Europe* (New York: Random House, 1990).

Index

Printed in the United States
838900004B